MW01622945

Nationalism as a Way of Life

While nationalism is a term that is often associated with instability, violence, extremism, terrorism, wars, and even genocide, in fact most forms of nationalism are nonviolent. Beyond politics, it is a set of discourses and practices that shape economic, social, legal, and cultural life all over the globe. This book explores the global rise and transformation of nationalism and analyses the organisational, ideological, and micro-interactional mechanisms that have made it the dominant way of life in the twenty-first century. In a series of case studies across time and space, the book zooms in on three key forms of lived experience: how nationalism operates as a multi-faceted meta-ideology, how national categories have become organisationally embedded in everyday practices, and why nationalism has become the dominant form of modern subjectivity. The book is aimed at readers interested in understanding how nation-states and nationalisms have attained such influence in contemporary world.

Siniša Malešević is Professor of Comparative Historical Sociology at the University College, Dublin, and Senior Fellow at the Conservatoire national des arts et métier (CNAM), Paris. He is the author of the award winning books *The Rise of Organised Brutality* (Cambridge 2017), *Grounded Nationalisms* (Cambridge, 2019) and *Why Humans Fight* (Cambridge, 2022). His work has been translated into fourteen languages.

Nationalism as a Way of Life

The Rise and Transformation of Modern Subjectivities

Siniša Malešević

University College Dublin

Shaftesbury Road, Cambridge CB2 8EA, United Kingdom

One Liberty Plaza, 20th Floor, New York, NY 10006, USA

477 Williamstown Road, Port Melbourne, VIC 3207, Australia

314–321, 3rd Floor, Plot 3, Splendor Forum, Jasola District Centre, New Delhi – 110025, India

103 Penang Road, #05–06/07, Visioncrest Commercial, Singapore 238467

Cambridge University Press is part of Cambridge University Press & Assessment, a department of the University of Cambridge.

We share the University's mission to contribute to society through the pursuit of education, learning and research at the highest international levels of excellence.

www.cambridge.org
Information on this title: www.cambridge.org/9781009570206

DOI: 10.1017/9781009570213

When citing this work, please include a reference to the DOI 10.1017/9781009570213

First published 2025

Cover image: Paul Campbell / iStock / Getty Images Plus

A catalogue record for this publication is available from the British Library

A Cataloging-in-Publication data record for this book is available from the Library of Congress

ISBN 978-1-009-57020-6 Hardback

In memory of dida Rajko and stric Zaba

Contents

Acknowledgements

I am grateful to many people who have helped me in different ways to complete this book. First, to my family, Vesna, Luka, and Alex, who keep tolerating all my academic adventures, never-ending book projects, and constant travels abroad. I am also thankful to friends and colleagues who have offered incisive comments, suggestions, and critique on individual chapters or the full book. I have also received very constructive feedback on presentations that were later redrafted as chapters of this book. I am thankful to different audiences at various academic venues over the years, including Academia Sinica, Taipei; ASEN summer school in Zadar; the Australian Defence College, Canberra; NIOD at the University of Amsterdam; Université libre de Bruxelles; University of Belgrade; Ben Gurion University; Breaking the Silence workshop, Bethlehem; Cambridge University; University of Graz; McGill University, Montreal; University of Copenhagen;, Eastern Sociological Society conference in Washington DC; Inter-University Centre, Dubrovnik; Scuola Normale Superiore, Florence; University of Zadar; Oxford University; Queen's University Belfast; Norwegian Defence University College, Oslo; University of Zagreb; and University College, Dublin.

I would especially like to thank Gerry Boucher, Saša Božić, John Breuilly, Benedikte Brincker, Miguel Centeno, Randall Collins, Sophie De Schaepdrijve, Jon Fox, Rasmus Glenthøj, Dejan Guzina, Jonathan Hearn, John Hutchinson, Atsuko Ichijo, Richard Jenkins, Dietrich Jung, Stathis Kalyvas, Danny Kaplan, Deborah Kaple, Ville Kivimäki, Gëzim Krasniqi, Krishan Kumar, Simona Kuti, Dan Lainer-Vos, Steve Loyal, Michael Mann, Slobodan Markovich, Harris Mylonas, Aogan Mulcahy, Niall O'Dochartaigh, Christian Olsson, Srdja Pavlovic, Kevin Ryan, Stacey Scriver, Eric Storm, Ori Swed, Jenifer Todd, Tamara Pavasović Trošt, Gordana Uzelac, Srdjan Vučetić, Iarfhlaith Watson, Brad West, and Andreas Wimmer. I am particularly grateful to Lea David, John A. Hall, Lorenzo Posocco, Rok Stergar, and the two anonymous Cambridge University Press reviewers who provided insightful comments on the entire manuscript.

Several chapters of the book are based on previously published work, but they have all been revised, expanded, and updated. I would like to thank the following publishers for their permission to draw on the previous publications: Chapter 4 is a revised version of (2021) 'Forging the Nation-Centric World: Imperial Rule and the Homogenisation of Discontent in Bosnia and Herzegovina (1878–1918)', *Journal of Historical Sociology* 34(3): 549–687. Chapter 5 is an updated version of (2024) 'Grounding Civic Nationhood: The Rise and Fall of Yugoslav Nationalism 1918–1991', *Canadian Slavonic Papers* 66(1–2): 8–35. Chapter 6 is an expanded version of (2022) 'Resurrecting National Greatness: The Changing Face of Golden Age in the Balkans', *Sociological Forum* 37(1): 1294–1317. Chapter 8 draws on (2025) Warrior Ethos and The Spirit of Nationalism, *Innovation* (39) 1:1–18. Chapter 9 is a revised version of (2024) 'Between Deep Comradeship and Nationalism: The Social Dynamics of Solidarity on the Battlefield', *Nations and Nationalism* 31(1): 47–63; and Chapter 10 is an updated version of (2022) 'Imagined Communities and Imaginary Plots: Nationalisms, Conspiracies, and Pandemics in the Longue Durée', *Nationalities Papers* 50(1): 45–60.

Finally, I would like to thank John Haslam from Cambridge University Press for his professionalism and support for my book projects over many years.

Introduction
Living in a Nation-Centric World

In 2024 two unrelated events received a great deal of public attention in Ireland. In May the Cork native non-binary performer Bambie Thug won sixth place at the Eurovision song contest in Malmö, which mass media have described as 'Ireland's most successful achievement since 2000' (O'Rourke 2024:1). The Eurovision contestant was considered to be highly unusual. Their performance combined unorthodox and syncretic musical styles including heavy metal and hyper-punk avant electro-pop (i.e., ouija-pop) with the stark staging visuals invoking images of witchcraft, occult, and neopaganism. Bambie Thug regularly accentuates the rebellious nature of their music: 'Historically, heavy metal, punk and rock has always been for the outcasts, the misfits and for the people who needed to rebel. Right now, our community is completely under attack' (Shutler 2023:1).

Nevertheless, despite this rebelliousness and the nominal commitment to nonconformity, Bambie Thug constantly emphasises their strong sense of nationhood. In many photographs published after their Eurovision success Bambie Thug was dressed in the fully fledged Irish tricolour with the sign 'crown the witch'. In their post-performance press conferences Bambie Thug would regularly emphasise how central is their sense of Irishness to this success: 'I'm beyond proud and beyond grateful for the love.... We're a tiny country and I don't think anyone screams louder than the Irish.... I am so proud to be Irish and to be representing this country and to have that war chant behind me.... I love you so much, we've just put Ireland on the map globally guys' (O'Rourke 2024:1).

Although the other event, taking place in September 2024, received less mass media coverage than the Eurovision contest, it too attracted a great deal of public attention – the winning of the Homeless World Cup by the Irish women's soccer team. This victory of the Irish national team, consisting of fifteen unhoused women, was hailed as 'heroic', 'amazing', and 'inspirational'. Although none of these women had any proper accommodation or fixed address in Ireland, the headlines in the major TV and newspaper outlets emphasised the centrality of their Irishness for this unprecedented success: 'The Girls in Green beat USA 5-2 in their Trophy Stage Final to cap off a fantastic tournament in style', 'Ireland ladies Homeless World Cup team are doing the country proud', and 'The victorious Irish women's homeless football team has returned from South Korea to a rapturous welcome at Dublin Airport' (FAI 2024; O'Donnell 2024). The mass media have zoomed in on the public elation and the even more emotional responses from the players: 'The team were joined by the men's squad and were greeted with cheers of "Ole, Ole, Ole" by family and well-wishers who gathered at Terminal One to welcome them home' (O'Donnell 2024:1). The commentators emphasised the homeless players' difficult road to the success by making links to their nationhood: 'They have experienced so many hardships in their lives yet here they are representing their country on the world stage and doing themselves, their families & friends and the nation proud' (FAI 2024:1). One report singled out a player who lost her father just before the tournament: 'My father boasted to so many people that his daughter was playing in the world cup so I felt like it was right to go, and I couldn't have asked for a better group to be there with. I'd say he would be bursting with pride and that's all I wanted to do is go out and make myself proud and make everyone else proud and I'm happy with that' (O'Donnell 2024:1).

What these two unrelated events have in common is that they are both firmly framed in the nation-centric terms. Not only do mass and social media articulate these two events through the prism of nationhood, but the participants of these events define their achievements within the identical, nation-centric, framework. Their individual success stories are automatically and unambiguously narrated as victories for and of the Irish nation. They express a sense of enormous pride of being members of their nation, and their accomplishments are simply assumed to be also the achievements of millions of other individuals whom they do not know and will never meet – the Irish nation.

The international successes in sports and entertainment regularly invoke a sense of collective effervescence where the citizens of nation-states routinely engage in the acts of national self-worship. However, on the first glance these two cases would not fit easily into these predictable patterns of national self-adulation. With their provocative appearance and the controversial performance, Bambie Thug challenges the conventional parameters of what is appropriate behaviour at international song contests. Their performance was deemed to be scandalous by many conservative groups throughout Europe, who objected to their 'sick and satanic routine', their 'demonic rituals', and 'disgusting witchcraft' (Williams 2024). Bambie Thug is very conscious that their performances attract such controversy, and they thrive on being rebellious, unconventional, and provocative: 'tell me I can't do it, I'll do it anyway.... [T]here's space for weirdness and diversity.... We are the rebels you need to hear' (Shutler 2023:1).

Nevertheless, this radical challenge to the existing norms and the intrinsic rebelliousness of this performer stop at the borders of nationhood. While they fiercely contest the conventional understandings of music, religion, sexuality, and even international politics (with their critique of Israel), they remain deeply conformist in reproducing nation-centric language and practice. While one can question and rebel against nearly every aspect of conventional life, nationhood remains outside that critique. By superimposing the rebellious sign 'crown the witch' on a garment made of the Irish flag, Bambie Thug's rebellion defines its ceiling – the deconstruction of nationhood remains off-limits. Moreover, the sense of being a member of one's nation remains the central nodal point of all activity. As Bambie Thug emphasises, 'I am so proud to be Irish', 'We're a tiny country and I don't think anyone screams louder than the Irish', and 'we've just put Ireland on the map globally' (O'Rourke 2024:1).

However, there is nothing unique in embracing nationhood by the rebellious artists. This pattern has been present with many other radical performers – from the deeply anti-conformist hippie singers to the punk and heavy metal bands to the recent politically defiant rappers and hip-hop artists. Although many of them challenge social inequalities, political corruption, gender disparities, conventional sexual mores, and racial injustice, they generally do not question the ideas and practices of nationhood. For example, when the punk band the Sex Pistols recorded their version of 'God Save the Queen', they were attacking nearly all aspects of the existing social, political, and economic order, including the institution of the monarchy, but not British nationhood as such. Paradoxically, this rebellious song eventually became another cultural product that glorified the British nation-state by emphasising its unprecedented liberties, where you can even poke fun of the national anthem. Hence, even the most radical performers remain within the confines of nation-states and their own nationalisms.

The same pattern of nation-centricity permeates the second public event – the Homeless World Cup victory by the Irish women's soccer team. In some respects, this is not unusual as sporting victories in the international arena have become an important instrument of national prestige. Hence, any international success, and especially winning a global trophy, is bound to be hailed as a major accomplishment that glorifies a particular nation-state and provides an opportunity for an act of collective self-adulation. Nevertheless, what is atypical in this case is that the winning team consists of individuals who have no home of their own. Although all the players are Irish citizens, none of them had a fixed address or place to call a home in Ireland. Although the sense of nationhood is often derived from the idea of home, a place where one feels safe, loved, and where one belongs, these players do not have actual homes. Instead, an abstract notion of a homeland replaces the real homes as the main nodal point of belonging. In this context nationhood is almost literally an imagined community, solely based on one's mental image of intra-group affinity and belonging. In Anderson's (1983:9) words these mental images of shared communion are 'saturated with ghostly national imaginings'. So, the individual players can embrace their abstract homeland but cannot return to their actual homes as they remain unhoused. This paradoxical situation is never referred to or even mentioned by the mass media reports where one's attachment to their respective nation-state is simply and automatically assumed to trump all other forms of belonging, including the attachment to one's locality and place of residence. The players themselves have also internalised this view and understand nationhood as something more significant than one's own home. In this context nationhood is not a substitute for the actual home but it replaces it completely as a source of identification, group solidarity, and collective prestige.

Both of these paradoxical examples indicate just how central nationhood is in the contemporary world. We live in the world where nation-state is the fundamental form of territorial political order and where nationalism is the hegemonic ideological discourse that justifies the existence of such an order. Nationhood is normalised, naturalised, and nearly universally perceived to be the principal form of organised collective belonging. While most other aspects of social life receive extensive scrutiny and generate intense polemics, the ideas and practices of nationhood largely remain taken for granted. For example, key social divisions such as the class, status, gender, sexuality, ethnicity, and 'race' are comprehensively analysed, problematised, and remain the central topics of intense debates across the globe. In contrast, the ideas and practices of nationhood receive much less analytical attention among sociologists and almost no critical scrutiny in public debates. Instead, nation-states are presumed to be the standard, logical, optimal, and only rightful form of social organisation, while nationhood is perceived to be an intrinsic and normal mode of collective existence. It is recognised that one can be a member of more than one nation-state (and possess several passports) and can have mixed loyalties or multiple identities. However, being voluntarily a-national or nation-less is largely not considered to be a serious political or social position. Losing one's membership in a nation-state or feeling alienated from one's nation would generally be perceived as a terrible misfortune.

However, as nation-states and nationalisms develop very late in human history, it is not completely clear how have they become so hegemonic in the contemporary word. Since its inception nearly 300 years ago nationalism has gradually expanded through a variety of social practices. This expansion was possible because nationalism is much more than a form of politics. It is a set of discourses and practices that strongly shape the economic, social, legal, and cultural life of billions of people all over the globe. The nationalist principles impact public policy, welfare provisions, migration laws, border control, economic planning, education systems, mass media discourses, military and policing practices, artistic trends, cultural policy, and consumption practices, among many others (Storm 2024; Fox 2025). Nationalism is not a marginal ideology to be associated with the militant movements, extremist groups, and populist politicians. It is the dominant operative ideology of modernity and as such it underpins the structural foundations of the world we inhabit today – the world of nation-states. Whether we like it or not, nationalism has become the dominant way of life.

Nationalism developed quite late as a sociological phenomenon, but once it took hold of state power its growth was largely continuous. The nationalist doctrine has managed to replace the competing ideological discourses of state legitimacy, including the divine origins of monarchy, imperial creeds, and the notion of civilising mission, among many others. From the end of World War II nationalism has gradually attained many hegemonic features and has become the dominant form of political legitimacy in the contemporary world. In addition to acquiring state power and enveloping official institutions and non-state organisations, this ideology and social practice has also penetrated civil society and the inter-personal networks of everyday life. Over the last 200 years one could witness an incessant proliferation of nationalism across the globe and within different social strata of individual societies. As I have argued before, and as elaborated more extensively in Chapter 1, the historical trajectory of nationalism has been shaped by the nearly continuous organisational, ideological, and micro-interactional grounding across time and space (Malešević 2020, 2019, 2013). Nationalism has protean features and, like a chameleon, can easily adapt to its surroundings. Scholars have traditionally invoked the image of the Roman god Janus to pinpoint the two contradictory faces of nationalism: as a force of collective solidarity but also as a mechanism of group aggression against those that do not belong to the nation (Nairn 2011, 1998). However, nationalism has many faces – it is a multifaceted political ideology, a habitual form of everyday practice, and a very plastic type of modern subjectivity.

Nationalism is a flexible discourse and social practice that can coalesce with far-right and the far-left ideologies, but it can also accommodate moderate positions across the political spectrum. Nationalist ideas are the cornerstone of such ideologically diverse movements as the far right Alternative für Deutschland in Germany and Sverigedemokraterna in Sweden and far-left groups such as the Tigray People's Liberation Front or the Communist Party of Cuba. Similarly nationalist principles feature prominently in centre right parties such as Les Républicains in France, GERB in Bulgaria, or Fine Gael in Ireland, and in centre left parties such as SMER in Slovakia, the Republican People's Party in Turkey, or the Plaid Cymru in Wales.

Even more importantly nationalism is not just a political ideology; it is also a social practice that is integral to many activities and processes present in a variety of social organisations and outlets of everyday life. For example, nationalist practices are often promoted by religious organizations (e.g., the Greek Orthodox Church, evangelical Christian movements in the United States, or the Bajrang Dal in India). Nationalist ideas can also underpin civil society activities (e.g., ethnic minority NGOs, cultural heritage associations, and national sport societies such as GAA in Ireland or Basque pelota clubs), private corporations (from selling distinct national products such as BMW or Guinness beer to promoting national tourist destinations such as the Eiffel tower, Taj Mahal, or Hagia Sophia), and different social institutions (such as Masonic lodges, war veterans' associations, or Boy Scouts).

Nation-centric practices are also integral to everyday life and habitual interactions between friends, family members, neighbours, peers, clans, and kinship-based groups. For example, wedding celebrations in the Balkans are often accompanied by the patriotic songs and the waving of national flags, while in Denmark birthday cakes regularly feature Danish national symbols such as the Dannebrog. The intimacy of friendship is also often interwoven with the shared experience of fervent cheering for one's national teams in various sporting competitions. In this sense nationalism has become a meta-ideological doctrine and social practice that infuses many aspects of everyday life in the contemporary world. Hence to better understand this complex phenomenon it is necessary to explore these many faces of nationalism to understand how and why nationalism has become the prevalent way of life in the early twenty-first century.

This book aims to explore the rise and transformation of nationalist subjectivities in the modern world. By zooming in on very different aspects of social change I intend to show how nationalism has gradually penetrated nearly every aspect of social relations and has largely become an incontestable and naturalised mode of living. More specifically, this book analyses a variety of historical and contemporary milieus, including religious-secular dynamics, imperial and post-imperial contexts, the formation of nationalist movements, the role of golden age myths in nationalist narratives, the impact of warfare on nation formation, the motivations of soldiers on the battlefields, the role of geopolitics in nation-building, civil-military relations, and the impact of conspiracy theories, to reveal the social and historical dynamics of nationalism as a way of life.

The focus is on tracing the organisational, ideological, and micro-interactional processes that have made nationalism such an influential discourse and practice in the contemporary world. This book builds on my previous studies on nationalism (Malešević 2020, 2019, 2013, 2006) but it differs from these publications in the two main ways: (1) it elaborates fully the key tenets of the grounded nationalism perspective and makes clear how this approach differs from other theories of nationalism and (2) it expands the historical and geographical scope of analysis by applying the grounded nationalism approach to a variety of case studies across time and space. In other words, I focus on the specific organisational, ideological, and micro-interactional mechanisms that reproduce nation-centric ideas and practices and make nationalism into a hegemonic way of life in the early twenty-first century. The book explores the key forms of lived experience: (1) how and why has nationalism become the dominant form of modern subjectivity – I explore the practices through which nation-centric idioms become normalised, routinised, and infused with social meanings that underpin how most people today see and experience the world; (2) how nationalism operates as a multifaceted meta-ideology – I aim to show why nationalism is much more than an ordinary political ideology such as liberalism, conservatism, or socialism; and (3) how and why national categories become organisationally embedded in everyday practices – I focus on the micro-context of kinships, friendships, and deep comradeships to demonstrate how dominant social organisations can successfully nationalise the micro-universe of everyday life.

In methodological terms the book is based on the analysis of primary and secondary data from different sources. Chapters 4 and 5 use primary data from archival research conducted in several archives in the Balkans. Chapters 5–10 rely on the qualitative analysis of various primary documentary resources including newspapers, school textbooks, official government records, military reports, websites of different civil society organisations, and artefacts from popular culture from all over the world.

Chapter 9 also analyses data collected from in-depth interviews with former soldiers who fought in the 1990s wars of Yugoslav succession. Chapters 1–3 and 11 mostly rely on secondary sources.

The Book's Structure

In Chapter 1 I briefly engage with contemporary approaches in the study of nations and nationalisms and offer a critique of structuralist and agency-centred explanations. I also articulate the theoretical framework that is then applied to the variety of case studies in the book. I outline the key features of my approach and describe how nationalist grounding operates on the coercive-organisational, ideological, and micro-interactional levels.

Chapter 2 explores the relationship between imperial and national subjectivities. Empires have dominated this planet for thousands of years, but in a relatively short period of time they have been completely delegitimised by nationalist projects. Hence, this chapter aims to explain how and why this has happened. Using historical examples of Japanese and Hungarian nation-formation the chapter traces the transformation of local, kinship-centred, and religiously based subjectivities into the nation-centric subjectivities.

In Chapter 3 I analyse the relationship between religion, state-formation, and nationalism. The focus is on the transformation of collective subjectivities in the Ottoman and post-Ottoman worlds. By zooming in on case studies of the Ottoman Empire and Turkey the chapter analyses what role religious and state institutions play in the development of distinct nationalist projects. Since both religion and nationhood were key sources of political legitimacy, the chapter explores how these two distinct types of collective subjectivities were reconciled in the social and political spheres. The chapter investigates the inherent tensions between the universalist doctrines of Sunni Islam and the unambiguous particularism of the modern nationalist projects in Turkey.

Chapter 4 explores the relationship between nationalism and imperialism. In this chapter I question the role of (nationalist) agency in the collapse of imperial order. Drawing on the primary archival research I focus on the case of Bosnia and Herzegovina under Austro-Hungarian rule (1878–1918). The chapter contests the view that the imperial state was severely undermined by the presence of strong nationalisms. I also challenge the notion that most of the Bosnian population remained 'nationally indifferent' during this period. Instead, I argue that understanding the character of Austro-Hungarian rule is a much better predictor of social change that took place in this period. Rather than stifling supposedly vibrant nationalisms or operating amidst widespread national indifference, the imperial state played a decisive role in forging the nation-centric world through its inadvertent homogenisation of social discontent.

Chapter 5 examines the role of golden age narratives in nationalism. By contrasting the experiences of the late nineteenth- and early twenty-first-century South-East European societies I explain how and why the images of the mythical past are articulated differently in these two historical periods. I argue that in the nineteenth century, golden age rhetoric was mostly a top-down phenomenon centred on transforming Balkan peasantry into the loyal members of their new nation-states. By the early twenty-first century this process has reached its institutional limits, and the golden age narratives have become a bottom-up phenomenon: the key agents of their creation and dissemination are members of civil society, social movements, and ordinary people. I focus on the structural processes that underpin this change to explain the historical dynamics of nationalist subjectivities.

In Chapter 6 I analyse the processes of nationalist grounding in ethnic and civic projects of nation-formation. I focus on the Yugoslav case to explore why both historical instances of civic-based nation-building have ultimately failed. This chapter focuses on the development and transformation of Yugoslav nationalism with the spotlight on its two main incarnations – the Yugoslav idea as articulated in the centralised and monarchic state of Serbs, Croats, and Slovenes (1918–1941) and the development of the Yugoslav project during the state socialist period (1945–1991). I argue that despite the nominal commitment towards building a civic nationhood, the Yugoslav project has paradoxically provided organisational, ideological, and micro-interactional mechanisms for the relatively continuous rise of ethnic nationalisms. The failure of Yugoslav nationalism stems in part from its uneven and misdirected grounding. It is this structural unevenness that also contributed to the relatively continuous proliferation of a much better-grounded ethnic nationalism.

In Chapter 7 I examine the impact war victories and war defeats have on the character of dominant nationalist discourses. Scholars of nationalism have extensively analysed how military defeats have shaped the collective memories of different nations. However, there has not been much comparative analysis of the relationship between nationalisms that transpire in the context of war victories and those that emerge in the environment of war defeats. This chapter looks at both phenomena. It argues that the scale and direction of nationalist narratives is rarely determined by war winning or losing but by the ability of social organisations to institutionalise a particular interpretation of specific wars. Instead of victories or defeats it is the coercive-organisational, ideological, and micro-interactional grounding that shapes the character of nationalism. This key argument is illustrated with a paired analysis of Croatia's memorialisation of the war victory in the 1991–1995 war of independence and Ghana's commemoration of the war defeat in the 1900 War of the Golden Stool.

In popular culture nationalism is often associated with battlefields. The combatants are regularly deemed to be inspired by a strong sense of patriotic duty. In Chapter 8 I challenge such views and aim to show that nationalism plays a marginal role in the combat zone. I argue that in most cases the warrior ethos is not linked directly to the nationalist ideas and practices. Instead, most combatants fight from a sense of moral obligation and emotional attachment to their micro-level groups. However, this is not to say that nationalism is irrelevant in the context of violent conflicts. On the contrary, I aim to show how nationalist ideas and practices permeate the organisational and ideological scaffolds of the wider social world. I argue that nationalism is primarily generated and reproduced in civilian institutions and other domains of civilian life.

Chapter 9 follows this line of argument by looking at the social mechanisms that facilitate the transformation of micro-level solidarities into coherent nationalist narratives. The aim is to explain a paradox: while the armed forces are highly nationalist institutions, most ordinary combatants detest nationalist rhetoric on the battlefield. Drawing on interviews with combatants who fought in the 1991–1995 wars in Croatia and Bosnia and Herzegovina together with the analysis of mass media reports, I examine how deep bonds of micro-solidarity forged in violent experiences are transformed into coherent nationalist discourses. I explore how social ties generated in the protracted face-to-face interactions can be enveloped by specific social organisations and then 'translated' into nationalist ideologies that project deep comradeship as 'national solidarities'. I aim to show that the direct war experience does not automatically generate strong bonds of national solidarity. Instead, nationalism is always a product of protracted coercive-organisational, ideological, and micro-interactional work.

Chapter 10 focuses on the historical relationship between nationalist subjectivities and conspiracy theories in times of profound crises. I argue that premodern conspiratorial narratives were mostly focused on eschatological and theological images, aiming to blame and delegitimise the religious Other. In these imaginary plots, large-scale pandemics were regularly interpreted as attacks on one's religious subjectivities. With the rise of nation-states and the decline of empires and patrimonial kingdoms, the periodic outbursts of epidemics gradually attained more nationalist interpretations. In these narratives the threatening Other was usually nationalised, and even traditional religious groups became reinterpreted as a threat to one's national subjectivities. In recent times, new technologies and modes of communication have created space for the emergence of global conspiracy theories. Some scholars have interpreted this as a reliable sign that nation-states and nationalisms have lost their dominance. However, this chapter shows that many global conspiracies in fact reinforce nationalist ideas and practices and, in this process, foster the perpetuation of national subjectivities.

In Chapter 11 I briefly explore how future human societies could exist without the nation-states and their foundational ideology of nationalism. I envisage several scenarios for the post-national world and analyse the long-term consequences of such scenarios. The Conclusion summaries the key arguments of the book.

Nationalism is so embedded in our lives that it is almost impossible for anyone living today to disentangle themselves from its engulfing tentacles. Moreover, as this ideology and social practice has become second nature to billions of people, there is no interest nor meaningful organised attempt to remove these tentacles. Most people enjoy the embrace of these tentacles and identify strongly with them. In many respects nationalism is the quintessential example of Weber's view that human beings are animals suspended in webs of significance that they themselves have spun (Geertz 1973:5). We have created this omnipotent nationalist web of significance that now shapes nearly every aspect of our lives.

1 Nationalism as a Way of Life

Introduction

The phenomenon of nationalism has been extensively studied by many different disciplines, including history, political science, international relations, social psychology, philosophy, anthropology, geography, and sociology. This research has produced abundance of excellent studies on different aspects of nationalism through time and space. There are now many valuable theoretical and empirical analyses of this phenomenon from all over the world. However, much of this scholarship remains divided along several axes. For one thing, there is a deep split between the structuralist and agency-centred perspectives. These differences are not just epistemological, in the sense that some theories prioritise structure over agency or vice versa in their explanations of this phenomenon, but they are also focused on different experiences of nationalism. Structuralists tend to explore the impact of geopolitical, economic, cultural, and military institutions, the role of states, political parties, and social movements in the development and proliferation of nationalism. In contrast, agency-centred theories zoom in on the use and reproduction of nationalist practices in everyday interactions of ordinary life (Mylonas & Tudor 2023; Özkirimli 2017; Smith 1998).

For another thing, the thematic differences are also pronounced within both analytical camps. For instance, the cultural structuralists are interested in tracing analytical parallels between collective myths, religion, commemorations, and nationalism. In contrast, the economic structuralists focus on the economic nationalist policies: the interventions of the governments in the economy such as the use of tariffs on goods and restrictions on the movement of labour or capital. The political structuralists tend to investigate state power, political systems, and the rise and decline of nationalist parties and movements. The military structuralists explore geopolitical transformations and the potential threat of war and how these processes impact nationalist mobilisation.

The agency-centred approaches also exhibit a significant difference in their research interests: while elite theorists analyse how the political entrepreneurs deploy potent symbols to mobilise nationalist action, the materialist approaches zero in on individual motivations and the dynamics of situational rationality in the decisions of agents to support specific nationalist projects. Neo-Darwinian perspectives analyse what they see to be the biological givens of ethno-nationalist identifications, while the symbolic interactionists explore how the social order is generated and reproduced through everyday interactions of ordinary individuals (Mylonas & Tudor 2023; Özkirimli 2017; Malešević 2006, 2004).

This cacophony of very diverse perspectives that often focus on different issues does not help us gain better understanding of how and why nationalism became and remains the dominant social force in the contemporary world. Hence, to analytically examine this multifaceted phenomenon it is necessary to epistemologically navigate between structure and agency to generate more comprehensive answers to these questions. In this context nationalism is not just a form of politics, an economic force, a cultural artefact, a military and geopolitical phenomenon, or a form of everyday life. It is all of this and much more. Nationalism is a dominant form of modern subjectivity that shapes nearly every aspect of social life in the contemporary world. In this chapter I aim to explore how nationalist grounding operates across three different but deeply interconnected processes that shape social reality: the coercive-organisational, the ideological, and the micro-interactional. I try to show how these processes make nationalist ideas and practices normalised, naturalised, and deeply embedded in our public institutions and our private lives. The first part of the chapter engages briefly with the strengths and weaknesses of the structuralist and agency-centred perspectives, while the second, much longer, part offers an alternative understanding of nationalism that tracks its historical grounding.

Beyond Structure

There is no doubt that nationalism is a structural phenomenon. As classical modernist scholarship made clear many years ago, nationalist ideas and practices are neither primordial nor transhistorical (Gellner 1983; Anderson 1983; Breuilly 1993; Hobsbawm 1990; Hall 1993). As a sociological phenomenon nationalism emerges in a specific historical period (modernity), and its development is shaped by very particular structural forces.

For some economic structuralists such as Gellner (1983) and early Nairn (1981) nationalism transpires in the context of changing economic foundations of social order that ultimately generates uneven industrialisation. For Nairn (1981:332) nationalist ideology is 'determined by certain features of the world political economy, in the era between the French and Industrial Revolutions and the present day'. In Gellner's view nationalism emerges in the period of transition from the agrarian to the industrial world. The economy of premodern societies is based on the control and exploitation of the land, which engenders deeply stratified social orders where culture is deployed to reinforce the difference between aristocracy and peasantry. In contrast, the economy of modernising societies is dependent on industrial production, which ultimately entails social and spatial mobility and culturally homogenous populations. As Gellner (1983:57) emphasises: 'Nationalism is, essentially, imposition of high culture on society, where previously low cultures had taken up the lives of majority.... It is the establishment of an anonymous, impersonal society, with mutually substitutable atomised individuals, held together above all by shared culture of its kind.'

Political structuralists such as Breuilly (1993), Hall (2013, 1993), Brubaker (1996), and Hearn (2006) focus on the role of the state in the development and proliferation of nationalism. In this understanding 'nationalism is a form of politics' and political action involves struggles over power. For Breuilly (1993:1) 'power in the modern world, is principally about the control of the state'. In this context nationalism is primarily a political phenomenon that emerges when modern nation-states gradually replace premodern imperial orders. Social modernisation generates a shift from the 'corporate' to 'functional' division of labour that facilitates the rise of the modern bureaucratic state with clear separation between public and private spheres. Nationalism emerges as a political project that promises to re-establish the state–society connection so that one's private interests are reconciled with public interests of citizens. For Breuilly (1993:19) nationalism 'involves the organisation of mass support for political purposes of the management of large groups which have suddenly intruded into a previously exclusive political arena'. Nationalism is a form of oppositional politics that challenges existing state structures and aims to attain state power. Brubaker (1996:21) develops this argument further by insisting on the contingent character of nation-formation.[1] In his view nations are not 'substantial, enduring collectivities'. Instead, nationhood is a 'category of practice' and 'an

[1] In his early work Brubaker (1996, 1992) developed politically structuralist explanations of nationalism. In his later work (2004, 2015) his approach is more micro-sociological, agency-centred, and interactionist.

institutionalised political and cultural form'. Using the example of the Soviet Union, Brubaker shows how Soviet nationality policy was first and foremost a political project that ultimately reified ethno-national categories. The regime institutionalised the territorial republics for different ethno-national collectivities. Soviet institutions consisted of a 'pervasive system of social classification, an organising principle of vision and division of the social world'. Hence, nationalist tensions that emerged in the 1990s were conflicts not between nations but between 'the institutionally constituted national elites' (Brubaker 1996:24–25).

The military-centred structuralists such as Mann (2023, 1993), Tilly (1992), Giddens (1986), or Wimmer (2013) also accept that nationalism is a political phenomenon. However, they emphasise that military power and wars have played a central role in the formation of nation-states and that organised coercion remains crucial in this process. For Mann (1993) and Tilly (1992), the intensification of inter-state warfare in early modern Europe spurred the process of nation-formation and unwittingly fostered the spread of nationalist fighting, tax collection, and military recruitment. To increase military budgets, the size of their armies, and the quality and quantity of their weaponry, the rulers had to stimulate the development of science and technology, build better administrative apparatuses capable of regular revenue collection, make the judiciary more efficient, create more centralised systems of governance, and build better transportation and communication networks. The governments also had to introduce the military draft, aiming to maximise the number of potential recruits. The long-term consequence of this process was the transformation of civil society and the rise of nationalism. To gain a degree of legitimacy and to receive a continuous supply of recruits and taxes, rulers had to make concessions to the ordinary population. Consequently, intensified warfare stimulated the rise of citizenship rights, the development of parliamentary systems, and the expansion of religious, national, and political freedoms and even welfare provisions. With increased literacy rates, the development of mass media, and a shared military experience, the ordinary population became highly receptive to nationalist ideologies. More recently, Wimmer (2013) has provided extensive empirical validation that nation-states and nationalism emerged in the context of major wars. He argues that the rise of nationalist movements played a central role in the development of warfare, which has ultimately brought down the old imperial order.

Finally, cultural structuralism, as articulated in the work of ethnosymbolists such as Smith (2009, 2008, 1986) and Hutchinson (2017, 1994), interprets nationalism through the prism of shared transgenerational cultural heritage and practices. For Smith (2009) nationalism is a form of civil religion that imposes specific moral obligations on its adherents. The myth of common descent together with the idea of national sacrifice invoke a sense of collective responsibility for members of the nation. In this context, periodic rituals such as the commemoration of the fallen solders or revolutionaries who died for the nation establish and sustain the shared moral universe of co-nationals. In Smith's view nations have 'sacred foundations' as they develop on premodern ethnic and religious attachments. In this view nationalism remains powerful because it addresses the same cultural questions that religion does: the meaning of existence, the sense of collective belonging, and moral guidance for social conduct, 'so it is in the sphere of "religion" that we must seek primarily the sources of national attachment' (Smith 2003:4–5). For Smith (1991:14) nationalism is a phenomenon that is shaped by different cultural structures such as common myths and historical memories, historic territory, mass public culture, and common legal rights and duties for all its members.

All these structuralist explanations offer persuasive arguments about the origins of nationalism. Nevertheless, as they focus on different aspects of nationalist experience, they tend to provide partial answers to what is an all-encompassing phenomenon. There is no doubt that nationalism is shaped by economic, political, military, cultural, and many other structures. However, all these structural forces presuppose the emergence and development of specific organisational capacities that can sustain and foster these structural transformations. In other words, structures cannot appear out of thin air; they must be created, sustained, and coordinated to make a specific change or just to keep these structures in place. The problem with most structuralist theories is that they simply assume the existence of structural entities. There is a tendency to reify social structures and treat them as given rather than attempting to explain their origin, formation, transformation, and possible disintegration. The structure is not a permanent and fixed entity; it is a dynamic social force that is composed of actions of specific human beings. As Rex (1980:119) noted a long time ago, social structures should be perceived as 'arising from the continuity in time of interlocking patterns of interaction' and as such they do not have constant and pre-set properties but are variable and changeable entities. In this context economic, political, military, or cultural powers are not primordial forces but something that gradually arises from the coordinated social action of thousands or millions of individuals over the course of human history. To account for the emergence of these social structures it is necessary to zoom in on the origins and development of specific social organisations that can generate this structural power. Thus, political movements, militaries, private corporations, and churches are all examples of social organisations that can shape the direction of specific nationalisms.

Hence, if social organisations are the key vehicles of structural transformations, the key question is, how did they develop and operate? I define social organisations as complex hierarchical entities that rely on the division of labour, discipline, control, and mobilisation of people and resources. Such entities tend to operate through the durable means of communication, transport, and knowledge generation that allow them to accomplish different tasks. Social organisations are the most effective medium for a coordinated social action and as such they have historically proved to be the principal agents of social change (Malešević 2017:44–47). Archaeological and paleontological studies indicate that complex social organisations developed late in prehistory and early history – around 12,000 years ago. For much of their existence on this planet, human beings have lived as nomadic hunter-gatherers with very loose group configurations that lacked stable and coherent organisational forms. Thus, it is only with the Neolithic revolution that social organisations become the cornerstone of social life.[2] Once they emerge on the historical stage, they soon attain a near-hegemonic position. The early forms of social organisations – from chiefdoms and city-states to the pristine imperial orders and other entities – quickly established their dominance over populations lacking complex social organisations (Scott 2017; Mann 1986). With the emergence of empires and the proliferation of wars of conquest, many nomadic populations were either obliterated or coercively assimilated into large state structures. Hence, the existence of complex and durable social organisations is a basic precondition for the development of large-scale economic, political, military, or cultural structures. Nevertheless, it is important to emphasise that social organisations are not uniform and motionless blocks of material but are entities composed of dynamic and variable human beings whose actions are never fixed and predictable but are prone to change. The historical record indicates that these actions are mostly shaped by coercion, legitimacy, and the sense of emotional attachment towards other people (Mann 2023, 1986; Malešević 2017, 2010; Collins 1986). In other words, the strength and durability of social organisations are

[2] Some scholars such as Graeber and Wengrow (2021) question the entire idea of Neolithic revolution and argue that agriculture did not replace nomadic lifestyles throughout the world but that many alternative ways of production and social organisation have emerged. However, this view has been challenged by other anthropologists and archaeologists, who mostly agree that the current geological epoch, the Holocene, is defined by the shift from hunting and gathering towards sedentary agricultural life that started 12,000 years ago (Bell 2021; Handler 2022).

dependent on their ability to successfully combine these three processes to maintain or expand their organisational powers. An ever-increasing coercive capacity, a widening ideological justification, and an ability to integrate these two with the micro-emotional ties of ordinary individuals have been crucial for the historical expansion of social organisations and ultimately for the development of dominant social structures that shape the contemporary world. Thus, the economic, political, military, or cultural structures that gave birth to nation-states and nationalisms as they exist today have all transpired and continue to shape human action on the back of specific social organisations. By focusing on the rise and transformation of social organisations, one can move away from the overly structuralist explanations of nationalism. By demonstrating in practice how all social organisations consist of, and depend on, the actions of thousands and in some instances millions of human beings, one can go beyond the deterministic approaches that neglect or downplay the significance of social action. In this way one can overcome the economic, political, military, and cultural determinism of classical structuralist approaches to nationalism without giving up on the significance of social structures. Furthermore, by emphasising the situational and contingent character of human action one can adequately account for the persistence, and the growth, of nationalism in the contemporary world. In contrast to the economic structuralists such as Gellner, political structuralists such as Breuilly, and military structuralists such as Tilly and Giddens, who all understand nationalism as a historically transitional phenomenon that is likely to soon fade away, the non-structuralist perspectives allow us to explain the continuous potency of nationalism in the contemporary world.

Beyond Agency

From the inception of nationalism studies as a distinct academic area in the late 1980s until quite recently, structuralist theories have completely dominated this field. Even the perspectives that recognised the significance of specific agents for the development of nationalism such as intellectuals and cultural elites (Kedourie 1960; Hutchinson 2005) or political entrepreneurs (Hobsbawm 1990; Tilly 1992) tended to see agency through the prism of wider structural processes. It is only in the last few decades that social action has gained more systematic analytical treatment and that the behaviour of individual agents has been recognised as central for understanding the dynamics of nationalism. However, agency-centred theories of nationalism also appear in several very different guises: biological, economic, political, discursive, and interactionist approaches. Biological theories, as articulated by van den Berghe (2001) and Gat (2013), draw on the neo-Darwinian framework and see nations as primordial entities defined by shared descent and endogamous patterns of collective reproduction. In this perspective nationhood is based on ethnic ties that have developed from shared kinship. As van den Berghe (2001:274) emphasises, 'ethnicity, thus, is simply kinship writ large'; ethnic groups and nations 'are super-families of (distant) relatives, real or putative, who tend to intermarry, and who are knit together by vertical ties of descent reinforced by horizontal ties of marriage'. For both van den Berghe and Gat, ethnic groups have existed since 'the dawn of history' and nations only represent politically conscious ethnic groups. These sociobiological accounts prioritise agency over structure as they focus on the biological motivations of individuals for social action. In this interpretation, nationalism is a form of ethnocentrism that has evolved over millions of years as an extension of kin selection. Human beings are perceived to be animals who are primarily driven by the biological need to reproduce. When they cannot reproduce directly, they do so indirectly by preferring kin over non-kin and close kin over distant kin. In this context nationalism operates as a mechanism of in-group favouritism.

The economic theories of nationalism such as the social exchange and the rational choice perspectives also focus on the role of individual motivation. However, instead of inherent genetic propensities they emphasise economic self-interest. For Banton (1983), Hechter (2000), and Laitin (2007), nationalism is a consequence of individual and collective decision-making processes. They see humans as being predominately rational and self-interested creatures whose actions are governed by the principle of utility maximisation. In this view a strong sense of national identification is regularly shaped by the collective coordination of individual benefits. The individual agents will emphasise their sense of national belonging or their similarities with members of their nation if this action can generate economic (or in some instances symbolic) gain. For Laitin (2007) national solidarity is a consequence of interest-driven individual action. Banton (1983) specifies that the principle of utility maximisation operates differently on the individual and on the group level: 'when people compete as individuals, group boundaries are weakened but when they compete as groups, boundaries are strengthened'. Hence, increased nationalism is perceived to be a direct consequence of the coordinated collective competition for resources, status, or power.

The agency-centred political approaches also identify individual self-interest as a crucial mechanism of social action, but they attribute this motivation to political elites rather than ordinary individuals. For Brass

(1991:111) ethno-national tensions and animosities are regularly a product of elite manipulation. Rather than having a primordial quality, national and ethnic attachments are for the most part an elite construct: 'they are creations of elites who draw upon, distort, and sometimes fabricate materials from the cultures of the group they wish to represent, in order to protect their wellbeing or existence, or to gain political and economic advantage for their group or for themselves'. Similarly, Snyder (2000) argues that nationalist mobilisation is often associated with the actions of political elites who radicalise political rhetoric to thwart democratisation. By focusing on the political orders that undergo transition from authoritarian rule he aims to show how political entrepreneurs utilise nationalist symbols for political mobilisation to acquire or cement their hold on power. In this perspective nationalism is perceived to be a political resource that elites can deploy willy-nilly to maintain their privileged political position.

In contrast to the political approaches that focus on the behaviour of elites, the discursive and the interactionist approaches study the actions of ordinary populations. The agency-centred discursive perspective on nationalism has been developed most systematically by Billig (1995) and Calhoun (2007, 1997). They both perceive nationhood through the prism of popular rhetoric and practice. Drawing on the tradition of discursive psychology, Billig (1995) has developed a novel approach that focuses on the reproduction of nation-centric ideas and practices in everyday life. In his view nationalism cannot be reduced to far-right politics, to political aspirations to create a new nation-state, or to some peripheral regions that struggle with social cohesion. Instead, nationalism is a phenomenon that affects all modern societies as it is embedded in everyday actions and discourses. He argues that 'crises do not create nation-states as nation-states'. Rather 'daily, they are reproduced as nations and their citizenry as nationals ... For such daily reproduction to occur, one might hypothesize that a whole complex of beliefs, assumptions, habits, representations, and practices must also be reproduced. Moreover, this complex must be reproduced in a banally mundane way. For the world of nations is the everyday world, the familiar terrain of contemporary times' (Billig 1995:6). For Calhoun (1997) nationalism is a discursive formation centred on the specific ways of speaking, thinking, and acting that prioritise nationhood. In contrast to most structuralists who see nations as objective historical realities, Calhoun (1997:5) rejects this objectivism and argues that 'nations are constituted largely by the claims themselves, by the way of talking and thinking and acting that relies on these sorts of claims to produce collective identity, to mobilise people for collective projects, and to evaluate peoples and practices'.

The interactionist approaches, most consistently developed by Brubaker (2011, 2004), Fox and Miller-Idriss (2008), and Skey (2011), explore how ordinary people deploy the nation-centric categories in everyday encounters with others. In his later works Brubaker (2015, 2004) advances a cognitive interactionist approach that blends a social constructivist paradigm with the up-to-date knowledge from natural science. In this approach nationhood is conceptualised as a relational category that is shaped by different social agents. In this context Brubaker (2004:77–78) argues that nations are not real, physical entities but are the product of human perceptions: 'they are not things in the world but perspectives on the world. These include ethicised ways of seeing (and ignoring), of construing (and misconstruing), of inferring (and mis-inferring), of remembering (and forgetting)'. It is through national categories and classifications that individuals 'recognize and experience objects, places, persons, actions or situations as ethnically, racially or nationally marked and meaningful' (Brubaker 2004:78). Fox and Miller-Idriss (2008) expand the interactionist perspective further by analysing the practices and values of ordinary populations including nation-centric consumption, nationalist forms of everyday performance, enactment, and the use of nation-centric categories in everyday language. Together with Skey (2011), Antonsich (2016), and Edensor (2002), they explore the different repertoires of everyday nationalism as articulated in culinary practices, tourist destinations, sporting events, beauty competitions, and so on.

This rich repertoire of different agency-centred theories of nationalism contributes significantly towards better understanding of this phenomenon. These micro-sociological perspectives show clearly that nationalism is not just a structural phenomenon but is something that is developed, shaped, enacted, and sustained by the individual actions of millions, and in some cases by billions, of people. As a sociological phenomenon nationalism is first and foremost a lived experience. There could be no nation-states and nationalisms without real-life human agency. Moreover, these organisational vehicles and ideological projects remain dependent on the ongoing commitment and shared perceptions of ordinary populations all over the world. There is no doubt that nationalism is a phenomenon shaped by the rhetoric of shared descent, the manipulation of political entrepreneurs, the influence of cultural elites, the economic self-interest of organised individuals, and the discursive practices and everyday interactions of ordinary people. Nevertheless, nationalism is more than this.

What is missing in most agency-centred perspectives is time dynamics. Nationalism is not a transhistorical phenomenon but something that only appears in a specific historical period and under very distinct social conditions. The problem with all ahistorical theories such as sociobiology, rational choice theory, and many strands of elite-centred approaches is that they analyse nationhood as a timeless universal phenomenon that is shaped by the same individual motivations as any other form of group category, including class, status, caste, or gender, to name a few. However, nationalism emerges on the historical stage only when many other social processes have already taken place – from the transformation of the economy to the development of centralised state structures and a society-wide bureaucratic system of governance, the spread of standardised vernaculars, the creation of mass-scale education, substantially increased literacy rates, and the development of mass media and military conscription, among others. In other words, the agency matters only in the context of the large-scale structural transformations that transpire over long periods of time.

The discursive and interactionist approaches tend to recognise the modernity of nationalism, but they too neglect the historical and structural context of nation-formation. As Knott (2023:230) recognises, everyday nationalism approaches 'require a degree of presentism to gain the thickness of data that comes from immersion in a particular field site at a particular moment, in turn sacrificing historical breadth for sociological and contemporary depth'. Nevertheless, if one ignores historical contexts, it is difficult, if not impossible, to understand where everyday nationalism comes from and how it operates. It is only by historicising nationalism and exploring its wider structural processes that one can trace the long-term trajectories of everyday nationalist practices. Furthermore, by focusing on the historical breadth one can also better understand the role coercive organisational power has historically played and continues to play in the development and reproduction of nationalism worldwide. The interactionist and discursive theories tend to overemphasise the ideational variables and ignore or downplay the coercive and geopolitical factors that make nation-states and thus nationalism possible and socially viable. Nationalism is not just a set of ideas and values; it is even more a corpus of social practices that are shaped by specific coercive-organisational powers. This epistemological idealism of interactionists is countered by another extreme within the agency-centred approaches that underpins the rational choice theory, sociobiology, and elite-centred perspectives: epistemological materialism. As I have argued elsewhere, neither of these two radical positions is adequate for understanding the complexity of social relations in general and of nationalism in particular. Instead, it is necessary to develop a softer, wider, and politically more supple understanding of social action that would generate better explanations of this phenomenon (Malešević, 2004:172–175). The multifaceted and multi-historical character of nationalism does not allow for simple generalisations that reduce everything to elite manipulation, self-interest, shared descent, institutional reproduction, or discursive framing. Nationalism is both a structural phenomenon and an ongoing product of human agency. However, this is not to say that one can easily integrate structure and agency and develop an epistemologically sustainable synthetic or syncretic perspective.[3] The main problem with all such syncretic attempts is that if you recognise that all variables are just as important, then a meaningful explanation is not possible. Craib (1992:10) illustrates this epistemological problem well: 'general synthetic theories close down the possibilities of investigation and explanation that are open to us. Theoretical work comes to be like putting together a jigsaw puzzle: before we start, we already know what the final picture will be like.' Any sociologically meaningful explanation entails that an analyst identifies the key factors that shape the direction of a particular event, process, or phenomenon. Hence saying simply that both agency and structure contribute equally to the development of nationalism would not help us much. Instead, the complex and sometimes contradictory relationships between structure and agency can be navigated through a theoretical framework that analytically accounts for both but still gives more weight to some explanatory factors over others. Hence, to better understand these complexities one has to focus on the three long-term and ongoing historical processes through which nationalisms operate: coercive-organisational, ideological, and micro-interactional grounding.

Making Sense of Nationalism

While the classics of nationalism studies such as Kohn (1958), Nairn (1981), or Gellner (1983) were focused on developing an all-encompassing theory of nationalism, many contemporary scholars are wary of such attempts as they believe that no universal theory of nationalism is possible. For example, Calhoun (1997:123, 8) argues that 'nationalism is too diverse to allow a single general theory to explain it all' and that 'nationalism is a rhetoric for speaking about too many

[3] In sociological theory these syncretic attempts to transcend the duality between structure and agency, and between the macro and micro perspectives, are associated with the structuration theory of Anthony Giddens (1984), Pierre Bourdieu's (1990) theory of habitus, Norbert Elias's (2000) figurational sociology, and Margaret Archer's (2008) morphogenesis, among others. For the epistemological critique of these syncretic perspectives, see Loyal and Malešević (2020) and Malešević (2004).

different things for a single theory to explain it'. Similarly, Breuilly (2016:80) points out that 'nationalist ideas and politics are found in a bewildering variety of modern situations, and it is impossible to develop a "theory of nationalism" which connects this diversity to particular internal conditions'. Brubaker shares this view: 'the great range and heterogeneous causal texture of the phenomena grouped under the rubrics of ethnicity and nationalism ... render problematic any effort to construct a general theory' (Brubaker et al. 2006:357; Brubaker 2004). Nevertheless, this blanket rejection of general theory seems epistemologically unfounded. If one conceptualises theory as an accumulated body of knowledge intended to explain some phenomenon based on the general principles that are independent of the phenomenon that needs to be explained, then a general theory of nationalism is possible. Rejecting the possibility of a general theory on the simple ground that nations and nationalisms are 'too diverse', have a 'great range', or appear in a 'variety of modern situations' does not seem to be a plausible argument. If we were to apply this same analytical yardstick to other social phenomena such as class, gender, race, status, or age, among many others, there would be no general sociological theories of any of these phenomena. Yet there are numerous general sociological theories of gender, class, age, race, or status. Why would nations and nationalisms be an exception here? Even if the focus is shifted towards the ideological doctrine or practice alone, it is still possible to develop a general theory of nationalism in the same way that has been done for the theories of racism, classicism, ageism, or gender-based ideologies. All these ideological discourses and practices also appear in many diverse guises, have a great range, and display huge variety across time and space.

The fact that nationhood and nationalism are heterogeneous and highly dynamic phenomena does not mean that they should be immune to general theorising. On the contrary, the enormous historical, geographical, and experiential diversity of nationalism together with its contemporary pervasiveness both provide a real analytical challenge to make sense of this all-embracing phenomenon. It is precisely because nationalism appears in so many different forms and is such a prevalent, omnipotent, and ever-expanding phenomenon that it requires a more general explanation. Calhoun's (1997:8) view that 'grasping nationalism in its multiplicity of forms requires multiple theories' does not seem convincing. If one is to apply the same criteria to other social phenomena that also appear in multiplicity of forms – for example, crime, inequality, education, violence, or social movements – then the outcome would be thousands of very specific micro-theories for each instance of this multiple experience. This approach would not be helping the explanatory cause. Hence, nationhood, nation-states, and nationalisms should be an object of general theorising, just as any other social phenomena.

It is necessary to identify some common threads and general principles that have led to the contemporary situation where nation-states are deemed to be the only legitimate form of territorial authority in the modern world and where nationalism has become the hegemonic and rarely contested view of the world. To explain this historical trajectory, it is crucial to ask general questions that require general answers: Why, when, and how did the nation-states replace the alternative forms of territorial organisation and establish an organisational monopoly on this planet? How and why did nationalism become the hegemonic ideology of modern world? Why do we still live in a nation-centric world? To provide meaningful answers to these general questions one cannot benefit from the multiple micro-theories. As nationhood and nationalism are not experiences that affect a small group of people, a particular region, or a unique social condition but things that shape the entire world and influence the behaviour of billions of people, it is paramount to offer a general explanation of these phenomena.

However, this is not to say that one, all-encompassing theory of nationalism can deal with all aspects of this vast research area. No theory can do that. The classical critics of abstract theorising in sociology such as Merton (1968) and Mills (1959) were right that it is impossible to construct a total theoretical model that would cover all segments of social life and would generate timeless universal truths. They demonstrated convincingly that the grand theories such as Parsons' systems theory or the Marxist theory of society were inadequate for explaining many aspects of ever-changing social relations. Such theories regularly lack a robust empirical foundation, are disconnected from everyday practice, and are too rigid to account for the deeply contingent and dynamic character of social life. Hence, the most popular alternative to grand theorising ever since has been the Merton's idea of the middle-range theory. In contrast to the abstract universalism of grand theory, the middle-range approach has been associated with two central aims: (1) to develop hypotheses from more specialised theories that can be tested in the empirical context and (2) to gradually accumulate testable knowledge in order to build a more general conceptual scheme that would bring together these specialised theories (Merton 1968:51). Thus, the middle-range perspective was not designed to reject the possibility of general theories. Instead, it was devised as a more effective and empirically more rooted method that would lead towards better general theorising. Merton's ideas have recently been developed further, aiming to use the accumulated knowledge from the middle-range perspectives to advance the general theories (Hedström & Udehn 2009).

While many contemporary theorists of nationalism reject the idea of general theory, a few have developed a satisfactory alternative. Among those who have not given up on the systematic theory building are Wimmer (2013, 2017) and Cederman (2024, 1997), whose deductive approaches represent a form of middle-range theory as applied to the study of nation-formation and nationalism. They both follow Merton's two main precepts of middle-range theorising as they formulate specialised theories that are then tested on the range of empirical material in order to cumulatively build more general explanatory models. Both scholars have produced deductive large-scale comparative analyses that successfully combine theoretical analysis with robust empirical validation by focusing on the entire world. These studies indicate clearly that the systematic application of middle-range theory can lead towards more general theories of nations and nationalisms. However, these approaches have also been criticised for their overreliance on the hard positivist methodologies that impact directly on their theoretical frameworks and their empirical findings. While both Wimmer and Cederman emphasise the relational and dynamic character of nationhood, their dependence on the very static quantitative research techniques shapes their key arguments: the process-centred theoretical models that posit plasticity of group categorisations and identifications are often tested using the conventional quantitative methods and traditional databases where ethnic groups and nations are regularly defined in essentialist and mutually exclusive terms.

Nevertheless, middle-range theorising does not have to be strictly deductive. It is possible to articulate the inductive middle-range models that would still lead towards a more general theory of nation-states and nationalisms. The positivist tradition, as exemplified by Wimmer and Cederman, is largely built around deductive principles that start with hypotheses and theory building, which are then tested in the empirical world. In contrast, the inductive perspective commences from observation of social life in order to identify some common patterns and then gradually proceeds towards theory building. The main advantage of this perspective is that it allows for a deeper understanding and better embedment of the key concepts within empirical reality; it also promotes more reflexive and process-oriented theory building as the researcher works with a range of probabilities that help expand one's knowledge, perception, and understanding of the social world. When social relations are not conceptualised as fixed, stable, static, and mutually exclusive collectivities, as inevitably framed by positivist methodologies, it is possible to better capture the ongoing social changes. By starting from observation and then moving to exploration before developing an explanatory framework the researcher can constantly navigate between empirical material and theory building. In this context theory building is not reduced to generating a simple formula that can be applied to all historical situations and all social relations. Instead, theory building is an ongoing and reflexive process that can be developed, reformulated, and improved on the basis of new information, previously unavailable data, and/or novel discoveries about the wider social world. This perspective also allows for greater methodological flexibility as it can successfully integrate very different research techniques, including participant observation, interviews, archival research, and documentary analysis. Thus, inductive middle-range theorising provides a steppingstone towards development of more reflexive and historically nuanced general theories of nation-states and nationalisms.

The analytical approach developed and applied in this book, as in my previous studies (Malešević 2019, 2013, 2006), uses the form of inductive middle-range theory to explain the historical dynamics of nationhood and nationalism. By focusing on the three processes of nationalist grounding (the coercive-organisational, the ideological, and the micro-interactional) I aim to explore the long-term transformation of social orders in order to understand the social dynamics of nation-states and nationalist subjectivities.

Organisational Grounding and Nationalist Subjectivities

Nationalist ideologies are usually associated with the spread of ideas that advocate popular sovereignty, cultural authenticity, political independence, or national solidarity. However, nationalism would never become such a potent and prevalent ideological discourse without the presence of robust social organisations. The development and expansion of specific coercive-organisational capacities over time has played a central role in the rise and spread of nationalism worldwide. Historians often emphasise that the early forms of nationalist projects were created through the interaction of middle-class intellectuals congregating in the social clubs, reading rooms, public cafes, pubs, teahouses, or private salons (Hroch 2015; Smith 1986; Leerssen 2006). Historical scholarship largely focuses on proto-nationalist ideas that were articulated in these micro-environments, but what was just as important was the organisational milieu where these ideas were fermented. Although these were all informal settings, their very existence provided an organisational shell for the development of specific associations that would promote the early proto-nationalist projects. Regular meetings in designated spaces transformed ad hoc interactions and free-floating ideas into the Goffmanian (1967) interaction rituals and institutionalised entities that gradually gave birth to relatively coherent proto-nationalist projects.[4] These were the seeds of the organisational grounding of nationalism.

Some of these regularised encounters led eventually towards the development of secret revolutionary societies that devised more elaborate plans for national independence or the protection of state sovereignty. Early forms of such societies include the Carbonari in southern Italy, who established their secret lodges in the early 1800s; the Charbonnerie in France; the Carbonaria in Portugal; and similar societies that developed in Spain, Brazil, Uruguay, Russia, and the Ottoman Empire. Members of these secret societies were mostly nobility, higher ranking officers, government officials, small landlords, and some representatives of the urban middle class. They advocated liberal and constitutional reforms and had developed vaguely defined proto-nationalist agendas. Nevertheless, the endurance of these secret societies had less to do with the quality and coherence of their ideological programmes and much more with their coercive-organisational capacity. They were effective in avoiding government's attempts to disband the societies and arrest the members by operating in small, covert cells that were scattered across different areas. They also implemented a strict recruitment system with the rituals of initiation and the creation of hierarchical structures of masters and apprentices. So, full membership (being a master) would be granted only after being tested for loyalty and after serving for six months or more as an apprentice (Birmingham 2003; Rath 1964). The early nineteenth century witnessed a proliferation of many secret societies that promoted various proto-nationalist ideas, including the Greek Society of Friends, the Macedonia Society, the Philorthodox Organisation, the Big Brotherhood, and the Fenian Brotherhood. All these groups developed a similar organisational structure that emphasised discipline, hierarchy, loyalty, and devotion to the cause. Hence, coercive-organisational power was central for the existence of such secret societies. This was a further step in the organisational grounding of nationalism.

The significance of social organisations for the development and spread of nationalist ideas and practices became even more pronounced with the rise of large-scale movements that advocated popular

[4] Collins (2004) explains well how relatively spontaneous social interactions can gradually transform into protracted interaction ritual chains. This process can eventually generate lasting social organisations.

sovereignty. Initially in mid-nineteenth-century Europe and Latin America, such movements mostly attracted young middle-class followers. For example, Giuseppe Mazzini's Young Italy, established in 1831, promoted the idea of Italian unification and organised resistance against the Austrian occupation. The movement was spearheaded by young intellectuals and at its peak was comprised of 60,000 mostly middle-class members (King 2019). Since the movement was proscribed, it had to operate abroad or in a clandestine form in the Italian regions. The movement was hierarchically organised and operated as a brotherhood with the members using nicknames instead of their proper names. Upon joining the movement, an individual was required to recite an oath and pledge allegiance to the movement, which aimed to establish a free, unified, and independent Italian republic (King 2019). Young Italy spurred the development of other, similar movements such as Young Germany, Young Poland, Young Switzerland, Young France, and later Young Turks, Young Bosnia, and Young Ireland. The movement also inspired similar brotherhoods in several Latin American, Asian, and African countries (De Donno & Srivastava 2006). The organisational backbone of these movements provided a sustained impetus for the development and grounding of nationalism.

However, by the end of nineteenth and beginning of the twentieth century, the nationalist movements had expanded substantially to include different social classes and large sectors of the population. The rise of the civil society sector opened new possibilities for social action. Nationalist ideas and practices were promoted in many different areas, including sports, religion, arts, entertainment, and electoral politics. Sporting events had gained great popularity, and early nationalist ideologues expounded the Latin proverb 'mens sana in corpore sano' (healthy mind in a healthy body) to the level of the nations as whole. Thus, gymnastics movements such as Sokol, established by the Czech intellectuals Miroslav Tyrš and Jindřich Fügner in 1862, promoted the idea that regular physical activity leads to morally, intellectually, and physically healthy nations. This movement quickly spread throughout Austro-Hungary and the Russian empire and was particularly popular in the Slavic lands of Poland, Belarus, Ukraine, Slovakia, Slovenia, Serbia, Croatia, and Bulgaria. Although the movement was nominally built around gymnastics, it organised many events that fostered nationalist ideals, including publishing its own journal, holding lectures in the Sokol libraries, and organising theatre performances as well as large-scale gymnastic performances (called *slets*) (Nolte 2002). The Sokols quickly became mass-scale social organisations that enticed wide support and mass participation. Initially the movement attracted professionals and students, but soon it gained a large following among the working-class population. Sokol events were highly organised and meticulously choreographed: the *slets* would start with welcoming ceremonies at the train stations, and included mass demonstrations, gymnastic competitions, speeches of the leaders, and theatrical performances (Nolte 2002). In the later nineteenth and early twentieth century, members of the movement were also involved in military training and would act as security guards at public events.

Similarly, in Ireland the Gaelic Athletic Association (GAA) was established in 1884 to promote Irish amateur sports, such as hurling, camogie, Gaelic football, Gaelic handball, and rounders, and specific cultural practices, including Irish traditional music and dance and the Irish language. The movement expanded quickly to include all sectors of Irish society as it became the beacon of Irish nationalism and resistance towards British control of Ireland. Rule 1.4a of the official GAA guide (Cronin & Rouse 2009:5) makes it clear that nationalism remains central to the organisation's identity: 'The Association shall actively support the Irish language, traditional Irish dancing, music, song, and other aspects of Irish culture. It shall foster an awareness and love of the national ideals in the people of Ireland and assist in promoting a community spirit through its clubs.' Just as with the Sokol movement, the success of the GAA has strong organisational roots. The organisational structure of the GAA is hierarchical, and it parallels parish-based membership, very similar to that of the Roman Catholic Church in Ireland (Cronin & Rouse 2009). Just like the Sokol movement, the GAA was very effective in penetrating different social classes and spreading its nationalist messages and practices throughout society. The equivalent of Sokol's large-scale gymnastic performances were the GAA games, as both attracted huge audiences.

Even before the establishment of the GAA, Ireland had witnessed mass-scale participation in political rallies organised by the opponents of British rule in Ireland. Daniel O'Connell's campaign for repeal of the Act of Union in 1843 mobilised hundreds of thousands of people at more than forty 'monster' meetings. As Gilmore (2019:75) shows, these enormous gatherings of people were well organised and were designed as 'a campaign to dominate public space in both small town and rural environments, based on a symbiotic relationship between the Repeal Association and Catholicism which deployed a nationalist iconography that deployed images of the natural world, and exhorted the Irish peasantry to peacefully demonstrate in favour of Repeal by invoking the natural advantages of Ireland that would be unleashed by self-government'. In both cases the superiority of social organisation was crucial for the spread of nationalist ideas and practices. The ever deeper nationalist grounding was spearheaded by the organisational power of Sokol, the GAA, and the Repeal Association.

By the early twentieth century many similar institutions were involved in the process of organisational grounding of nationalism. For example, the Boy Scouts and Girl Guides movements were created in part to promote nationalist masculinity and femininity. As Pryke (1998:309) argues, the founder of the two movements, lieutenant general Robert Baden-Powell, 'conceived the Boy Scouts as a youth movement to arrest national decline through bolstering physical fitness, morality and cross-class unity of British boyhood'. The movement promoted self-discipline and self-improvement and was 'centred on the nation's chivalrous past'. The Girls Guide movement followed similar principles but was also centred on reproducing patriarchal matrix, the gendered division of labour, and the policing of female sexuality. Very quickly such movements sprung up all over the world, and scouting is still a highly popular and state-supported practice.

Religious institutions also played an important role in the organisational grounding of nationalism. In Britain some Protestant movements were strongly associated with the promotion of nationalist militarism. For instance, the Boys' Brigade was established in 1883 by Presbyterians in Glasgow and with branches in England and Wales, and the Anglican Church Lads Brigade was created in 1895. Both organisations recruited Christian youth who wore uniforms, carried dummy rifles, and participated in military marches. They also glorified the virtues of British imperial nationalism (McLeod 2015). Although initially hostile towards nationalism, which was perceived as a liberal and secular ideology (Warren 2024), the Catholic Church eventually provided an organisational milieu for the promotion of nationalist projects in Poland, Ireland, and many other European regions with a significant Roman Catholic population. The Church's organisational capacity was instrumental in giving space to the nationalist movements of resistance against Russian, Austrian, and Prussian/German rule in the case of Poland, or British domination in the case of Ireland. This is not to say that the Catholic Church officially sanctioned such activities but only that its institutions were used, covertly or overtly, by the nationalist movements. A similar pattern is discernible in Eastern Orthodox churches where the top clergy were also initially opposed to the demands expressed by Greek, Serbian, or Bulgarian nationalists against Ottoman rule. With the reform of the Ottoman millet system, church leaders were generally unwilling to undermine their own, relatively privileged, position within the empire (Kitromilides 2010; Malešević 2013). It was only in the later years, mostly from the mid to late nineteenth century, that the Orthodox churches gradually became the beacons of the Greek, Serbian, Bulgarian, and other nationalisms. Nevertheless, institutional access to the church and church-organised events including masses, baptisms, weddings, and religious celebrations all provided space for the congregation of nationalist groups, which facilitated the development of specific political organisations.

However, the most important entity for the organisational grounding of nationalism is the state. Once nationalism becomes the official state doctrine, its proliferation is mostly reliant on the organisational vehicles of state apparatuses. As soon as the nation-state was established as the only legitimate form of political sovereignty and territorial authority, its administrative scaffolds were deployed for the continuous embedment of nationalist ideas and practices. The monopoly on the legitimate use of violence together with the tight control of taxation, education, and the judiciary enhanced the organisational capacity of nation-states. Furthermore, as the states developed their infrastructure, including better communication and transportation networks and the ability to centralise power and expand their administrative structures across the entire polity, they have attained an unparalleled capacity of surveillance and control over their citizens. These coercive-organisational advancements were all instrumental in the drive towards the standardisation of administrative practices and regulations and the uniformisation of the state institutions. Moreover, once the nation-states gained a hegemonic position in the world order, they have also fostered the cultural homogenisation of their citizenry. These processes have at times been intentional, an exercise in social engineering, but in most cases they were a by-product of organisational inertia and institutional routines. In other words, the organisational grounding of nationalism was a consequence of structural processes and agency too. There is no doubt that political elites, intellectuals, government officials, teachers, and many other individual and social agents have consciously and often enthusiastically promoted different nationalist agendas and were focused on bringing about more nation-centric societies in which they lived. Yet these individual and collective initiatives could succeed only if the requisite structural conditions were already in place. The peasants could not become Frenchmen if there were no institutions enabling this transition (Weber 1976). Once the national languages have been standardised and their everyday use legislated, the organisational grounding of nationalism was in full motion. With the introduction of compulsory primary education and increased literacy rates, the actions of nationalist ideologues were less significant. Instead, this process attained a nearly automatic form of self-reproduction: the structural processes that were put in place fostered an ongoing nationalisation of the public space. As Max Weber (1992) made it clear many years ago, once in motion, the iron cage of rationalisation spreads very quickly and standardisation becomes the norm. Meyer et al. (1997) have demonstrated empirically that these isomorphic processes, which make state institutions very similar and uniform, do not stop at the borders of nation-states. Rather, institutional standardisation is a global phenomenon through which institutions of all nation-states start resembling each other – from the schools using standardised curricula to similar rationalised demographic record keeping, uniform constitutional frameworks, similar welfare systems, regularised census taking, and so on. These findings are fully in line with Gellner's (1983:124) characterisation of nationalism as an ideology that 'claims to defend folk culture while in fact it is forging a high culture ... [I]t preaches and defends cultural diversity when in fact it imposes homogeneity both inside and, to lesser extent, between political units.' Hence, the organisational grounding of nationalism operates through very similar if not identical organisational vehicles.

All modern nation-states end up building structural foundations that provide impetus for nationalist grounding. Once all these organisational ingredients are in place, nationalist self-reproduction starts operating in routine and mostly unnoticeable ways. Billig (1995) has identified how these banal practices work in everyday contexts and how nationhood is habitually reproduced through the existing institutions: 'The metonymic image of banal nationalism is not a flag which is being consciously waved with fervent passion: it is the flag hanging unnoticed on the public building' (Billig 1995:8). However, the scholarship on banal nationalism has overemphasised the reproduction of national symbols such as flags hanging on public buildings; banknotes, coins, and stamps displaying images of one's nation; nation-centric weather reports; or the cheerleading sports pages of newspapers. Although symbols are significant as they crystalise and simplify nationalist messages, much more important are the social organisations that reproduce nation-centric social practices. There would be no national flags hanging on public building if there were no social organisations such as the ministries of culture, education, or judiciary that are situated in such buildings. There would be no banknotes, coins, or stamps featuring nationalist imagery without the national central banks and national postal services. The same applies to the nation-centric weather reports and nationalist newspapers – they too can have significant influence only because there are specific social organisations such as mass media and meteorological services that generate such messages. The banal reproduction of nationalism operates less through symbols and much more through social practices that are integral to many activities and processes that shape our everyday lives. Althusser (1994 [1970]:126) had noted long ago that ideological state apparatuses are effective because they successfully imbued our daily practices: if an individual 'believes in God, he goes to church to attend Mass, kneels, prays, confesses, does penance … if he believes in Duty, he will have the corresponding attitudes, inscribed in ritual practices … if he believes in Justice, he will submit unconditionally to the rules of the Law, and may even protest when they are violated, sign petitions, take part in demonstrations'.

One does not have to be a hard structuralist like Althusser to recognise how central are the social organisations for reproducing and embedding social practices that shape one's everyday life. In this context the state monopolies on the legitimate use of violence, taxation, legislation, and education play a central role in the reproduction of nationalism. All state organisations – military, police, judiciary, civil administration, educational, economic, border control, or welfare – are directly involved in the continuous organisational grounding of nationalism. The very existence of the military and police institutions is linked to the preservation of the nation-state from potential external and internal enemies. In this context the police and the military defend the nation-centric values that prioritise the nation-states over anything else. The judiciary and the civil administration are also centred on upholding the views of social order that privilege nationhood over other forms of collective allegiance. The legal and administrative system is designed in a such a way that only members of the nation-state are entitled to certain legal rights and welfare provisions. The nationalist principles impact nearly every aspect of social life, including public policy, migration laws, border control, economic planning, educational systems, mass media discourses, cultural policy, and even consumption practices. The power and endurance of nationalism reside in its organisational capacity. All these institutions remain central to everyday life because they possess a strong coercive-organisational backbone. One can oppose these institutions and protest specific policies, but in the world of nation-states it is almost impossible to reject or try to disband these social organisations that compose the nation-state. There would be no nationalism without this incessant organisational grounding.

Ideological Grounding and Nationalist Subjectivities

The isomorphic qualities of nationalism, emphasised by Weber, Gellner, and Meyer, are crucial for sustaining its organisational capacity.

Institutional standardisation and bureaucratic uniformity foster the development and expansion of nationalist practices within and across individual societies. Isomorphic homogenisation encourages a more cohesive social order. The state promotes organisational uniformity, but this is also perpetuated through non-state agents, including private corporations, religious institutions, and civil society groups, among many others. The key organisational principles identified by Ritzer (1993) in his McDonaldisation of society, such as efficiency, calculability, predictability, and control, which are associated with food production, apply just as much to the spread of nation-centric practices and are equally present in state and non-state organisations. Nevertheless, if the dominant institutions of nation-states all start to resemble each other throughout the world, then it is not clear why this planet is comprised of more than 200 such entities rather than a single state. Weber's iron cage of rationalisation leaves no room for the emergence and proliferation of distinct nation-states. If bureaucratisation infiltrates social relations so that rational calculation, control, and teleological efficiency permeate all aspects of human life, then why are there more nation-states today than a hundred years ago? The same critique applies to the theories of Gellner and Meyer. If modernisation fosters the organisational imitation and the inevitable shift from Agraria to Industria and beyond, why has this transition resulted in a multi-polar world of independent nation-states rather than a single world polity? To answer these questions, it is central to recognise that nationalism is not just a structural and coercive-organisational force but also an ideological doctrine that generates specific social meanings.

Nation-states are not just coercive social organisations; their existence and spread are also dependent on securing and maintaining a degree of popular legitimacy. In other words, nation-states could not exist without nationalisms – ideological discourses that justify the existence of nation-states by invoking the idea that a nation is a principal unit of human solidarity and political legitimacy. There is no doubt that nationalism is a form of social practice, but this practice is framed around specific ideas, values, and principles that its adherents find important and meaningful. Although modern nation-states may organisationally resemble each other in some important ways, the nationalist doctrines deployed to justify their existence thrive on promoting the idea that each nation is distinct and unique. While the geopolitical and historical changes can explain the specific trajectories of nation-state formation all over the globe, they cannot account for the strong sense of attachment that most people have towards their own nation-states. So, to better understand the strength of such identifications and the formation of nation-centric subjectivities, it is crucial to analyse the ideological grounding of nationalism.

The conventional views of ideology often overemphasise its manipulative character. Ideologies are often associated with social control, exploitation, illusion, wishful thinking, fantasy scenarios, brainwashing, or false consciousness. In this understanding ideology is often opposed to truth or the scientific view of the world. However, as I have argued before, such simple dichotomies are not very helpful. They ignore the complex social realities where scientific knowledge and true statements can also be used for manipulation, exploitation, and control. Furthermore, proving that some value systems are not based on factual reality is unlikely to undermine such beliefs. There are many epistemological problems with such sharp and often empirically unsustainable dichotomies (Malešević 2002:47–67). Hence, the focus should shift from the fixed set of prescriptions and doctrinal principles that compose particular ideologies and towards the process of ideologisation as such. While ideology stands for the set of established ideas and predetermined precepts, ideologisation is a dynamic, contingent, and relational historical process that shapes human experiences. It is through the ongoing process of ideologisation that the key institutions of the nation-states justify their very existence and also mobilise mass public support in times of crisis. In this they rely on the organisational capacities of the state apparatus, including the educational system, judiciary, police, military, welfare agencies, and so on. However, ideologisation is also generated and perpetuated through a variety of non-governmental institutions – from private corporations, religious institutions, social movements, and public and private mass media outlets to civil society groups. This is a centrifugal process in a sense that it often radiates from the epicentre of doctrinal power and spreads unevenly across different social strata. Key ideological precepts are formulated by cultural, political, economic, or military elites and are then spread by relying on the ever-increasing organisational capacities of states and non-state entities. In some ways this ideological unfolding of specific ideas and practices resembles a washing machine – it spins very quickly around, and it spreads (ideological) droplets from centre towards the periphery. However, unlike the washing cycle that separates different substances in this process (clean clothes from dirty water), the ideologisation merges different ideas and practices and spreads them to the wider sectors of population. Although ideologisation regularly originates among the elites, the process itself is not one-way, top-down form of simple indoctrination. Instead, once in motion ideologisation is a contingent, ongoing, dynamic, and unpredictable process that is dependent on popular reception and is often reshaped and sustained by different groups and individuals across society. Just like the washing machine in motion, centrifugal ideologisation permeates the entire social order. Once it starts, the washing cycle does not differentiate between the individual ingredients – the detergent, the clothes, the water, or the dirt. Similarly, once centrifugal ideologisation is in action, it spreads throughout society and does not differentiate between political and cultural elites and the rest. This is the structural element of ideologisation: the process might be initiated by the specific (elite) agents but once in motion it acquires distinct structural properties that affect all.

The ideological grounding of nationalism remains dependent on coercive-organisational grounding in the sense that the state apparatuses and non-governmental institutions, associations, and movements are the key vehicles for the dissemination of nation-centric images, ideas, and practices. Nevertheless, the ideational and practice-based content is just as important for the persistence of nationalism. All nationalist ideologies invoke ideas that emphasise the unique qualities of their respective nations. Nationalist ideologues often present their nations as being exceptionally fraternal, brave, resilient, just, or freedom loving. Nationalist doctrines often combine universal ethical principles with some very specific values that are attributed to one's own nation. Thus, among the general moral principles, one can regularly encounter ideas such as that every nation should have a state of its own, that everybody should be ruled only by their co-nationals, or that political sovereignty should reside with the people who inhabit a particular state (Smith 2008).

These universal principles are often framed in particular terms so that general moral values are transformed into the nation-centric principles. For example, while the United States is just one of many nation-states in the world, in the nationalist discourse its very existence is framed as historically unique, exceptional, and irreplaceable. This is, in the language of the US national anthem, 'the land of the free and the home of the brave'. In this understanding the universalist idea of popular sovereignty and the willingness to protect this sovereignty become exclusively American traits. As articulated in the words of cultural elites such as the famous US war reporter Elmer Davis: 'This nation will remain the land of the free only so long as it is the home of the brave.' The idea of American exceptionalism is regularly invoked by the political, economic, and military elites too. For US president Harry Truman, 'America was not built on fear. America was built on courage, on imagination and an unbeatable determination to do the job at hand.' In the words of John F. Kennedy, 'Let every nation know, whether it wishes us well or ill, that we shall pay any price, bear any burden, meet any hardship, support any friend, oppose any foe to assure the survival and the success of liberty.' For the US general Douglas MacArthur, 'Americans never quit', and for Elon Musk, 'America is the spirit of human exploration distilled' (www.brainyquote.com/topics/patriotism-quotes). Very similar nation-centric pronouncements can be found among the politicians, writers, artists, industrialists, and generals from other nation-states. From Charles de Gaulle's 'France cannot be France without greatness' to Novak Đoković's description of Serbs as 'the heavenly people', influential individuals tend to invoke and reproduce ideas of national exceptionalism.

In these discourses, nations are anthropomorphised and often attributed distinct wills, emotions, and moral qualities that only individual human beings could possess. Obviously, millions of people could not have the same patterns of behaviour, share the same moral qualities, or have the same wills. Nevertheless, in nationalist discourses nation-states are regularly depicted as uniform and homogeneous actors – they are victims, martyrs, or heroes. The ideological grounding operates in a way that combines the actions of influential agents with the continuous structural reproduction of nation-centric content that is reproduced through the mass media, educational systems, and the public sphere. In ideological terms nationalism thrives on morality, as it is regularly couched in the language of universal ethical principles such as the idea of collective liberation, national sovereignty, political equality, international justice, fraternity, and national emancipation. However, despite its nominal universalism this language of morality is deeply particularistic. As Gellner (1988:272) perceptively notes, ideologies prioritise shared moralities and social cohesion over factual reality: 'Referential unificatory truth … corrodes belief systems. Social cohesion cannot be based on truth. Truth butters no parsnips and legitimises no social arrangements. There are at least two reasons for this. One is the failure of the genuine knowledge to be social subservient. The second is that publicly accessible truth fails to separate members of a community from non-members.' Thus, the depiction of one's nation as exceptionally heroic, uniquely ethical, incomparably hardworking, or as a group that has experienced a higher level of suffering and martyrdom than any other nation is something that cannot be measured using standard analytical parameters. These ideological frames of reference enhance social cohesion and as such cannot be delegitimised by truth. Moreover, the nationalist discourses imbue a sense of shared collective meaning. They project the idea that one's nation is irreplaceable and that being a member of that nation makes all its members exceptional.

Both Anderson (1983) and Smith (2003) argue that nationhood resembles religion in the sense that it offers an escape from oblivion: while every individual is mortal, nations are perceived to be eternal or at least highly durable entities. Thus, a strong sense of identification with the nation provides what Smith (2003), echoing Edmund Burke, sees as 'a sacred communion of the dead, the living and the yet unborn'. He also emphasises the centrality of shared myths of common descent and the public commemorations of one's ancestors. Anderson (1983:5) too insists that nationalism is different from the conventional political ideologies such as liberalism or socialism and that it is more akin to religion or kinship as it speaks in the language of shared meanings and cultural durability. In his view, nationalism does not supersede religion, but 'nationalism has to be understood by aligning it, not with self-consciously held political ideologies, but with the large cultural systems that preceded it, out of which – as well as against which – it came into being' (Anderson 1983:12).

Ideological grounding relies on ever-increasing coercive-organisational grounding, as grand national vistas cannot be effectively transmitted and reproduced without large-scale organisational apparatuses such as schools, universities, workplaces, television, radio, newspapers, and, more recently, the internet and social media. However, while these structures sustain ideological grounding, they do not create a nation-centric citizenry. Such structures can operate only if there is a response from the agency. In other words, nationalist grounding is also a process through which modern subjectivities are formed. Ideological grounding fosters the formation and reproduction of nationalist subjectivities as the nation-centric idioms become normalised, naturalised, and routinised in everyday life.[5] Modern subjectivities tend to become infused with the specific nation-centric meanings that underpin how most people see and experience the world.

In the twenty-first century we are all born into the world where nation-states are the dominant and only legitimate form of state organisation and where nationalism is their primary ideological glue. Key nationalist principles such as popular sovereignty, cultural authenticity, or political independence are deployed to justify the existence of nation-states domestically and in the global environment. In the world of nation-states, the rulers have the right to govern only if they are perceived to be following these nationalist principles and, in this way, fully and adequately represent their populations of co-nationals. The rulers of

[5] For an excellent analysis of how nationalism has become naturalised as an everyday social practice all over the world, see Storm (2024). Storm also examines the nationalisation of the physical environment, including public spaces, museums, monuments, street names, statues of national heroes, preservation of cultural heritage, and landscapes, as well as the domestic sphere.

nation-states invoke the same nationalist principles to legitimise their existence internationally. In the world of nation-states, all polities are expected to align with the UN charter that prohibits its members to use force 'against the territorial integrity or political independence of any state'.[6] As this structural context has been in place for eighty years now, an overwhelming majority of the world's population has been socialised to live in this nation-centric universe and has no living experience of other, non-national worlds. Nationhood is the norm; everything else is an exception or aberration. Continuous ideological grounding fosters this understanding of social reality where nations are perceived to be the natural vessels of social life.

Micro-Interactional Grounding and Nationalist Subjectivities

Nationalism could not spread throughout the world and penetrate different social strata without having robust coercive-organisational and ideological platforms. Ideological and organisational grounding play a central role in the reproduction of nationalist ideas and practices. However, as humans are complex, dynamic, reflective, and thinking creatures, they require more than organisational and ideological powers to embrace fully the nation-centric understanding of the world.

As human beings are active agents who shape and are shaped by ever-changing social environments, their nationalist perceptions of reality could not simply be imposed from above. Instead, nationalism is a social phenomenon that entails constant reflection, social engagement, emotional commitment, the presence of moral imperatives, and a strong sense of micro-group attachment. In other words, nationalism not only is a product of macro-historical forces but also is something that is created, maintained, and reproduced in the micro-interactional settings of everyday life. This micro-world is constantly in the making, and although sustained and shaped by coercive-organisational and ideological structures, it develops its own autonomous dynamics.

Since Billig's (1995) pioneering work, scholars have paid more attention to the habitual aspects of nationalist experience. Billig has made it clear that the strength of nationalism does not reside in periodic outbursts, virulent rhetoric, or aggressive displays. Instead, nationalism

[6] Article 2.4 of the charter of the United Nations states that 'All Members shall refrain in their international relations from the threat or use of force against the territorial integrity or political independence of any state, or in any other manner inconsistent with the Purposes of the United Nations.'

persists through the continuous reproduction of national symbols and practices in the public and private spheres. Although his focus was mostly on the reproduction of nationalist images in the public domain, he also identified a variety of the nation-centric experiences taking place in everyday life – from hanging national flags in front yards and balconies to the use of collective 'we' in daily interactions and the celebrations of sporting successes in familiar settings.

Sociologists of everyday life, such as Fox (2018, 2017), Fox and Miller-Idriss (2008), Skey (2011, 2009), and Knott (2015), have focused extensively on nationalist experiences in everyday interactions. They identified a variety of nation-centric practices that ordinary people perform, consume, or undertake – from the discursive reproduction of nationhood in routine conversations to the daily ritual performances of nationhood to everyday nation-centric consumption patterns. As Fox (2018:863–864) puts it, while Billig focuses on 'the taken-for-grantedness of nationalism, which translates into a largely unnoticed, unseen, and unremarked upon nationalism', the sociologists of everyday life are 'interested in nationhood as a practical accomplishment, where actors creatively and wilfully invoke and manipulate nationhood for their own purposes'. In other words, nationalism is not just reproduced by social organisations is just as much an object of individual and collective self-reproduction – 'how ideas about the nation are reproduced by ordinary people doing ordinary things in their ordinary lives' (Fox 2018:862).

More recently Collins (2022, 2014) has pushed this argument further by emphasising the temporal dynamics of nationalist rituals. He sees nationalism as an interaction ritual chain through which individuals generate and amplify symbols of their membership. When successful, such ritual experiences help foster shared emotional energy and reinforce the group boundaries. Nevertheless, as Collins argues, this emotional intensity, often reflected in a collective effervescence, exhilaration, enthusiasm, and 'rhythmic entertainment', cannot last for long. Hence, nationalist exuberance operates through the 'time-bubbles' – ' the conflict-mobilized national solidarity' that is reflected in 'an emotional mood produced by a sudden event focusing public attention into a massive interaction ritual'. In his view, such instances of intense emotional commitment usually last from three to six months (Collins 2022).

These novel agency- and micro-centred approaches help us understand better how nationalism operates beyond and below the coercive-organisational and ideological powers. These perspectives also provide more insight on how human subjectivities are developed and transformed in the nation-centric world. By emphasising the contingent, dynamic, and voluntary aspects of social action, these perspectives show convincingly that nationalist subjectivities are not bound, linear, fixed, and inexorable but are constantly in the making, unfinished, and partial. Nevertheless, there are two issues that have not been adequately addressed by these new agency-centred perspectives: (1) it is not clear why nationalism and not something else is the dominant form of modern subjectivity and (2) how are the individual motivations, practices, and beliefs linked with wider organisational and ideological processes?

To tackle these two issues properly it is necessary to challenge some misconceptions of the agency-centred perspectives. Billig (1995:44) is rightly critical of perspectives that see nationalism as an extraordinary phenomenon that disrupts the normal routine: 'ordinary life in the normal state (the sort of state that the analyst tends to inhabit) is assumed to be banal, unexpecting politically and non-nationalist. Nationalism, by contrast, is extraordinary, politically charged and emotionally driven.' He rightly dismisses such views and shows that nationalist practices are often ordinary and integral to much of social life. However, by rejecting this narrow view of nationalism and by emphasising its predominately routine character, Billig downplays an important aspect of all nationalist experiences: their emotional valence. The fact that nationalism is regularly reproduced through the habitual activities does not mean that this phenomenon is emotionless. On the contrary, the emotional commitment and a sense of moral responsibility are central to nearly all forms of nationalism. Nevertheless, the emotional dynamics involved here are not usually associated with externally generated processes such as elite manipulation, war mongering, or anti-immigrant movements that Billig rightly criticizes. Instead, emotions and moral commitments that matter for the existence of nationalism are located in networks of micro-group solidarities that shape much of everyday life. Human beings are emotional and moral creatures who thrive on a sense of loyalty and attachment to their micro-groups – their close friends, family members, lovers, peer groups, work colleagues, trusted neighbours, and others. It is in this micro-universe of strong social ties that most humans attain solace, a sense of security, and emotional fulfilment. Hence, to fully understand how nationalism operates, it is crucial to explore how coercive-organisational and ideological grounding link with micro-interactional grounding. Habitual reproduction is an important aspect of nationalist phenomena, but this routine can operate successfully only because nationhood is part and parcel of everyday life. It is through micro-interactional grounding that nationalist narratives become integrated into the well-established bonds of friendship, deep comradeship, and kinship. These micro-group solidarities are rooted in the strong emotional and moral ties that social organisations regularly mimic to project the bonds of micro-level solidarities onto the macro-plane. Through nationalist grounding these intense emotional and moral ties with one's micro-group are ideologically transformed into society-wide attachments that encompass millions of anonymous individuals.

While Billig downplays the role of emotions in the reproduction of nationalism, Collins does the opposite. For Collins (2014:54) nationalism is 'an intensely felt bond of solidarity' that is often characterised by shared rituals such as public commemorations, celebrations of national holidays, or the spontaneous displays of national symbols. He emphasises the emotional bonds that are forged in such shared ritual experiences. In this view national solidarities can be very intense but usually do not last for more than a few months and in some instances only several days. While Collins is right that emotional bonding, active participation, group synchronicity, and shared rituals are important for the reproduction of nationhood, his perspective lacks the historical and structural foundations. If nationalism was just 'an intensely felt bond of solidarity' that can easily evaporate after the end of a ritual-intense periods, why does nationhood, and not any other form of collective attachment, generate a continues sense of collective reverence? The point is that in modernity nationhood is not like any other group identity; it is the hegemonic form of subjectivity. This dominance has concrete coercive-organisational and ideological bases: the monopoly of the nation-state as the only legitimate form of territorial organisation, and nationalism as the principal form of political legitimacy. Thus, Collins' micro-sociology of interaction ritual chains has to be situated within the wider macro-sociological realities of ideological and coercive-organisational grounding of nationalism. Nationhood is not just an emotional symbol; it is also a product of specific historical contexts and structural transformations. If this were not the case, nationalist rituals would appeal not only to citizens of contemporary nation-states but would have the same emotional resonance among the fourth-century Visigoth chiefdoms or the thirteenth-century Kilwa sultanate. This profound difference cannot be explained without analysis of historical and structural transformations.

The everyday nationhood perspective of Fox, Skey, and Knott recognises the importance of both emotional commitments and habitual reproduction of nationalist practices. More than other new approaches, it also emphasises the centrality of grassroot perceptions and behaviours. This bottom-up approach has generated valuable findings on the motivations of ordinary individuals and their reflexive deployment and use of national symbols and practices in everyday contexts. However, this perspective also has little to say about the wider historical dynamics that link organisational structures and ideological processes with the everyday realities of the micro-world. There is no doubt that nation-centric conversations among friends, the consumption of national products, and involvement in everyday nationalist rituals foster the existence of nation-centric world. Nevertheless, such actions maintain but do not create nationalism from scratch. Rather, nationalist ideas and practices must be there in the first place, and these are generated through ongoing coercive-organisational and ideological grounding. In other words, there would be no rituals, conversations, or consumption practices that reproduce, deploy, and manipulate images of nationhood without the organisational and ideological scaffolds through which nationalism is engendered and disseminated. The everyday practices of individuals feed into these structural processes, and it is through the envelopment of the micro-universe of everyday life that these structural forces develop and expand. Hence, nationalism becomes the dominant way of life only when coercive-organisational and ideological grounding is successfully merged with micro-interactional grounding.

Furthermore, the focus on how 'ordinary people' are doing 'ordinary things in their ordinary lives' (Fox 2018:862) might imply a degree of uniformity in behaviour and thinking that is rare. As Feinstein (2024:738) emphasises, most contemporary societies display high levels of polarisation over what the key elements of nationhood are and how they should be practiced: 'intense national emotions may emerge even without confrontation with external actors if the public sees focal events as reassessing and potentially amending tenets of the collective national identity and narrative'. Thus, it is important to recognise that despite nationalism's enormous influence in everyday life, its micro-interactional grounding is neither uniform nor even. Instead, this is an ongoing process that can be more or less successful. As I show in Chapter 5 with the example of monarchist and state socialist Yugoslavia, the process of nationalist grounding can be ineffective in different ways – resulting in organisational, ideological, or micro-interactional under-grounding or mis-grounding. Micro-interactional grounding can also be deep or shallow, and when shallow it can dissipate quickly in times of big crises. Hence, the key issue here is to differentiate between diverse forms of micro-group solidarities and the ability of states and other social organisations to successfully penetrate this micro-world. In this sense Smith (2008:565) is right that undifferentiated 'ordinary people' might be an 'un-sociological category that needs to be broken down into its constituent parts, be they individuals, or various organized groups of people (e.g. movements, parties), or different interest and status groups (castes, classes, ethnic communities)'.

A better differentiation of this micro-universe would help with identifying the social mechanisms through which micro-interactional grounding merges with coercive-organisational and ideological grounding. There are many ways through which this process operates. For example, micro-interactional and ideological grounding can combine effectively to police the boundaries of nationhood: close kinship groups and friendship networks can enforce moral pressure and emotional intimidation to prevent dating practices and possible marriage arrangements outside one's nation. They can also foster the nation-centric rites of passage for younger members of their group so that they would observe specific national and/or religious practices. Wedding and funeral rituals featuring national flags or other symbols prominently can reinforce national boundaries and ideologically frame the personal and family events as nation-centric rituals. Micro-interactional grounding can also be gauged in shared micro-practices such as telling nation-centric jokes at parties and barbeques or singing national songs at sporting events with friends and family members.

Micro-interactional grounding is most effective when it is mostly imperceptible – when friends, neighbours, lovers, and family members do fun things together – such as sharing meals, going to the same pubs, drinking together, engaging in shared recreational activities, or playing in schoolyards while displaying, communicating, singing, joking about, gossiping against, or chatting through and within national images and practices. The micro-universe of everyday life is not just about the reproduction of nationalist symbols or the unconscious reception of banal nationalist discourses, as explored by Billig, or about the individual experiences and practical accomplishments of 'ordinary people'. It is first and foremost about the emotional commitments and moral imperatives of the micro-groups. Nationalism regularly trumps other ideological discourses in the contemporary world because it is more effective in deploying the coercive-organisational and ideological powers to penetrate the micro-level solidarities and project the shared inter-personal emotions and ethical values onto the macro-universe of nationhood.

Conclusion

For more than 99 per cent of the time of our existence on this planet, our predecessors have lived in a world where there were no nation-states and where one could not identify in national terms. Yet today we inhabit a globe that is carved into 205 sovereign states recognised by UN, and the overwhelming majority of the world's population identifies strongly with their nation.[7] In the contemporary world, the nation-state is regarded as the only legitimate form of territorial rule and nationhood as the most popular mode of large-scale collective identification. Moreover, the nation-centric understanding of social reality has become fully normalised and naturalised. State institutions, non-governmental agencies, private corporations, civil society groups, religious orders, and many other organised entities are involved in the continuous reproduction of nationhood as the dominant form of subjectivity. National categories saturate much of everyday life. This hegemonic position of nation-states and nationalisms in the contemporary world remains a puzzle for social science and humanities. There are now numerous excellent theoretical and comparative historical analyses of these phenomena, but there is very little consensus over the key questions on the origins, development, and resilience of nation-states and nationalisms. In this chapter I have attempted to bring some order to these debates by identifying the strengths and weaknesses of the structuralist and agency-centred perspectives. Furthermore, by zooming in on the coercive-organisational, ideological, and micro-interactional processes of nationalist grounding, I have tried to point out why nationalism remains the dominant form of modern subjectivity in the contemporary world. The next step is to apply this theoretical framework to many case studies across time and space.

[7] Out of 205 states recognised in UN, 193 are full UN member states, 2 are UN General Assembly observer states (Holy See and the State of Palestine), and 10 are 'other states' that are not members of UN. According to recent global surveys, a sense of attachment to one's nation remains very strong and in many parts of the world has increased over the last two decades (Duina 2018; Medrano 2009; Antonsich 2009).

2 Between the Imperial and the National Worlds

Introduction

The social and political worlds we inhabit today are profoundly different from the worlds of our grandparents. The parents of baby boomers and generation X still lived in a world dominated by powerful imperial orders. At the beginning of the twentieth century, royal households such as the House of Yamato, the Romanovs, the Habsburgs, the Qing dynasty, the House of Hohenzollern, and the House of Osman, among others, justified their political absolutism by invoking the theory of divine origins of rule. Even in states where the power of the monarchs was curtailed by parliaments or constitutions such as the House of Orange-Nassau, the House of Windsor/Saxe-Coburg and Gotha, or the House of Burbon, royal prerogatives were used extensively to legitimise the imperial expansion.[1] Hence, in the early twentieth century the most powerful polities in the world were still empires rather than nation-states. In direct contrast after 1945, the nation-state had gradually become the only legitimate form of territorial organisation of political power. As the influence of the nation-state model expanded throughout the world, the ideology that sustained empires – imperialism – was also delegitimised and replaced by a very different ideological doctrine: nationalism. How and why did this happen?

In this chapter, I explore the relationship between the imperial and national projects by zooming on the historical transformation of collective subjectivities. The first and second part of this chapter aim to explain why the nation-state model of polity organisation has replaced imperial forms of territorial rule. Although empires have been the dominant form of territorial organisation for more than 5,000 years, by the mid-twentieth century this model of rule had been completely delegitimised, and since then the nation-state has been recognised as the only legitimate

[1] These polities are better known under the following names: Japan, Russia, Austro-Hungary, China, Germany, the Netherlands, the United Kingdom, and Spain.

form of territorial organisation. The third part of the chapter analyses the internal dynamics within social orders that have gradually moved from imperial to national forms of socio-political legitimacy. Using a paired analysis of Hungarian and Japanese nation-formation, I explore how large-scale structural changes impacted the transformation of collective subjectivities. The chapter traces the gradual transition from the predominantly locally and eschatologically based subjectivities towards the hegemony of nation-centric subjectivities.

The Imperial and the National Worlds

In one respect the history of nationalism mirrors the history of Christianity in the Roman empire. Romans had tolerated religious pluralism and accepted the deities of the peoples they conquered into their pantheon of gods. Initially Christianity was treated in the same way, but as the Christians did not recognise other deities, they represented a threat to the empire and were persecuted. However, after prolonged struggle Christianity eventually replaced all other religions and became the only legitimate religious practice in the empire.[2] In a similar vein, nationalism was perceived as a threat in pre-revolutionary France and many other parts of Europe. As this ideology invoked the notion of popular sovereignty, it directly challenged the ideological foundation of their royal rule – the idea of the divine origins of monarchs. Hence, nationalists were initially persecuted in Europe. Nevertheless, once this ideological doctrine become the principal source of state legitimacy, it gradually replaced all alternatives. Moreover, from the mid-twentieth century onwards, the nation-state model of polity organisation attained a global monopoly by delegitimising imperial orders, patrimonial kingdoms, city-states, and other forms of territorial organisation. At the same time nationalism acquired a near hegemonic status as the only justifiable form of political sovereignty.

To understand how this extraordinary transformation happened, it is important to focus on the ideological, organisational, and micro-interactional grounding of the imperial and national worlds. I will argue that this historical shift was not so sudden and unprecedented but emerged gradually, and often through existing organisational and ideological channels. In other words, nation-states and nationalisms do not

[2] Christianity was recognised as the legal religion of the empire with the Edict of Milan in 313 CE during the reign of Emperor Constantin. Only a few decades later, Emperor Theodosius issued the Edict of Thessalonica in 380 CE, which made Christianity the official religion of the Roman empire (Dwyer 1998).

have the deus ex machina features that have been attributed to them by classical modernist scholars such as Gellner (1983) or Hobsbawm (1990). In Gellner's (1996:366) famous account, modernity starts from year zero: 'the world was created round about the end of the eighteenth century, and nothing before that makes the slightest difference to the issues we face'. In this understanding nation-states and empires are mutually incompatible forms of polity. For Gellner (1983) they represent two distinct and profoundly different socio-economic systems. The imperial Agraria is deeply hierarchical and driven by Malthusian logic where people 'starve according to rank' and where the ruling aristocrats value descent and honour and despise physical labour. In contrast, the national Industria is based on continuous economic growth, the development of science and technology, and pervasive social mobility. While the former is a stagnant and deeply stratified world dominated by the military caste, the latter promotes meritocracy, economic development, and the political equality of its citizens. As Gellner (1988:158) emphasises, with the rise of Industria and nation-states 'Production replaced Predation as the central theme and value of life.' Nevertheless, the starkest difference between these two worlds is in the cultural sphere: while the agrarian empires use cultural difference to reinforce established social hierarchies, nation-states foster cultural homogeneity as this underpins their industrial base. For Gellner this deep cultural schism between the nobility and the rest is an unsurmountable obstacle for industrialisation, and thus modernity is only possible when nation-states replace empires.

Gellner is right that the empires and nation-states represent different forms of social, economic, and political life. An empire is a large-scale and composite political entity with a centralised and expansionist power structure. This form of polity is deeply hierarchical: it is composed of a dominant core and subordinated peripheries, and it maintains a system of status hierarchies within the populations and territories it governs (Breuilly 2016; Hall 2017). In imperial political systems, the moral order privileges status descent and vertical over horizontal forms of group organisation: from the emperor at the top to different layers of nobility, with commoners at the bottom of the social pyramid. The imperial state orders are typically characterised by cultural heterogeneity, elaborate lineage and descent hierarchies, and multi-layered power arrangements. An empire is a conquest-oriented polity that has no permanent and fixed borders; instead, it keeps open-ended frontiers. In organisational terms an empire is an asymmetrical entity that practices different forms of governance for different territorial units under its control. It also deploys a diverse sets of rules, regulations, and rights for different populations.

In ideological terms an empire is usually legitimised through universalist principles that range from cosmological, mythological, religious, and personalised to civilisational creeds. Much of this universalism stems from the perception that an empire is the epicentre of the world. As Munkler (2007:5) points out, 'empires have no neighbours which they recognize as equals'.

In contrast, nation-states have clearly defined and stable borders.[3] Their rulers justify their position by invoking the notion of popular sovereignty rather than the principle of divine authority. Nation-states are rooted in the idea that all their citizens are of equal moral worth and as such oppose the notion of natural hierarchies based on birth rights. Unlike the imperial world, which is generally characterised by heterogeneity, nation-states foster a sense of cultural homogeneity. In some cases, this means enacting policies that encourage assimilation, while in other instances the focus is more on generating a shared public sphere and common sense of national belonging (Malešević 2013:64–74).

However, these obvious organisational and ideological differences do not imply that empires and nation-states have nothing in common. By positing a stark dichotomy that leaves no room for the elements of compatibility between the two, Gellner and other classical modernists cannot explain adequately the transformation of the imperial into the national worlds. To understand how this change was possible, one cannot simply dismiss the past. Instead, the focus should shift from the economic foundations that Gellner prioritises towards the political processes that have made this transformation possible. In this context the organisational elements of continuity are just as important as those associated with organisational discontinuity. Nation-states do not appear ex nihilo but emerge slowly and gradually on the existing organisational scaffolds of the imperial orders, patrimonial kingdoms, city-states, city-leagues, tribal confederacies, complex chiefdoms, and many other historical forms of polity.

Furthermore, nation-states do not completely and permanently replace empires. Instead, this is a protracted and reversable historical process characterised by different geographical, geopolitical, and social oscillations. In some contexts, a number of imperial features remain within nation-state structures. As Kumar (2021, 2017) and Cooper (2005) show convincingly, there are many organisational overlaps between the nation-states and empires. For Cooper (2005:153–203) there is no natural and inevitable progression from empires to nation-states. Instead, they are

[3] Obviously, nation-states might have profound border disputes, but no nation-state, unlike empires, has unlimited frontiers.

both 'variable forms of political imagination'. In Kumar's (2021:83) view the historical record indicates that in some instances 'nations can be seen as miniature empires', while in other contexts empires appear 'as glorified nation-states'. Many nation-states such as Great Britain, France, Spain, or Japan[4] were originally constituted as empires and have used this designation for many years, while some large nation-states such as the United States, China, or Russia retain many imperial prerogatives such as the capacity to militarily intervene abroad and trample on the sovereignty of other nation-states, the ability to dictate the economic policies and trading agreements, the power to pursue coercive state-building throughout the world, or the capacity to impose and maintain distinct geopolitical status hierarchies.

To trace the elements of organisational continuity, it is crucial to first differentiate between ancient or capstone empires and modern imperial orders. The central feature of capstone empires such as the Roman empire under Augustus (27 BCE–14 CE) or the Chinese empire under Wu of the Han dynasty (141 BCE–87 BCE) is that the imperial power is highly centralised at the top, but lacks the organisational and ideological capacities to penetrate the societies under its control. Hence capstone emperors tend to rule through local intermediaries and are not interested in nor able to forge unified social orders (Hall 1986). In contrast, modern imperial orders such as the British empire during the reign of Queen Victoria (1837–1901) or the French empire under Napoleon I (1804–1814) had developed substantial coercive-organisational capacities and a degree of ideological legitimacy to permeate the social orders under their control. The proliferation of warfare and capitalism allowed some Western European empires to build stronger and more centralised state structures at home while continuing colonial expansion abroad. Hence, empires have never been invariable entities. Instead, they have always been highly dynamic polities that have been changing and evolving. By focusing on the processes of organisational, ideological, and micro-interactional grounding one can detect how imperial state structures provided the structural and ideational contours for the emergence of nation-states.

The Dynamics of Organisational Grounding

Organisational grounding is a historical process that involves the relatively continuous and cumulative expansion of coercive-organisational powers

[4] In a formal sense Japan is still an empire, although from 1947 the emperor's traditional name and his political role have been radically altered. The former Mikado ('emperor') has been renamed as Tenno ('heavenly sovereign') and he has lost all political power.

that can foster large-scale social transformations. This is a continuous, although uneven and dynamic process that generates an environment where social organisations can force individuals to work on the realisation of specific organisational goals. The directed social change entails the presence of durable social organisations that can facilitate this process. Unlike individuals or small groups, large-scale social organisations entail a patterned and often institutionalised form of collective relationships created to pursue specific organisational objectives. Social organisations are defined by established social hierarchies with decision-making regulations, codified formalised relationships between members and clear rules of membership, and the elaborate division of labour with specialised tasks and functions for all members (Malešević 2022, 2017, 2010). Organisational grounding has historically involved a variety of social organisations that can range from private corporations, social movements, and religious institutions to different forms of state structures. The gradual expansion of organisational grounding has played a significant role in the historical transformation of pristine city-states into patrimonial kingdoms and empires. For example, one of the earliest imperial projects, the Akkadian empire under Sargon, developed through the conquest of several city-states in Mesopotamia in the twenty-fourth to twenty-third centuries BCE (Foster 2016). Subsequent world empires grew and expanded based on their ever-increasing organisational capacities (Kumar 2017; Burbank & Cooper 2010). This process was shaped by the ability of social organisations to increase their infrastructural reach through improved transportation and communication networks, as well as by controlling their populations and policing access to key resources. The proliferation of inter-state wars has played a central role in organisational grounding as the rulers of the early modern polities were forced to develop ever larger and more efficient administrative apparatuses. The enlarged bureaucratic apparatus together with better infrastructural capacities were indispensible for maximising revenue collection and for increasing conscription rates to finance and supply soldiers for protracted European wars (Mann 1993; Tilly 1992). This process had crystalised in the eighteenth and early nineteenth centuries, but the organisational transformation of states had started much earlier and was not unique to Europe (Hobson 2004; Teschke 2017; Spruyt 2017; Tin-Bor Hui 2005).

Tilly (1992) argues that from the seventeenth century onwards the increased inter-state warfare fostered the growth in army size, while other scholars have traced this process earlier: to the fourteenth century (Strayer 1970) or between the fifteenth and sixteenth centuries (Bean 1973). Zhao (2015), Ferejohn and Rosenblut (2010), and Tin-Bor Hui (2005) show convincingly that this process started much earlier in China and Japan. During the Warring States period (475–221 BCE) intensified war-making fostered state centralisation where the outcome was not the muti-state system but an imperial order (Tin-Bor Hui 2005). In Japan the state attained a monopoly on the legitimate use of violence long before Europe: the result of the series of protracted and destructive wars in the sixteenth and seventeenth centuries was a highly centralised government capable of disarming its citizens (Ferejohn & Rosenblut 2010). The key point here is that classical modernists such as Gellner or Hobsbawm cannot account for the long-term transformations that shifted the balance from imperial to national worlds. Organisational grounding is a protracted historical process that has gradually shaped the state formation long before the emergence of nationalism. Imperial structures did not suddenly give a way to the nation-states; instead, nation-states emerged progressively on the organisational spine of empires, patrimonial kingdoms, city-states, and many other social and political entities.

This organisational change can best be analysed by zooming in on the historical experience of contemporary polities that were shaped through the imperial-national continuum. For example, both Hungary and Japan are political entities that have developed from premodern organisational scaffolds. In contemporary nationalist discourses, both are often referred as 'thousand-year-old nations'.[5] Modernist scholars such as Gellner or Hobsbawm are absolutely right that such primordialist descriptions have no basis in historical record but reflect an attempt to impose contemporary nationalist categories on the pre-national and non-national past. A common name and some elements of alleged linguistic continuity do not constitute nationhood in any sociologically meaningful sense. Being a 'Hungarian' or a 'Japanese' in a political sense is a very modern construct. However, by dismissing the primordialist account one should not throw the baby out with the bathwater. Instead, to understand how nationhood emerges in the modern conditions it is crucial to explore its premodern organisational scaffolds. Thus, both Hungarian and Japanese nationhoods are the outcomes of long-term organisational grounding.

[5] Many contemporary historians in Hungary and Japan still use this primordialist discourse to describe their respective nations. For instance, in a paper entitled 'The Hungarians in Europe: A Thousand Years on the Frontier', Fodor and Pok (2020:115) write about Hungarians as follows: 'the basic characteristics that made them a people displayed an unparalleled continuity. Over three thousand years, they have managed to retain their system of symbols (above all the language) and distinguish and separate themselves from other peoples, as manifested in their enduring name for themselves, Magyar'. Similarly, several history textbooks in Japan depict mythical figures, who allegedly lived 2,000 years ago, such as Emperor Jimmu and Prince Taishi (Shōtoku Taishi) as the fathers of the Japanese nation (Bukh 2007; Rose 2006).

In other words, there is no alleged ethno-national continuity of the premodern and modern 'Hungarians' or 'Japanese'. Instead, like all other national projects, these are also modern political creations. Nevertheless, nationhood does not emerge ex nihilo; it is a phenomenon shaped by durable organisational logic. The key contours of this process can be traced by examining the Hungarian and Japanese organisational grounding.

Archaeological research indicates that in the ninth century the military coalitions of several Eastern nomadic tribes including Ungri and the Kabars engaged in periodic looting raids in the Carpathian basin. They often fought the local, mostly Avar and Onogur population, and eventually established a permanent settlement in the region (Molnar 2001). It seems that the invading military alliance was able to maintain control of the Carpathian basin by adopting the existing organisational structure of the Avar Khaganate. In this highly hierarchical organisation, the khagan was the principal power holder who relied on the nomadic aristocracy of elite warriors. This organisational structure was flexible and often integrated a variety of other tribal groups, which is reflected in the Turkic names of tribes, chieftains, and other leaders (Révész 2014; Pohl 1998). This organisational structure was later transformed in a more complex and durable entity: the Kingdom of Hungary under Stephen I, who was crowned king in 1001. The Árpád dynasty ruled the kingdom for the next three centuries. The elements of organisational continuity from the Avar Khaganate were visible in the county system of the kingdom, which seemed to resemble the administrative structure established in the times of the Avar rulers (Révész 2014; Pohl 1998). The Kingdom of Hungary was a typical medieval polity where the ruling nobility practiced aristocratic endogamy, and was part of the trans-European Christian and Latin-centred elite world where cultural difference was used to differentiate the nobility from the ordinary peasantry. In other words, this was a social universe divided by lineage and birthright where there was no society-wide sense of cultural or political identification. There were neither political nor cultural Hungarians in the premodern world.

Nevertheless, the development and reproduction of the coercive-organisational apparatus of the Hungarian polity has played a significant role in the organisational grounding of the Hungarian nationhood that will eventually emerge in modern times. The institutions and administrative structure of the kingdom together with the military legacy will later became the steppingstone for the nation and state formation. By the fourteenth and fifteenth centuries the kingdom was a formidable military power that was engaged in the protracted Ottoman wars. With the resounding defeat at the Battle of Mohács by the Ottomans, the kingdom experienced a dramatic decline and was divided into three entities ruled by different imperial orders: Ottoman Hungary, Royal Hungary under Habsburg rule, and the semi-independent Principality of Transylvania (Molnar 2001). With the gradual weakening of the Ottoman empire and the Habsburgs occupied with various conflicts, Francis II Rákóczi led from 1703 to 1711 an uprising of Hungarian noblemen against Habsburg rule. Although later nationalist interpretations paint this conflict as a war for national independence, this was predominantly an aristocratic-based struggle over dynastic claims. Francis II Rákóczi was the prince of Transylvania, who had a legitimate claim over the St Stephen crown. This was an aristocratic rebellion. When the Hungarian Diet met in 1705 to elect Rákóczi as the ruling prince of the Confederated Estates of the Kingdom of Hungary, its members were all noblemen: 6 bishops, 36 aristocrats, and about 1,000 representatives of the lower nobility (Molnar 2001). However, this violent conflict against the Habsburgs eventually contributed towards the development of Hungarian proto-nationhood. This rebellion was a failure, as the leaders of the uprising were defeated and took an oath of allegiance to the Habsburg emperor in 1711. Nevertheless, the legacy of this uprising played an important role in galvanising the 1848–1849 revolution, which had many hallmarks of a nationalist uprising. The revolutionaries radically reshaped the existing organisational structure of the state: the feudal Estates General was transformed into a democratic representative parliament; the new suffrage law introduced a parliamentary election system; and the privileges of the nobility were abolished (Molnar 2001). Following Emperor Franz Joseph I's arbitrary revocation of these new laws, the revolution transformed into a war for Hungarian independence. The military defeat of the revolutionary forces created an unstable political situation that was partially resolved through the 1867 compromise that created the Austro-Hungarian monarchy where Hungary was officially named the Lands of the Crown of Saint Stephen. After the collapse of the empire in the wake of World War I, Hungary become an independent kingdom. After World War II the country was constituted as the Hungarian People's Republic and in 1989 became a unitary parliamentary republic.

What comes across as central to Hungarian nation-formation is the existence of the organisational backbone that made this long-term historical process possible. Organisational grounding starts with the structure of the Avar Khaganate, then the feudal kingdom of Stephen I, Royal Hungary under Habsburgs, Ottoman Hungary, the Principality of Transylvania, the Austro-Hungarian empire, the People's Republic, and the independent nation-state of today. Without this gradual but relatively continuous, yet highly contingent, development of the coercive-organisational capacities there would be no modern-day Hungarians. The long-term organisational grounding rather than the mythical 'cultural continuity' made the emergence of modern Hungarian nationhood possible. The alternative historical trajectories of Avars, Pechenegs, Scythians, Sarmatians, Visigoths, and thousands of other historical groups that have disappeared or were assimilated into larger entities indicate how important the organisational structures were for the eventual development of nationhood.

Another example of successful organisational grounding is the Japanese national project. Japanese conventional historiography refers to the Japanese as a people that have existed for more than 2,000 years (Benner 2006). The foundation of Japan is traced to the mythical Emperor Jimmu, an alleged descendent of Amaterasu, the Sun Goddess, who is perceived to be the direct ancestor of the current ruling dynasty (Totman 2014).[6] However, this imperial mythology does not have much bearing on the actual nation-formation process, as Japanese nationhood is just as modern as the rest of the world. Nevertheless, as in the Hungarian case, nation-formation did not happen suddenly in the nineteenth century but was a consequence of long-term organisational grounding.

The relatively unique and isolated geographical position of the Japanese islands has proved detrimental to external invasions for centuries. Hence, the principal conflicts in the early periods of history were between neighbouring tribes. By the end of the Yayoi period (300 BCE–300 CE), coercive-organisational grounding intensified, and most tribes were integrated into larger kingdoms. According to the earliest available sources such as the Book of Han and the Book of Wei, many small kingdoms were eventually absorbed by the kingdom of Yamatai in 240 CE. The process of organisational grounding continued for the next several centuries whereby intensified warfare fostered the development of a more centralised structure of governance. During the Nara (710–794 CE) and Heian (794–1185 CE) periods, Japanese rulers had built a formidable administrative base. The transportation system was improved so that new roads were built to link the capital Nara (and then Kyoto) to the provincial capitals. A new and improved mode of regular tax collection was introduced, and the government also sponsored the minting of the coins, although their use was still sporadic. However, by the end of this period the government was facing a financial crisis and was forced to

[6] This mythological thinking 'postulated that all Japanese people were descendants of the same divine ancestress, the Sun Goddess Amaterasu' (Benner 2006:21).

reduce the number of civil servants and to abolish universal conscription (Ooms 2009; Brown 1993). Although the Heian period is now associated with intense cultural and religious development and the rise of new forms of art, poetry, and literature at the imperial court, it was also a period when the warrior caste started gaining more influence. Despite Emperor Kammu's attempt to enhance his authority by moving the capital to Kyoto (Heian-kyō), he mostly remained a nominal ruler during this period. The real power was in the hands of the Fujiwara nobility, who controlled the substantial military force. For the next several centuries the warrior caste continued to increase their power while the emperors became figureheads.

From 1185 to 1333 Japan was ruled by the Kamakura shogunate. The shoguns were military dictators who established full control of the country. The first shogun, Minamoto no Yoritomo (1147–1199), initiated a new form of governance that expanded the coercive-organisational capacity of the state. The shoguns appointed and oversaw military governors (*shugo*) who oversaw individual provinces. In addition, they controlled the economic system through the appointment of stewards of the manors (*jitō*). These individuals were paid by the manors for their military service. The military government also introduced its own legal code (Goseibai Shikimoku), which regulated civilian and military responsibilities (Mass 1999). This militarisation of political life together with the growing centralisation of rule had a significant impact on the development of Japanese nationhood. Although for much of its existence the shogunate was a feudal and highly stratified system of rule, in the long term it fostered organisational grounding that made Japanese nation-formation possible. The gradual standardisation and centralisation of the transportation networks, communication systems, military, police, and the legal system that took place under different shoguns contributed substantially to the transformation from the imperial to the national world.

The shogunate order remained in place for nearly seven centuries and ended during the Meiji Restoration when Tokugawa Yoshinobu relinquished his position in 1867. The pivotal moment for organisational grounding was the decision by the shogun Toyotomi Hideyoshi to initiate a society-wide weapons ban with his 1588 'sword hunt'. Using a pretext to melt swords to build a giant statue of the Buddha, Hideyoshi played a key role in the gradual pacification of Japan. This process was finalised by other rulers, and by 1630 the entire country was completely disarmed. Hence Japanese rulers attained a monopoly on the legitimate use of violence long before the European states. This early pacification together with the increased centralisation and isolation from the rest of the world generated an organisational environment that was highly conducive to the development of Japanese nationhood. Nevertheless, there was still no fully-fledged Japanese nationhood until the end of nineteenth century. The Tokugawa period (1603–1867) played a crucial role in providing the organisational structures for the gradual transformation of the imperial into the national realm. This was a period of political stability, two and a half centuries of peace and continuous economic growth. Tokugawa Ieyasu oversaw a social order that established full control over local lords (*daimyo*), who were obliged to reside in the capital Edo (Tokyo) for several months every other year. In addition, the numerous samurai, a warrior caste who constituted up to 8 per cent of the total population, were required to take up residence in Edo where many ended up as civil servants, thus boosting the organisational spine of the state – the administration (Masashi 2000).

The last shogunate pursued a policy of self-isolation from the world (the Sakoku period) while also preventing social mobility at home. The peasantry, which constituted more than 80 per cent of population, was not allowed to seek employment outside their farms (Laver 2011). All these organisational changes eventually stimulated a shift towards nationhood. However, in the mid-nineteenth century the majority of the ordinary population still identified more in local, kinship-based, and religious than in national terms (Laver 2011). The period of Meiji restoration (1868–1912) transformed Japan from a deeply hierarchical feudal and agriculture-dominated society into a social order focused on intense modernisation and industrialisation. Although Japan nominally remained an empire, its internal social structure changed substantially, and this was most pronounced in the rise of a society-wide sense of shared nationhood. Reformers prioritised development of state infrastructure, including the 1871 formation of a national army with universal conscription and an administrative reorganisation that abolished old domains and introduced a more efficient prefecture system of bureaucratic organisation. The new government also unified the tax and monetary system and introduced a society-wide universal system of education. Japan was opened to international trade and foreign influence in many spheres of life. In 1889 the first (Meiji) constitution was adopted, and the new parliament was instituted (Teikoku Gikai) with limited voting franchise. These organisational changes had a decisive impact on the ordinary population. With compulsory conscription, intensive urbanisation, and industrialisation Japan was able to quickly build a formidable military force that defeated two large powers in subsequent wars (China in 1894–1895 and Russia in 1904–1905). These military victories raised the international standing of Japan, but they also fostered the development of cross-class sense of nationhood. In the early twentieth century, Japan was a society undergoing a rapid societal transformation that was particularly visible in ever-intensive militarisation, industrialisation, and a focus on territorial conquests. The defeat in World War II, followed by US occupation, stimulated a further shift from the imperial to the national order. With the 1947 constitution Japan became a constitutional monarchy, while its organisational and political structure shifted in the direction of a regular nation-state. Hence, just as in the case of Hungary, Japanese nationhood is a modern creation, but the organisational grounding that made nation-formation possible is a long-term historical process. The fully-fledged Japanese nationhood transpired only in the twentieth century, but this would not have been possible without the organisational spine that can be traced back to a variety of social orders from the history of Japan.

The Sinews of Ideological Grounding

Many scholars have emphasised that empires and nation-states differ profoundly in their legitimising ideologies (Breuilly 2016, 1993; Gellner 1983; Anderson 1983). While the rulers of empires justify their power through different forms of imperialism, the legitimacy of governance in the nation-states is derived from the notion of popular sovereignty. The imperial systems often rely on specific religious creeds to frame their political domination as a God-given right, or they legitimise their rule through the notion of a civilizing mission. For example, the rulers of the Roman empire invoked the notion of humanitas as a system of values associated with legality, civilised behaviour, education, urbanity, and the continuous drive for cultural advancement (Woolf 1998). Their ambition was to spread these values throughout the known world by conquering the 'barbarian' lands and turning them into a civilisation. Similarly, in their nineteenth-century colonisation of Africa and South-East Asia, the French empire relied on the idea of *mission civilisatrice.*[7] This project implied the inherent superiority of French civilisation, which would be deployed in the colonies to help uplift the 'uncivilised' indigenous population. The focus was in particular on education and the acquisition of French-language skills (Steinmetz 2023). The discourse of imperialism is characterised by universalist

[7] This concept was originally formulated by the enlightenment philosopher de Condorcet (1988:269), who argued that Europeans have a duty to help indigenous populations, who in their aim to 'civilize themselves wait only to receive the means from us, to find brothers among Europeans, and to become their friends and disciples'.

language and practices. The key distinction here is between those who live in the empire ('the civilised') and those who live outside its borders ('the barbarians'). Hence, imperial projects aim to reshape the 'uncivilised' world in their image. In contrast, rulers of nation-states recognise the rights of other nation-states to exist and as such they also respect that citizens of other nation-states subscribe to different value systems. Hence, in contrast to the universalism of empires, nation-states promote value particularism – their own brand of nationalist ideology. As Gellner (1983:56) noted, 'in a nationalist age, societies worship themselves brazenly and openly, spurning the camouflage. At Nuremberg, Nazi Germany did not worship itself by pretending to worship God or even Wotan; it overtly worshiped itself.'

There is no doubt that empires differ from nation-states in their legitimising practices. Nevertheless, by differentiating sharply between these two forms of polity it is difficult to understand how nationalism replaced imperialism as the principal ideological doctrine of state power. To better understand this historical shift, it is important to recognise that this was a gradual, contingent, and ongoing process that was often riddled with many contradictions. Just as organisational grounding involves a slow and protracted progression that eventually transforms empires, patrimonial kingdoms, and city-states into nation-states, the same applies to ideological grounding.

The process of ideological grounding is centred around the principal belief systems espoused within a particular social order. This is an open-ended activity through which different ideological and proto-ideological doctrines permeate different social groups within a specific society. It is through this process that the rulers acquire normative justification for their right to rule. These principles can also be used to delegitimise the counter-elites as well as to mobilise support among different social groups in times of crisis. Ideological grounding is not a static set of values; it is an ongoing historical process through which particular ideas and practices are produced and disseminated to justify the existence of a specific organisational form. In other words, ideological grounding is not culture; instead, it is a process based on the selection of specific cultural markers that can facilitate justification of a particular action and aid group mobilisation. In the premodern world such values are usually associated with the universalism espoused in mythological or religious creeds. Hence, imperial rulers are often presented as the defenders of a shared faith. For instance, the Ottoman sultans were bestowed titles such as 'the Commander of the Faithful and Successor of the Prophet of the Lord of the Universe, Custodian of the Holy Cities of Mecca, Medina, and Kouds' (see Chapter 3). Similarly, King Henry VIII was styled as the

'King of England, France and Ireland, Defender of the Faith and of the Church of England and also of Ireland in Earth the Supreme Head' (Wooding 2015). Furthermore, although entire social orders were associated with a single belief system such as Christianity, Islam, Hinduism, Confucianism, legalism, animism, or totemism, to name a few, the lack of organisational capacity and deeper ideological penetration often generated a cacophony of social values. Even though the majority of population might have been regarded as Christian, Hindu, animist, or something else, their everyday cultural practices were usually diverse and syncretic and as such would differ significantly from the official doctrine of their social order. Many anthropologists and historians have analysed differences between the elite cultures associated with the aristocracy and the vernacular cultural practices and values as experienced in the villages and small, mostly illiterate communities (Crone 2003; Hall 1986). Hence in the premodern world it was very difficult, if not impossible, to forge cross-class and society-wide shared ideological values and practices. Nevertheless, such societies were still able to generate proto-ideologies that fostered a degree of cohesion among the elites. For example, in feudal Europe or fifteenth-century Mesoamerica, rulers had to justify their political and military decisions to their fellow aristocrats, while at the same time they could have ignored the will of the ordinary population. The sheer discrepancy in power between the aristocratic elite and the rest is well visible in the ability of premodern rulers to change the official doctrine of their social order. For example, when Henry VIII decided to break links with the Catholic Church and establish an independent Church of England, he was able to enact this unprecedented ideological and organisational shift despite strong opposition among some fellow aristocrats and much milder resistance among the commoners (Wooding 2015).

However, none of this is to say that one can trace nationalism to the premodern world. Ideological grounding has very little to do with cultural content and much more with ideologisation as a process. Hence, there is no cultural continuity between the premodern and modern worlds. Instead, there is an element of continuity in the way ideological processes operate. Ethno-symbolists such as Smith (2009, 1986) and Hutchinson (2017, 2005) and perennialists such as Hastings (1997) and Grosby (2005) invoke the centrality of long-term cultural identities for the development of nationalism. Hasting (1997:12) argues that 'ethnicities naturally turn into nations or integral elements within nations at the point when their specific vernacular moves from an oral to written usage to the extent that is being regularly employed for the production of a literature'. Similarly, Smith (1986:157) insists that 'in the modern era, ethnie must become politicised ... and must begin to move towards nationhood'.

Nevertheless, these teleological accounts leave no room for the historical fluctuations or reversibility of ideological change. More problematically, they wrongly insist on the premodern and modern continuity of cultural values and practices. As there are obvious and marked cultural discontinuities between the cultural practices of the medieval peasantry and those of the citizens of modern nation-states, the focus should not be on this alleged but chimerical cultural continuity, but on the structural processes that make the transformation from the premodern into the modern world possible. While one can accept that there is no sudden ideological rupture between the imperial and the national worlds, this does not mean that elements of endurance are to be found in the allegedly robust cultural identities or ethnies. Instead of cultural contents such as shared myths and collective memories, as emphasised by Smith (2009), the focus should be on the ideological processes that facilitate this social change. The brief historical analysis of the Hungarian and Japanese cases indicates clearly how this process works.

The perennialist and ethno-symbolist accounts regularly interpret Hungarian and Japanese nation-formation through the prism of the long-existing ethnic cores around which nations developed in the early modern period. For Smith (2013) the Hungarian and Japanese nations emerge from the long-lasting Hungarian and Japanese ethnies. Smith identifies Hungarian knights as representatives of the ethnie who are now associated with 'the persistence of various collective vernacular memories, myths [and] traditions', while for the Japanese he insists that there is 'evidence of the persistence of at least some ethnic ties and boundaries for millennia, despite periodic transformations of their cultural contents'. Nevertheless, there is really no point in focusing on the shared cultural practices when in the premodern world nobility and commoners inhabit profoundly different cultural universes. It is more fruitful to attend to the symbols and ideational resources that were liable to ideologically transform. For example, the contemporary coats of arms and national flags of Hungary and Japan were built on the premodern heraldry associated with the specific aristocratic families. The current coat of arms of Hungary (Magyarország címere), adopted in 1990, was developed from the aristocratic emblem of the Árpád nobility from the early thirteenth century. The coat of arms also features another medieval family symbol, the Holy Crown of St Stephen. The colours of the Hungarian flag can also be traced to the Árpád nobility. Similarly, the Japanese flag (Nisshōki or Hinomaru) was initially a symbol of a particular clan and was later adopted as an imperial emblem. During the Genpei War (1180–1185) the imperial court used a flag with a golden sun circle, while the Genji (Minamoto clan) used a white flag with a red circle. The warlords who won the war saw themselves as the successors of Genji and adopted the Hinomaru flag (Befu 2001).

In contrast to the ethno-symbolist and perennialist views that see these symbols as forms of cultural continuity between ethnies and nations, it makes more sociological sense to focus on the ideological practices that such symbolism enacts. The proto-ideology behind the premodern flags and coats of arms was a shared common descent of respective noble families. The aristocrats used such symbols to differentiate themselves from the commoners but also to project their superior position into the past. A Hungarian aristocrat such as Francis II Rákóczi could use such heraldry to establish a direct lineage to the first king of Hungary, Stephen I (1000–1038), to justify his claim to the throne. However, other aristocrats were able to invoke this lineage too and to contest the competing descent claims. For instance, in the sixteenh century two aristocrats had made legitimate claims to the Hungarian throne – János Szapolyai (1487–1540), who was Voivode of Transylvania, and Archduke Ferdinand I of Habsburg (1503–1564). They both invoked a lineage to Stephen I and used similar heraldic symbolism to enforce their claims. They were both elected king by rival factions of the Hungarian nobility, but eventually Szapolyai was crowned the king of Hungary in 1526 (Engel 2001).

In the premodern context such symbols of shared lineage also often had a religious resonance as some notable rulers, including Stephen I as St Stephen, were later beatified and attained sainthood. Hence, by establishing a direct family link to a saint the new rulers could legitimately position themselves at the top of the social pyramid. In a very similar vein the Japanese nobility, *daimyo*, adopted their own distinct symbols of lineage that projected a shared descent with a noble family from the past. For example, the Satake clan used a family crest of white *sensu* (a folding fan) on a black background to establish a direct descent with the Minamoto clan. In particular the link was made between Satake Masayoshi and the prominent eleventh-century warrior Minamoto no Yoshimitsu. The Toki clan used the family crest of a black lotus flower, and they too made a claim of descent from the Minamoto clan and the Seiwa Genji (Befu 2001). In this context the shared heraldry performed a specific ideological role: to symbolically link the aristocratic rulers with their predecessors. All such links were based on the aristocratic lineage that was centred on the elite and had no ethno-national connotations whatsoever. It is only in the modern contexts that these family crests gradually acquire the cross-class and nationalist meanings. Once nationalism becomes a dominant frame of reference the traditional aristocratic symbols become re-interpreted as the national coats of arms and the national flags. Hence, what used to be the family crest of thirteenth-century Árpád nobility becomes the central symbol of the Hungarian nation. Something that was previously an exclusive property of a handful of noble individuals is gradually transformed into a political symbol associated with millions of Hungarians. The same applies to the Japanese experience: the flag of the sun was an emblem of the Minamoto clan in the twelfth century, and today it is a national flag that more than 125 million Japanese perceive as the symbol of their nation. Here too the central role these symbols perform is ideological. In the premodern context, the focus was on identifying a vertical model of legitimacy – one could establish the political and even religious primacy through direct lineage with the aristocratic predecessors. In modernity the emphasis shifts towards a horizontal model of legitimacy – all Japanese or Hungarians are entitled to popular sovereignty because they can equally make a claim of shared common descent. In this context political symbols such as the flag or coat of arms do not have much to do with cultural practices but are primarily the ideological requisites that generate political legitimacy. The ideological grounding is a long-term historical process that makes the transition from aristocratic lineage to nationalist identification possible. There is an important element of continuity here, but this is not a cultural continuity invoked by the ethno-symbolists and perennialists. Instead of spontaneously shared myths and collective memories, what is at stake here is the ideological process through which aristocratic symbols once used to differentiate nobility from peasantry are gradually transformed into the cross-class and society-wide symbols of nationhood.

In modern contexts ideological grounding is regularly dependent on and also helps to reinforce organisational grounding. The ever-increasing coercive-organisational capacities of states and many non-state entities foster the development of transportation and communication systems, the enhanced bureaucratic apparatus of the state, the increased military and policing capacities, and the expansion of legal structures, among others. All these large-scale transformations provide new organisational channels for deeper ideological grounding. More specifically, the introduction of compulsory education, the rise of literacy rates, the spread of mass-scale publishing, and the proliferation of 'high culture' institutions all advance ideological grounding. Hence, in modernity nationalist principles and practices permeate the majority of state institutions and are just as much present in civil society and other non-state contexts. All these outlets promote nationhood as a transhistorical community of fate and the only legitimate mode of modern subjectivity. In contrast to the deeply hierarchical imperial creeds, nationalist discourses promote the moral equality of all citizens and invoke the principles of collective emancipation, liberation, and national authenticity. Nationalist discourses are often rooted in the language of morality, which is framed in terms of attaining equality, justice, and freedom. With the development of mass education, society-wide media, military conscription, national court systems, and large-scale civil service, modern states are in position to continually disseminate and reproduce the nation-centric visions of social reality. This ideological transformation is also clearly observable in the Hungarian and Japanese cases. In the beginning of the nineteenth century Hungary was a less developed part of the Habsburg empire, and its literacy rates were significantly lower than in Austria. It is estimated that in the early nineteenth century only 12 per cent of the population of Hungary could read and write, while in Austria the literacy rates were much higher (Reis 2005; Cvrcek 2020). In this period the Hungarian society was still sharply divided between the wealthy and literate nobility, who mostly communicatd in Latin and German, and the large, generally illiterate peasantry, who used a variety of local vernaculars. However, by the end of the century the ideological grounding had dramatically intensified, and in 1900 more than 80 per cent of the Hungarian population was literate (Reis 2005; Cvrcek 2020). The language reform intensified in the nineteenth century when Ferenc Kazinczy and other authors and linguists introduced thousands of new words and simplified old expressions. In 1844 Hungarian replaced Latin as the official language. The linguistic standardisation continued for the next century when many traditional dialects were homogenised into a standard Hungarian language.

The combined processes of organisational and ideological grounding had transformed a predominantly feudal social order into a modernising society suffused with rising nationalist ideologies. The nineteenth and early twentieth centuries were decisive periods in the formation of Hungarian nationhood as a sociological phenomenon. The compulsory general primary education that was introduced already in 1774 was fully codified in 1868 with the first Education Act. In 1883, the secondary school system underwent a significant reform and was fully institutionalised across the country (Rébay & Kozma 2015). The rising literacy rates were soon reflected in the number of new newspapers, magazines, and periodicals published in the Hungarian language. While there were only five literary and political journals published in the Hungarian language in 1840, by the end of the century there were hundreds of new newspapers and periodicals (Simmonds 1841:127). This period also witnessed the development and expansion of key cultural institutions that foster mass-scale nation-formation, such as the Academy of Sciences (established in 1825), the National Theatre (opened in 1837), the National Museum (1808), National Széchényi Library (1802), and the Hungarian State Opera House (1884). Over the last two centuries these cultural, educational, and journalistic institutions were the key social mechanisms for ideological grounding. In particular the mass media and educational system have played a crucial role in nationalist socialisation. Contemporary Hungarian society has attained near full literacy (99.1 per cent), and nearly all of the population has completed some level of education. The educational cycle starts at the age of three and is compulsory until the age of sixteen. The mass media in the Hungarian language is very vibrant today. In 2016 there were 31 dailies, 262 weeklies, 176 bi-weeklies, 1,358 monthlies, 542 bi-monthlies, 1,129 quarterlies, 363 bi-annuals, and 2,792 other publications (www.whitereport.hu/2016).

The consequence of this long-term and highly successful ideological grounding was the transformation of a predominantly feudal and deeply stratified social order into a nation-centric society. Organisational and ideological grounding facilitated this transition: while in the late eighteenth century very few individuals identified primarily in national terms, today an overwhelming majority see themselves first and foremost as Hungarians. According to a recent poll, when asked, 'Do you identify yourself as European or Hungarian?', 83 per cent of population identified as Hungarian and only 15 per cent described themselves as European (Statista 2021). In 2021 another survey found that 'eight out of ten Hungarians are proud of being Hungarian, and 85 percent of them have a strong national identity', while 63 per cent of respondents were extremely proud to be Hungarian (Kopp 2021).

A similar pattern can be observed in the Japanese case. Although Japan had relatively high literacy rates already by the second half of the Edo period (1603 until 1868), this process has intensified after the Meiji Restoration. Several sources indicate that 35–40 per cent of males and 10–15 per cent of females were literate by the end of Edo period (Perez 2009; Tocco 2003).[8] Literacy levels increased in the Bunka

[8] As Masashi (2000:45) explains, these unusually high levels of literacy in a largely feudal order are atypical but are a product of Japan's system of rule, as this was 'a society in which the information that was important for people took the form of the written word'. Rulers issued their orders through written documentation only: 'the samurai did not carry out their authority directly in person; rather, their domination of society took the form of a system of laws and ordinances, which were issued in the form of written documents and bulletins', and 'the government accepted no reports, petitions or appeals that were not written down'.

period (1804–1818) where there were up to 1,300 private schools (Iwasaki 2008:5). Similar to Hungary, the political elite were fully literate – the samurai class attained a nearly 100 per cent literacy rate much earlier. The Meiji reforms had an important impact on the development of the modern educational system and have quickly fostered an increase in literacy rates. In 1872 the Japanese government introduced a new educational system (Gakusei, the First National Plan for Education) modelled on the European and American experiences with a six-year compulsory primary education. It is estimated that by the beginning of the twentieth century 90 per cent of the Japanese population were literate (Iwasaki 2008:5). The modernisation of the Meiji period was also centred on national homogenisation. As Zielenziger (2006:249) points out: 'The Imperial Rescript on Education issued in October 1890 demanded that all schooling be grounded in Confucian ethics. This proclamation asserted both that filial piety and loyalty were "the fundamental glory of Our Empire" and that a "national essence", whose values had been manifest in Japan's distant, primordial past should be the foundation for its future actions and beliefs.'

By 1909, 98 per cent of Japanese children were in full-time primary education (Masashi 2000). During the Taishō and early Shōwa periods (1912–1937) the focus had shifted towards the secondary and university levels, and the education system has become more centralised. In the 1930s and early 1940s, under the far-right minister of education Sadao Araki the curriculum became more militaristic and aggressively nationalist. After World War II, the new educational system was modelled on the US example, and a focus on practical skills was put in place. The number of primary and middle school students who went on to high school increased from 42.5 per cent in 1950 to 91.9 per cent in 1975 (Morley 1999). Just as in Hungary, in 2024 the Japanese population reached full, nearly 100 per cent, literacy.

The deeper ideological grounding was also facilitated by the ever-increasing number of cultural institutions, the mass production of books, and the proliferation of numerous mass media outlets. Similar to the Hungarian case, Japan's leading academic and cultural institutions had been established in the nineteenth century: the Japan Academy (Nihon Gakushiin), Kabuki-za national theatre (1889), the Tokyo National Museum (1872), the National Diet Library composed of the Imperial Library (1872), the House of Peers (1889), the Imperial Diet (1890), and the University of Tokyo (1877), among others. Although Japan has a long history of producing printed works it was only during the later years of the Edo period that books had acquired a mass audience. In the Edo period the focus was on the woodprint publications of Buddhist scriptures and Chinese classics. A rudimentary form of newspaper, *kawara-ban*, with tile-block-print editions, was also available for larger audiences (Iwasaki 2008:5). However, the mass scale publishing of newspapers, magazines, and books intensified at the beginning of the Meiji period. The most influential nation-wide modern Japanese newspapers have all emerged in this period: *Yokohama Mainichi Shimbun* (1871), *Tokyo Nichinichi Shimbun* (1972), *Yomiuri Shimbun* (1774), *Nihon Keizai Shimbun* (1876), and *Asahi Shimbun* (1879). Initially the newspapers were sold in bookstores, but from 1903 the majority of newspapers and magazines have been distributed through direct home delivery, so that in 2016, 95 per cent of mass media included home delivery (Web Japan 2024:1). The Meiji period was also a springboard for the large-scale book publishers such as the Kōdansha and Hakubunkan publishing houses. For example, from 1895 to 1933 Hakubunkan published *Bungei Kurabu*, which was the first literary magazine for a mass audience. Newspaper, magazine, and book publishing have increased exponentially from the late nineteenth to twenty-first century; today Japan is one of the world's leading countries in terms of printed works. For instance, in 2002 the total circulation of national and provincial newspapers was around 10 million copies (Iwasaki 2008:6). The number of books published has also increased substantially: 75,412 books and magazines were published in 2017 (Web Japan 2024:2). The continuous and cumulative rise of organisational and ideological grounding has transformed the population: the nineteenth century feudal order dominated by the military aristocracy gave way to a nation-centric society. According to the most public polls the overwhelming majority of the population identifies strongly and primarily in national terms. For example, in 2008 a national survey showed that 92 per cent of respondents declared that they were proud to be Japanese (Glosserman & Snyder 2008). In a 2014 survey on national identity, 96 per cent of respondents expressed strong emotional attachment to Japan, and a further 61 per cent were in favour of 'strong patriotic feelings' (Murata 2014).

The Hungarian and Japanese examples illustrate well how the process of ideological grounding operates over long periods of time. Rather than witnessing an unimpeded transition from ethnies to nations, one could observe how ideological grounding played a central role in the highly contingent and ongoing process of nation-formation. Instead of the cultural durability expressed in shared collective memories, nation-formation is shaped by very specific ideological practices and organisational mediators.

The Micro-Interactional Universe and the Rise of National Subjectivities

The shift from the world of empires and patrimonial kingdoms to the world of nation-states could not happen without the large-scale structural processes of organisational and ideological grounding. However, these structural transformations would not last without a profound change taking place in the everyday perceptions and self-understanding of ordinary people. Nationalism could gradually supplement and then eventually replace imperial, religious, mythological, civilisational, and other proto-ideologies only when it was able to fully penetrate the grassroots. In other words, the transition from imperial to national subjectivities was also dependent on a process of micro-interactional grounding. This process affects the domain of everyday life and the face-to-face interactions with people from the same communities, residential areas, kinship-based networks, neighbourhoods, and peer groups. Recent studies from micro-sociology and social psychology have demonstrated on numerous occasions that this grassroots level impacts human behaviour profoundly. We are reflexive creatures who thrive on the emotional support from significant others (Malešević 2022; Collins 2022, 2008, 2004; Turner 2007, Turner & Stets 2005). Our social actions are often shaped by our micro-level relationships with people who matter to us, such as close family members, friends, lovers, comrades, peers, and neighbours. The emotional dynamics of human behaviour are regularly framed around one's aim to impress, please, protect, obey, or establish some other form of meaningful relationship with the individuals who matter to us. In this context long-term ideological grounding would not succeed without micro-interactional grounding. The top-down ideologisation as exemplified in the spread of mass media, the institutionalisation of compulsory education, increased literacy rates, and the development of the public sphere often emerges in parallel with the transformation of micro-level solidarities. The ideological power must fully penetrate the micro-sphere of everyday life as experienced in the change of inter-personal relationships in order to make the transformation from imperial to national subjectivities possible.

In the pre-national world, micro-level solidarities were typically shaped by one's lineage, social status, and the place of birth. The children of nobility socialised with the other aristocratic families, maintained kinship networks, developed friendships, and later in life were likely to attain deep comradeships with other members of the nobility through the shared experience in fighting wars (Halden 2020). They inhabited a relatively isolated micro-world that revolved around the events and rituals associated with their own social class. They also tended to practice strict rules of aristocratic endogamy. A recent comparative study of marriage strategies among the European nobility from the sixteenth to nineteenth centuries indicates that aristocrats usually married within the same title range, with the German nobility being characterised by a particularly high degree of homogamy: 'In the 1500s, British nobles were about 1.2 times as likely to marry someone who shared their same title as they were to marry someone who did not. The same odds were about 3.1 for German nobles' (Marcassa et al. 2020:1).

At the other end of this social pyramid was the micro-world of the commoners who would usually reside, marry, live, and work in the same village or community of their birth. The everyday life of such communities was shaped by very different working practices, rituals, marriage arrangements, and social experiences. Although endogamy was a norm here as well, a limited form of exogamous marriage was also practiced. For example, in England the evidence of merchant payments that indicate that a woman was married outside the manor testify that this practice did exist. However, in most instances such marriages, as in the case of the Ramsey Abbey estates, usually happened within a fifteen-mile radius and were mostly within the same class (Ward 2002). This deeply stratified character of everyday life had a decisive impact on collective subjectivities. Hence, the micro-level solidarities of the nobility had very little if anything in common with the micro-world of the peasantry. The Japanese and Hungarian cases illustrate this well.

Premodern Japanese society was a deeply hierarchical feudal system where the aristocratic elite were culturally detached from the rest of the predominately peasant society. In some respects, this was a capstone model of imperial rule where the military class 'sat atop a series of separate "societies", which it did not wish to penetrate or mobilise: perhaps the key to its behaviour was its fear that horizontal linkages it could not see would get out of control' (Hall 1986:52). In other words, the rulers of the premodern Japan lacked the coercive-organisational capacity to penetrate the microcosm of everyday life in the villages. Hence for more than a thousand years Japan had a deeply stratified social order where the emperors, shoguns, and samurai inhabited a very different inter-personal world from that of the peasantry.

During the Heian period (794–1185) shoguns become more powerful than the court officials, and for the next seven centuries, until the end of the Edo period in 1868, the military class held political power whereby the sons of shoguns would inherit their titles. The shogun rule was characterised by a strict class hierarchy with the *daimyo* (hereditary warlords) and samurai having a privileged position over the artisans, merchants, and vast peasantry. Over the centuries the *daimyo* class developed distinct cultural values and practices that underpinned the micro-interactional environment of their everyday lives. These feudal lords were not just warriors but also fostered a rise in unique culture associated with nature paintings, calligraphy, handscrolls, tea ceremonies, Zen meditation, poetry, and the mastery of the arts of peace. Most of all the key mechanism of micro-interactional grounding was to be found in the cult of bushido – 'the way of the warrior'. The Bushido ethic was built on a combination of the Confucian ethics, Zen Buddhist precepts of stoicism and serenity, and Shinto principles of fidelity and loyalty (Benesch 2014). Although this martial moral code was later institutionalised and formalised by the Tokugawa shogunates, for much of Japanese history there was no single code governing behaviour of the *daimyo* and samurai. Instead, there were multiple warrior codes with enormous variation across different samurai clans and different time periods. In other words, bushido was a set of moral prescriptions shaping a micro-universe of different elite groups. The key principles associated with this moral code, such as frugality, loyalty to one's lord, duty, virtue, obedience, self-sacrifice, honour until death, sincerity, and the mastery of martial arts, constituted a normative universe of military aristocrats. These ethical precepts were central in shaping the imperial subjectivities of the elite as each new generation of samurai and *daimyo* was socialised through the glorification of this ethical code. Furthermore, just as in other feudal social orders, this cultural resource was used to dissociate the nobility from the peasantry. In the famous text, allegedly published in the sixteenth century, 'The Military Mirror of Kai', which was widely read by the samurai, bushido rules were deliberately described in a metaphorical language that was not accessible to the ordinary population. One of the central aims here was to differentiate the elite from the commoners (Wert 2014). However, as each clan had its own version of bushido, these general codes usually had different local applications. For example, some samurai clans practiced *tsujigiri* (crossroads killing) where they would attack a commoner to test their weapons or martial skills; other clans practiced *kiri-sute gomen* – the right to injure or kill a member of the lower class whose actions were deemed to dishonour a samurai – or seppuku, the use of the ritual suicide to die honourably (Benesch 2014).

Unlike this micro-universe of the class-based martial ethics, the commoners did not possess a codified set of moral prescriptions for everyday life. Instead, most of the Japanese population were impoverished peasants whose everyday life was confined to the village of their birth. Even in 1750, 92 per cent of the population of 27 million people lived in the countryside. During this period there were more than 63,000 villages, most consisting of 400 or fewer people. Each village family was required to pay the land tax of one *koku* of rice per year (around 150 kilograms), a target difficult to attain for many who often were on the brink of starvation. These everyday hardships, together with the shared living spaces in the small and cramped villages, fostered the development of collectivist values and practices centred on the village community. In the majority of cases the council of elders ran the village and most everyday activities were done collectively – from planting, harvesting, hunting, and fishing to processing, food preparation, house building, and dredging of irrigation canals. These shared everyday experiences shaped a sense of micro-group attachments that were primarily based around one's kinship and village. In the early medieval period, most peasants were animist or polytheists but eventually became Buddhists. However, as Toshio (1996) emphasises, most peasants espoused syncretic beliefs that combined magic and religion with local worship practices. Peasants often established their own village worship halls that reflected local social practices. 'As agricultural production dependent not only on the efforts of individuals but on the communal village ties, agricultural rituals were generally performed as village rituals.... As centres of village life, village worship halls served primarily as gathering places for villagers, more than as temples run by clerics' (Toshio 1996:293). Thus, despite the universalist teachings of Buddhism, the village worship halls reflected much more the particularistic beliefs and practices of each village. In many respects this was a world of local, vernacular cultures where each village had its own set of values and practices. However, the strong local sense of attachment to one's village and kinship group did not undermine the deeply hierarchical character of the Japanese feudal system: 'in all villages class and status divisions were comparatively complex. In early medieval times and in the less-developed regions of the country, the medieval village was characterized in general by the direct, comprehensive rule of local lords, with the lord, his family, and his retainers dominating both independent and dependent peasants' (Toshio 1996:292). Hence, this was an environment where one's subjectivities were determined by one's place of origin and their status descent. This was an imperial and deeply hierarchical world where for the majority of the population the process of micro-interactional grounding remained at the level of one's village.

Despite enormous cultural differences a very similar structural pattern operated in the premodern Hungary. This too was a deeply hierarchical social order where the aristocracy were regarded as having a higher moral worth than the rest of the population. Furthermore, the everyday lives of the nobility and the peasantry were profoundly different. Hungarian aristocrats practiced endogamous marriage policies and were intermarried with other European noble families. The most influential aristocrats, such as Esterházys, Batthyánys, or Pálffys, were in possession of huge estates and were also owners of numerous serfs who worked on their lands. The Hungarian nobility was relatively large, with up to 5 per cent of the population possessing a patent of nobility (Peter 1992:79). As in other European societies, the upper nobility was associated with the ideas and practices of chivalry. As in the case of bushido in Japan, this was not a uniform set of values, but a general code of conduct associated with the aristocratic way of life. Over time chivalry became more refined and more institutionalised, focusing on a shared set of social and moral principles. The ethical codes of chivalry were particularly associated with the institution of knighthood and involved military bravery, a deep commitment to self-improvement in military skills, and service to others. This moral system developed over several centuries and became centred on the warrior ethos, refined courtly manners, and knightly piety, all of which signified honour and noble origins. From the early fourteenth century, 'barons of the realm' were appointed as knights at the court by King Charles I Robert. This status-centred microcosm of knighthood was reproduced through generations as the children of knights would serve first as pages (*parvulus*) and then as 'juveniles-at-the court' in the royal households. In a very similar way to Japan, the Hungarian nobility deployed distinct cultural practices in everyday life to differentiate themselves from the commoners: specific martial skills such as handling the sword, elaborate dance routines, distinct mannerisms, the use of non-vernacular languages (Latin and later German), and so on. Although chivalry and other aristocratic values and practices were a pan-European phenomenon spread throughout the whole of Christendom, their everyday expressions had a distinctly local flavour. In other words, while the European aristocrats were part of the same social strata and as such had a sense of attachment to this class, their more meaningful micro-level solidarities were often shaped through everyday interactions with a small number of their fellow nobility. They often had a shared experience of fighting in wars and tournaments, participated together in ceremonial oath-taking events, would often go together on pilgrimages, and would generally spend much of their time in the same everyday activities (Dvorakova 2002).

The Hungarian peasantry lived a very different social life. Until the full abolition of serfdom in 1848, many peasants were overburdened with their obligations to the local lords, while also attempting to provide for their own subsistence. The land toiled by the serfs was owned by the gentry, the Church, or the king. The feudal system of obligation whereby the peasants work on the land owned by the lords was codified as *telek-s* (mansio, fundus, sessio) (Hofer & Fel 2008:24). The *telek* system also included a serf's obligations towards the Church and the state with the tithe of grain, livestock, wine, and other produce being regularly delivered to the lords, clergy, and state authorities. This enormous burden occasionally generated resistance of the serfs, with the most notable revolt being the 1514 peasant uprising led by György Dózsa (Molnar 2001). However, the feudal state was able to crush such peasant rebellions through force and the introduction of the obligatory corvée of one day per week.

During the sixteenth and seventeenth centuries the Hungarian peasantry was affected by the 'second serfdom' whereby they were under a landlord's jurisdiction and needed the permission of their lords to leave their villages. They were also required to provide a tribute in kind (mostly grain, dairy, or poultry) and corvée labour on the lord's farms. Typical villages included peasant houses and the land they farmed, the *határ*. It is only in the later periods that the *határ* was clearly separated from the landlord's demesne. After the reforms of Maria Theresa (1767) and Jospeh II (1785), the personal subordination of peasants to their lords was abolished, and from then onwards the villages were run by the village judges and several jurors (usually four to twelve). These were either elected by the villagers or selected from the nominees of the landlord (Gray 2009:65). As in many other parts of Europe the peasantry were nominally Christian but practiced syncretic beliefs that combined pagan practices, magic, superstition, and religious teaching. For example, many villagers sought the help of *táltos* (shamans) and believed in the evil eye (*rontás*), the healing power of charms and incantations, and many other pagan practices. Hungary was a prominent site of conflicts between early reformation and counterreformation. These deep religious rivalries created an ambiguous ideological environment that fostered syncretic and locally framed beliefs among peasants.

A recent anthropological study of the Hungarian village of Atany shows how these local interpretations of religion persisted for centuries and as such have played an important part in the collective self-understanding of the villagers. Shared Calvinist beliefs were central to the development of strong communal bonds within the wider rural area: 'Marriage ties outside the village and the resulting bonds of kinship and friendship connect Atany with the Protestant villages of the neighbourhood' (Hofer & Fel 2008:26). During the Habsburg rule the Protestant areas experienced discrimination and many Calvinist churches were closed. This external intrusion fostered a stronger sense of micro-group solidarity among the inhabitants of Atany. In 1765 the villagers organised a protest against the bishop of Eger, who came in person to the village to take over the church for the Catholics (Hofer & Fel 2008:30). However, despite strong communal ties, Atany, like other Hungarian villages, remained deeply stratified between the landed gentry, petty nobility, and the peasantry. The petty nobility were often the mediators between the peasantry and the lords. More importantly, they developed a distinct set of cultural practices and in this way planted the ideological seeds for the later transformation of imperial into national subjectivities. As Hofer and Fel (2008:28) emphasise, the lower gentry 'performed the same manual work as the serfs' but 'they took part in the administration and the political life of the county; some of them went to secondary school; and their attire, their manner, and sometimes also the design and furnishings of their houses followed the style of the nobility' as did their 'forms of greeting, address, polite behaviour, and Christian names'. Most of these cultural practices of the petty nobility were later re-articulated as 'Hungarian values' that were imitated by many commoners. Nevertheless, for much of the premodern period the Hungarian aristocracy and peasantry populated very different micro-social worlds. It is only through large-scale structural transformations such as coercive-organisational and ideological grounding that these two worlds would eventually start to interact and integrate.

In the conventional historiographic and theoretical narratives, nationalism is an ideology that reaches its apex in the nineteenth century. In this understanding, national identities suddenly and completely trump the imperial, religious, kinship-based, and local sense of attachments. In the view of Gellner, Hobsbawm, and other classical modernists, this transformation was caused by unprecedented socio-economic changes. However, these approaches cannot adequately explain the historical dynamics of the micro-world. How and why have the micro-universes of the aristocrats and the peasants started coalescing and developing into a single, relatively homogenous, and nation-centric reality? While the tectonic structural shifts played a crucial role in making the world of empires and patrimonial kingdoms into the universe of nation-states, these changes were not sufficient to reshape everyday interactions. Hence, to understand how nationalism came to dominate daily life it is necessary to zoom in on the processes of inter-personal grounding. The examples of Hungary and Japan will illustrate this historical shift.

When nationalism appears on the historical stage it is predominantly an ideology of a very small social stratum – the middle class. In most instances nationalist ideologies develop in urban settings among the sons and daughters of merchants, bankers, traders, artisans, and other urban professionals. Large-scale structural transformations such as coercive-organisational and ideological grounding were important in expanding the size and impact of this stratum while also reducing the political significance of nobility and the size of the rural population. Nevertheless, what was just as important were the changes taking place in the inter-personal domain. Nationalism was successful not only because it eventually captured the state administration, mass media, educational systems, military draft, police structures, or judiciary but also because it gradually became the dominant way of life. In Hungary nationalism did not suddenly and completely replace the Habsburg imperial project; it was a protracted, highly contingent, and uneven social process that started in the mid-eighteenth century, but gained its full form only in the nineteenth and twentieth centuries. Furthermore, as Maxwell (2019) convincingly demonstrates, from 1789 to 1867 Hungarian nationalist ideas and practices developed not only through the political parties, social movements, trade unions, and networks of highly engaged intellectuals and artists, but also through a variety of everyday practices. More specifically, Maxwell shows how nationalism slowly but effectively became a lived experience of different social classes. For example, he focuses on drinking, smoking, shaving, and clothing practices as objects of national contestation. The nationalisation of tobacco was initially linked to tariff disputes between the landowning big producers and the central government in Vienna. However, this tax dispute was gradually transformed into an established cultural practice whereby the Hungarian elites and the middle classes would smoke tobacco produced in Hungary to signify their attachment to the Hungarian nation. Even poems contained verses that promoted virtues of Hungarian pipe smoking, as 'smoking tobacco had come to signify friendship, honesty, and social solidarity … [that is,] civic virtue and 'nationality'' (Maxwell 2019:82). Some of these practices were later imitated by ordinary Hungarian men, and the popular press spearheaded campaigns to promote the idea of Hungarian tobacco culture. A similar pattern emerged in the context of alcoholic drinks. Maxwell dissects changing attitudes towards specific drinks, for example, the glorification of Tokaj wine as being distinctly Hungarian in contrast to non-Hungarian (i.e., Austrian or Slovak) spirits and beer. This too started as an elite practice but was eventually embraced by the ordinary population, who made the consumption of Hungarian wine a social practice that enhanced micro-level solidarities – casual drinking with close friends and family members. Even shaving practices gradually attained nation-centric features. An analysis of newspapers and other magazines indicates how the idea of the moustache was completely nationalised in the nineteenth century so that 'a Hungarian without a moustache' resembled 'a rose without thorns' (Maxwell 2019:131). Although wearing a distinct form of moustache was initially a prerogative of the aristocracy and high-ranking military officers, gradually men from other social strata embraced this practice, and facial hair was established as a potent national symbol. During pronounced political tensions, not wearing a moustache in Hungary could be interpreted as a sign of obedience to the Habsburg rule. Thus, nationalism had gradually penetrated many aspects of everyday life – from habitual patterns of drinking and smoking to distinct clothing and shaving practices. Status symbols previously associated solely with the nobility had gradually transformed into popular symbols and daily practices associated with millions of ordinary Hungarians.

This process has only intensified through the twentieth and early twenty-first century. Once organisational and ideological grounding created the structural conditions for the full-scale transformation of the imperial into national subjects, interpersonal grounding has reached its pinnacle. Although Hungary was under communist rule for more than four decades, this period has not undermined the proliferation of nationalism. On the contrary, despite its nominal proletarian internationalism, the Hungarian Socialist Workers Party, and its predecessor the Hungarian Communist party, pursued strong nationalist policies such as honouring nationalist heroes such as Kossuth, Petofi, Szchenyi, and Rakoczi, appropriating traditional national holidays such as March 15 and October 6, and justifying the expulsion of the German minority (Swabians) after World War II. This 'socialist patriotism' relied extensively on nationalist symbols in everyday life (Pap 2023; Mevius 2005). Communist authorities legitimised their regime by invoking the more radical version of egalitarianism that underpins all nationalist projects: 'The higher development of socialist patriotism does not mean preserving the possible privileged position of one class or another, but it also reduces the distance between classes, bringing the different social strata closer together, even at a more advanced historical-economic level of the division of labour' (Pap 2023:999). This was also a period when Hungary had reached near full literacy and the overwhelming majority of its population had been exposed to nation-centric discourses in compulsory education and mass media. The intensified urbanisation of the communist period also fostered the development of stronger bonds between the micro-level groups now residing in big cities such as Budapest, Debercen, Miscols, or Székesfehérvár. With nuclear families and small circles of trusted friends becoming a norm, the nation-centric understanding of everyday realities was perpetuated through a variety of shared everyday practices. Nationalist imagery and activities were not just present in institutionalised spaces such as kindergartens, schools, workplaces, party meetings, or retirement homes, but the nation-centric contents were just as visible in daily interactions in pubs, restaurants, coffeeshops, sporting events, and leisure activities, as well as in cuisine, everyday talk, consumption practices, and ritualistic events (Pap 2023; Mevius 2005; Brubaker et al. 2006). After the collapse of state socialism, the rhetoric of 'socialist patriotism' was replaced with the fully blown ethno-nationalism that permeates equally in the public and the private sphere (Horváth et al. 2012; Fox & Vermeersch 2010; Brubaker et al. 2006). In this primordialist discourse the Hungarians are a nation with a thousand-year-long history. As the guidebook of the new museum, the House of the Hungarian Millenium, states: 'The greatest celebration in the history of our people, when we celebrated 1000 years history, we suggest that our country, the Kingdom of Hungary, was made in 896, this was the moment when we arrived here and established a new home' (Posocco 2022:41). The nation-centric rhetoric infuses all aspects of everyday life. As Andras (2014:1) reflects on Hungary under Orban's rule: 'Nationalism is not just in Hungary's backyard, it is in every corner of the house from the basement to the roof. It gets inside with the air and has completely soaked through the orifices of the building: the front door, the windows, the chimney, the front yard.... Nationhood is constantly and vigorously flagged: national symbols are everywhere. Even protesters and activists opposing the regime's politics feel a pressing need to take back the national symbols – currently appropriated for official use – because those not regarded as Hungarian enough are excluded from the notion of the nation.' These banal nationalist practices, which Billig (1995) has analysed so well, find their micro-interactional counterparts in the daily routines of the ordinary population, for being and acting as a Hungarian has become second nature to most people. Hungarianness is naturalised and normalised as the dominant way of life.

The rise of Japanese nationalism follows a similar pattern. The Meiji restoration was central in spearheading coercive-organisational and ideological grounding as it generated an unprecedented structural transformation within Japanese society. The result of this process was a much more centralised state, more developed civil service, enhanced transportation and communication networks, an effective reform of the military, and the accelerated industrialisation of the economy. The modernising Japanese state was also hostile towards traditional cultural beliefs and practices that ideologically sustained the feudal order, such as the symbolic privilege of the samurai and the untouchable status of *burakumin*. The new policies fostered a degree of egalitarianism in social conduct. Thus, with the 1871 Dampatsurei edict the samurai class were required to cut their hair short and abandon the traditional *chonmage* hairstyle. The prohibition of Christianity and the ban on Japanese citizens traveling abroad were lifted too. Nevertheless, the transformation from imperial to nationalist subjectivities was dependent on the changes taking place in the micro-interactional universe. It is in this grassroots sphere that one could observe the most profound transformations. As Shimazu (2006) argues convincingly, the emergence of the *kokumin* (the Japanese national subject) was a protracted process that intensified during the Russo-Japanese war of 1904–1905. Analysing the diaries of Japanese conscripts, Shimazu (2006:41) finds that 'the Russo-Japanese war was the defining event in consolidating the identity of ordinary Japanese as kokumin'. The war mobilisation and the recruitment process involved a long journey ('journey of a lifetime') for many ordinary young men, most of whom had never left their villages before. The war experience generated a deep ideological shift for many, as their predominantly local and village-centred attachments had eventually transformed into nationalist subjectivities. The horizontal bonds of soldiers built in the calamity of war gradually merged with a strong sense of belonging to the Japanese nation. The process of micro-interactional grounding fused successfully with organisational and ideological grounding in the theatres of war. However, this was not a straightforward or resistance-free process. On the contrary, as Shimazu (2006:43) emphasises, the macro and the micro worlds started colliding: 'Being a responsible "national subject" (kokumin) necessitated the sacrifice of the family, which led to a conflict of interest between the loyalty to the state (chusetsu), and filial piety (ko).' Many young recruits were reluctant to leave their villages and towns and go to war: 'We were sent off with banzai, leaving the familiar hometown, with little hope of being able to walk on this ground again, with thoughts of parting from aging parents and younger brothers and sisters, mixed emotions closing in, leaving as in a dream with the noise of banzai' (Shimazu 2006:49). Nevertheless, the long and protracted journey to the theatres of war that involved mass participation of ordinary people cheering 'their' soldiers and organising elaborate nationalist farewell rituals had an impact on their self-perceptions as members of the Japanese nation: 'This has tremendously powerful effects on the soldiers, as it united them with the ordinary people of Japan, giving the perception that the country was united as one behind this war. This journey of farewell made them pinfully aware of their role as "Japanese" soldiers defending their country. The overwhelming emotional sense of belonging to the nation converted even the sceptics to fight for the kokka [nation]' (Shimazu 2006:62). Furthermore, their shared war experiences and hardships on the battlefields played a central role in transforming the ambiguous peasant recruits into fully-fledged Japanese subjects.

The micro-interactional grounding of nationalism only intensified in the second half of the twentieth century and the beginning of the twenty-first century. The highly impressive post–World War II economic development of Japan has generated a sense of self-confidence and superiority among most of the population. Nevertheless, the economic success was experienced in distinctly nation-centric terms and perceived to be an indicator of Japanese exceptionalism. As Sugimoto (2010), Yoshino (1992), and Dale (1988) emphasise, this myth of unique Japanese national qualities, often referred to as Nihonjinron, has shaped many aspects of everyday life. Sugimoto (2010:4) associates the Nihonjinron perspective with the view that all Japanese people share the same key values regardless of their social position and that no other society in the world is as culturally homogenous and unique as the Japanese nation. This perception also promotes an idea that these shared cultural attributes have always existed among the Japanese. The Nihonjinron discourse is strongly premised on micro-interactional grounding as it frames the Japanese nation through the prism of kinship. In this understanding Japanese life is based on the archaic and vertical family model that reproduces the transhistorical parent-child patterns (親分・子分, kobun) whereby all Japanese favour clan-based solidarities (氏, uji) (Dale 1988). The Nihonjinron view also emphasises the uniqueness of the Japanese group-centred view of everyday life, as formulated in the concept of *kanjin*, which stands for the inclination towards strong micro-group solidarity, symbiosis, and harmony (Sugimoto 2010). As Surak (2012) shows, Japanese nationalism has successfully combined the familial and the national in the notion of the family-state (*kazoku kokka*). Although these values are promoted through various organisational and ideological channels, they are also reproduced in the micro-interactional contexts of everyday life. For example, research on Japanese everyday behaviour indicates that the majority of population share and reproduce these nation-centric views (Brooke 2022; Tanabe 2021; Coulmas 2007; Yoshino 1992). In 2003, 95 per cent of respondents expressed the view that they 'feel glad that they were born Japanese' (Coulmas 2007:3). More importantly, most respondents perceive their nation in strictly primordialist and uniquely homogenous terms. For instance, interviews with undergraduate students indicate that regardless of their political orientation, most students subscribe to such essentialist views: 'the Japanese nation (kokumin) has been built and nurtured over the years by one ethnic group in an island. The Japanese are ethnically homogeneous (tan'itsu minzoku). [The core of the nation is] the allegiance based on blood' (Fukoka 2017:354).

Everyday nationalism is also reproduced in daily interactions with family members, friends, and peers. It is also a part of regular consumption practices, family-based rituals, and daily micro-interactional routines (Yoshino 1992). Ichijo and Ranta (2016) have analysed the everyday practices of cooking and food consumption among the Japanese and have traced their nation-centric framing. They show convincingly how some foods are styled as being distinctly Japanese and how the shared food consumption practices enhance the sense of being Japanese in everyday life. Even imported foods such as pasta can be nationalised and made part of the national imagination. Ichijo and Ranta (2016) analyse how Japanese-style pasta establishes the parameters of everyday nationalism: its Japanese-ness is created and maintained through the banal practices of shared cooking, consuming, and talking about the Japanese features of this food. Since cooking and food consumption often take place in intimate family settings or among networks of close friends and peers, eating rituals play an important role in the micro-interactional grounding of nationalism.

Conclusion

Most constitutions of modern nation-states locate a specific national collectivity as the epicentre of social and political power. Moreover, such legal documents are regularly framed as if reflecting the unanimous view of millions of individuals. Hence, the Hungarian constitution opens with the statement: 'We, the members of the Hungarian nation … with a sense of responsibility for every Hungarian, hereby proclaim the following' (Hungarian Constitution 2011). Similarly, the Japanese constitution states: 'We, the Japanese people, pledge our national honour to accomplish these high ideals and purposes with all our resources' (Japanese Constitution 2024). These formulations stand in stark contrast to the legal documents issued by premodern rulers to justify their right to rule. Thus, the Yōrō Code, which was promulgated in 757 and was nominally in place until the Meiji restoration's constitution of 1889, specified that all power belongs to the emperor of Japan and that imperial descent determines the process of secession (Lu 1997:30). Similarly, medieval royal codes stipulated that Hungarian kings had to be the descendants from the Royal House of Arpad, with the Catholic Church providing legitimacy through the rituals of coronation (Zupka 2016). Thus, while in premodern contexts the polity was a property of the royal family and ultimately of the specific emperor/king, in modern nation-states political sovereignty belongs nominally to all its citizens. These very different sources of political legitimacy reflect the profoundly different character of the social order in the premodern and modern worlds. By zooming in on the processes of coercive-organisational, ideological, and micro-interactional grounding, this chapter has explored the long-term transformation of collective subjectivities. More specifically, using the examples of Japan and Hungary, I have tried to explain how and why nation-states replaced the empires and patrimonial kingdoms as the dominant form of territorial organisation. Furthermore, the chapter also explored how premodern forms of subjectivity, centred on one's locality, religion, lineage, and descent, have transformed into national subjectivities. My argument emphasises the gradual, durable, and highly contingent character of this historical process and questions both dominant explanatory paradigms of ethno-symbolism and classical modernism. Nationhood is neither a product of cultural continuity nor a phenomenon that emerges ex nihilo. Instead, nation-states and nationalisms are processes that are shaped by long-term organisational, ideological, and micro-interactional grounding.

3 From Religious to Nationalist Subjectivities

Introduction

Nationalism has often been described as a distinctly secular ideology (Gellner 1983; Hobsbawm 1990). However, recent scholarship has challenged this view by pointing to the fact that many nationalist movements deploy religious symbols, invoke religious traditions as a foundation of the national narrative, or even make religious affiliation a key principle for membership in the national community (Brubaker 2015, 2004; Asad 2003; Spohn 2003). In this chapter I explore the relationship between religion and nationalism by examining the imperial and the post-imperial contexts. I argue that although religious symbols and rhetoric can be an important part of nationalist discourse, their social meaning and function change substantially in modernity. In other words, while the religious beliefs and practices were the organisational, ideological, and micro-interactional cornerstones of the premodern world, they do not possess this capacity in the world of nation-states. Religious symbols can operate as effective mechanisms within nationalist ideologies, but in the world of nation-states, religious markers are regularly subsumed into nationalist subjectivities. I illustrate this argument with a historical-sociological analysis of Ottoman and post-Ottoman social realities. This case study is chosen because it is one of the most complex examples of how modern national subjectivities have developed.

The first part of this chapter explores the roles Sunni Islam, different strands of Christianity, and Judaism have played in the everyday life of the Ottoman empire. I analyse the religious subjectivities of the ruling aristocracy and the ordinary population of the empire. The second part of the chapter focuses on the post-imperial world and zooms in on the transformation of religious into nationalist subjectivities in twentieth- and twenty-first-century Turkey. I argue that this ideological change was slow, protracted, and uneven, but once most of the population became fully nationalised, religious ontologies are fully integrated into nationalist subjectivities. I also aim to show that nationalism did not suddenly replace religious attachments, but that the religious markers were gradually integrated into the new national subjectivities.

The Religious Universe of Empires

For much of history, emperors have invoked specific religious creeds to justify their right to rule. This was often reflected in imperial titles that invoked a sense of divine. As Rietbergen (2018:140) points out, 'any form of supreme power needed to continuously and closely associate itself with the sacred'. In Japan this was *tenno* ('Heavenly Augustness') and *kotei* ('August Supreme Deity'). In China such role was played by *huangdi* ('Lord on High') and *tianzi* ('Son of Heaven'). In the Islamic empires al-Khalifat al-Rashidun ('Rightly Guided Caliph'), Amir al-Muʾminin ('Commander of the Faithful'), 'Shadow of God on Earth', and 'Guardian of the Holy Cities' were titles that imbued a sense of the sacred. Similarly, in Christendom this role was performed by Pontifex Maximus and Vicarius Christi. European emperors continued this tradition with the Habsburg Apostolic Majesty, the Holy Roman Emperor, the Rey Católico of the Spanish emperors, English kings as the Defenders of the Faith, or French kings as Rex Christianissimus and Roy Tres-Chrétien (Rietbergen 2018).

Ottoman rulers had styled themselves also as 'the Successor of the Prophet of the Lord of the Universe, Custodian of the Holy Cities of Mecca, Medina and Kouds (Jerusalem)'.[1] This religious legitimacy was central to any claim to power in the premodern world. The rulers who could not invoke a sense of divine providence would not be able to justify their right to govern to their own subjects, to other domestic aristocrats,

[1] The full titles of Ottoman rulers were extensive and captured all their territorial possessions: 'Sultan [given name] Han, Sovereign of the Sublime House of Osman, Sultan us-Selatin [Sultan of Sultans], Hakan [Khan of Khans], Commander of the Faithful and Successor of the Prophet of the Lord of the Universe, Custodian of the Holy Cities of Mecca, Medina and Kouds [Jerusalem], Padishah [Emperor] of the Three Cities of Istanbul [Constantinople], Edirne [Adrianople] and Bursa, and of the Cities of Châm [Damascus] and Cairo [Egypt], of all Azerbaijan, of the Maghreb, of Barkah, of Kairouan, of Alep, of the Arab and Persian Iraq, of Basra, of El Hasa strip, of Raqqa, of Mosul, of Parthia, of Diyâr-ı Bekr, of Cilicia, of the provinces of Erzurum, of Sivas, of Adana, of Karaman, of Van, of Barbaria, of Habech [Abyssinia], of Tunisia, of Tripoli, of Châm [Syria], of Cyprus, of Rhodes, of Crete, of the province of Morea [Peloponnese], of Bahr-i Sefid [Mediterranean Sea], of Bahr-i Siyah [Black Sea], of Anatolia, of Rumelia [the European part of the empire], of Bagdad, of Kurdistan, of Greece, of Turkestan, of Tartary, of Circassia, of the two regions of Kabarda, of Gorjestan [Georgia], of the steppe of Kipchaks, of the whole country of the Tatars, of Kefa [Theodosia] and of all the Neighbouring Regions, of Bosnia, of the City and Fort of Belgrade, of the Province of Sirbistan [Serbia], with all the castles and cities, of all Arnaut, of all Eflak [Wallachia] and Bogdania [Moldavia], as well as all the dependencies and borders, and many others countries and cities' (Özgen 2008).

as well as to the aristocratic rulers of other polities. Military strength was not enough in itself to maintain one's rule; religious legitimacy was just as important. For example, when former enslaved mercenaries, slave soldiers, and their descendants, Mamluks, took power in Egypt and Syria, they had difficulty attaining political legitimacy in the eyes of other rulers. Thus, when Sultan Baybars, Abu al-Futuh "Father of Conquests' (1228–1277), demanded recognition from other Muslim rulers he was scorned and called 'a dog and a slave' (Broadbridge 2008:13).

The unprecedented rise of the Ottoman empire was grounded in the combination of military might and religious legitimacy. The backbone of the imperial project was the warrior aristocracy, which effectively blended the martial *ghazi* interpretation of Islam[2] with an innovative military organisation centred on continuous territorial conquest (Kumar 2017; Jones 1987). One of the key organisational mechanisms behind the exceptional military successes of the early Ottoman armies was the institution of *devşirme*. This system of 'blood tax' was based on the forcible recruitment of non-Muslim children into the top echelons of the Ottoman military and civil service. By converting mostly Balkan Christian children, some of whom came from the nobility, and raising them in Istanbul, the imperial order forged a new social stratum that lacked local family connections and was completely loyal to the emperor. The existence of *devşirme* created a quasi-meritocratic system of military and administrative slave recruitment that freed the rulers from the potential intrigues and conspiracies of the local aristocracy. As janissaries and bureaucrats who came through the *devşirme* were trained and educated in specialised institutions that were separated from the rest of the society, they tended to be more loyal to the sultans than the local aristocrats were. This novel system of military and administrative recruitment had proved organisationally superior to European alternatives. Hence, in a relatively short period of time the Ottoman armed forces were able to conquer vast territories on three continents: Europe, Asia, and Africa.[3] The empire also adopted innovative and efficient models of administrative organisation including the *mukâṭa'a* system (with *timars*, *emanets*, and *iltizāms*) where the aristocrats were given a portion of the sultan's revenue in exchange for their service to the state. In the *timar* system the sultan granted land or revenue to the

[2] The early Ottoman rulers used the term *ghazi* in their titles as this term was closely associated with a religious calling: 'The Ghazi is the sword of God, he is the protector and the refuge of the believers. If he becomes a martyr in the ways of God, do not believe that he has died, he lives in beatitude with Allah, he has eternal life' (Wittek 2013:44).

[3] During the rule of the sultan Süleyman I (1520–1566), the Ottoman empire reached the peak of its power and stretched from the outskirts of Vienna over North Africa to the Red Sea, the Caspian Sea, and the Persian Gulf.

aristocracy as compensation for military service. The *timar* holders were entitled to all profits from the revenue source for their personal benefit (Howard 2017). However, this system was not based on reciprocity, as the sultan could take any positions and properties at will. In later years the Ottomans instituted the millet system, which allowed for a substantial degree of religious autonomy to non-Muslims on the condition that they follow the established rules within their own communal religious hierarchies. These and other administrative inventions have played an important role in the expansion and stability of the Ottoman empire. Significantly, they were all deeply rooted in religious principles shared by the majority of the population.

The World of Aristocracy

The Ottoman aristocracy, *askeri*, was a highly privileged stratum within the empire. The elite strata were composed of the top military (*seyfiye* or *askeriye*), the civil servants in charge of administration and the imperial treasury (*kalemiye*), clergy and religious scholars (ulema), and court officials (*mülkiye*). All four groups were exempt from paying taxes in return for their services to the sultan. As Halden (2020) emphasises, this system of elite organisation was mostly informal, improvised, and ad hoc. The Ottoman system of stratification allowed for a degree of social mobility. As all members of the nobility were considered to be slaves of the sultan, they could be demoted and removed from the elite on the whim of the emperor. Moreover, the sultan was the ultimate owner of all possessions and even the lives of his aristocrats. State sovereignty resided exclusively in the person of the emperor. The Ottoman nobility were expected to continuously demonstrate loyalty to the sultan, be devout Muslims, and observe the established system of customs and cultural practices of Ottoman society. Membership in the elite was symbolised through honorific titles such as *mevlana*, *fakih*, *halife*, *molla*, and *efendi* (for the religious elite); *agha* and *beğ* (for military administrators); and *çelebi* for distinguished individuals within the upper strata. The nobility were also differentiated from the ordinary, tax-paying population (*reaya*) by the clothing they wore, as the state regulated what different social, religious, and gender groups could wear. For example, non-Muslims, women, and members of the lower classes were prohibited from wearing specific clothes, or from using some fabrics, textiles, or colours. The dominant system of social stratification was often justified through the paternalistic image of 'circle of justice' (*daire-i 'adalet*) with the sultan depicted as being dependent on those of the military stratum, who in turn were dependent on those in the treasury, while the economic power of the treasury was grounded in the taxes collected from the *reaya*, and the *reaya*'s freedom was dependent on the justice of the sultan (Howard 2017).

The military elite of the Ottoman empire were composed of two main groups: the traditional Seljuk aristocracy and the janissary order. From the fourteenth century until their abolition in 1826, janissaries were members of an elite military force and the first modern standing army in Europe. Initially recruited through the *devsirme* system of blood tax, this elite force was characterised by complete loyalty to the sultan and by a highly disciplined and ascetic lifestyle. In the early years janissary soldiers were expected to be pious Muslims and celibate until retirement[4] (Howard 2017; Imber 2002). All janissaries were required to be fully obedient to their officers, and respectful of military hierarchy. They were also expected to despise luxury and demonstrate a unity of purpose. Janissaries were also associated with strict piety and a high sense of moral responsibility towards their fellow soldiers and their dependents. Ordinary soldiers could not wear beards and had to reside in the military barracks. In the spirit of Islam they were forbidden to drink alcohol or gamble. Janissaries were highly regarded for their military skills and prowess and were particularly known as excellent archers and in later years also as precise firearm shooters. Janissaries received extra pay to support the regular armed forces in military actions. In later years they were often involved in Ottoman politics and staged several palace coups.

The everyday life of this elite force was shaped around military training and religious practices. Janissaries were members of the Bektashi order of Islam, a Sufi syncretic movement that was tolerant of difference. Since the majority of janissaries were originally teenaged Christian boys, they were generally more receptive to the Bektashi religious practices that tolerated and integrated some Christian beliefs. Hence, the early stage of the *devsirme* process shaped the dynamics of micro-interactional grounding. It included a prolonged shared training, usually lasting seven to eight years, whereby the boys would work with farmers in order to develop a work ethic and a strict sense of discipline, and to learn 'the rudiments of Islam, through living in an Islamic environment', and the Ottoman Turkish language (Imber 2002:139). Bektashism was the ideological cornerstone of the janissary world. When they were not in the military training the soldiers would visit coffeehouses run by other janissaries. These coffeehouses were places where Sufi practices and rituals

[4] Initially the Janissary membership was limited to Christian, mostly Slavic, teenage boys who were converted to Islam, but from the early eighteenth century Muslims from the mainland were also allowed to join.

were enacted on an everyday basis. They often sung together Bektashi hymns and organised Bektashi parades. The coffeehouses were regularly inscribed with Bektashi prayers and proverbs. Bektashi beliefs and practices were retained well into their retirement age and have served as a strong form of social bonding for the janissary soldiers. This potent religious ethic was also displayed in the establishment of waqfs, charitable institutions, aimed at providing financial support for the needy and particularly for families of deceased or incapacitated janissaries. In this context every soldier had to donate a percentage of his salary to the waqf of his regiment. A strong sense of micro-level solidarity was also visible in the regular donations that wealthier janissaries made during Ramadan to their poorer comrades and their families. Hence, in ideological terms the janissary world revolved around absolute loyalty to the sultan, to the Bektashi version of Islam, and to the janissary military order. Once janissaries became the dominant military and political group in the empire, from the mid-sixteenth till the early nineteenth century, the traditional Seljuk nobility lost much of their influence and had migrated to Anatolia and south-eastern Europe (Howard 2017). This political transformation had a significant impact on imperial power: as janissaries could no longer be pitted against the traditional Ottoman nobility, the sultan's power decreased vis-à-vis the janissary order.

The religious elite also possessed significant ideological and political powers. As the very existence of the Ottoman empire was justified in religious terms and the emperor was perceived as 'the Successor of the Prophet of the Lord of the Universe' and 'the Custodian of the Holy Cities of Mecca, Medina, and Kouds', he required continuous approval from the ulema. Since the ulema were the principal arbiters of which actions were in accordance with the Sharia, divinely inspired moral, social, and political regulations, their ideological support was crucial for the emperors. Nevertheless, as Sharia focused mostly on questions of morality in personal behaviour, political rulers retained a substantial degree of freedom in interpreting the Islamic understanding of the state and public law. In this context they could clash with the ulema, whose principal role was the interpretation of Sharia and who as such believed that in religious matters, they had more power than the sultan. This was particularly the case with the Shaykh al-Islam, who held the highest rank among the ulema. He was a moral authority responsible for issuing fatwas, the written interpretations of Sharia, which was understood to be a religious obligation for all Muslims in the empire. From the sixteenth century the ulema were integrated into the wider religious structure of the empire, Ilmiye. The principal role of Ilmiye was to promote, protect, and preserve the key tenets of the Islamic religion. Thus, they were responsible for the implementation of Sharia in the courts, the schools, and the public sphere. The institutions of Ilmiye generated the two principal types of religious authority: the town judges (*kasabat kadis*) and the high dignitaries (*mollas*). Both of these professions required completion of religious education in Islamic schools, or madrasas. While the former offered instant and secure employment, the latter entailed a continuous education and teaching in madrasas with the prospect of gaining a high-level religious position – *mevleviyet*. In principle the religious elites had the right to invalidate any secular law or a specific imperial ruling that was perceived to contradict the Sharia. However, this right was rarely practiced as the ulema were fully integrated into the imperial social order and could lose their positions on the order of the sultan.

The non-Muslim religious elites also had a privileged position in the imperial social order. Although the millet system fully developed only in the eighteenth century, the idea that each confessional community should have autonomy in practicing their own religious laws can be traced back to the fifteenth century[5] (Masters 2001). The millets were associated with personal law, under which each religious community would rule their co-religionists using the laws of their own religion such as Sharia for Muslims, halakha for Jews, or canon law for Christians. The religious elites of each millet had substantial power over their flocks. With each millet having nearly full autonomy to set their own laws, collect and distribute their own taxes, and control education and religious affairs, millet leaders were powerful individuals. This system of religious pluralism with non-territorial autonomy allowed the Ottoman empire to maintain internal peace and continue territorial expansion. As Aral (2004) argues, Ottoman rulers were not interested in controlling the public sphere as long as the religious communities stayed away from politics. However, these wide religious freedoms were still limited by the legal supremacy of the Sharia. For instance, any criminal case involving a Muslim and non-Muslim was decided by Sharia regulations.

In addition to the military and religious elite, the Ottoman empire also developed a court elite, which gradually transformed into imperial officials and civil servants in charge of the treasury. Nevertheless, for much of its existence the empire lacked a coherent administrative system. The civilian administration mostly consisted of scribes who

[5] The millet system has its ideological roots in the Qur'anic teaching that Jews and Christians were people of the holy book, *dhimmi*, who should not be forced to convert to Islam but could practice their own religion while paying the *jizya* tax for the ruler's protection and military exemption.

were recruited through familial and patronage networks. In the early years of the empire there were only a handful of scribes (*katib*), who were more focused on developing their own elaborate styles of expression and establishing a degree of personal authority within the Islamic scholarship and arts than in performing specific governmental roles (Woodhead 1982).[6] The top echelon of the court administration was often appointed to the imperial council by the grand vizier – the personal representative of the sultan. The imperial council (*divan*) helped the grand vizier in running the everyday affairs of the empire. Usually, the council was composed of the vizier's cabinet, including the chief of chancellery or lord privy seal, the treasurers (*defterdars*) of Anatolia and Rumelia, as well as the leading religious and military authorities (Kia 2011). Scribes and other clerical staff were under supervision of the *reisülkütab*, the chief of scribes, whose office was responsible to the grand vizier. In the 1530s there were only 110 scribes in Istanbul, and they enjoyed a highly privileged position: 'Each Ottoman high official maintained a large household, a kind of imperial palace in miniature, as a manifestation of his prestige and power. His retinue consisted of several hundred officers, ranging from menial domestics and bodyguards to companions and agents' (Kia 2011:58).

The first large-scale institutional reform in the Ottoman world was initiated by Sultan Selim III (1789–1807) and his successor Mahmud II (1808–1839), both of whom attempted to adopt some Western European practices and create a more effective administrative system. At that time there were only 1,500 scribes, mostly working in the treasury, land registry, and the headquarters of the grand vizier. In addition, there were a few hundred scribes supporting the provincial governors and military officers. Hence, until the mid-nineteenth century this large imperial order had to rely on a tiny administrative apparatus of fewer than 2,000 scribes. It was only with the centralising reforms of Mahmud II in 1830s that the Ottoman empire acquired a table of civil ranks, established secular schools for the administrators, introduced salaried appointments, and made civil service jobs more secure. The edict of Gülhane, enacted by Sultan Abdulmejid I in 1839, initiated the Tanzimat reforms and transformed the position of all Ottoman subjects, including the administrators (Findley 1989, 1980).

Before the Tanzimat reforms, scribes were also mediators between the institutions of the empire and the ordinary population. One of their roles was to decipher the complex and convoluted language of the imperial

[6] Many scribes were poets and writers who did not differentiate between their artistic ambitions and their governmental responsibilities (see Woodhead 1982).

edicts and other state documents and communicate them to the mostly illiterate subjects of the empire. Although their everyday activities were focused on secular tasks, the majority of scribes had a religious education from the madrasas and espoused Islamic principles in their everyday conduct.

Thus, members of the Ottoman elite broadly shared a similar worldview that combined the religious with the imperial ethos. In this Weltanschauung the authority of the sultan was linked to his commitment and ability to govern the empire by relying on Islamic principles. Although political sovereignty resided solely within the person of the sultan, he would not be able to rule without the tacit consent of Ottoman religious, military, and administrative elites. It is this shared religious and imperial doctrine that made the sultan's power legitimate.

The World of the Commoners

In most imperial orders, aristocratic elites share very similar beliefs and lifestyles. They regularly intermarry, go through the same rites of passage, jointly fight in wars, pray together, and participate in the same imperial and religious rituals. As Kumar (2017) shows, regardless of their internal differences, all empires invoke a sense of superiority whereby their rulers and other aristocrats perceive themselves as the epicentre of the world. Imperial elites rely on the concept of *translatio imperii* to justify the existing social order: they perceive their world as a continuation of previous empires. One is superior on account of imperial continuity with ancient imperial orders. So, Ottoman sultans made a claim that they were the inheritors of the Roman empire, something that their fellow aristocrats in the Ottoman world wholeheartedly embraced (Kumar 2017:91). This historical grounding of superiority was amalgamated with a societal sense of superiority vis-à-vis the commoners. As in other imperial orders, the aristocracy developed distinct cultural practices to dissociate themselves from the ordinary population. In the Ottoman world *askeri* had very little or no interaction with commoners, and even the shared Muslim religion was not a particularly significant source of trans-class group cohesion. While the Ottoman elite did generally practice their Islamic duty of providing *zakat* (i.e., a small proportion of their wealth) to those in need, this did not mean that they identified in any way with the Muslim peasantry living in the empire. Being a nominal part of the umma, a community of believers in Islamic principles, had little impact on the existing social hierarchies within the imperial world. Instead, this was a deeply stratified social order where *askeri* lived in a world very different to that of ordinary peasantry.

The overwhelming majority of the Ottoman population were *reaya* – illiterate peasants. They were the tax-paying stratum. Most of *reaya* resided in small villages and worked on land that nominally belonged to the emperor. Nearly all arable land was designed as *miri*, meaning land owned by 'the public treasury of the Muslim community' and 'in its name to the caliph or the ruler'. In 1528 more than 87 per cent of arable land was recorded as *miri* (Kia 2011:95). However, the sons of the farmers who tilled the land and lived on the farm could continue using the land as hereditary tenants, provided that they continue with their farming responsibilities.

The peasantry were also required to fulfil their feudal obligations such as pay tithe and the annual tax to the *sipahi* – cavalrymen who were given control over the land (*timar*) by the sultan in exchange for their military service. *Sipahis* acted as representatives of the imperial government. The farmers were not allowed to move away from their villages in order to settle in another village or a town. Ottoman villages were run and organised through a patriarchal social structure. The male head of the household was the principal taxpayer and was regarded by the state authorities as the only representative of the household.[7] Everyday village life was shaped around agricultural labour cycles and religious holidays, with a very strict division of labour around gender and age. Religious beliefs together with local customs were central to nearly all social relations. The authority of the male head of the household was rarely questioned, and family patriarchs usually made all major decisions for the household. The Ottoman peasantry has often been described as being prone to fatalistic attitudes to life, with 'resignation to the will of God, loyalty to the sultan, honesty, sobriety, passive contentment, and cleanliness' (Kia 2011:101).

In most cases, networks of extended families lived the same village and worked on the same fields, thus reinforcing the micro-interactional grounding. The endogamous patterns of marriage indicate that most peasants did not have much opportunity to meet and socialise with people from other villages or towns. Hence, marriages between cousins and other extended family members were common, contributing to the development of close-knit micro-group bonds within village communities. Shared kinship and the village were the key social parameters of group identification. Much of everyday social life was shaped around interactions with extended family members and people from the same village. The same individuals would work together in the fields, would

[7] As Kia (2011:95) points out: 'In Ottoman survey registers, taxation for each household was listed according to the name of the husband who represented his family.'

participate in the same religious and communal rituals, and would also spend their free time together. 'When they were not in the field, men gathered at the village coffeehouse (or teahouse) at one another's houses to discuss the latest news. While doing so they drank tea or coffee and played chess or backgammon. Women visited each other's homes, where they also partook in refreshments, discussed the latest happenings in the village, and watched each other's children' (Kia 2011:100).

This pattern of shared communal life was common for all religious groups within the empire. With the formalisation of the millet system, the heads of the households in non-Muslim villages and settlements were required to address all legal matters with their own religious authorities. Nevertheless, in most other respects the everyday life of commoners in the six millets (Orthodox Christian, Armenian, Syriac Christian, Jewish, Roman Catholic, and Circassian) was not profoundly different to that of those who inhabited the Sunni Muslim villages. The majority of the population remained illiterate until the end of the empire. Peasant children usually received basic religious and practical instruction from their family or the village imams, rabbis, or priests. Muslim boys were taught how to pray and recite suras from the Quran by heart. Similarly, Christian and Jewish children were expected to memorise their prayers without learning how to read and write.

Although the Abrahamic religions had a monopolistic position in the Ottoman villages and towns, a majority of the ordinary population were highly receptive to syncretic beliefs. Despite the hostility of all Abrahamic religious authorities towards superstition and pagan traditions, many Muslim, Christian, and Jewish peasants practiced some pagan rituals and believed in various superstitions. Charms, amulets, talismans, and magical formulas were highly popular in everyday life, and many peasants were keen to acquire these devices in order to cure various illnesses, to lay a curse, to bring good lack to the family members, or to compel somebody to do something against their will. The ordinary Muslim population was inclined to believe in the magic powers of written charms or any material objects that were linked directly with the prophet Muhammad. For example, the dust from the tomb of the prophet Muhammad in Medina was regarded as having miraculous qualities. The same attitude was expressed towards pieces of the curtain from the sacred Ka'ba and the holy water from the sacred well of Zamzam in Mecca. They were all viewed as having supernatural properties that could heal or bring good luck (Lane 1973:255). Written charms were even more present in the everyday life of commoners. Verses from the Quran were regarded as having a powerful and magical influence on human interactions. Many illiterate peasants would carry written verses from Quran with them for protection. In some cases a miniature leather version of the Quran was carried as part of one's regular clothing. Many 'written charms included the names of saints and angels, or magic squares, or diagrams and combinations of numerals' and 'were worn by adults and children, hung on cradles and round the necks or on the foreheads of animals, and suspended in houses and shops; in fact they were used everywhere as protection from evil' (Lewis 1971:52).

The Christian and Jewish population of the empire also shared a strong belief in the magical power of amulets, talismans, and charms. Instead of verses from Quran, the focus was on the psalms from the Bible, crucifixes, rosary beads, sorcery, icons of specific saints, or holy water for Christians, and verses from Talmud, gems, amulets, and casting spells for Jews (Weiker 1992). One of the most popular superstitions shared across all religious groups was the notion of the evil eye. This supernatural belief was centred on the idea that a curse can be brought about by a malevolent glare. The evil eye was often associated with envy, and if somebody had good fortune it was necessary to counter or pre-empt the evil eye curse. For example, if someone praised the unique skill, beauty, or strength of another person, it is crucial that this admiration was prefaced by the religious pronouncement such as 'God bless him', 'mashallah' ('God has willed it'), 'tabarakallah' ('blessings of God'), 'b'li ayin hara' ('without an evil eye'), or by the pagan or religious practices of crossing oneself, knocking on wood, spitting three times, and so on. If such statements were not made and the individual in question became ill or lost their prowess, the person who gave the compliment would be deemed responsible for bringing the evil eye curse on that individual. Many rituals were devised to counter this curse, including wearing specially designed or blessed amulets, talismans, or charms. Some parents would disguise their children to avoid envious reactions and the evil eye curse. Others would smear garlic on their foreheads or those of their children, or would wear it around their necks. The Ottoman Sephardic Jews would use the colour blue to ward off the curse (Koén-Sarano 2015:297). These forms of folk religion represent the syncretic belief systems that combined established religious teachings with some pagan practices, superstition, and local traditions. As such they were very common not only in Ottoman lands but also in many other premodern imperial orders all over the world.

A key feature of the Ottoman world was that imperial coercive-organisational, ideological, and micro-interactional structures did not encourage society-wide cohesion. Despite nominal commitment to the same religious beliefs, most imperial orders were capstone states – deeply stratified and hierarchically ordered social systems where culture was used to reinforce existing social hierarchies. As Hall (1986) emphasises, in capstone empires rulers maintain centralised power structure only by relying on local intermediaries. As the premodern states lack the coercive-organisational and ideological capacities to deeply penetrate the social order under their control, they operate as a capstone on top of different societies. Hence, the emperors had to rely on local aristocrats to maintain the social order, to extract resources and taxes, and to mobilise the population in times of war. However, they had no interest in nor means to mould their imperial subjects into a relatively homogenous society.[8] In this context the imperial world is by definition spilt between the two ideologically very different strata – the elite and the commoners. In the Ottoman empire *askeri* and *reaya* had largely lived in a parallel ideological universe where the nominal religious unity was never translated into a shared way of life. In this world there was no organisational, ideological, nor micro-interactional capacity for the development of society-wide nationalist subjectivities.

Fashioning the Nation-Centric Universe

Arguing that there were no sociological preconditions for the emergence of nationalism in the world of empires does not mean to suggest that nationhood emerges suddenly and *ab ovo* in the modern world. As emphasised in the previous chapter, rather than being a revolutionary undertaking that abruptly redesigns the structure of the social order, nationalist ideas and practices fermented gradually and developed on the contours of existing organisational, ideological, and micro-interactional scaffolds.

In conventional historiography the early nineteenth century is often depicted as an age of nationalist revolutions. For example, both Greek and Serbian historians regularly refer to this period as a time of national revolutions: the 'Greek revolution of 1821' (Milios 2023; Moutsoglou 2020) and the 'Serbian revolution of 1804–1835' (Stojanovic 2004; Popov 2004). These accounts tend to interpret the collapse of the Ottoman empire through the prism of rising nationalisms of Balkan populations who allegedly rebelled against the 'Turkish yoke'. However, as several recent accounts show, rather than being a cause of imperial collapse, nationalism was much more a consequence of these

[8] In Crone's (1989:57) words, 'the capstone government was a response to the problem of organising a large number of people over large areas with inadequate resources ... it made emperors specialists in what has been called extensive power, that is the ability to organise large numbers over large distances for minimal co-operation'.

highly contingent historical processes (Kotsonis 2025; Kitromilides 2010; Malešević 2019; Anscombe 2014; Roudometof 2001). Conventional historiographic accounts often mischaracterise the direction and scale of social change in the early nineteenth century. They typically overemphasise the strength of nationalism while also downplaying the elements of organisational continuity between the imperial projects and the new nation-states. In contrast, I argue that in most cases nationalism was not the gravedigger of empires. Instead, nationalism was often the unintended consequence of imperial politics. Moreover, in most instances nationalism was a very weak sociological force in the early nineteenth century. This ideology developed and expanded only after the formation of independent nation-states. By focusing on the example of Turkey I will try to show how nationalist subjectivities have slowly and gradually replaced imperial and religious subjectivities to become the dominant categories of everyday life.

By the second half of the eighteenth century, the Ottoman empire had been experiencing a steady geopolitical decline. A series of revolts, uprisings, and military defeats, including the war with Russia 1768–1774 and conflicts with France and later Britain in North Africa, resulted in substantial territorial losses. Open trade policies and the gradual dependence on foreign loans generated a huge public debt and impoverished the population of the empire. After the failed military reforms of 1789, the rulers decided to abolish the janissary order in 1826. With the Young Turk uprising in 1908, the empire entered its last stage.

The dominant faction of the Young Turks movement, the Committee of Union and Progress (CUP), spearheaded the revolt against the absolutist rule of Sultan Abdulhamid II. The new government initially fostered the establishment of the constitutional order, a multi-party democracy, and the liberalisation of the public sphere. However, with the ever-changing geopolitical conditions CUP became more radicalised, and after the 1913 coup it ruled the empire as a dictatorship. Conventional historiography often emphasises the radical discontinuity between the traditional Ottoman order and the policies instigated by the CUP. While the previous sultans promoted an inclusive imperial Ottomanism, the CUP was a radical nationalist organisation bent on creating a monoethnic Turkish nation-state (Howard 2017). However, until the Balkan wars of 1912–1913 the CUP was not a particularly nationalist organisation. In fact, their principal ideology was Ittihadism (İttihatçılık), which combined statism, social Darwinism, the cult of science, and conservativism. CUP leaders perceived themselves as the scientific elite responsible for healing and modernising the Ottoman society (Akçam 2007:57). Initially, the CUP advocated the preservation of the sultanic system and the position of Islam as the state religion. This view was driven in part by the fact that an overwhelming majority of the Ottoman population did not see themselves in ethno-national but primarily in religious and kinship-based terms. It is only later that the CUP became radicalised and focused on implementing ethno-nationalist agendas, which ultimately ended in genocidal violence against the Armenian, Greek, and Assyrian populations of the empire. Furthermore, this movement did not spring out of nowhere and could not start from organisational scratch. Instead, CUP nationalist policies were built on the coercive-organisational, ideological, and micro-interactional scaffolds of the late Ottoman order. In other words, there is much more continuity than discontinuity in the grounding of Turkish nationalism.

Coercive-Organisational Grounding

By the time of the Young Turk uprising, the Ottman military had already undertaken several significant reforms and had modernised its organisational structure. The Tanzimat reforms (1839–1876) fostered a degree of modernisation in the administrative, judiciary, military, and civil spheres. The reforms introduced legal equality for all imperial subjects, with the Gülhane Decree (1839) proclaiming 'security for life, honour and property'. The reforms also promoted a regular system of revenue collection and a more formalised system of military recruitment. The Tanzimat period is also associated with reform of the banking sector, constitutional change, the introduction of the postal system, telegraph and railway networks, and the transformation of the religious into a more secular legal system. The state also become involved in promoting some civil liberties, including freedom of religion (Reform Edict of 1856). By promoting the ideology of Ottomanism, the rulers attempted to centralise the state and increase political legitimacy. During the Tanzimat period the military organisation was transformed and improved: a new system of regular recruitment was introduced with fixed military service and more effective levying of the army (1844). Sultan Abdulmejid I reorganised the military hierarchy, introduced new military tactics, opened the first military academies, adopted new military technologies, and imported modern European weaponry (such as rifles and heavy artillery). New military factories were built to produce weaponry. The Ottoman navy was rebuilt, introducing steam-powered ships and ironclads. The reformed military structure included six armies and four detached corps, the navy and other auxiliary units totalling more than 660,000 soldiers (Agoston 2005). These reforms continued under Abdul

Hamid II, who was inspired by German military reforms and who appointed two German officers, including Lt Colonel Otto Köhler, as principal military advisers. During his reign, the Ottoman military professionalised its officer corps and developed an effective system of military education (Agoston 2005).

The Tanzimat reforms in administration, judiciary, and policing also increased the coercive-organisational capacities of the Ottoman state. In the Edict of Gülhane, Sultan Abdulmejid I was very explicit that his focus was on the transformation of the civil service, aiming 'to bring the benefits of a good administration to the provinces of the Ottoman Empire through new institutions' (Celik 2020). These reforms created a modern civil service, the new municipality of Constantinople, and a new city planning council, and introduced the first state-wide census (1844). Key elements of policing were put in place with the reorganisation of the civil and criminal code (1840), the introduction of identity cards for all citizens (1844), and the adoption of the nationality law (1869), which created a common Ottoman citizenship regardless of one's religion. A new police force was created (*zaptiye*) and the prison systems were modernised (Celik 2020). The CUP government would not have been able to initiate the transformation of the imperial order without these organisational changes. Hence, the CUP only intensified and expanded the coercive-organisational grounding. In addition to the regular military and police, the new regime established a paramilitary force, the Turkish Strength Association, which encouraged young men to join 'in order to save the deteriorating Turkish race from extinction'. This paramilitary organisation was billed as a place where young Turks would 'learn to be self-sufficient and ready to die for the fatherland' (Akmese 2005:169). The CUP had further militarised the Ottoman state by creating a number of new coercive organisations such as the National Defence League, Ottoman Navy League, Ottoman Red Crescent Society, Turkish Hearth, and Ottoman Strength Clubs. From 1914 all male children aged ten to seventeen were required to become members of the Ottoman Strength Clubs, an organisation established by the Ministry of War (Akmese 2005). The CUP regime also continued to expand the police, civil service, and judiciary, albeit in a distinctly authoritarian way. The organisational grounding of Turkish nationalism was a slow and protracted process that started much earlier than the CUP regime.

Ideological Grounding

The elements of continuity were also visible in the ideological sphere. The Tanzimat reforms provided the ideological seeds for the development of nationalism. Although the focus was on Ottomanism rather than the Turkish national project, the reforms played an important role in fostering nation-centric practices. For example, the Tanzimat reforms were crucial for the birth and expansion of what Gellner (1983) calls 'the high culture' that gradually replaced the vernacular and localised cultural worlds. Thus, the Academy of Sciences was established in 1851; the first modern universities, academies, colleges, and teacher schools were created in 1848; and the new Ottoman flag and national anthem were designed and institutionalised in 1844. During this period religion too started becoming more politicised and directly linked with the new vision of Ottomanism. The CUP rule only radicalised this vision further. Hence, instead of an ambiguous and vague idea of Ottomanism, the CUP was moving more and more towards Turkish ethno-nationalism. Although initially the CUP leadership attempted to accommodate some minority groups who had representatives in parliament, the 1912–1913 Balkan wars environment fostered a further radicalisation. Eventually, the CUP abandoned the multi-ethnic idea of Ottomanism and promoted the ethno-nationalist vision of the 'Turkish race' that was traced to the mythical homeland of Turan. The chief ideologue of the movement, Ziya Gökalp, advocated the idea of Pan-Turkism – the cultural and political unification of all Turkophone populations. In this understanding Turks were the dominant nation within the empire, who needed to rediscover their glorious past that allegedly could be traced to their heroic 'Turanian' predecessors – Attila, Genghis Khan, Tamerlane, and Hulagu Khan, among others. Gökalp advocated territorial expansion and ethno-national homogenisation. In one of his famous poems, 'Turan', he states: 'The land of the Turks is not Turkey, nor yet Turkestan. Their country is the eternal land: Turan' (Karsh & Karsh 1999:101). Although Gökalp formulated a secular vision of Turkish nationalism where the focus was more on language and ethnic origins, the CUP's nationalism project still relied extensively on religious markers. As it was not completely clear yet who exactly were the Turks, the religion remined the central mechanism of national categorisation.

Micro-Interactional Grounding

Nevertheless, religious markers retained the greatest importance at the grassroots level – in the domain of micro-interactional grounding. The ideological shift from Ottomanism to Turkish nationalism would not be possible without the regime's penetration into the micro-world of everyday life. The CUP regime had devoted a great deal of attention towards reaching the inter-personal sphere of the ordinary population. The micro-universe of everyday life was largely shaped by locality, kinship, and folk religions. As the majority of the Ottoman population were still illiterate and lived in the vast rural areas, their everyday perceptions and interactions were shaped by syncretic beliefs, superstition, and oral traditions. The state religion mediated by the written word of holy books and clergy (including muftis, qadis and teachers) largely remained an urban experience that most peasants would rarely encounter. Hence, folk religion, defined by saints, holy men, sacred landscapes, trees, caves, stones, and tombs, was more prevalent in village life. In addition, there was no religious purism or fundamentalism in the countryside. The focus was on the sense of protection and preservation over the purity of the doctrine. Syncretic practices were prevalent from the Balkans to the Middle East: Christian families would give Muslim names to their third child if the first two did not survive; Muslim villagers would baptise their newborn children; the Druze would pray to the Virgin on the Mountain shrine; Christians and Jews would recite prayers on the Prophet Muhammad's birthday; and so on (Grehan 2014). The deep ties of kinship networks, village neighbourhoods, and clans were also central sources of collective identification in everyday life. Thus, the CUP regime had to find a way to permeate these relatively isolated and intermingled micro-worlds in order to foster a nationalist ideology. One of the key structural changes that allowed for greater penetration of nationalism has happened through religious transformation. With increasing urbanisation, modernisation, and slowly rising literacy, the state was able to 'purify' the faith. The intensive modernisation advocated by the CUP contributed towards emphasis on written religious texts. Scriptures gradually replaced the folk saints, and religious identification became a public and state-sponsored affair. In this context religion played a significant role in the eventual nationalisation of the ordinary population. By transforming religious beliefs from the oral, syncretic, and diverse local traditions towards relatively uniform, scripture-based faiths, the state created organisational and ideological conditions for the mass-scale politicization of difference.

In this context the CUP regime devised a highly militaristic educational system that aimed to transform ordinary peasants into nationally conscious and enthusiastic soldiers. Drawing on Colmar von der Goltz's idea of 'nation in arms', the CUP leadership perceived war as the natural and principal activity of the modernising state. As an advisor to the Ottoman army after 1908, Goltz was able to implement his social Darwinist ideas on a grand scale. The CUP regime subscribed to the survival of the fittest and also accepted Goltz's idea that military norms should govern civil society. To generate a degree of public support, the

CUP used the concept of jihad to motivate the Ottoman soldiers to fight and die for the Islamic empire (Aksakal 2016). Hence, some religious tenets were successfully used to bring together the moral and emotional precepts of the microcosm of everyday life with the ideological project of the nationalising state. Young children entered this militarised educational system as Sunni Muslims with strong familial and local attachments, and at the end of their education their religious upbringing was eventually suffused with Turkish nationalism.

The Nationalising State

The series of military defeats culminating in the World War I loss have delegitimised both the CUP rulers and the character of the Ottoman empire. During the Balkan wars the empire had already lost more than 30 per cent of its territory and up to 20 per cent of its population. By the end of World War I, the Ottoman empire had shrunk beyond recognition. It lost more than four-fifths of its total territory and approximately the two thirds of its population in the European provinces. It also lost its territories in North Africa and the Middle East. The 1920 Treaty of Sevres partitioned the empire between France, the United Kingdom, Italy, and Greece, while the 1923 Treaty of Lausanne made some territorial concessions. The end of World War I brought more instability, which quickly resulted in a new conflict – the Turkish war of independence (1919–1923). Already well known for his successful military campaign in the defence of Gallipoli during World War I, General Mustapha Kemal Pasha led the resistance against partition. He eventually became the leader associated with military successes in the Turkish war of independence. By successfully resisting the partition of Anatolia and Eastern Thrace and by taking control of Istanbul, Kemal had managed to become a war hero who soon also led the revolution against the sultan. In October 1923, Kemal Pasha Atatürk abolished the Ottoman empire and proclaimed the Republic of Turkey.

The fifteen years of Atatürk's rule have traditionally been depicted as a radical break with the Ottoman legacy. In some respects, this is true, as Kemalism brought about all-encompassing changes in the political, economic, social, legal, and cultural organisation of the state and society. Atatürk's government was determined to create a secular and unitary republic that would resemble Western European nation-states. In this context the government introduced a strict separation of the state and religious institutions, promoted the role of science and technology, and advocated a degree of gender equality and economic statism. The new regime adopted the Swiss Civil Code, the Italian Criminal Code, and the

German Commercial Code with the aim of transforming the traditional legal system. It also fostered the rise of Turkish nationalism in the public sphere, mass media, educational system, state administration, military, police, and legislative system. The new constitution of 1924, modelled on the French example, established a novel legal structure aimed at modernising the Turkish state and society. Political sovereignty was not linked to the sultan as the caliph of all Muslims any longer; instead, the Turkish nation became the ultimate source of all political power in the republic. This shift towards popular sovereignty was also reflected in the new Kemalist slogans such as 'Ne mutlu Türküm diyene!' ('How happy is the one who says I am a Turk!'), which replaced Ottoman slogans such as 'Long live the Caliph' or 'Long live the Sultan' (Brockett 2011).

In 1935 the French model of *laïcité* (secularism) was fully incorporated into the legislative system, and all references to Islam were removed from the Constitution. Religious schools and courts were also disbanded, and the secular system of family law was introduced. With the abolishment of the caliphate in 1924, a new Directory of Religious Affairs (Diyanet) was created as a state institution that exercised oversight over all religious activities. In 1937 Kemalism was incorporated into the Constitution as the official state ideology.

Coercive-Organisational Grounding

Nevertheless, despite this pronounced hostility towards the *ancien regime*, the new Turkish republic could not start from scratch, but had to build on the already existing coercive-organisational, ideological, and micro-interactional scaffolds of the Ottoman state. In other words, the process of nationalist grounding predates Kemalism as its structural seeds had already been planted with the Tanzimat reforms, military reforms of Selim Ill and Mahmud II Young Turks, Abdul Hamid II's social changes, and CUP militarist policies, among others. Hence, like the CUP regime, Atatürk continued to rule through a one-party state – with the Republican People's Party being the only legal political association. The Kemalist government also continued with the coercive-organisational developments of the state administration, legal system, military, and police, something that had been initiated during Tanzimat and was rigorously pursued by the CUP regime. In many ways the Kemalist military reform followed in the CUP's footsteps. The military was perceived to be the guardian of the Turkish state. The Turkish military and bureaucracy were largely composed of former Ottoman officers and civil servants: 93 per cent of the staff officers came from the Ottoman army and 65 per cent of the Ottoman civil servants constituted the administration of the new Turkish republic (Mooney 1984:18). Also similar to the CUP regime, the Kemalist state adopted the doctrine of raison d'état as the principal military policy. This was also legalised in the 1935 Army Internal Service Law, which stipulated that 'the military was constitutionally obliged to protect and defend the Turkish homeland and the republic' (Capezza 2009:1). In addition, article 148 of the Military Penal Code defined the military as 'the vanguard of revolution' that reserves the right to 'intervene in the political sphere if the survival of the state would otherwise be left in grave jeopardy' (Capezza 2009:1). The central role of the military was also visible in the fact that the chief of staff did not report to the minister of defence but directly to Atatürk.

This continuous militarisation and the state-centric policy inherited from the CUP regime were also present in the economic sphere. The Kemalist state intensified the existing statism, which eventually became the state-controlled economy. In 1934 the government instituted a five-year plan that centred on establishing state monopolies in industry, banking, finance, commerce, and other sectors of the economy. The focus was on achieving industrial self-sufficiency and removing all vestiges of foreign dominance in the economy. Hence, coercive-organisational grounding was built on top of existing developments that were initiated long before the creation of the Turkish nation-state.

Ideological Grounding

The elements of continuity were also present in the ideological domain. Although the Kemalist regime differed from its predecessors in fostering radical secular principles, its nationalist ideology was built on existing ideas and practices. Similar to CUP chief ideologues such as Gökalp,[9] who advocated the idea of ancient Turan and 'Turkish race', the Kemalist ideologues invoked a primordialist idea of the Turkish nation that was traced back to Central Asia. Although Kemalists were more focused on the idea of Turkishness within the confines of the nation-state, the regime was sympathetic towards pan-Turkist organisations such as the Turkish Hearths. The mass media, the educational system, and the state administration also promoted such primordialist ideas, including the discredited Turkish history thesis (Türk Tarih Tezi) and the pseudolingustic Sun Language Theory (Güneş Dil Teorisi), the latter of which advocated that all world languages originated from a proto-Turkic primeval language

[9] Although Gökalp died in 1924, his ideas continued to influence many political leaders and intellectuals of the Kemalist state.

(Aydingün & Aydingün 2004). One of the leading Kemalists, Ahmet Ağaoğlu, was particularly invested in promoting the Turkish history thesis, which insisted that all Turks had Hittite origins and had migrated from Central Asia to China and then India, where they established major civilizations such as Mohenjo-daro and Harappa and created numerous 'Turkic' empires such as Scythian, Xiongnu, and Göktürk (Cagaptay 2004). The Kemalist government inherited the CUP's social Darwinist view of the nations as entities being constantly at war with each other and promoted military education as the way to keep Turkish young people strong, healthy, and prepared for battle. Drawing on the French example, the Kemalist regime defined Turkishness in nation-state-centric terms and made no provisions for minorities. Atatürk was explicit in his assimilationist rhetoric: 'Within the political and social unity of today's Turkish nation, there are citizens and co-nationals who have been incited to think of themselves as Kurds, Circassians, Laz or Bosnians. But these erroneous appellations – the product of past periods of tyranny – have brought nothing but sorrow to individual members of the nation, with the exception of a few brainless reactionaries, who became the enemy's instruments' (Mango 1999:20).

The nationalising Kemalist state was particularly keen to reshape the cultural policy and transform the education system. In 1928 the Arabic alphabet was replaced with Latin script, and a few years later the government established the cultural institutions that were responsible for the protection of Turkish language from foreign influences: the Turkish Language Association (1932) and the Turkish Association of History (1931). The transition from Arabic to Latin script had a significant impact on literacy rates as many people had to learn a new script. Hence, in 1927 only 8.1 per cent of population was literate. By 1935 this number has jumped to 15 per cent and gradually increased to 32 per cent in 1960 and 46 per cent in 1970 (Ekinci 2015). There were huge gender and regional differences in literacy rates. Male literacy was substantially higher: in 1950, 48.4 per cent of men were literate versus 20.7 per cent of women. The urban and Marmara province-based population, with Istanbul, had a literacy rate of 67.5 per cent in 1950, while southeast Anatolia had only 20.8 per cent in the same year (Taeuber 1958). To increase the literacy rates the government made literacy courses compulsory for those aged sixteen to thirty. Large-scale literacy campaigns were organised in the late 1920s, and in 1928, 1.5 million reading certificates were distributed (Akgül 2019). Primary education (for five years) was also introduced by the government, and university reform was undertaken following the advice of Western European academics and advisors. Consequently, the number of students in full-time education increased substantially. The number of pupils attending primary school more than doubled – from '342,000 to 765,000; the number of students attending middle schools increased from around 6,000 to 74,000; and the number of students attending high schools increasing from 1,200 to 21,000' (Akgül 2019:34). All these measures in education gradually contributed to nationalist grounding.

The new regime also reshaped the public sphere by creating space for the development of institutionalised national culture and mass media throughout the country. From the early 1930s the government sponsored the opening of People's Reading Rooms and People's Houses, institutions dedicated to the promotion of the Turkish language, literature, art, history, and sports. In addition, the Kemalist state established Village Institutes in the countryside, which were focused on various cultural activities including reading rooms, musical performances, theatres, book and magazine publishing, translations of world literature, and many other activities (Kirby 2000:145). Nation-centric and republican-focused plays were also staged all over the country.

Micro-Interactional Grounding

The Kemalist project was also focused on micro-interactional grounding. By using all the instruments of one-party rule and by pursuing the relentless modernisation of all sectors of society, the regime was eager to penetrate the micro-world of everyday life. Since shared religious practices were central to everyday life in most villages and towns, it was crucial to find a way to replace traditional beliefs with a secular alternative. In this context the Kemalist state attempted to nationalise existing religious practices and imagery. As the overwhelming majority of Turkish population were conservative peasants who opposed secularism and radical modernisation, it was necessary to integrate this population within the wider ideological project. Hence, the regime promoted the idea of 'peasantism' as the essence of being Turkish. In other words, the Kamalist project rejected the conventional divide between the urban and rural population and invoked the notion of *halkçilik*, a populist concept that denied class differences in the name of the 'interest of the people'. The peasantry were glorified as a symbol of the nation. Peasants were depicted as the feeders of the nation and providers for the military. In many of his speeches Atatürk would refer to peasants as 'the masters of Turkey' and said that 'the real warden and governor of Turkey is the villager, who is the real producer' (Sezer 2022:54). Peasants were discouraged from moving to urban areas with the view of avoiding potential social conflicts. The creation of the Village Institutes and People's

Houses was an attempt to replace the authority of the traditional ulema with that of the nationalising state (Yildrimaz 2017). Nevertheless, the aim was not to completely dispense with religious practices, which would have been an impossible undertaking. Instead, the government attempted to reframe religious symbols as national symbols. For example, the national flag and many other state and civil society symbols retained Islamic imagery, such as the crescent moon and stars, *kathim* (the Islamic value of patience and self-restraint), or traditional Islamic calligraphy. Although the regime advocated nominally a separation of religion from the state, in reality this relationship was much more blurred. Clergy were placed under state supervision and paid by the state. Instead of diminishing the power of religion, the Kemalist regime was keen to control and use it in its nationalist project. Drawing on Gökalp's ideas, the regime attempted to fuse religion and nationhood. Thus, the emphasis was on the translation of the Quran into Turkish and the use of Turkish version only in religious education. The Turkification also meant removal of all Arabic and Persian influences in everyday life and the 'purification' of the Turkish language. In this context the state attempted to penetrate the grassroots and control the daily activities of the village communities.

The government envisaged an ideal type of village that would constitute a modernised vision of rural Turkey. As Sezer (2022:12) points out: 'Forming a modern Turkish village was a significant field of building practice, closely bound with the realisation of the modernised and nationalised rural ideal.' The state attempted to substitute the traditional religious practices with new, nation-centric rituals. The modernisation of rural areas went hand in hand with demographic engineering, as the Kemalist state implemented a 'population exchange' with the Greek government, the deportation of the Kurdish population from Anatolia to other regions of the country, and the sponsored immigration of Turkish-speaking and other Muslim populations from the Balkans to Turkey. The government also invested heavily in the nation-centric socialisation of young villagers, as the People's Houses and Village Institutes provided educational programmes and new schooling models for village children (Sezer 2022:16). However, despite the substantial energy, resources, and personnel devoted to this project of turning Sunni Muslim peasants into nationalist Turks, the success was rather limited. This top-down project of state engineering generated a great deal of resistance, and the regime was not very effective in fully penetrating and transforming the micro-world of the peasantry. In much of the countryside, traditional religious practices still trumped nationalist ideology.

Nationalism and Religion in Contemporary Turkey

Post-Atatürk Turkey was characterised by uneven social development where periods of democratisation were interspersed with military coups and interventions in 1960, 1971, 1980, and 1997.[10] From the 1940s until the failed military coup of 2016, the army was the dominant and largely independent political force in Turkey. In the early post-Atatürk period, the influence of the army expanded substantially, while defence spending rose to half of the budget during the World War II years. The relative liberalisation of the public sphere had an impact on the proliferation of the independent mass media, which galvanised society-wide debates on the direction of social development. State-sponsored educational reforms fostered increased literacy rates. Hence, there was a continuous and substantial increase from 1935 to 1955: literacy rates expanded from 20.4 per cent in 1935 to 30.2 per cent in 1945 and 40 per cent in 1955 (Rustow & Ward 2015). This trend intensified in the 1970s and 1980s: in 1975 the literacy rate was 61.6 per cent, and in 1985 it increased to 76 per cent (Macrotrends 2025).

Although the Kemalist ideology remained hegemonic throughout the twentieth century, successive governments have relaxed a number of staunchly secularist policies from Atatürk's years. For example, new religious schools were permitted to open, and religious instruction became a part of the regular curriculum. Readings of the Qur'an appeared on radio programmes and later also on private TV channels. Arabic has replaced Turkish in the calls to prayer. From 1980s onwards there was a noticeable revival of religion in the public sphere, civil society, and everyday life. External observers have noted more visible Islamic dress in the cities, instances of gender segregation in public spaces, the expansion of Islamic schools, the proliferation of Sufi orders, and the emergence of Islamic banks. This religious revival was also reflected in the political sphere with the formation of new social movements and political parties promoting Muslim ethical principles. The most influential such party in the 1980s and early 1990s was the National Salvation Party, led by Necmettin Erbakan, which in 1980 advocated the restoration of Sharia. After the ban in 1981 this movement, together with the former National Order Party, was re-established as the Welfare Party (Refah Partisi). This Islamist movement continuously increased its support to the point of becoming the largest party in the

[10] The 1997 military memorandum was not a classical coup, but since the military forced the government to resign without dissolving the parliament or suspending the constitution, this event had many features of a military coup.

1995 election. The party's support base was unusually wide, including not only voters from the countryside and small towns but also from major cities. The 1997 coalition government led by Erbakan was forced out of office by the intervention from the Turkish military, and the Welfare Party was banned in 1998. However, this military intervention could not stop the tide of religious revival. Only a few years later a new party with an Islamist programme, the Justice and Development Party (Adalet ve Kalkınma Partisi, AKP), led by Recep Tayyip Erdoğan and Abdullah Gül, became the dominant force in the political life of Turkey. For the past twenty years of Erdoğan's rule, Turkish society has been characterised by a pronounced rise of religion and nationalism in the public sphere. Although this development has often been perceived as a radical break with the secularist past, there is in fact more organisational, ideological, and micro-interactional continuity in the development of Turkish nationalism than usually acknowledged.

Coercive-Organisational Grounding

In the last two decades the Turkish nation-state has continued to expand its coercive-organisational capacities. Following the military reform at the end of the 1980s, the Turkish armed forces have substantially increased their capability. Turkey possesses the second largest military in NATO – the size of its military personnel of 890,500 is larger than that of the United Kingdom, France, Italy, Germany, or other powerful NATO members. The Turkish armed forces are composed of 355,200 active personnel (260,200 in the land forces, 45,000 in the navy, and 50,000 in the air force), 378,700 reserve forces, and 156,800 in the coast guard and gendermerie (IISS 2023:141–144). The Turkish armed forces are also present in many countries in the Middle East, Europe, and Africa, including Albania, Azerbaijan, Bosnia and Herzegovina, Kosovo, North Cyprus, Libya, Qatar, Syria, Iraq, Somalia, Lebanon, Mali, Central African Republic, and the Democratic Republic of the Congo. After the United States, Turkey has the largest deployment of military forces abroad, which amounts to over 60,000 personnel (IISS 2023:164–168). In 2024 Turkey's military budget was more than $40 billion, which was a 150 per cent increase over its 2023 budget (Reuters 2023). There is also a strong element of continuity in the way the military is organised and run. For example, just as in the times of Atatürk, the military branch commanders continued to report to the prime minister instead of the defence minister, and after the 2017 constitutional reform they now report to the president.

A very similar organisational pattern is present in the police, civil service, and legal system. All of these coercive organisations have increased their capacity over the last two decades. The General Directorate of Security, which runs the police force, is a complex bureaucratic entity that is composed of 81 directorates of provincial police, 751 police directorates of towns, 22 border gate police directorates, 18 free-zone police stations, and 834 police stations in 81 provinces. The size of the police force has constantly been increasing, reaching 329,00 personnel in 2020. In 2021 Turkey had 568 police officers for every 100,000 people, while the EU average ratio was 335 officers per 100,00 people (Bianet 2023). The Turkish civil service has also expanded substantially over the past twenty years. The AKP-run government has employed 3 million new civil servants, which represents a 119 per cent increase since 2003. In 2020 there were close to 4.8 million administrators, while in 2003 there had been around 2 million. The civil service now accounts for 17.7 per cent of the total workforce in Turkey (Turkish Minute 2021). The legal system has also expanded, but after the 2017 constitutional changes, political power is now centralised in the office of the president, thus removing some key checks and balances that the judiciary provided before. The ever-increasing authoritarian rule together with the centralisation of power allowed for the continuous purge of individuals from the civil service, police, military, educational system, and mass media. It is estimated that after 2016 more than 140,000 people had been removed from their jobs, and many have also been arrested.

The continuous increase in the coercive-organisational capacities is also visible in the development of the transportation and communication networks. Over the last twenty years the Turkish government has built numerous new roads, railways, airports, and ports, thus enhancing its transport capabilities and fostering coercive-organisational grounding. Since 2016 the transport sector has been continuously increasing, to reach 8.6 per cent of the Turkish GDP (Statista 2024). Other indicators also point to substantial developments, including the rise of rail freight (38.2 million metric tons in 2021) and road cargo transport, which increased by 14 per cent in 2021 (Statista 2024). The same process is evident with the proliferation of new systems of communication. The communication technologies market continues to expand – from $9.1 billion in 2021 to $13 billion in 2022. The information technology market has experienced a similar trajectory – from $6.9 billion in 2021 to $11.7 billion in 2022. Both sectors have also witnessed a substantial increase in employment – 7 per cent for communication technology and 17 per cent for information technology (International Trade Administration 2024). Hence, coercive-organisational grounding follows a similar pattern that has been in operation for many years: the state's coercive power and its ability to penetrate the social order have continued their upward trajectory.

Ideological Grounding

Despite some doctrinal oscillations on the issue of secularism, ideological grounding has also continued to expand and more deeply permeate Turkish society. Although the AKP's rule has been characterised by more pronounced use of religious symbolism and some Islamic practices in the public sphere, this did not happen at the expense of nationalism. On the contrary, Erdoğan's rule has been firmly built on the nationalist foundations of Kemalism, and the only noticeable difference is that this nationalism has nominally acquired some religious and quasi-imperial features. The religious imagery deployed in contemporary Turkey rarely appeals to the universalism of umma and is much more used to frame the Turkish nationalist project. As Posocco (2022:48) and White (2009) show, the AKP's rule has been typified by the rise of Turkish Muslim nationalism, which 'leverages on the Ottoman, Turkic and Islamic heritage of Turkey'. As White (2009:9) emphasises, in Erdoğan's Turkey 'everything from lifestyle to public and foreign policy are up for reinterpretation, not necessarily according to Islamic principles (although Islamic ethics and imagery may play a role), much less Islamic law (in which few Turks have any expertise), but according to a distinctly Turkish post imperial sensibility'. In other words, Turkish nationalist grounding has not experienced a decline or significant alteration. Rather, it has markedly intensified under AKP rule. However, this is only in small part a result of political engineering by Erdoğan's establishment and much more a long-term consequence of the structural transformations. This ideological grounding was only possible in a substantially changed Turkish society, and these social changes have been taking place progressively over the last hundred years. For example, the literacy rates that have been gradually and substantially increasing throughout the second half of the twentieth century have now reached their historic maximum – near full literacy. Hence in 1975 the literacy rate was 61.63 per cent, in 1985 it rose to 75.97 per cent, in 2004 it grew further to 87.37 per cent, and in 2019 it was 96.74 per cent (Macrotrends 2025). Another two pillars of ideological grounding – the mass media and the educational system – have also continued to expand and integrate millions of people. For example, while there were only 5,100 schools in 1923 with 361,500 students, by 2001 Turkey had 58,800 schools and 16 million students. In 2023 there were almost 19,000 public and private secondary schools and 209 universities and academies (Statista 2024). In 2019 the primary school enrolment was 97 per cent, indicating how deeply the state has penetrated the social order.

The last twenty years have also witnessed a staggering expansion of mass media and social media. Although the government controls most of the media, censors directly or indirectly the media landscape, and occasionally bans critical media outlets or imprisons journalists, Turkey still possesses a large and diverse mass media sector. For example, in 2003 there were 257 licenced TV stations and over 1,100 radio stations; many other outlets operated without a licence. In 2019 there were 536 TV channels and more than 1,200 licenced and unlicenced radio stations (RTÜK 2024). Nearly all Turkish citizens possess a TV set (99.1 per cent in 2014) and regularly watch TV news (97.3 per cent in 2014) (Gallup 2014). There are also numerous newspapers and popular dailies such as *Hürriyet*, *Sabah*, and *Posta*, all with over 300,000 daily sales in 2016 (Gazete tiraj rakamları 2016). In addition, many citizens receive their news and other information from online sources, and 75 per cent use social media. According to a 2014 Gallup survey, 48 per cent of the population received their information from television, 32 per cent combined TV news and the internet, while 20 per cent receive news from a variety of media platforms (Gallup 2014). In 2022 there were 72.5 million internet users, which is 84 per cent of population (BBC 2023). This mass and social media diffusion contributes substantially towards the reproduction of nation-centric views of the world. In the last several decades the successive Turkish governments have also invested extensively in the development of 'high culture' to promote Turkish nationalism. Posocco (2022) has extensively analysed the rise of new museums under AKP rule, such as the Istanbul Museum of the History of Science and Technology in Islam, the Panorama 1453 museum, and the Kabatepe Simulation Center and Museum, and has demonstrated how they all deploy advanced technologies to project a primordialist vision of the Turkish nation.

Despite the authoritarian nature of AKP rule, contemporary Turkish civil society is very vibrant and it too contributes to the proliferation of nationalist discourses. As in most other modern social orders, the opposition regularly challenges the government using nation-centric language: rulers are rebuked for not adequately pursuing national interests or for not properly implementing nationalist programmes. Wide-scale social protests and election campaigns, together with oppositional activities in the mass and social media, have generated an environment where nationhood acquires a sacred status. Nearly all major political parties and social movements invoke the sense of Turkishness as the key attribute of social and political life.[11] Thus, both state institutions and non-state organisations reproduce the nation-centric ideological discourses in their everyday activities. The ideological centrality of nationalism is also visible in the legal system: the criticism of Turkish nation is punishable by prison sentence,[12] as articulated in article 301 of the 2008 Turkish penal code. A version of this law has been part of the penal code since 1926 (with slight amendments in 1961 and 2003 and a change in wording in 2005 and 2008), and the code was approved or amended by successive Turkish parliaments.

Micro-Interactional Grounding

In addition to coercive-organisational and ideological grounding, Turkish nationalism has continued to develop and expand through micro-interactional grounding. While the early Kemalist state provided the organisational and ideological seeds that initiated this process, it was unable to fully penetrate the grassroots. Hence the process of 'nationalisation of the masses' (Mosse 1991) was still slow and uneven. In contrast, the contemporary Turkish nation-state operates in a different social environment where the majority of population has been exposed to and lived with nation-centric everyday practices for decades. While in the early and mid-twentieth century many citizens of Turkey still identified more in religious, kinship, clan, or village-based terms, today nationhood trumps all these forms of group attachment. According to several recent polls on Turkish identity, an overwhelming majority of citizens express a strong sense of attachment to their nation. In 2018, 86 per cent of respondents said that being a Turk is important to them, with 56 per cent agreeing with the statement that being Turk is very important to them. Indeed, the survey indicated that the 'majorities of men and women, as well as majorities of all age and education groups, feel that being a Turk is very important to them' (Halpin et al. 2018:16). The survey results also show that the majority of the population shares strong

[11] The partial exception here is the Peoples' Democratic Party (HDP), which is a left-wing movement that advocates for the greater social and political rights of Kurdish population. However, even this party uses the nation-centred language in its political campaigns, although it promotes a more civic, inclusive, and left-wing form of nationalism.

[12] According to article 301 of the Turkish penal code, 'A person who publicly denigrates the Turkish Nation, the State of the Turkish Republic or the Grand National Assembly of Turkey and the judicial institutions of the State shall be punishable by imprisonment from 6 months to 2 years' ('Parliament Passes the Revised Article 301 with 250 Votes Against 65', bianet.org). The earlier, pre-2008, version of this article was even more draconian and centred specifically on possible insults to 'Turkishness'.

nationalist views that are rooted in a sense of historical superiority. Hence 84 per cent of those surveyed in 2021 agreed with the statement that 'my country's culture is superior to others' (Balta & Grigoriadis 2024). In another public poll conducted in 2018, this figure is lower but still fairly high. When asked whether 'believing that Turkey is better than other nations' is very important to their sense of being a Turk, 47 per cent deemed it very important, and in total 75 per cent considered it either very or somewhat important (Halpin et al. 2018:15–16). Turkey is also regarded by many of its citizens as being superior among the other Muslim-majority nation-states and as such was perceived to be their leader. So, 72 per cent agreed (including 41 per cent strongly agreeing) with the statement that 'Turkey is a natural leader of the Muslim world' (Halpin et al. 2018:20). Many respondents also believed that supporting 'kinfolk outside of Turkey' is also either very important (49 per cent) or somewhat important (31 per cent) to being a Turk (Halpin et al. 2018). Similarly, the majority of the surveyed population saw the legacy of the Ottoman empire in a very positive light and agreed with the statement that their Turkish identity is linked with their pride in the Ottoman Empire – 53 percent deemed this to be very important, and in total 79 percent judged it to be either somewhat or very important (Halpin et al. 2018:15–17).

What is particularly relevant is that this strong sense of attachment to the nation is firmly linked with religion. Thus, the data show that 'being Muslim' is generally regarded as being a very important aspect of Turkish national identity: 67 per cent of respondents consider this to be very important, while in total 91 per cent believe it to be either very important or somewhat important. In addition, 80 per cent of respondents expressed the view that 'Islam plays a central role in my life and is essential to my understanding of Turkish identity' (Halpin et al. 2018:15–18). Nevertheless, this strong attachment to religion is understood not in universalist terms but primarily as a cultural marker of Turkishness. The survey results indicate that many respondents have rather negative attitudes towards other Sunni Muslims in Turkey, including Arabs and particularly Syrians, Kurds, Domari, Romani, and Abdals, as well as in the neighbouring nation-states. For example, when asked about their attitudes towards refugees in Turkey, 78 per cent agree (with 49 per cent strongly agreeing) with the view that 'Turkey spends too much time and money caring for refugees from other countries and should focus more on its own citizens' (Halpin et al. 2018:18). The overwhelming majority of respondents (79 per cent) view fellow Sunni Syrian refuges in a 'totally unfavourable' light (Halpin et al. 2018). Another survey conducted in 2022 provides a similar pattern of values:

67.8 per cent of the respondents believe that individuals born in Turkey should be given preference over immigrants when it comes to jobs, housing, and health care (Balta & Grigoriadis 2024). The neighbouring Muslim-majority countries such as Iran, Syria, or Iraq generally are not regarded positively in Turkish public opinion. In addition, this commitment to the religious markers of identity is not an expression of anti-secularism. On the contrary, the majority of the Turkish population is firmly in favour of the separation of church and state. According to a recent poll, 70 per cent of respondents agree (including 38 per cent who strongly agree) with the view that 'Turkey should be a secular state that respects the rights of people from all religious backgrounds to practice their faiths with no official state religion' (Halpin et al. 2018:26). Furthermore, 79 per cent are committed to the preservation of democratic principles as they agree with the following statement: 'Democratic rights such as a free press, free speech, and the right to speak one's views are vital and should not be sacrificed for any reason' (Halpin et al. 2018:25).

Hence, religion is an important element of Turkish nationhood, but this is a very different understanding of religion to that of the premodern world. There is not much regard for umma here; religious markers are fully submerged into the nationalist narrative. This nation-centric understanding of religion is a distinctly modern phenomenon shaped by the ability of nation-states to deeply penetrate society and particularly to envelop the micro-level solidarities of the ordinary population. Nationalism becomes a way of life only when it successfully links the micro-level bonds of kinships, friendships, and other micro-level solidarities to the wider narratives of nationhood. The scale and intensity of social change that has taken place in Turkey over the last several decades has provided a social environment where coercive-organisational and ideological grounding fostered and then effectively fused with micro-interactional grounding. Speedy, yet uneven, modernisation, including rapid urbanisation, industrialisation, and post-industrialisation; the development of the service economy and especially tourism; the rise of universities; and the development of the technological sector, has transformed the traditional universe of micro-level solidarities.

The process of urbanisation has substantially intensified in the last thirty years: while in 1989 only 57 per cent of the population lived in urban areas, in 2022 this number was nearly 80 per cent (Statista 2022). The intensified industrialisation and shift to the service economy in the last few decades have stimulated economic growth. As Pamuk (2023:5) shows, tax revenue collection has increased substantially, and consequently, the government expenditure in GDP has grown from '5–6 percent around

1850 to 15 percent at the end of the 1930s, to 20 percent at the end of the 1970s and to more than 30 percent in 2020'. The commodity exports also increased enormously: 'from $2.3 billion or 2.6% of GNP in 1979 to $13 billion or 8.6% of GNP in 1990, and to $170 billion or 24% of GDP in 2020' (Pamuk 2023:20). All these changes, together with ever-increasing coercive-organisational and ideological grounding, have contributed to the development of micro-interactional grounding. The scale of urbanisation and industrialisation, full participation in the workforce, and increases in education, among other advances, have had a direct impact on the transformation of the family structure, residential and local solidarities, and patterns of deep friendships. As Esen (2024) shows, the new demographic data indicate that Turkish society is undergoing a substantial socioeconomic transformation, with individuals marrying later in life, postponing having children, and having fewer children than before. The population is also aging, and divorce rates have increased. Between 2008 and 2023 the average household size shrank from 4.0 to only 3.14 people. The number of single-person households has dramatically increased, from 14.4 per cent in 2015 to 19.7 per cent in 2023. The number of single-parent families has gone up, from 7.8 per cent in 2015 to 10.6 per cent in 2023, with 10 million people in this category (Esen 2024:1). The traditional extended families that characterised much of Turkish history have shrunk to only 13.2 per cent in 2023, and while the nuclear family remains dominant, it too has experienced decline – from 44.8 per cent in 2015 to 39.2 per cent in 2023 (Esen 2024:2). In this changed social context family and friendship ties tend to be decoupled from their traditional, village-based, micro-universes and are more easily integrated into urban nation-centric narratives. The data show that the family remains the most important source of one's attachment. Nearly two thirds of respondents (68 per cent) consider a belief in strong families to be very important for them, and 22 percent deem it somewhat important (Halpin et al. 2018:20). A similar figure is reported for respondents who see their families as their main source of happiness – 69.9 per cent (Esen 2024:2). The process of nationalist grounding makes this strong link with families a part of the nation-state project. In the discourse of nationalism, the family is regularly farmed as 'a natural unit of the nation'.

Conclusion

This chapter has focused on the transformation of collective subjectivities over several centuries with a spotlight on the relationship between religion and nationhood. Using the example of the Ottoman empire and the Turkish nation-state, I have argued that nationalism is not necessarily a secular ideology that suddenly and irrevocably replaces dominant religious belief systems. I have also tried to show that traditional religious beliefs and practices cannot operate in the world of nation-states in the same way they had in the premodern imperial world. Instead, in modernity nationalist subjectivities gradually transform and reshape religious attachments. The coercive-organisational, ideological, and micro-interactional grounding of nationalism fosters social change where religious subjectivities progressively become integrated and subsumed by nationalist subjectivities. In the premodern imperial world, religion was the dominant source of political legitimacy, and in a highly stratified form a principal social practice of everyday life. In contrast, in the modern universe of nation-states religions regularly lose this ontological power and often become the potent cultural markers of national identification and group categorisation. The example of the nationalising Turkish state indicates clearly that the relationship between nationalism and religion is shaped more by long-term structural forces than by top-down political engineering. Despite its organised hostility to religion, the Kemalist project could not eradicate religious subjectivities that were rooted in micro-level solidarities, nor it could fully dispense with religious symbolism. Similarly, regardless of its nominal commitment to the full revival of Islam in everyday life, Erdoğanism had to reconcile with the legacies of the secular state where religion and imperial nostalgia have only become visible markers of what is a staunchly nationalist project.

4 National Movements and Imperial Discontent

Introduction

Nationalism and imperialism are typically understood to be mutually exclusive ideological projects. In south-eastern European historiography empires have often been described as 'prison houses of nations' that were destined to collapse and give way to 'authentic' nation-states. Furthermore, national movements have regularly been identified as playing a central role in the destruction of imperial orders and creation of nation-states. However, much of recent research has questioned these assumptions. Several historians and historical sociologists have demonstrated that there is more continuity than discontinuity in nineteenth-century imperial and national projects (Malešević 2019; Stephanov 2018; Kumar 2017; Hall 2017; Stergar & Scheer 2018; Judson 2016). Moreover, this scholarship has successfully deconstructed traditional understandings of the late Habsburg, Ottoman, and Romanov worlds by explaining how empires have often unwittingly fostered development of institutional and ideological structures for the proliferation of nationalisms. Hence these studies show convincingly that nineteenth- and early twentieth-century nationalisms and imperialisms were not inevitably on collision course but have often coexisted and reinforced each other.

This chapter follows in the footsteps of this new research. However, my aim is to push this analysis further by questioning not only traditional historiographic paradigms of 'popular longings' for national independence but also the influential notion of 'national indifference' that has dominated recent analyses. The focus here is on the development of national movements and the function they have played in the transformation of modern subjectivities. More specifically, the chapter focuses on the role of Austro-Hungarian imperial structure in the homogenisation of discontent in late nineteenth- and early twentieth-century Bosnia and Herzegovina. I contest the view that the imperial state was undermined by the existence of strong national identities. Nevertheless, I also challenge the idea that the majority of the Bosnian and Herzegovinian population remained 'nationally indifferent' during this period. Instead, I argue that understanding the character of Austro-Hungarian rule in Bosnia and Herzegovina is a better predictor of social change that took place in this period. Rather than stifling supposedly vibrant national identities or operating amidst widespread national indifference, the imperial state played a crucial role in forging nation-centric understandings of social reality. However, this is not to say that the Habsburg state administration created nationalist resistance ex nihilo. Instead, the nationalisation of discontent was a largely unintended consequence of the uneven and increasingly coercive policies of the Austro-Hungarian state. I argue that the disconnect between the coercive, ideological, and micro-interactional powers, which underpinned Austro-Hungarian rule in Bosnia and Herzegovina, contributed substantially towards the homogenisation of very different forms of resistance. By framing all forms of anti-state discontent as a form of nationalist rebellion, the Habsburg state contributed substantially towards the nationalisation of different acts of discontent. The first part of the chapter briefly reviews recent debates on nationalism, imperialism, and state formation and articulates the key argument. The second part provides some information on the historical context, while the final, longest part offers an in-depth analysis of the social mechanics of Austro-Hungarian colonial rule and its management of social discontent in Bosnia and Herzegovina.[1]

Beyond 'Popular Longings' and 'National Indifference'

Traditional European historiography often depicted the late nineteenth and early twentieth century as the heyday of nationalism. In this

[1] This chapter is based on primary sources collected during archival research conducted in 2018 and 2019 in the Archives of the Republic of Srpska (RS), Banja Luka, Bosnia and Herzegovina. The documents analysed include official government communications and correspondence: documents issued by the central government in Sarajevo (Zemaljska vlada Sarajevo), county Banja Luka administration (okružna oblast Banja Luka), other county administrations in Bosnia and Herzegovina (i.e., okružna oblast Travnik), various district administrations (katarski ured or seoski katarski ured Bosanska Gradiška, Banja Luka, Kostajnica, Kotor Varoš, Sanski Most, Prnjavor, Bosanska Dubica, Tešanj, Bosanski Novi, Prijedor, Derventa, Odžak, Kozarac, Bihać, Doboj), and city administrations (Sarajevo, Mostar, Banja Luka). Other documents analysed in the chapter include official reports from military headquarters in Sarajevo (Vojna komanda Sarajevo) and military administration in Banja Luka, the military court in Sarajevo, municipal courts, police reports from the central police administration in Sarajevo (komanda žandarmerije, žandermarijski korpus), reports from local police stations in Banja Luka and adjacent districts (žandarmerijska postaja, redarstvena straža), documents from the financial inspectorate in Sarajevo, prison reports, documents from municipal courts, and information provided by the Austro-Hungarian consulate in Belgrade.

conventional narrative, strong nationalist movements spearheaded the collapse of imperial orders and in this way fulfilled the popular aspirations of ordinary people to live in their own sovereign and independent nation-states. The collapse of the Ottoman, Habsburg, and Romanov empires has often been interpreted through the prism of rising and uncompromising nationalists who challenged and ultimately overthrew these imperial 'prison houses of nations' (Nairn 2011; Gerolymatos 2002; Snyder 1968). Even some highly influential contemporary scholars of nationalism such as Connelly (2020), Wimmer (2018, 2013), and Hroch (2015) insist that nationalist leaders and nationalist movements caused the collapse of imperial orders. Although they challenge the traditional accounts of 'popular longing' for one's own nation-state, they still see rising nationalism as the primary trigger of imperial downfall. For Wimmer (2013:75), 'nationalists create nation-states, whether or not nations have already been built', while Hroch (2015:37) argues that national movements forged modern nations as they were 'driven by human intent in the shape of subjective "nationalistic" dreams and hopes'. These approaches share the traditional historiographic emphasis on the role of agency in the formation of nation-states. In this understanding, the focus is on nationalist agitators, who allegedly succeed in mobilising popular support against imperial rule. Nevertheless, while traditional historiography tends to operate with the perennial view of nations as something that has always existed and just needed 'awakening', contemporary scholars of nationalism such as Wimmer and Hroch are well aware that nationhood is a modern phenomenon.[2] Hence in their interpretation nationalist movements need to change public perceptions and transform ordinary individuals into nationally conscious citizens.

Nevertheless, this well-entrenched view has recently been questioned by several historians and historical sociologists who argue that the collapse of imperial world was not caused by nationalists and ordinary individuals who wanted the creation of nation-states. Instead, these scholars point out that imperial collapse and nation-state formation were the outcome of contingent geopolitical changes, wars, revolutions, economic breakdowns, and a variety of other social factors (Tesser 2024; Van Ginderachter & Fox 2019; Malešević 2019; Hall 2017; Judson 2016, 2006; Mann 2012; Zahra 2010). Furthermore, these new studies show that nation-formation was a protracted and contested process that largely took off not before but after the establishment of independent polities.

[2] For criticism of Wimmer's and Hroch's perspectives, see Malešević (2019:111–134) and Malešević (2019, 2013).

Thus, instead of being driven by intense nationalist sentiments or clearly defined nationalist programmes that would ultimately cause imperial collapse, the populations of new polities became nationalised only after these events have taken place (Malešević 2019, 2012; Judson 2016). As Hall (2013:230) argues, it was the actions of 'states [that] actually created nationalist movements where none existed before'. In many cases the empires themselves unwittingly created a space for the emergence of nationalisms and nation-states.

One of the key concepts developed to make sense of the popular attitudes that were present during this period of historical flux in Europe is the notion of national indifference. As Zahra (2010) and Judson (2006) argue, national indifference was a phenomenon associated with the large number of individuals who were reluctant to identify as members of a single and officially recognised nation and preferred to describe themselves in local, regional, religious, kinship-based, residential, cosmopolitan, or other terms. These 'nationally ambivalent populations' either would reject the official categorisations or would consciously switch between two or more identifications depending on the changing social conditions. Zahra and Judson have traced this mass phenomenon to Europe in the second half of nineteenth and the beginning of the twentieth century. However, after World War I there was a visible decline of such identifications. Zahra (2010:104) describes this historical experience as a form of 'national agnosticism'. Individuals who expressed such nationally ambiguous identities have often been belittled by the nationalists and the state officials as 'amphibians', 'borderland souls', or 'hermaphrodites'.[3]

These approaches equally challenge the perennialist and modernist accounts of nation-formation. On the one hand, they show that there was nothing inevitable in the emergence of a uniform sense of nationhood in the nineteenth century and that the premodern ethnies were not destined to become modern nations, as argued by Smith (1986) and Armstrong (1982). On the other hand, Zahra and Judson also show that the classical modernist theories of nationalism, including those of Gellner (1983), Anderson (1983), and Hobsbawm (1990), are not sensitive enough to account for the ambiguities of nation-formation. Hence national indifference was not a sign of insufficient modernisation or the lack of premodern ethnic cores. Instead, as Zahra (2010, 2008) and Judson (2016, 2006), argue rather than being a remnant of the premodern world, national indifference was a product of modernity. In the

[3] The early formulation of 'national indifference' in the Habsburg world can be traced to King (2002).

words of Zahra (2010:105): 'this imagined noncommunity was brought to life and institutionalized through nationalists' own persistent efforts to eradicate it'. Hence national indifference emerged as a response to changing social and political realities of nineteenth-century Europe; as such this was not a 'binary opposite of political engagement, a reflection of popular ignorance, or a premodern relic', but 'a response to modern mass politics' (Zahra 2010:118).

These new perspectives rightly and successfully challenge the traditional and contemporary accounts of the relationship between empire and nation-state. They show convincingly that there is nothing automatic, inevitable, or irreversible in the collapse of empires and creation of nation-states. They also demonstrate that the collective and individual attachments are highly malleable, situational, and can assume very diverse forms. Nationhood is never a teleological development but a highly contingent, unpredictable, reversible process characterised by social unevenness, historical oscillations, and multifaceted transformations (Brubaker 2015; Malešević 2019, 2006).

However, these new perspectives do not tell us enough about the organisational, ideological, and micro-interactional processes that underpin different trajectories of nationhood and national ambivalence. Although these approaches move in the right direction, as they recognise that national movements and nationalist individuals do not necessarily play a central role in the establishment of nation-states, we still do not know enough why some individuals and groups become fully nationalised and others develop ambiguous collective identities. Moreover, it is not clear whether national indifference is a temporary phenomenon that only arises in situations where nation-formation is in flux and where states have not fully monopolised the use of coercive power over their territories and populations. The notion of national indifference has also been criticised for conflating different individual and collective experiences, including a fluid sense of national attachments, a conscious rejection of national categories, an unconscious sense of being a-national, and specific behavioural practices such as living in mixed-marriage families or being bilingual (Van Ginderachter and Fox 2019:7; Kamusella 2016).

In this chapter I aim to go beyond the national indifference literature to explore the organisational, ideological, and micro-interactional processes that shape the transformation of non-national, anti-national, and proto-national categories into the nation-centric forms of thinking and acting. I argue that the transition from the a-national to nation-centric understanding of social reality is largely moulded through the coercive-organisational and ideological powers and their successful embedment into the networks of micro-level solidarities. Thus, the collapse of imperial structures and the formation of nation-states in late nineteenth- and early twentieth-century Europe had less to do with the ambitions of nationalist agitators and the national aspirations of ordinary people and much more with the coercive-organisational capacities and ideological penetration of competing social organisations – the imperial states, provincial governments, local authorities, clandestine societies, insurgent organisations, social movements, and other organised entities. The success and failure of nationalist and a-national discourses is largely determined by their organisational, ideological, and micro-interactional powers.

As I have argued previously, both modern empires and nation-states possess sizeable coercive organisational capacities and are also capable of effective ideological penetration of the societies under their control. Nevertheless, they usually differ in their ability to enact micro-interactional power: while nation-states often can successfully envelop the networks of micro-level solidarities, nineteenth-century and early twentieth-century empires usually were unable to penetrate the micro-world fully or even partially (Malešević 2019:70–89). Consequently, the nation-state as a form of polity trumped the imperial structures and has gradually become the only legitimate form of territorial rule. In this context nationalism has also replaced imperialism as the most potent and most popular society-wide ideological discourse of the contemporary world (Malešević 2019, 2013). Nevertheless, this was neither a teleological nor an uncontested project. Instead, nationalism and imperialism have also coexisted and reinforced each other for much of the nineteenth and early twentieth century. They have also been challenged by many other ideological projects. Furthermore, the formation and proliferation of the nation-centric categories of identity was not an exclusive prerogative of the state. In addition to the top-down developments, national categorisation also developed through other social organisations, including religious institutions, private corporations, political parties, and other groups working within the sphere of civil society (Stephanov 2018; Kumar 2017; Stergar & Scheer 2018).

However, once the nation-state model attained a hegemonic position at the global level, imperialism became delegitimised and discredited as a valid ideological project. Thus, since the second half of the twentieth century no polity relies on an imperial doctrine to justify its existence. While it is now clear that this large-scale transformation has taken place over the last two and half centuries, it is less clear how this historical process unfolded in the intricacies of everyday life. Hence to capture segments of this process in motion this chapter focuses on the role of the Habsburg state and its challengers in reshaping the ideological landscape of Bosnia and Herzegovina between 1878 and 1918. The chapter focuses on three key processes that defined the historical trajectories of nationalism and imperialism in this part of Europe. I analyse how the competing coercive-organisational, ideological, and micro-interactional powers have shaped the conflict between the imperial and the national projects and why nation-centric understandings of social and political realty ultimately won.

Obviously, there are many other factors and processes that have impacted the dynamics of imperialism and nationalism in late nineteenth- and early twentieth-century Bosnia and Herzegovina. In addition, this small micro-level study is not intended to capture the enormous geographical and historical variety that has characterised social and political change in this region. This chapter has a rather modest aim: to trace the social dynamics of the national and imperial projects in the everyday experiences of the ordinary population in Bosnia and Herzegovina. The aim is not to provide a comprehensive explanation of Austro-Hungarian policies towards Bosnia and Herzegovina nor to track the complex and changing developments within the nationalist movements in the region. Instead, the main ambition of the chapter is to analyse how specific actions of the Habsburg state shaped the character of the resistance on the ground. I argue that the imperial state contributed heavily towards turning instances of popular dissatisfaction into nation-centric forms of political resistance. In this context I explore the role of coercive-organisational, ideological, and micro-interactional powers of the imperial state and their impact on the ordinary population.

The coercive-organisational capacity is characterised by one's ability to successfully direct and coordinate people, resources, communication, transport, and a variety of other social roles and services. This process entails disciplinary capability and the use of coercive means to implement stated goals. The defining features of coercive-organisational capacity are effective division of labour, clearly articulated hierarchical chains of command, a degree of meritocratic social mobility, compliance with the rules, and the expectation of loyalty and obedience to the organisation (Malešević 2017, 2010). Historically the states have been the most significant containers of coercive-organisational power as they control military, police, security apparatuses, and the judiciary, all of which are purveyors of disciplinary might. However, most complex and durable social organisations possess a degree of coercive capacity, as they also operate through hierarchical systems of control and coordination. Hence the most effective non-state organisations adopt pyramid-like structures, with a hierarchical division of labour, control, and expectation of compliance with the organisational rules and objectives. The increase in coercive-organisational capacity has historically been visible through a variety of indicators such as the size of the administrative apparatus, communication systems, transportation networks, control of finances (i.e., taxation), policing of borders of organisation and control of its membership, and increased systems of surveillance (Mann 2012; 1993).

Ideological power is rooted in the normative codes and principles that justify the existing social organisations and their actions. Since all durable and complex social organisations cannot operate through coercion alone, they devise and use specific ideological narratives to legitimise what they do and why they exist. With the development of coercive-organisational powers through time, ideological power has also expanded, as it is able to utilise the new and improved infrastructural capacities. For example, the development of transportation, communication, and administration has ultimately impacted the standardisation of vernaculars and dramatically increased literacy rates and the cultural homogenisation of the population. These changes fostered the emergence of the public sphere, compulsory education, mass media, and other cultural spheres that have played a vital role in the proliferation of ideological narratives. With the rise of coercive-organisational capacities, ideological penetration was intensified and was able to reach throughout the social and political orders (Malešević 2019, 2013; Mann 2012, 1993).

Finally, the micro-interactional powers have also shaped the beliefs and behaviour of ordinary individuals. Since human beings are meaning-oriented creatures who thrive on the emotional and moral attachments of small and intimate groups, much of their action is governed by the intricacies of this micro-world. In other words, most individuals are embedded in networks of micro-level solidarity where they form strong bonds with their close family members, lovers, intimate friends, kinship groups, and peer groups. These personalised micro-bonds motivate individuals to support or reject the particular course of action, and in times of social crises and conflicts these micro-bonds influence individuals' willingness to sacrifice themselves for their significant others. Since these micro-level networks of solidarity are durable and intensive, most social organisations aim to penetrate this micro-world and utilise the existing emotional and ethical ties to advance their own organisational aims. Hence successful social organisations aim to envelop the micro-level solidarities and integrate them into their own ideological projects (Malešević 2019, 2013). In this context they often mimic the language of intimacy and face-to-face interactions and address members of their organisations in terms of comradeship and close kinship. Thus, nationalist ideologies regularly frame individuals as 'our Italian/Thai/Senegalese brothers and sisters', who willingly sacrifice themselves for their 'motherland' or their 'fatherland' and who are determined to protect their 'Italian/Thai/Senegalese mothers, daughters, and children' and who fight with their 'Italian/Thai/Senegalese comrades and friends'.

Historically, states tended to have more coercive-organisational and ideological powers than non-state organisations. From the pristine city-states to the patrimonial kingdoms, empires, and other forms of polity, state power has traditionally been defined by centralised authority, hierarchical division of labour, and control of the military, judiciary, and administration. Although the premodern polities usually did not have enough organisational capacity to establish a monopoly on the legitimate use of violence, the modern state system is built on the principle that the state possesses such monopolies and also tends to control taxation, the judicial system, and in many cases the educational system too (Weber 1968; Elias 2000; Gellner 1983). Nation-states differ from the premodern polities in the sense that they can develop, operate, and maintain high levels of coercive-organisational and ideological powers while also penetrating deeply into the corners of micro-solidarity. Although nineteenth-century empires possessed formidable coercive-organisational capacities and coherent ideological projects, they were largely unable to fully envelop the networks of micro-solidarity (Malešević 2019:70–89). Non-state organisations such as private business corporations, religious associations, social movements, political parties, cultural institutions, or insurgent military organisations usually have less coercive and ideological powers than the states. However, they can still develop strong and resilient organisational and ideological powers and can successfully penetrate the micro-interactional world. For example, during the civil war in Colombia the state apparatus could not envelop the networks of micro-solidarity among the peasants in several provinces of that country. Although the state possessed much more powerful coercive-organisational and ideological capacities than the FARC insurgents, it was still unable to penetrate the micro-world. In contrast, FARC was successful in developing and maintaining an effective administrative apparatus, which together with the deeper ideological penetration enveloped fully the networks of micro-level solidarities across the territories under its control and even in villages that were outside its direct control (Gutierrez 2021).

This discrepancy between state and non-state powers is particularly relevant for nationalism. For one thing, since the states possess much larger coercive-organisational and ideological capacities, they can institutionalise and disseminate nationalist ideas and practices over a much wider space. With the control of legislation, they can standardise and impose specific cultural policies and linguistic practices (i.e., prohibiting some languages and dialects and privileging others). They can also allocate funding for the organisation of particular national commemorations while ignoring other historical events. States can influence the process of language standardisation and the imposition of uniform teaching practices in the educational system. They can also support mass media that is partial to the specific interpretations of the national past and present. To counter this asymmetry, many nationalist movements and organisations tend to focus on civil society and the domestic sphere, trying to influence ordinary individuals through subtle diffusion across the networks of micro-solidarity. When successful, nationalist movements can establish a degree of hegemony across large sections of society. For example, in Francoist Spain, Catalan and Basque nationalists could never match the coercive-organisational powers of the Spanish state, but they were often much more successful in controlling the nationalist narratives in civil society and the domestic sphere. Hence many ordinary individuals living in Catalonia and the Basque country were not persuaded by the coercive-organisational and ideological powers of the Spanish state that they are Spaniards only. Instead, despite prohibitions on language use and the deployment of many other coercive measures, the Spanish state could not penetrate the hubs of micro-level solidarity, and thus the repression often had a countereffect as it enhanced the Catalan and Basque nationalisms (Conversi 1997).

While nationalist movements and organisations possess some coercive organisational capacities, nationally indifferent individuals usually lack any such powers. While there is an abundance of national organisations and societies for protection of one's culture, language, traditions, religion, and history, there are no associations for 'imagined non-communities' (Zahra 2010:106). Thus, it is difficult to historically trace the individuals and groups who have constituted such 'imagined non-communities' in the Habsburg worlds. Nevertheless, such instances of national ambiguity and indifference can be observed through governmental records and documents produced by nationalist associations, both of which tend to describe behaviour of people who do not fit easily into the ideological categories imposed by these competing social organisations.

In this chapter I explore how the coercive organisational and ideological powers of the imperial Austro-Hungarian state have historically clashed with popular discontent across Bosnia and Herzegovina between 1878 and 1918. I also analyse the social dynamics of national ambivalence and how inadvertently the coercive imperial structures have contributed to the development of a nation-centric understanding of social and political reality. I argue that the coercive and ideological actions of the Habsburg state played a central role in the nationalisation of Bosnian and Herzegovinian discontent. Rather than the nationalists being responsible for the collapse of the Austro-Hungarian imperial rule, it was the actions of the Habsburg state that fostered homogenisation of very diverse forms of grievances into a relatively coherent proto-nationalist narrative. The increased coercive-organisational capacity of the Austro-Hungarian state apparatus has unwillingly contributed to the increased organisational power of Bosnian resistance, while the enhanced ideological penetration throughout society has galvanised the ideological homogenisation of resistance. At the same time, despite its substantial efforts the Habsburg state has never managed to successfully envelop the networks of micro-level solidarity in the urban and even less in the rural areas of Bosnia and Herzegovina. Ultimately it was not the nationalists who delegitimised the imperial rule, but the imperial state and its administration, who were responsible for codifying and enhancing the nation-centric categories of identification in Bosnia and Herzegovina. This codification was central in framing all forms of popular discontent as acts of nationalist resistance.

Historical Context

After four centuries of Ottoman rule (1463–1878), Bosnia and Herzegovina was occupied by the Austro-Hungarian empire. Following the congress of Berlin's (1878) decision, Austro-Hungarian troops crossed the Sava river in the summer of 1878 and soon encountered strong resistance from 79,200 Bosnian volunteers and around 13,800 regular Ottoman troops (Schindler 2004:532). Although the majority of insurgents were Bosnian Muslims, there was also a sizeable number of Orthodox Christians, who objected to the Habsburg occupation and joined the resistance led by local agitator Hadži Lojo (Salih Vilajetović). After two months of intensive fighting involving continuous deployment of new Austro-Hungarian troops and significant losses, the resistance was crushed. At the end of this military campaign the Habsburg state was forced to engage 278,000 soldiers, which amounted to 'more than a third of the Habsburg Monarchy's ground forces' (Schindler 2004:537).

Once fully occupied the new colony was run by the joint ministry of finance of Austria and Hungary. Although Bosnia and Herzegovina remained nominally a part of the Ottoman empire until the Austro-Hungarian formal annexation in 1908, the new rulers moved quickly to take a control of all aspects of social life in the country. Fearing continuous resistance from the Bosnian Muslim and Orthodox populations, the new government reorganised the main religious institutions where all clergy became Austro-Hungarian state officials. Leading Muslim clergy lost their connection to Istanbul as their traditional subordination to the sultan had been replaced with the state-mediated organisation of the Islamic community in Bosnia and Herzegovina. Similarly, the Habsburg rulers signed a treaty with the Ecumenical Patriarchate of Constantinople through which the Serbian Orthodox Church in Bosnia and Herzegovina became integrated into the Austro-Hungarian state (Hajdarpašić 2015; Okey 2007). In the early years of Habsburg rule, the ambition was to transform Bosnia and Herzegovina into a model colony that would fully reflect the Austro-Hungarian commitment to the ingenuity and progress. The imperial minster of finance and long-term chief administrator of Bosnia and Herzegovina (1882–1903), Benjamin von Kállay, was a principal proponent of the Habsburg civilising mission in the new colony. His administration was eager to industrialise, urbanise, and modernise the country while also attempting to contain all forms of resistance to the imperial rule.

Hence between 1878 and 1914 Bosnia and Herzegovina experienced significant social and economic development in industry, infrastructure, and education. Building on the well-established Ottoman fiscal and agrarian laws and the functioning road system,[4] Habsburg rulers had created a new model of administration, built a wide network of railways, and fostered the development of mining, forestry, food-processing, and carpet making, as well as tobacco and salt production. As Palairet (1993:138) explains: 'The lack of infrastructure, markets, and industrial labour skills limited the attractions of Bosnia to private investors, so the administration embarked on a far more interventionist industrial policy than was ever pursued either in Austria or in Hungary.' This state-led industrialisation relied mostly on German and Austrian investors, who developed an export-centred economy. Consequently, the country experienced a high annual growth rate of 12.4 percent over the period 1881–1913 (Palairet 1993:143). Although the country was a less developed part of the empire, by 1907 Bosnia and Herzegovina was 'three times as industrialised as Serbia in 1910 and five times as industrialised as Bulgaria in 1910/11' (Palairot 1993:149).

This focus on economic development went hand in hand with the ideological and coercive-organisational fight to pacify any form of political resistance. In this respect Kállay's principal ambition was to use

[4] The Ottoman administration has reorganised and created a better administrative system in the country in the last period of its rule (1850–1876) (Palairot 1993:137).

ethnic and religious differences in Bosnia and Herzegovina to form a single political identity. Hence the Habsburg administrators forcefully promoted the idea of a single, multi-confessional Bosnian nation. Drawing on the Ottoman attempts of Topal Osman Pasha, a grand vizier who in the 1860s advocated the notion of multi-faith Bosnians, Kállay supported and provided an institutional backing for the all-Bosnian national project of Bosnianhood (Bošnjaštvo). This concept stood for the idea that all inhabitants of Bosnia and Herzegovina constitute a single nation who speak the same Bosnian language and possess the same rights despite professing three different religions. In this context Kállay encouraged development of all Bosnian cultural institutions such as interconfessional primary and secondary schools, book publishing, mass media, national museums, and galleries. The schools were required to use state-approved textbooks promoting the Bosnian language and an idea of shared Bosnian history (Okey 2007:55–73). However, the notion of Bosniahood was not conceptualised or implemented in the sense of civic nationalism. Instead, Kállay's administration conceived of Bosnianhood as a segment of 'dynastic patriotism' that would generate a sense of loyalty towards the empire. This policy was in tune with the actions of the Habsburg administration in other parts of the empire (Cole & Unowsky 2009:1–10).

At the same time, Habsburg authorities discouraged or prohibited distribution and circulation of books, magazines, and newspapers from Serbia and neutralised any attempts to promote Serbian or South Slav national ideas among the Bosnian Orthodox and Catholic populations. Kállay believed that 'the Bosnian begs were direct descendants of medieval leaders who accepted Islam to retain their predominance in the land', and as such he identified the Bosnian Muslim landowners as the backbone of the all-Bosnian nation (Okey 2007:60). Thus, the Habsburg civilising mission combined a policy of intensified economic development with the fostering of imperial 'dynastic patriotism' associated with the idea of Bosnianhood.

Nevertheless, this policy soon was beset with many problems on both fronts: economic modernisation remained uneven and deeply polarising, while the project of building a single Bosnian nation within the confines of imperial rule ended in a complete failure. Although the Habsburg rulers invested substantially in industry, infrastructure, and education, their interventionist policies largely benefitted only a very small sector of the population. Most individuals employed in the administration and the state-run industries were middle-class immigrants from other parts of the empire (Lyon 2014:30), while the Bosnians and Herzegovinians, being mostly employed in low-paid jobs, experienced no substantial benefits.

Despite the impressive growth rates in industry, this sector constituted only 5.79 per cent of labour force, while over 90 per cent of population in Bosnia and Herzegovina were involved in agriculture (Palairot 1993:139). One of the key problems that Habsburg rulers inherited from the Ottomans was the issue of land ownership. During the Ottoman period, Muslim landowners controlled most of the arable land, while much of the Christian population were serfs. Austro-Hungarian rule introduced some changes, including liberalisation of the traditional lord–serf relationships, but it never attempted to institute radical land reform. Hence according to the 1910 Austro-Hungarian census the landownership structure was very similar to the one that was in place before Habsburg rule: Bosnian Muslim landlords owned 91.1 per cent of land, while the Orthodox Christians owned only 6 per cent, Catholics 2.6 per cent, and others 0.3 per cent (Austrian Census 1910). Furthermore, as Okey (2007:65) shows, despite its proclaimed lofty goals Kállay's administration did not embark on the society-wide cultural transformation but tended to focus almost exclusively on Sarajevo and a few other towns. Instead of systematically building new primary schools throughout the country, the Habsburg administration prioritised the creation of secondary schools in Sarajevo: '74.5 percent in the budget for 1889 was devoted to the handful of secondary institutions ... [I]n the years 1882 to 1890 the government spent more on the Sarajevo Gymnasium ... than on all primary schools in the same period' (Okey 2007:66). Furthermore, most students went not to state schools but to private schools usually run by religious organisations (Pejić 2018). Consequently, literacy rates remained abysmal. The 1910 Austro-Hungarian census shows that the overall literacy rate for Bosnia and Herzegovina was only 12.16 per cent (industrially less developed Bulgaria had a literacy rate of 42 per cent). In 1911/12, only 17 per cent of children who were eligible were enrolled in primary schools throughout Bosnia and Herzegovina (Palairot 1993:151).

This uneven and thin modernisation generated deep social discontent and division, with large sections of population being profoundly dissatisfied with Habsburg rule. One of the folk proverbs popular among the peasantry during this period was 'Sjaši Murta da uzajši Kurta' ('Murat [Ottoman] gets off the horse so that Kurt [Austrian] can get on the horse', horse meaning the Bosnian peasants). Thus, Habsburg rule was characterised by periodic acts of resistance, including protracted strikes, destruction of property, banditry, uprisings, assassinations, and protests. In addition, many dissatisfied citizens emigrated from Bosnia and Herzegovina to Serbia, the Ottoman empire, other parts of the Habsburg empire, or the Americas. Despite its nominal commitment to continuous development, the empire extracted more resources and labour from the country than it brought in (Ruthner 2018; Lyon 2014). One of the guiding principles of imperial rule was that all advancements in the colony had to be financed by the colony itself. In this context local entrepreneurs were completely overpowered by the imperial economy: 'Austro-Hungarian policy practically excluded native capitalists from participating in the industrialisation of the province … [T]he Salom brothers and Alkalay [were the only two] local entrepreneurs who were able to establish industry of any significance in the Bosnia and Herzegovina under Austro-Hungarian rule' (Sugar 1963:214).

The intermittent and asymmetrical modernisation together with Habsburg unwillingness to undertake land reform also undermined the second pillar of their rule – the project of forging a unified pro-imperial Bosnian nation. Since Kállay and other administrators privileged Muslim landlords and mostly ignored the pleas of the Orthodox Christian peasantry for land reform, they unwittingly created a space for resistance and radicalisation. It is no accident that nearly all members of Young Bosnia, including Gavrilo Princip and other anti-imperial organisations, were children of peasant serfs who grew up in dire poverty during Habsburg rule (Hajdarpašić 2015; Vojinović 2018). Imperial administrators never attempted to address the deep social inequalities that uneven modernisation produced. Moreover, while they gained some support from Muslim landowners, the Habsburgs were continuously distrusted by ordinary Muslims. Muslim peasants, although smaller in size than their Christian counterparts, were equally dissatisfied with the lack of land reform. The small Muslim middle class was heavily underrepresented in the civil service, industry, education, military, police, communications, and other public jobs (Lyon 2014:30–31). Although all Bosnians and Herzegovinians were underrepresented in public service (out of 14,000 civil administrators only just over 4,000 were local employees), Muslims were completely absent in most middle-class professions: 'Almost all directors of train stations, post offices, officials in state institutions and administration, doctors, judges, attorneys, pharmacists, and public-school teachers were Christians or Jews' (Lyon 2014:31). Even the Bosnian Catholic population was mostly dissatisfied with their situation. Habsburg rule was beneficial in terms of increased religious freedom and social status within an essentially Catholic-dominated empire, but their socio-economic position had not improved: 'Catholics were the poorest section of the population and were sharply affected by rising prices and taxes in an unresolved agrarian situation' (Okey 2007:109). The continuous existence of these deep social, economic, and political grievances combined with the entrenched religious differences impacted negatively on the development of a single, pro-imperial, nation project. Hence forging a unified nation where religious and class divides overlapped and where the imperial rule was mostly resented was an impossible task. Kállay's successor Istvan Burián recognised the failure of this project and conceded cultural autonomy to all three ethnic/religious groups in Bosnia and Herzegovina. Burián's administration even decided to change the official name of the language spoken in the country – from 'Bosnian' to 'Serbo-Croat' (Hajdarpašić 2015:186).

Imperial Rule and the Mobilisation of Discontent

Conventional historiography often depicts the anti-imperial resistance as a product of the conscious or intentional action of nationally aware individuals and groups who aimed to replace coercive and exploitative foreign rulers with the new, native-ruled state based on the idea of popular sovereignty. In this context, traditional historical accounts tend to overemphasise insurgent actions such as the 1914 assassination of Archduke Franz Ferdinand by Gavrilo Princip and other members of Young Bosnia. In this well-established narrative Princip is depicted as a hardened Serbian nationalist deeply dissatisfied with the annexation of Bosnia and Herzegovina by Habsburgs in 1908, which would prevent unification of Bosnia with Serbia (Butcher 2014; Clark 2012). In this interpretation he and his co-conspirators were also infuriated by the repressive actions of the imperial state against the Serbian cultural and religious organisations (many of which were banned in 1913). The argument is that this strong nationalist commitment was behind the plan to assassinate the heir to the Austro-Hungarian throne (Butcher 2014: Clark 2012). Clark (2012:50–51) insists that Princip and other members of Young Bosnia were fanatical Serbian nationalists who 'dwelt at length on the suffering of the Serbian nation, for which they blamed everyone but Serbs themselves, and felt the slights and humiliations of the least of their countrymen as if they were their own'.

Nevertheless, these rather simplified and stereotypical historiographic accounts are deeply grounded in the teleological understanding of empires as being destined to be replaced by nation-states. In this retrospective, nation-centric interpretation, it is the determined and unwavering nationalists who are the dramatis personae of history and who ultimately bring down the rotten imperial orders. There are numerous historical articles and books that refer to Princip's assassination as 'the shots … that brought down the not just the monarchy but the whole European order' (Barker 1998:68). However, these post hoc nation-centric explanations are not rooted in historical evidence. Young

Bosnia was not a fully-fledged Serbian nationalist movement but an association of discontented youths who were equally inspired by anarchism, socialism, anti-imperialism, and South Slav pan-nationalism (Hajdarpašić 2015; Vojinović 2018). Nationalism did not bring down the Austro-Hungarian empire; it was the empire itself that inadvertently fostered the rise of nation-centric understanding of social reality in Bosnia and Herzegovina.

Imperial policies played a central role in homogenising diverse forms of discontent into relatively coherent anti-Austro-Hungarian activities. Moreover, the actions of the colonial bureaucracy fostered the unification of resistance around the nation-centric categories of identity. In other words, it was the empire and not the nationally conscious agitators that spearheaded the break-up of the imperial state and the emergence of nation-centric understandings of social and political life.

The Austro-Hungarian empire contributed towards the nationalisation of discontent in three principal ways: (1) through systematic coercive-organisational activities, (2) via ideological and counter-ideological penetration of society, and (3) through its inability to capture the networks of micro-level solidarities.

Coercive-Organisational Power

All colonial rule relies heavily on coercive power. Austro-Hungarian control of Bosnia and Herzegovina was achieved through the military means and was also sustained by the sizeable military and police presence in the country. Despite its popular image as an orderly and civil state, or as Kumar (2017:145) calls it, 'the most lovable' of all empires, Austro-Hungary possessed a formidable coercive bureaucratic apparatus that was regularly deployed to police and punish any forms of resistance to the imperial rule (Trode 2022). Local authorities imposed bans on many social and political activities, confiscated political literature, curtailed and monitored most forms of political agitation, spied on suspicious individuals, forced military draft on the resisting peasantry, broke up and barred workers' strikes, and also periodically arrested and imprisoned all those who persistently challenged the imperial rule. Nevertheless, these coercive actions usually did not differentiate between various forms of anti-state behaviour and were typically implemented uniformly against all types of political or social transgression. During the occupation and annexation periods, the rulers had constantly expressed concern and were fearful of any form of dissent. Hence the police often rigorously penalised a variety of individual and collective forms of discord and resistance: workers' strikes, desertions from military draft, countryside banditry, religious agitation, illegal imports of suspicious magazines and books from Serbia or the Ottoman empire, individual insults of the Habsburg royalty, suspicious travel plans abroad, and unwillingness to declare oaths of loyalty to the empire. Austro-Hungarian authorities regularly monitored activities of all potential dissidents including known political agitators, supporters of workers' rights, religious leaders, traders, and even ordinary peasants. For example, in 1883 the authorities in the county of Banja Luka reported on the activities of several individuals with very different social and cultural backgrounds. The report indicates that the brothers Hrvaćanin had applied to open a grocery shop in Bosanska Dubica, but since one of the brothers, Mujo Hrvaćanin, is described as a 'committed supporter of the Youth party', the report advised against granting such a licence (9/2/Z44/1883). In another document produced in the same year and in the same county, authorities expressed concerns about the activities of the Serbian Orthodox priest Mihajlo Opačić, who is described as 'a well-known agitator' (10/6/1883). The government invested significant resources in monitoring and policing everyday life in Bosnia and Herzegovina. This is well illustrated in several reports where local authorities ask for new appointees who would help with monitoring and spying on suspicious individuals. Hence in 1910 county of Banja Luka authorities report that 'to facilitate the information collection on the presence of politically and otherwise suspicious individuals we require a person responsible for the sorting of letters' (21/3/1910).

Many reports written by the local authorities and police indicate that all forms of dissent were addressed in similar, mostly coercive ways. The Austro-Hungarian administration closely monitored and, in some instances, also banned travel within and outside Bosnia and Herzegovina. For example, in 1886 a local authority in Travnik dispatched a warning to Sarajevo that 'seven individuals from Herzegovina and several Montenegrins have travelled through Glamoč to the region around [river] Una where there was the rebel leader Stefan Marinković' with the aim 'to organise an uprising around Unac [river]' (8/1/1886). The authorities also monitored travel to Serbia and the Ottoman empire. Hence in 1891 several reports indicate that 'many Serb peasants from different parts of the country have travelled to Serbia and that many others are planning to go', with a note that 'we are monitoring the situation and the results will be reported soon' (22/8/1891; 3/12/1891). The same suspicion is expressed in reports documenting the travel of Muslims to the Ottoman empire and Middle East. In 1895 local authorities noted that 'two suspicious Muslims from Bosnia have travelled to Istanbul' and that they should be monitored. Similarly, in 1903 the report from the Sarajevo government's central office indicates that individuals who are returning from the haj in Mecca can only enter Bosnia via Bosanski Brod where they will be thoroughly examined (11/4/1903). Despite clear cultural, religious, and class differences between the individuals involved in these reports, the Austro-Hungarian authorities tended to treat all these mostly non-political acts as suspicious. These policies contributed to popular discontent and also prevented emergence of 'nationally indifferent' populations.

The authorities applied more coercion in situations where acts of individual resistance directly affected the government's plans for the economy and the military. For example, periodic labour strikes were often depicted as political acts intended to undermine the government. In this context, strike leaders were regularly deported or imprisoned. In 1894 a group of workers organised a strike in Karanovac near Banja Luka. The workers were dissatisfied with the pay and housing conditions, but the local government was adamant that the strike was a political act orchestrated by infiltrators from the outside; strikers were arrested and 'taken to Banja Luka in order to deport them to their own place of origin' (10/5/1894). In a similar vein, a labour strike that took place in 1906 in Banja Luka was also interpreted through the prism of political activism. One of the speakers at the workers' assembly, teacher Vladimir Škarić, was accused of anti-government activities and his salary was terminated. He was also informed that he had been suspended from teaching and that the county court prosecutor had initiated a court case against him with the recommendation that he be deported from Banja Luka (23/5/1906). In 1908 after the case of disciplinary action against him was suspended for lack of evidence, Škarić was warned to avoid speaking against the government in the future or he would be 'rigorously punished' (18/6/1908) .

The dodging of military conscription was another area where the government utilised coercive powers to punish the noncompliant. In 1891 in response to the desertion of three soldiers from Bosnia and Herzegovina, the government's central office in Sarajevo issued a command to all local offices to prioritise the apprehension of all deserters (21/7/1891). In 1895 the central government's office sent a document found during the arrest of a deserter from Mostar, Ahmet effendi Kajtaz. This document indicates that 'during his trip to Belgrade Ahmed agha Mesić from Tešanj has established links with the worst enemies of our government and that in his treasonous agitation was collecting signatures for support from Russia' (5/4/1895).

Local authorities would also deploy coercive power to police speech and public activity. The reports often refer to public displays of animosity towards Austro-Hungarian rule and the monarchy. Public pronouncements such as insults of the emperor-king and the royal family were regularly noted and punished. For example, in 1907 the county of Banja Luka forwarded the notification to the prosecutor against Niko Kasalović for 'insulting his majesty' (16/10/1907). Just a few days later another notification was forwarded to the persecutor against Vid Lazić from Klašnice also for 'insulting his majesty' (19/10/1907). In 1914 the central government issued a list of fifty individuals who had been persecuted for insults against the royal house (14/7/1914, Box 1).

The police were engaged to monitor public activities of individuals who were considered to be radical or suspicious. The focus was on local residents who were known to be opponents of Austro-Hungarian rule in Bosnia and Herzegovina. For example, one document from 1894 reports on 'the political behaviour of Sava Pišteljić', who was described as 'extremely radical' and who was monitored regularly. However, 'interceptions of his correspondence have not generated anything of substance' because 'secret messages are communicated through other channels' (20/8/1894). The external activities of Bosnian and Herzegovinian citizens were also monitored by the government. Hence the Austro-Hungarian consulate in Belgrade reported that the magazine 'Greater Serbia' had published several articles from correspondents living in Bosnia: 'The contributors from Bosnia include Vaso Vidović, a trader from Bosanska Gradiška, who took part in the Nevesinje uprising' (6/8/1888). More prominent individuals such as Vaso Pelagić, a socialist writer, and Petar Kočić, a nationalist writer and a parliamentarian, were treated with more caution. The same policy was applied to well-known individuals visiting Bosnia and Herzegovina from Serbia. For example, when a professor from Belgrade University, Jefto Dedijer, was researching in Bosnia, his activities were monitored with great care and caution: 'Jefto Dedijer, docent at the University of Belgrade is traveling through Bosnia while undertaking his research. Considering his political views, it is necessary to inconspicuously monitor his movement. We must avoid the situation that transpired last time when the police patrol arrested him for the collection of statistical data which proved to be a very harmful act' (23/10/1912).

The authorities were also monitoring activities of Bosnian and Herzegovinian citizens who emigrated to Serbia and were still involved in anti-Austro-Hungarian activities. For example, in 1888 reports describe former traders who took part in the 1875 Nevesinje uprising against the Ottomans and who now lived in Serbia and agitated against the imperial rule (6/8/1888).

The reliance on more coercive measures intensified during the war[5] when many Bosnian and Herzegovinian individuals were interned or imprisoned for obstructing the war effort or supporting Serbia. For example, during 1914 and 1915 a large number of influential and educated individuals considered to be sympathetic towards Serbia were interned and kept away from influencing the ordinary population in Bosnia and Herzegovina. Several reports refer to the internment policies: 'interning teacher Vlado Škarić, Ilija Mihić and Pero Popović who have worked in the Serbian Sokol society and Serbian reading room. They are politically very unreliable.... In addition, 12 Arbanas [Albanians], 17 Serbians and 20 Montenegrins' had been interned (18/8/1914, Box 2). In another report regarding 'interned Serbs from Bosnia and Herzegovina': 'the administrators have too much work and cannot interrogate all interned individuals' (12/5/1915, Box 1). '[W]ith the start of war many Serbs were interned to Arad, deemed to be politically suspicious. Although this was a deliberate policy the speed of this action might have inadvertently led to imprisonment of some innocent people. Hence the district administration will undertake a revision to identify some individuals' (8/2/1915, Box 1).

In 1915 the central government issued clear and strict guidelines on treatment of different groups in the Bosnian and Herzegovinian population: 'During the recruitment medical check-up in January 1915 priority should be given to recruiting the dissatisfied elements of Serbian nationality while protecting Catholics and Muslims. The harsh treatment should be particularly enforced in the districts of Gradiška and Petrovac where the wealthy individuals, so called peasant leaders should be recruited. The district leaders will coordinate these actions with the presidents for the military boards so that this can be done skilfully. This recruitment of Serbs is not necessary for military reasons but primarily to weed out as many suspicious elements as possible' (3/1/1915, Box 1). Hence what is clear here is that the coercive policies of the Habsburg administration had further polarised the population of Bosnia and Herzegovina by differentiating sharply between different ethnic groups and in this way nationalising the Serbian Orthodox peasantry.

Others were arrested and imprisoned for opposing the war or speaking against the Austro-Hungarian empire. For example, one report indicates that the judge from the country court in Sarajevo ordered the arrest of teacher Ćasić and the student teacher, a son of the school

[5] It worth noting that this process had already started with the Balkan wars of 1912–1913 and had only intensified during World War I. See Grunert 2020.

principal, Cvjetko Popović, and their transportation to Sarajevo (11/1/1915, Box 1).

The wartime reports focus on potential spies and saboteurs and regularly invoke imprisonment for any anti-government activities. For example, the police often identified and described suspicious individuals: 'Gustav Pavišić, a butcher's apprentice, from Sremski Karlovac is suspected of espionage and should be arrested on the spot' (8/1/1915, Box 1).

The central administration also compiled a list of deserters who joined the Serbian military: 'Deserters from the army who have joined the enemy include Jovo Žerjavić, Boško Vukotić, Meho Mizić, Mustafa Smajlikić i Hakija Ramić' (13/10/1915, Box 2) or 'deserters from Bosnian Herzegovinian troops who have joined the enemy side. There are more than 100. All their property must be confiscated' (13/10/1915, Box 2) or 'Velimir Vukić from Prijedor, a soldier 2. BH regiment has deserted. He was in Milan where he had a medical treatment and since then he was not in contact. His property must be confiscated, and his citizenship revoked' (30/10/1915, Box 2). What is interesting here is that the government officials tend to homogenise different reasons for desertion into a single anti-state act. In this process they amalgamated together social, political, economic, and ideological concerns and inadvertently contributed towards the homogenisation of popular discontent.

The Austro-Hungarian government also demanded public expressions of loyalty to the empire. Thus, on Emperor's Day 'around 500 citizens' declared their loyalty to the monarchy (18/8/1914, Box 2). This event was followed by 'speeches and singing of the anthem' (21/8/1914, Box 2).

With the start of war, the central authorities also targeted Serbian Orthodox clergy, many of whom were deemed to be collaborating with the enemy: 'the charges have been initiated against Mladjen Popović, the Orthodox priest from Skender Vakuf, Kosta Čavić, a priest from Maslovari and Dušan Mladjenović, a priest from Kotor Varoš for holding suspicious meetings with the recruits. Popović was talking to the peasants about the assassination on St Vitus day and was shooting from the revolver. The police have inspected his house and confiscated books and other things. Čavić and Mladjenović [and Popović] have been arrested and transported to Banja Luka' (13/8/1914, Box 2).

The Austro-Hungarian state relied extensively on coercive-organisational power to maintain its rule in Bosnia and Herzegovina. In this process the coercive apparatus has often approached and treated diverse forms of resistance in a comparable way. Official documentation indicates that the central authorities regularly treated the real, potential, and imagined threats to Austro-Hungarian rule as if they were the same – the class-based grievances, the religious and ethnic tensions, the rural versus urban animosities, the hostilities between native and non-native population, and so on. Hence instead of developing different remedies for different social problems, the central authority tended to amalgamate all grievances together, thus inadvertently fostering unification of different forms of resistance. The coercive treatment of class, ethnic, religious, and ideological resistance contributed substantially towards the nationalisation of the wider resistance movement and ultimately contributed to the forging of proto-nationalist organisations that supported the break-up of the empire (Malešević 2019; Hajdarpašić 2015; Okey 2007). It is these coercive policies that played a central role in turning peasants into nationally conscious individuals. The historical evidence shows that most citizens of pre-Habsburg-era Bosnia and Herzegovina tended to identify much more in terms of religion, kinship, and status than nationhood (Hajdarpašić 2015; Okey 2007). This was even recognised by the nationalist agitators, who regularly complained that 'our peasant has no developed inner life, he has no ideas that could guide him ... we must impose the idea of "Serbdom" on the peasant' (Hajdarpašić 2015:124–125). However, during Austro-Hungarian rule the population of Bosnia and Herzegovina became much more receptive towards nationalist ideas (Juzbašić 2002; Vojinović 2018). The coercive policies of the Habsburg administration fostered the politicisation of ordinary individuals, thus preventing the emergence of 'imagined non-communities' or nationally indifferent populations, as was the case in other parts of the Austro-Hungarian empire (Zahra 2010).

Ideological Penetration

In addition to coercive-organisational capacity the empire also relied extensively on ideological power. Bosnia and Herzegovina was envisaged as a model colony and Austro-Hungarian authorities developed and implemented a distinct version of a civilising mission in the country (Okey 2007). The new rulers promoted a version of enlightened monarchism that emphasised the values of economic progress, social prosperity, modernisation, industrialisation, and the values of the Austro-Hungarian imperial project. In this context Bosnia and Herzegovina was to be developed and 'civilised' under the tutelage of its Austrian and Hungarian colonisers.

Initially the focus was on amalgamation of the three main religious groups into a unified Bosnian nation that would underpin 'dynastic patriotism' and be loyal and dependent on empire (Cole & Unowsky 2009:1–10). However, as this project relied too much on privileging

Muslim lords while mostly ignoring the needs of the impoverished Christian (and Muslim) peasantry, it soon faltered. The empire was suddenly confronted with highly dispersed forms of popular resistance. Although most of the opposition had no articulated ideological doctrines, some European ideas had gradually trickled down to the main Bosnian cities and occasionally taken the form of diverse and small proto-ideological movements centred on nascent types of anarchism, anti-imperialism, socialism, pan-South Slavism, and ethno-nationalism (Hajdarpašić 2015; Vojinović 2018). Nevertheless, this cacophony of doctrines could not significantly undermine the powerful Austro-Hungarian state and its imperial ideology. The bigger problem for authorities was the potentially rising impact of the external ideological currents, including the broader developments within Europe and more focused geo-political pressures by Russia, Serbia, and the Ottoman empire. Hence from the beginning of the twentieth century Austro-Hungarian rulers invested more resources and energy into countering ideological influences from abroad. Some of these measures were coercive, such as banning books, magazines, and newspapers from abroad; expelling suspicious visitors; or arresting local dissidents. For example, authorities regularly issued bans and confiscation orders for books and magazines that were considered to be threatening to the social order. In July 1914, the central government in Sarajevo issued an order that all 'anarchist and nationalist books from the libraries will be confiscated. The list of such books has been provided' (28/7/1914, Box 2). Other measures focused more on incentives to local population, such as rewarding acts of loyalty and denouncing potential protesters and deserters, providing financial and other support to groups and individuals who were considered to be sympathetic to Austro-Hungarian rule, and delegitimising new ideological discourses that would challenge imperial rule.

This ideological carrot and stick approach was useful in influencing some sectors of population but also proved counterproductive for containing the resistance. In fact, as the authorities tended to treat all forms of resistance as if they were coming from the same sources, they unwittingly contributed to the proliferation of relatively coherent ideological discourses and to amalgamation of different resistance groups into a more homogenous anti-imperial movement. The unsuccessful experiment of forging a multifaith Bosnian nation also politicised dissent and worked against development of national indifference as was the case in other parts of the empire (Zahra 2010; Judson 2006). The imperial administration unwittingly reinforced the creation and proliferation of national categories of identification.

In the early years of Austro-Hungarian rule, the focus was on accommodating religious elites. For example, in 1883 county of Banja Luka authorities reported on the state's support for the Islamic charitable endowment (waqf) of Ferhad Pasha mosque in Kola, 'which left a very good impression on the Muslims' (10/6/1883). The central government was also eager to emphasise its privileged treatment of the leaders of the Serbian Orthodox Church: 'the archbishop Mandić from Sarajevo must be shown full respect and ... the government officials provide him any help he needs during his travels' (29/5/1899).

At the same time, the government was concerned with the presence of influential individuals who were previously involved with resistance to the Austro-Hungarian occupation. For example, county of Banja Luka authorities reported on 'Ahmed Agha from Banja Luka who now lives in Kosovska Mitrovica and is temporarily located in Istanbul and who was a former standard bearer for Hadži-Lojo [the leader of rebellion against AH rule in 1878] ... and Hajrudin Agha from Rožaj, now based in Novi Pazar. They should be both be apprehended, and it is necessary to find out all about their activities' (30/3/1894). The government was also dissatisfied with the substantial and continuous emigration of Muslims from Bosnia to the Ottoman empire and was committed to ending or slowing down this trend.[6] In this context informers were employed to assess the motivation of emigrants. The report from the Austrian consul in Skopje discusses the behaviour of Muslim emigrants from Prnjavor and Bosanska Gradiška: 'They sent an appeal to Muhadžir board in Istanbul and wrote that the government official in Prnjavor tried to dissuade them from emigration and has spoken against their pure sovereign sultan' (27/6/1899). Other documents indicate the government's unease with mass emigration and suggest the adequate course of action to counter the agitation for migration to the Ottoman lands. 'Informants from Prijedor and Sanski Most indicate that many Muslims are planning to migrate.... Hadži Hasan Džihić has returned from the Ottoman empire while his family has settled there.... He is visiting villages Suhac, Agići and Hozići (Bosanski Novi) and advocates for emigration ... but the people should say that he is speaking against the migration' (5/11/1899).

Although the government encouraged the movement of professionals from other parts of the empire to Bosnia and Herzegovina, this was not the case with ordinary, landless immigrants. Moreover, to attract support from the local population and to prevent further emigration the

[6] For more about the emigration of the Muslim population to the Ottoman empire, see Hadžijahić (1950).

government discouraged mass immigration: 'Polish and Ruthenian families have been coming daily. They demand cleared lands for settlement. Even though there is no clear land some do not want to return to Galicia. There are 73 families with 420 souls in Rakovac and they did not receive the land. It is necessary to ban entering Bosnia to Galicians who do not have a permit from the central government' (18/11/1899).

The authorities were hostile to the presence of mass media from neighbouring countries and particularly from Serbia. Thus in 1892 the central administration declared that 'political magazine "Zlatibor" from Užice [Serbia] has been banned in Bosnia and Herzegovina. It has re-started the publication and it must be confiscated' (20/10/1892).

The central government offered a variety of rewards for reporting any anti-government activities. For example, in 1892 the Sarajevo central office instituted an award of twenty-four forints to 'anybody who reports and helps the government find the deserters from the Bosnian and Herzegovinian troops' (17/10/1892). The government also employed informants in Serbia and other neighbouring countries who would regularly report on activities of suspicious individuals. The police unit in Zemun reported on several suspect individuals: 'Isajlo Tomić was in Zemun on 17/6 and went to Okučani on 19/6. He has not met anybody but was in a hotel National where he has written letters to minister Kállay, duke Nikola, Maša Vrbica, Marko Bačković from Užice and Pavle Jovanović, the editor of Srbobran' (26/6/1894). 'The embassy in Belgrade has issued passports for Dr. Vojislav Veljković, Professor Bogdan Popović and solicitor Dragutin Protić for travel to Trieste, Dalmatia, Metković, Sarajevo and Brod. These well-known proponents of Greater Serbia should be treated with hospitality but also inconspicuously monitor who they meet. Their movements have to be reported to the government and the districts they visit' (26/7/1894). The same attitude was present when new Orthodox priests were appointed from Serbia to Bosnia: 'Kosta Vuković was appointed to parish Sočanica in the district of Derventa. His behaviour needs to be monitored and by the end of July the report on his activities has to be submitted' (21/1/1895).

The government's focus was not only on Bosnian Serbs but also on suspicious activities of Bosnian Muslim leaders. The central government in Sarajevo reported on actions of several prominent Muslim leaders: 'Derviš bey Ljubović was in Belgrade to ask that Bosnians and Herzegovinians stay in Belgrade as they are wanted by the Austrian government. He has documents showing that they [Bosnian Muslim leaders] want Serbian government and that they aim to travel further to Europe to ask for help. Hasan Osmanović went to Mali Zvornik to collect money, and Adem agha went to see a refugee from Trebinje, [Orthodox] priest Sava Pješčica, who was expelled by the [Austrian] government. Adem agha Mesić is collecting signatures and is sending them to Faladzić and Ljubović and they are preparing to send the appeal to Russia, for Bosnian people cannot survive now and need to be cared [for] by Serbia' (5/4/1915, Box 1).

Ideological justification plays an important role in sustaining political power. Hence the Austro-Hungarian state invested heavily in the ideological cement that would bind Bosnian and Herzegovinian society together and the province itself to the empire. In this process the imperial administration attempted to counter alternative and threatening ideological doctrines ranging from anti-imperialism, socialism, anarchism, and religious ideologies to pan-Slavism and ethno-nationalism (Hajdarpašić 2015; Vojinović 2018). Government policies centred on creating a unified Bosnian nation loyal to the imperial project largely backfired and, in this process, inadvertently politicised resistance, thus making potentially nationally indifferent populations into proto nationalists. Although this particular ideological project was later abandoned, the introduction of national categories into the everyday practice of government officials remained in place. The Austro-Hungarian bureaucracy was responsible for the proliferation of nation-centric categories of identity throughout the imperial realms (Stergar and Scheer 2018; Judson 2016) and Bosnia and Herzegovina was not an exception. In fact, as the Habsburg government perceived a rising Serbia and the recovering Ottoman empire as credible threats to its territorial claims in Bosnia and Herzegovina, it displayed suspicion of national irredentism and invested great deal of energy in countering nationalism. However, by framing its enemies and potential domestic threats in nationalist terms it inadvertently reinforced the ideas of nationhood.

Furthermore, as the imperial administration proved unsuccessful in delivering on its original social and economic promises, its rule gradually became contested and openly challenged by variety of groups. To counter this challenge the rulers intensified their ideological struggle and increased their coercive control. In this process they unwittingly contributed to the homogenisation of diverse forms of discontent and also fostered greater ideological development and rise of the anti-imperial movements. Hence nationalism did not destroy the empire. Instead, the ever-increasing imperial ideologisation of resistance inadvertently fostered the rise and proliferation of nationalist ideologies as the preeminent oppositional force.[7]

[7] As Stergar (2012:52) rightly notes, the imperial authorities often failed to differentiate between different forms of nationalist and other grievances. Not all nationalisms and

Disconnected Micro-Solidarities

Successful governance relies not only on coercive-organisational and ideological powers but also on the ability to fully penetrate and manage the networks of micro-solidarity. As I have argued before, the coercive and ideological powers that lack micro-interactional grounding are unlikely to last. The inability to penetrate the micro-world of locality, kinship, friendships, peer groups, and other forms of face-to-face networks of solidarity often undermines the strength of social organisations and leads to situations where such entities are replaced by other, better integrated, organisational forms (Malešević 2019, 2017, 2013).

Despite some modest accomplishments in the early years of its rule, the Austro-Hungarian empire had never succeeded in penetrating the microcosm of everyday life in Bosnia and Herzegovina. Early developments such as building better and more extensive transportation and communication networks, increasing the number of educational institutions, industrialising the economy, introducing more effective taxation systems, and improving urbanisation had all created better structural conditions for the penetration of micro-level solidarities. Nevertheless, the imperial governance was never able to build on these initial developments to envelop the micro-networks of the Bosnian and Herzegovinian society. Much of this structural development was highly uneven. The focus was on Sarajevo and a few other urban centres, while the vast countryside was largely ignored (Okey 2007). In addition, imperial rulers abandoned their original plans of substantive reform of institutions and decreased financial investment and support in the province. As much of recent scholarship shows, this 'model colony' was structured to be a self-financing entity and the imperial authority took more resources, finances, and taxes from Bosnia and Herzegovina than it brought in (Ruthner 2018; Lyon 2014). The unwillingness of the government to undertake land reform and their orientation towards the socio-economic status quo had also intensified class polarisation. Near the end of its rule Austro-Hungarian authorities initiated a modest political reform, including the establishment of the parliament and the organisation of semi-democratic elections in 1910. However, as these elections also privileged the upper

other ideological currents were against the imperial state: 'One could even argue that this somewhat peculiar coexistence was not so much threatened by nationalism as it was threatened by the inability of important parts of the state administration and the military to acknowledge it. For that reason, all nationalist activities were interpreted as signs of disloyalty, which should be vehemently opposed by the state.'

classes, their outcome contributed further to socio-economic and political polarisation.[8]

The authorities maintained a degree of control and some penetration in the micro-world of the urban areas but were unsuccessful in the countryside, where 90 percent of population lived. Thus, to pacify the villages the rulers tended to rely more on coercion and ideological messages, which often generated discontent and proved to be counterproductive in attracting support among the population. The Bosnian and Herzegovinian peasantry was generally suspicious and distrustful of all state authorities, and new coercive or ideological measures would usually tend to backfire (Hajdarpašić 2015; Okey 2007). For example, when the government intensified its programme of military conscription the ordinary population found a way to avoid it. Using health issues as an excuse many individuals avoided the draft. For instance, in 1899 in the town of Bosanska Dubica, 59.3 per cent of all military age men failed to pass the medical test and only 5.28 per cent were deemed healthy for military service (14/1/1899).

Instead of attempting to understand and accommodate problems in the countryside, the government often crudely interfered in the everyday life of ordinary people. For instance, an ordinary visit to a family living abroad was regularly treated with suspicion: 'A local resident, a Montenegrin Isailo Tomić is supposedly traveling to Zemun to visit his family. Since he is an unreliable individual, it is paramount to monitor his meetings and his correspondence in Zemun' (18/6/1894). Local authorities employed an extensive network of informers to spy on the everyday activities of Bosnian citizens and kept records on the character and behaviour of many individuals. For example, a local Orthodox priest was identified as a troublemaker and someone who 'is prone to drinking and to conflict with others … [H]e often travels to Prijedor and incites peasants against the priest Radić in Jalovac so that he could take up his post' (30/11/1897). Similarly, another citizen was deemed problematic and his application for a gun permit was denied: 'Mujo Spahić Čalić from Konjuhovci has applied for a gun permit. He is prone to drinking and socialises with the Orthodox radicals in Prnjavor' (20/6/1900). Reports were also compiled about undesirable social activities. One report indicates that a person who immigrated from Lika (Croatia) to Sanski Most

[8] The electoral system divided the population into three categories: (1) major landowners, priests, civil servants, and college-educated citizens who with ewer than 7,000 votes elected eighteen seats; (2) merchants, artisans, and small owners where fewer than 5,000 votes elected twenty seats; and (3) the rest of population where close to 350,000 citizens elected thirty-four deputies (Grunert 2020; Okey 2007).

had distributed leaflets about migration agents for America, F. Missler in Bremen, and Zagreb. The authorities noted that 'if these leaflets are found in other districts' they should be confiscated (20/5/1901). In a similar vein, government officials investigated information that 'imam Bešlić has received a medal from the Ottoman government for his activities relating to the emigration of Mohammedans' to Istanbul (4/3/1901).

The government would also interfere in commercial transactions that could affect its long-term population policies. For example, the prospective sale of land by would-be Muslim emigrants to the Ottoman empire had to be in line with the state's policy on ethnic residence: 'Some emigrants were selling their land and properties to Christians [in Bosanska Gradiška] – the former policeman Zeniva and tradesman Malić. These properties were bought by the mayor Sokol so that Christians would not move into the Muslim parts of the town' (16/3/1901). Local authorities also issued temporary orders to prevent emigration from Bosnia: 'The stoppage of applications for emigration and selling of land has left a good impression on peaceful elements [in Prijedor] while those who demanded passports show dissatisfaction and are revolting' (21/3/1901). Here again one can see how the imperial administration deployed, utilised, and reproduced national categories in everyday life.

The government relied on such information to police ordinary individuals and also to enforce its policies. In some cases, local authorities collected information on non-payment of taxes and brought in the police force to punish the non-complaint citizens: 'the village leader [knez] of Agići is asking for the police assistance to deal with the revolt against paying of taxes and unwillingness of many to pay the tax' (17/12/1901).

However, one of the central issues affecting everyday life was the continuous presence of semi-serfdom in Bosnia and Herzegovina. Many reports from the local and central government indicate that the peasants were deeply dissatisfied with serfdom: 'In four districts of Tešanj serfs did not allow aghas to attend the wheat harvest. The country office has undertaken measures to prevent this from happing in the future' (6/8/1910). 'The confidential sources have provided information that the serfs in the village of Krmine have no intention of giving one third of their hay to their aghas. They are saying that their parliamentary deputy told them that from 1.8.1910 there is no obligation to give one third [to the aghas]. The district representative has to go to Krmine to inform the peasants [that the law has not changed]' (23/7/1910). Similarly, 'The serfs in Turjak, enticed by somebody, do not intend to give one third from their hay and fruit to subasha of Džinić serfs. The police have been informed to act against the peasants' (11/7/1910) or

'Risto Dragičević, his three friends and his wife have been arrested for not giving a one third [of their hay] to Džinićs and for cursing and threatening them' (11/11/1914, Box 2). The continuous presence of semi-serfdom further politicised ordinary peasants, and instead of becoming or remaining 'nationally indifferent' their social and economic discontent was gradually transformed into proto-nationalist resistance (Hajdarpašić 2015; Vojinović 2018; Okey 2007).

With the start of World War I, Austro-Hungarian authorities became even less capable of penetrating the micro-universe of the Bosnian countryside and unable to gain trust among the population. Traditional suspicions towards ordinary people became even more pronounced and the government deployed more coercive measures to police the citizens. Any sustained communication with individuals living abroad or any prolonged travel would trigger suspicion of spying for the enemy. For example, the central government in Sarajevo warned that 'the wife of a [Bosnian-Herzegovinian] official, Milica Knežić from Mostar who now lives in Banja Luka, is still under suspicion for spying for Serbia. Her connections and letters to the Serbian consul in Vienna make her even more suspicious. She needs to be interrogated, and if there is evidence [for spying] she should be brought to the military court' (19/8/1914, Box 2). Similarly, some wealthy individuals were targeted for potential spying: 'the former director of the factory Max Steinlechner and Rudolf Čilić who claims to be an engineer have been traveling with the car to Trieste, Rijeka, Pula, Dalmatia, and Russia. They are keeping contact with Dr Radulović from Belgrade and are spending money. They should be arrested immediately as they are suspected of being spies' (22/8/1914, Box 2).

Nevertheless, most coercive policies targeted the ordinary Orthodox population. The imperial government banned the use of Cyrillic script outside church, and in 1914 Serb Orthodox confessional schools were closed. In some cases, citizens were arrested for expressing sympathy towards Serbia or for insulting the Austro-Hungarian royal house: 'the list has been sent of 50 citizens and peasants who are to be tried for insults of the royal house and other criminal offenses' (6/10/1914, Box 2). '[T]he police office in Bosanska Gradiška has arrested Vaso Babić, a trader, who said that Serbia has occupied 7 towns in Bosnian and is now targeting Dalmatia. He has been deported to the war military court' (18/10/1914, Box 2). However, as war progressed the government adopted a variety of coercive policies that targeted the entire population, thus contributing substantially towards the ethno-national homogenisation of the Bosnian Serb population. For instance, many prominent individuals had been arrested or interned without any proof of their collaboration with the enemy: '343 politically suspicious individuals have been deported and interned to Arad' (18/8/1914, Box 2); 'the [Orthodox] priest Dušan Subotić together with the materials found in his possession while searching his house, has been sent to the court' (2/8/1914, Box 2); 'the indictment against the local leader [*knez*] Teodor Mijatović for inciting the Serbian-Orthodox population against the Catholics has been issued. He has been replaced from his position and sent to the court' (15/8/1914, Box 2). These coercive measures not only alienated Orthodox Christians; they also contributed to almost universal hostility among peasants against the imperial state. It was the imperial state that nationalised their grievances. The continuous humiliation of ordinary people worked against the development of 'imagined non-communities' (Zahra 2010) and in fact forged imagined national communities where they did not exist before.

Some Austro-Hungarian government officials also publicly voiced their distrust of and aversion to the Orthodox population: 'the district leader Komadina … speaks of Serbs as a dangerous element among whom there are no sincerely loyal individuals … [S]ince the start of war numerous Serbs have been arrested for insults against the Monarchy, so we cannot trust Serbs' (24/8/1914, Box 2). In a similar vein, another document issued by the Banja Luka district authority depicts the behaviour of Serbian Orthodox Church leaders as deceitful: 'The statement issued by the metropolitan bishop of Banja Luka and Bihać and the Orthodox clergy is not to be trusted. It does not seem likely that they are teaching the loyalty and allegiance to their people towards the Emperor. For this contradicts their previous activities so it looks like a pretence' (8/8/1914, Box 2). Government informers also focused on monitoring the actions of the Orthodox population. One such report documents responses among the ordinary population following the declaration of war: 'Croats and Muslims are loyal and delighted, while Serbs are withdrawn and silent. … Serbs are poorly responding to the calls for the collection of war support funds except for Prnjavor' (18/7/1914, Box 2).

In this context the government issued orders to monitor the behaviour of ordinary individuals: 'Security measures against irredentist activities are to be put in place. The curfew will be introduced for bars and the youth will be forbidden to go out and socialise at night' (16/7/1914, Box 2). The central government also introduced strict policing of educational and cultural activities of the Orthodox population. For example, primary school teacher Stevo Uzelac and Filip Jorgić from Odžak were arrested and brought to court because 'Uzelac was teaching children Serbian songs, and Jorgić gave a book 'Patriotic songs' from [Jova Jovanović] Zmaj to a pupil as an award' (9/8/1914, Box 2).

These coercive actions, including the arrests and interment of teachers and priests, had largely been counterproductive, as they deepened mutual mistrust and generated rumours and fears among the ordinary peasants. This is well illustrated in the government's documents where the informers sent to gauge the feelings of the Orthodox peasantry towards Serbia describe the consequences of government's coercive polices: 'the information provided by the informer, a Serb who visited villages who describes attitude among the Serbs, indicates that they are all delighted in their expectation that the Serbian army will come to Bosnia and that they will join them. They are sad that their priests and teachers have been arrested. The reservists have been instructed not to shoot at the Serbian army but to surrender.... There are rumours that the Orthodox priests have been arrested and that people will be forced to convert to Roman Catholicism. It is necessary to ask the bishop in Banja Luka to send 13 priests that have not been arrested to the villages where there are no priests now' (25/8/1914, Box 2). 'The arrests of Serbs have generated fear among peasants' (14/8/1914, Box 2).

There is no doubt that during their rule Austro-Hungarian authorities were unable to fully penetrate the networks of micro-solidarity in Bosnia and Herzegovina. While some initial attempts made in Sarajevo and other large towns yielded a degree of moderate success, attained mostly through economic and social modernisation, these meagre achievements soon evaporated. Nevertheless, the imperial rule never succeeded in embedding and legitimising its place in the everyday life of the countryside. Deciding early on not to invest substantial material and organisational resources in its 'model colony' (Lyon 2014) and facing periodic crises throughout the empire, rulers opted to rely on coercive and ideological powers at the expense of micro-interactional grounding. This policy contributed substantially towards the proliferation of popular dissatisfaction with the imperial rule among the peasantry, an overwhelming majority of the population, who bore the brunt of everyday hardship. The uneven and intermittent modernisation that largely preserved the economic and social status quo from the Ottoman period alienated the majority of the population (Vojinović 2018; Okey 2007; Juzbašić 2002). While the peasantry were dissatisfied with the lack of serious land reform, local merchants and other urban populations resented the empire's privileging wealthy investors from outside Bosnia and Herzegovina. It is this pronounced popular dissatisfaction that left no room for political indifference or the emergence or persistence of 'national amphibians' or 'borderland souls' (Zahra 2010). The policies of the imperial state destroyed any rudimentary sense of identification with the empire among the majority of the ordinary population in Bosnia and Herzegovina. Although in the early years of their rule Habsburg colonial administrators attempted to appease and accommodate sections of Bosnian and Herzegovinian society, as the empire was beset with a variety of social, economic, and political problems it gradually ruled ever more through coercive practices. At the same time, Austro-Hungarian administrators largely abandoned any attempt to penetrate micro-level solidarities in the countryside of Bosnia and Herzegovina. All of these contributed to popular dissatisfaction, which was particularly prevalent among the peasantry and impoverished urban strata (Juzbašić 2002; Sugar 1963; Hadžijahić 1950).[9]

However, much of the popular dissatisfaction still lacked coherent ideological and organisational articulation. The ever-expanding reliance on coercive and ideological powers ultimately fostered the development of relatively coherent resistance to imperial rule. The inability of the government to penetrate the networks of micro-solidarity together with the intensified use of coercion and ideological power across the board and without differentiation contributed substantially towards the crystallisation of popular discontent around anti-imperial and nation-centric discourses and practices.

Conclusion

Nationalist movements have often been identified as playing a central role in the collapse of empires and de-legitimisation of imperial doctrines. While traditional historiography took for granted that there was a 'popular longing' for independence, more sophisticated analysts such as Hroch (2015) and Wimmer (2018) identified committed nationalist organisations as being decisive in bringing about sovereign nation-states. However, the transition from the mainly imperial to the predominantly national worlds is a protracted, contingent, and messy historical process that owes much more to the actions of imperial state structures than to the ambitions and plans of nationalist movements. Not only do new nation-states regularly transpire from changed geo-political conditions, the behaviours of Great Powers, and the deeds of rulers that govern neighbouring polities, but the imperial state itself often unwittingly creates and boosts nationalist ideas and practices (Stergar & Scheer 2018). Thus, the end of Austro-Hungarian rule in Bosnia and

[9] As Judson (2016) and Deak and Gumz (2017) have argued convincingly, from the summer of 1914 the military dictatorship had largely abandoned established norms and legal procedures and governed the empire by relying much more on force and the military mode of rule.

Herzegovina also had very little to do with domestic nationalist movements or 'age-old longings'. Instead, the empire collapsed through the military defeat in the Great War. Nevertheless, by the time of its downfall the majority of the population of Bosnia and Herzegovina was deeply dissatisfied with imperial rule, and some citizens were involved in formal or informal forms of nationalist resistance (Vojinović 2018; Okey 2007; Juzbašić 2002). In other words, instead of becoming or remaining 'nationally indifferent' (Zahra 2010), most ordinary individuals were inadvertently politicised by the coercive, ideological, and micro-interactional actions and inactions of the imperial state. Although much of this popular dissatisfaction was not nationalist in origin, as it was generated from various forms of discontent (e.g., religion, class, residence, status), it was the state's policies that ultimately homogenised these diverse forms of frustration into a proto-nationalist movement.

This outcome was a direct product of imperial governance, which relied extensively on coercive and ideological powers to subdue rising discontent. In this process state authorities inadvertently fostered homogenisation of very diverse types of grievances – class inequalities, religious dissatisfaction, individual disparities, rural versus urban tensions, linguistic issues, ethnic frictions, and so on – into a single and society-wide anti-imperial sentiment. The excessive reliance on coercion and ideology without being able to penetrate micro-level solidarities generated a situation where all forms of popular dissatisfaction eventually converged into an anti-imperial from of discontent. This resistance gradually attained proto-nationalist and in some cases fully-fledged nationalist contours. However, it was not individual nationalists nor nationalist movements that spearheaded the process of nationalisation of society. Instead, it was the imperial state that stimulated and enforced the nation-centric understanding of reality.

5 The Golden Age and Nationalist Narratives

Introduction

The myth of the 'golden age' is a bedrock of many nationalist narratives. Many scholars have analysed this phenomenon, with two theoretical perspectives dominating contemporary debates: culturalist and instrumentalist approaches. Whereas culturalists understand golden age myths through their quasi-religious function, instrumentalist perspectives emphasise the manipulative character of this phenomenon. In this chapter, I challenge both approaches and argue that the 'golden age' is not just a cultural or utilitarian phenomenon, but a historically dynamic political project associated with the changing political aims of different groups. Hence to better understand the social dynamics of nationalist narratives it is necessary to analyse how they emerge, develop, and change through time.

This chapter compares the changing images of the golden age in the Balkans.[1] I aim to show how the articulation of golden age narratives changes through time and space. In the late nineteenth century, the focus was on creating centralised polities and nationalising a predominantly illiterate and localised population. In this context the nationalist imagery of 'vast medieval kingdoms' was invoked from above to foster the transformation of peasants into nationally conscientious citizens. In contrast, in the early twenty-first century, populations of these countries have been fully nationalised, and narratives of the golden age are now developed and propagated more from below than from above. The competing versions of golden age myths are deployed by a variety of social and political actors, including political parties, social movements, civil society groups, and ordinary individuals. Many of these narratives represent more radicalised versions of existing golden age mythologies. This

[1] The chapter is based on the qualitative text analysis of many nineteenth- and twenty-first-century documentary resources from the Balkans, including archival research of newspapers, primary and secondary school textbooks, official government records, websites of various civil society organisations, and artefacts from popular culture.

chapter explores the relationships between different narratives of the golden age and the changing social and political dynamics of Balkan societies. The comparative historical analysis of Balkan case studies is highly relevant for understanding the general long-term dynamics of golden age narratives. It is here that one could observe how the wider structural transformations, which affected the entire world over the last 300 years, have shaped the political character of nationalism. Balkan societies have often been described as dominated by 'ancient hatreds'. However, this chapter shows that such ahistorical and anti-sociological views misunderstand not only the changing character of the Balkan societies but also the historical trajectories of nationalisms in the world as a whole.

The Sociology of the Golden Age

The idea of the golden age predates nationalism by thousands of years. It originated in different religious traditions and was particularly developed in Hinduism where Satya Yuga (Golden Age) was considered to be the first and the best of the four world ages in a cyclical vison of the world. In the Hindu religious tradition, the four ages were assessed in terms of their dharmic (virtue) qualities with Satya Yuga at the top and Kali Yuga (Dark Age) at the bottom of the value ladder. Satya Yuga was thought to be the age of truth or sincerity when human actions are governed by gods and when innate virtuousness dominates (Michaels 2004). A similar idea was developed in ancient Greek poetry, but instead of a cyclical concept of time the golden age was understood in linear terms as something that only existed in the beginning of time. Hesiod's *Works and Days* (800 BCE) identifies five different stages of people as points of decline, with the golden age being the original period of prosperity, social accord, and stability, and the remaining periods indicating the continuous decline of human race – silver, bronze, heroic, and iron ages.

This idea was developed further and popularised by Roman poets Ovid and Virgil, who associated the golden age with an idealised image of the Greek province of Arcadia. This place was envisaged as a pristine, pure, and harmonious land of peace and tranquillity but also something that has been lost in time. With the rise and spread of Abrahamic religions, the golden age was linked to the origin myths (i.e., the idealised state in the Garden of Eden) and the periods of cultural, religious, economic, and scientific prosperity (i.e., the reign of the Abbasid caliph Harun al-Rashid in Islam). In all these traditional narratives the golden age was portrayed as a period when human beings inhabited a morally superior state of existence. Despite some pronounced differences these narratives espouse a similar universalist idea where the golden age is associated with a flawless and immaculate image of human social order. In these idealised visions of the past, all human beings have the same origins – the primeval world of inherent goodness, sincerity, prosperity, harmony, and peace.

In direct contrast to these universalist classical visions the modern idea of the golden age is distinctly particularistic. Instead of universal Satya Yuga or the Garden of Eden, one encounters institutionalised narratives that often idealise and glorify specific nations and their glorious pasts. Since the nation-state has become hegemonic and the only legitimate mode of territorial organisation in the contemporary world (Malešević 2019, 2013; Wimmer 2018), golden age discourses have also attained a nation-centric from. Moreover, with the global rise of nationalist ideologies from the nineteenth century until present, the golden age idiom has proved to be one of the most important nodal points of nationalist narratives.

Several scholars, such as Smith (2013, 1997, 1991), Hutchinson (2017, 2009), Hobsbawm (2021, 1990), and Bauman (2017, 2002), have developed influential theories of social change where the concept of the golden age plays a crucial interpretative role. However, these theories articulate very different understandings of the golden age. While for Smith and Hutchinson this concept underpins the shared collective memories and as such is an indispensable cultural reservoir of nationhood, for Bauman and Hobsbawm the golden age is primarily a tool of social engineering invoked by economic and political elites to dominate the majority of population.

The Golden Age as a Cultural Reservoir of Nationhood

In Smith's (1997:47) view, the idea of the golden age is a cornerstone of nation-building as it links the past and the present: 'the collective appropriation of antiquity, and especially of shared memories of the "golden age", contributes significantly to the formation of nations. The greater, the more glorious that antiquity appears, the easier it becomes to mobilise people around a common culture, to unify the various groups of which they are composed and to identify a shared national identity'. For Smith (2013:17), the myth of the golden age is integral to shared ethno-history and as such is an essential ingredient of most nationalist narratives: 'The notion of a golden age is both a time of heroic virtue and an epoch of pristine or ancient grandeur ... for the 'true essence' of the nation is revealed in its days of greatest virtue and glory, with everything thereafter partaking of a sense of national decline.' He argues that one of the key functions of golden age mythology is to provide a sense of authenticity where nationhood can rediscover its 'true self': 'the immemorial existence of the nation is a guarantee of its authentic nature, its origin, unmixed and uncontaminated personality' (Smith 1997:56). This myth also helps establish a link with previous generations, thus reaffirming the idea of 'unbroken continuity' between nation's heroic ancestors and loyal descendants.

Continuity with the glorious past is important in terms of national dignity: 'an appeal to the golden age elevates the inner, or "true", essence of the community vis-à-vis both outsiders and the present degradations of the community' (Smith 1997:56). In this sense a shared myth of the golden age fosters a sense of being among the selected few, a chosen nation with a glorious history. For Smith, narratives of golden age are central cultural sources of collective identification as they generate shared collective meaning for members of the nation. By visualising the past through the prism of noble, brave, and virtuous progenitors, one attains a feeling of immortality. While individuals inevitably die, nations are envisaged as immortal.

John Hutchinson (2017, 2009) develops this line of thinking further by linking the idea of the golden age with warfare. He argues that the collective remembrance of previous wars enhances national identities. In particular, narratives of ultimate sacrifice made by predecessors fortify a sense of strong attachment to one's nation, thus providing 'the sacred foundations of nationhood'. In this understanding 'war may generate a set of historical myths that lodge in the consciousness of populations so that they become a framework for explaining and evaluating events' (Hutchinson 2009:402).

Among these historical myths the notion of the golden age looms prominently. For example, Hutchinson identifies two typical examples of golden age myths: 'England's defeat in 1588 of the Spanish Armada, which was linked to the cultural glories of Shakespeare and the King James Bible', thus underpinning English nationalism, and the Spanish conquistador nationalist myth, 'which celebrated the Christian Reconquista of the Hispanic peninsula in 1492 and the Spanish "discovery" and conquest of the Americas' (Hutchinson 2009:402–403). For Hutchinson, the link between warfare and the golden age can also be conceptualised through the tragic memories of historical disasters where military defeats represent the dividing line between the miserable present and the glorious past. Hence 'Greeks lamented the fall of their holy capital, Constantinople, and the Byzantine Empire in 1452, just as Serbs mourned their defeat in the battle of Kosovo Polje in

1389 as marking the beginning of their captivity in the Ottoman Empire. For the Irish, their conquest in the 17th century by the Protestant English under Oliver Cromwell and the loss of their lands and religious freedoms marked a long night of persecution' (Hutchinson 2009:403). Therefore, for both Smith and Hutchinson the myth of the golden age is a potent cultural resource that makes national identities durable.

The Golden Age as a Tool of Mass Pacification

In direct contrast to these cultural perspectives, Bauman (2017, 2002) and Hobsbawm (2021, 1990) articulate more materialist and instrumentalist interpretations of the golden age phenomenon. For Hobsbawm (1990:10) nationalism is a phenomenon enacted through social engineering: it is 'constructed essentially from above, but which cannot be understood unless also analysed from below'. In this approach nationalism is a product of structural transformation, including technological changes, economic development, and political transformations. Nationalism could not emerge before modernity, as its very existence presupposes presence of printing, standardised vernaculars, mass-scale literacy, and institutionalised schooling.

In his understanding of nationalism, Hobsbawm (2021) devotes much attention to what he calls 'the invention of tradition'. This concept stands for 'a set of practices, normally governed by overtly or tacitly accepted rules and of a ritual or symbolic nature, which seek to inculcate certain values and norms of behaviour by repetition, which automatically implies continuity with the past' (Hobsbawm 2021:108). Typical examples of invented traditions are the nineteenth-century decision to rebuild the British parliament building in the Gothic style to establish a visible link with the past or the supposedly immemorial Scottish Highland tradition of kilts, tartans, and bagpipes, which was also invented in the nineteenth century. He argues that this mass invention of national traditions allowed rulers to channel popular discontent through intensified ritualist practices. By participating fully in these nationalist commemorations, ordinary citizens would experience a sense of shared identity and as such would become loyal and docile towards the state. In this context golden age myths played a prominent role in pacifying potential popular resistance: many invented traditions were framed in reference to the alleged shared glorious past. Hence narratives of the golden age provided the political and economic elites with powerful resources to control the masses. For example, public ceremonies such as Bastille Day, Sedantag, or St Wenceslas Day were all invented traditions aimed at invoking the golden era of national greatness of the French, Germans, and Czechs, respectively.

Zygmunt Bauman (2017, 2002) also understands nationalism through the prism of social engineering. However, unlike Hobsbawm, who mostly focuses on the nineteenth and early twentieth century, Bauman examines golden age myths in the twenty-first century. While Hobsbawm sees the nineteenth century as the pinnacle of golden age narratives, Bauman is puzzled about why such narratives persist and increase in the contemporary period. For Bauman, the rise of nationalism in the twenty-first century is a symptom of deep economic and social crisis. He argues that in the liquid modern condition of today where human beings are highly individualised consumers rather than engaged citizens of their societies, there is simply no room for envisaging a better future. Instead, the ever-present neoliberal capitalism breeds an environment of constant insecurity in education, housing, and labour markets where individuals look towards the idealised past to address these insecurities.

Hence instead of progressive utopias one encounters regressive retrotopias where the 'hope of reconciling security with freedom' leads to 'rehabilitation of the tribal model of community' and 'return to the concept of a primordial/pristine self' (Bauman 2017:9). In this context golden age myths proliferate as they offer a sense of certainty and safety. The retrotopias stand in opposition to an unbearable present where 'public hopes of improvement in the uncertain and ever-too-obviously un-trustworthy future' are replaced with 'the vaguely remembered past, valued for its assumed stability and so trustworthiness' (Bauman 2017:6). In this understanding retrotopia is a pallid nostalgia for an imagined past, an attempt to overcome the structural anxieties of today by idealising the national past.

In Bauman's (2002:84) view neoliberal globalisation has severely undermined the strength and capacity of nation-states, with private corporations dominating the world economy and weakening a sense of territorial attachment: 'nation-building coupled with patriotic mobilisation has ceased to be the principal instrument of social integration and state's self-assertion'. Thus, in the contemporary world, national identifications are detached and de-territorialised. In this new environment nationalist nostalgia also becomes highly individualised where permanent insecurity breeds popular demand for retrotopian myths of past national greatness: 'it is the genuine or putative aspects of the past, believed to be successfully tested and unduly abandoned or recklessly allowed to erode, that serve as main orientation/reference points in drawing the roadmap to Retrotopia' (Bauman 2017:12). Retrotopian narratives are invoked by both establishment and anti-establishment elites, who both engage in social engineering by default: 'Once stripped of power to shape the future, politics tends to be transferred to the space of collective memory – a space immensely more amenable to manipulation and management, and for that reason promising a chance of blissful omnipotence long (perhaps irretrievably) lost in the present and in the times yet to come' (Bauman 2017:54). Therefore, for both Hobsbawm and Bauman golden age narratives represent an attempt to pacify deeply dissatisfied populations – images of glorious history offer a sense of superiority and an opportunity to replace one's present discontent with the glorification of the mythical past.

The Historical Dynamics of the Golden Age: Beyond Culturalism and Instrumentalism

The two dominant sociological perspectives on the golden age offer astute yet very different explanations of this phenomenon. While the culturalist approaches of Smith and Hutchinson insist that golden age myths are powerful because they offer a sense of collective continuity and immortality, the instrumentalist approaches of Bauman and Hobsbawm perceive golden age narratives as a device of social control. Whereas the former view the golden age motif as a social glue that makes social order possible, the latter emphasise the instrumental quality of these nationalist myths. Although both perspectives contribute to a better understanding of this sociological phenomenon, neither adequately captures the social and historical complexity of golden age narratives.

First, despite their pronounced differences, the two perspectives share an understanding of the golden age as a form of collective nostalgia. For Smith, myths of the golden age invoke a glorious past in order to generate a collective status reversal – our nation might be weak or poor now, but we are still superior as we possess a magnificent past that nobody can match. Similarly, Bauman interprets the proliferation of nostalgic retrotopias as an attempt to cope with the unbearable present: the only way to deal with the contemporary anxieties is to return to the imagined glorious past we once had. Nevertheless, this is too literal a reading of golden age narratives. Golden age imagery is much more than a simple sentimental story of longing and yearning for an imaginary past. Instead, it is an ideological project that underpins and sustains all nationalist narratives, including both those that challenge and those that aim to preserve the status quo. In this sense the ideology of golden-ageism is more focused on the future than the past. Nationalist projects draw on imagery from the past, but there is no actual intention to reinstate older forms of social order. Instead, the focus is firmly on regulating future relations within one's society. Invoking specific moments from the supposedly glorious past is not meant to suggest that the nation could or even should literally attempt to return to previous times in history. Rather, golden age narratives serve as ethical parameters of desirable forms of nationhood. Rhetorical statements about past glories are really ideological nodal points centred on future actions (Malešević 2002). In other words, most of those who propagate narratives of the golden age do not actually believe that one can resurrect the past but instead see these narratives as ideological blueprints that would govern formation of specific policies for the future. This feature of golden age myths is most clearly visible when one analyses how they change through time. Hence comparing contemporary instances of golden age rhetoric with those from previous historical periods will shed more light on the motivation behind golden age narratives.

Second, the phenomenon of the golden age cannot be reduced to exorbitant nostalgic imaginations of radicals and right-wing extremists, as instrumentalist perspectives may suggest. Not only do narratives of the golden age predate the era of nationalism, but more importantly most social movements and social organisations across the political spectrum invoke some form of golden age idioms. For example, many communist organisations depict prehistoric times of propertyless and egalitarian 'primitive communities' as a form of golden age – primitive communism (Gailey 2016). Similarly libertarian and anarchist movements often glorify the time before the establishment of pristine states as the era of ultimate freedom (Doherty 2007). However, what is more significant here is that nationalist imagery of golden age is not something that is restricted to extremist groups but is in fact integral to most social organisations operating within the framework of the nation-state. Simply put, golden age idioms permeate social life in the contemporary world as they often underpin nation-centric narratives that legitimize the existence of nation-states (Malešević 2019, 2013). Hence the instrumentalist approaches are inadequate in accounting for the continuous presence of golden age idioms in the contemporary world. This is not something that only appears in times of deep crises. Instead, this is a phenomenon that is a permanent feature of social and political life in all contemporary nation-states and in everyday interactions of people living in such nation-states. Golden age myths are not temporary products of extremist and reactionary groups; they are integral to many social and political processes that shape life in the world of nation-states.

Third, both dominant perspectives operate with a reductionist understanding of golden-ageism. Whereas Smith and Hutchinson offer a functionalist interpretation of this phenomenon where every instance of golden-ageism is explained through the same prism of shared cultural meanings and a sense of immortality, Hobsbawm and Bauman reduce all golden age myths to the utilitarian value they have for economic and political elites. As such the two perspectives cannot explain the sheer cultural and historical variability of this phenomenon: Why do some societies generate and utilise more of such myths than others? Why do some historical periods witness little reference to the golden age while others experience a proliferation of such narratives? How can one explain the particular timing and intensity of such narratives? Neither the culturalist nor the instrumentalist perspectives can provide adequate answers to these questions. To better explain these changing dynamics of golden-ageism it is crucial to explore the organisational capacity and ideological power of those involved in the production and dissemination of golden age idioms.

Finally, the two dominant perspectives cannot help us to understand the relationship between the macro and micro worlds of golden-ageism. While all nationalist organisations espouse some version of the golden age idea, only some of these organisations have been successful in galvanising mass-level support. As Gellner (1983) noted, for every successful nationalist movement there are hundreds that have failed to attract public attention. There are numerous groups and social organisations that propagate a variety of golden age narratives, yet only a few of these attain wider recognition. To understand how specific narratives acquire public support, it is necessary to explore the social processes through which nationalist idioms penetrate and envelop the microcosm of everyday life. The key issue here is to analyse how macro-level myths of the golden age become successfully embedded into micro-level discourses of ordinary individuals and small groups.

Although the culturalist and instrumentalist approaches help us understand some aspects of the golden age phenomenon, they seem inadequate for explaining the changing character of this phenomenon. For example, instrumentalist perspectives are helpful in understanding the processes that underpinned nineteenth-century nation-building, but they are inadequate for explaining how nationalism has changed over the last two centuries and what role golden age myths play in twenty-first-century nationalist practices. Similarly, culturalism is useful in tracing the form and content of key golden age myths, but it cannot adequately explain the role of different social groups in their creation and reproduction. Since the golden age is not just a cultural or economic phenomenon but a political project often pursued by different social organisations, it is crucial to explore how these idioms emerge, develop, and change through time.

Nineteenth-Century Balkans: Institutionalising the Golden Age

Nationalism is a malleable and adoptable ideology that constantly changes through time and space and in this process widens its appeal across different social strata. While in the early and mid-nineteenth century only small sections of the global population were likely to strongly identify in national terms, today nationhood has become the dominant form of collective subjectivity (Malešević 2019, 2013; Breuilly 1993). For example, many recent surveys and public polls regularly show that identification with one's nation is extremely high throughout the globe, and in some cases support for statements such as 'I feel proud to be … [American, Greek, Japanese]' or 'I identify strongly with my nation' is recorded to be over 90 per cent or more (Duina 2018: Tang & Barr 2012; Antonsich 2009).

In the 1850s nationhood was a phenomenon associated with upper- and middle-class individuals, whereas the rest of the population still identified primarily in terms of locality, kinship, and religion (Gellner 1983; Anderson 1983). In direct contrast, in the early twenty-first century nationhood is a cross-class phenomenon that has enveloped the entire globe. This profound historical change is also reflected in the framing and reception of golden age narratives. Whereas before nationalist idioms of glorious past could not easily appeal to a wider audience, today golden-ageism underpins popular understandings of what it means to be a member of a particular nation. This transformation was gradual and slow. It was mediated by large-scale structural changes taking place throughout the world in the last two centuries. Among these changes three processes stand out: the increased coercive-organisational capacity of states and other entities to restructure social order, the widened ideological penetration of different social organisations within the societies, and the expanded ability of large-scale social organisations to envelop the networks of micro-level solidarity. These three processes have contributed substantially towards the widening appeal of nationalist idioms throughout societies. One of the central such nationalist idioms is the myth of golden age, which now reinforces political legitimacy of most nation-states. By focusing on the changing form and content of golden age narratives over time one can also analyse the changing character of nationalism.

This transformation can be traced more clearly with the example of a single world region such as the Balkans where the process of nation-state formation experienced turbulent and violent trajectories over the last two centuries. By zooming in on the changing articulation and reception of golden age narratives in the nineteenth- and twenty-first-century Balkans, one could explore the historical dynamics of nationalist narrative formation.

Conventional historiography identifies the Balkans as the region where 'national revolutions' took place earlier than in most other parts of the world. Traditional accounts have centred on the two Serbian uprisings of the early nineteenth century and the Greek War of Independence (1821–1832), which have often been described as 'revolutions for national liberation' (Gerolymatos 2002). However, recent scholarship has challenged such interpretations by demonstrating that the main participants in these uprisings were not motivated by nationalist ideologies. Instead, the uprisings were a contingent product of parochial concerns, dissatisfaction with the economic hardship and the behaviour of local Ottoman administrators, and wider geopolitical changes (Anscombe 2014; Roudometof 2001). In addition, the majority of ordinary people who either took part in these violent events or were directly affected by them were illiterate peasants who had no understanding what a nation is. Hence invoking nationalist golden age narratives in this context did not make much sense.

The imagery of the heroic past became much more relevant once the Balkan states achieved partial or full independence in the nineteenth century. Thus, the governments of Greece, Serbia, Montenegro, Bulgaria, Romania, and later Albania all invested heavily in propagandistic campaigns that glorified their ethnic predecessors. For example, post-1881, Romanian rulers devoted substantial resources to propagate an idea that the two unified principalities of Moldavia and Wallachia that composed the new kingdom of Romania represented a direct link with the 'glorious ancient Romanians' traced back to the Dacian tribes and ancient Romans as well as medieval rulers such as Michael the Brave (1558–1601) and Stephen the Great (1440–1504) (Hitchins 2014).

This emphasis on glorious ethnic predecessors was particularly pronounced in nationalist narratives that were generated by state officials and nationalist intellectuals in Serbia, Bulgaria, and Montenegro. In all three cases golden age myths were centred on their respective medieval kingdoms – the Bulgarian empire under Simeon the Great (893–927), the Serbian empire under Tsar Dušan (1308–1355), and the Montenegrin principality of Dioclea under Mihailo (1046–1081) and Constantine Bodin (1081–1101).

In the Bulgarian case the focus was on demonstrating 'the unbroken continuity' between the principality of Bulgaria (1878) and later the kingdom of Bulgaria (1908) with the medieval empire of Simeon the Great. Hence the mass media, school textbooks, national calendars, novels, public sphere discussions, and many other avenues were saturated with narratives and visual images of the great medieval Bulgaria. For example, school textbooks depicted Simeon the Great as a Bulgarian nationalist who was the first to unify all the Bulgarians in one state: 'Now the whole Bulgarian nation, which inhabits almost the whole Balkan peninsula, was united for the first time in one state, under the rule of one king's will [Simeon I]; now it made up one whole, towards which all our kings aspired and toward which we, too, aspire now' (Ganchev 1888:24). Simeon's empire was hailed as one of the largest states in Europe at that time and also as an entity that was socially and economically among the most advanced polities of its era. In nationalist narratives Simeon's reign was regularly depicted as the golden era of Bulgarian culture – the time when Bulgaria was a beacon of the literary and spiritual life of the Slavs (Lalkov 1997). This period has often been described as a time of cultural renewal with the introduction of the new Cyrillic alphabet and the development of the Bulgarian Orthodox Church.

By the mid- and late nineteenth century, Serbian society was characterised by similar attempts to establish continuity with the glorious past. Just as in the Bulgarian case here too the emphasis was on tracing the links between the internationally recognised independent principality of Serbia (1878) and later kingdom of Serbia (1882) with the medieval empire of Tsar Dušan from the Nemanjić dynasty. State officials, intellectuals, journalists, priests, and educationalists, as well as members of the military and police, were all involved in propagating narratives of Dušan's empire as the cradle of Serbian nationhood. The focus was on the size of the empire, which at its peak in 1355 stretched throughout most of the Balkans – from the Danube to the Gulf of Corinth. Emperor Dušan was also credited with the renewal and increased prosperity of the Serbian Orthodox Church, which was upgraded from archbishopric to the patriarchate. The emperor was also praised for introducing the first legal system, Dušan's Code, which combined civil and canon law. This period was associated with economic prosperity and military might. Late nineteenth-century Serbian mass media and school textbooks contain numerous references to the golden age of Dušan's empire. Dušan's Code was regularly described as 'as the most precious monument that the medieval period has left us' (Novaković 1870:x). Similarly, school textbooks from the late nineteenth century depict the medieval Serbian state as the 'golden age of Serbdom'. One nineteenth-century textbook author proclaims: 'Neither before nor after was Serbia so powerful and famous' as under Dušan's rule. And the 'Serbian empire flourished' under this man of 'tall stature, a handsome face, resolute and brave' (Jelavich 1990:221).

Very similar processes were also present in post-independence Montenegro. Although the principality of Montenegro was established in 1852, full international recognition was only confirmed at the Berlin congress in 1878. The principality became a kingdom in 1910. During this period the government, intellectuals, priests, teachers, and other influential state officials were involved in the processes of establishing ideological continuity between the medieval states of Dioclea and later Zeta and the newly created Montenegrin state. Just as in the case of Serbia and Bulgaria, the public sphere was saturated with imagery that glorified the golden age of Montenegrin statehood, as represented by medieval rulers such as Mihailo Vojislavljević, his son Constantine Bodin, and Jovan Vladimir. These rulers were credited with military capability, enlightened politics, skilful diplomacy, and economic prosperity. Printed media and textbooks published in this period emphasise that the Pope bestowed the title 'King of Slavs' on Mihailo as a result of his decision to leave the Byzantine influence and side with the Western Church. Mihailo was also celebrated for conquering new lands such as Rascia, which was taken from the Byzantine empire in the 1060s. Bodin was also associated with the further territorial expansion of Dioclea, transforming it into one of the most powerful polities in the region. Hence the Montenegrin case is very similar to that of Bulgaria and Serbia. In all three medieval statehood was depicted as the golden age of nationhood. This is visible throughout the public sphere in late nineteenth-century Montenegro. For example, the mass media and educational system were full of descriptions of ancient glories: 'The whole world knows ... that Montenegro has always been independent since time immemorial.... Its fields and its rugged mountains have been covered in blood of the Montenegrin people.' 'Montenegro was never conquered and the whole magnificent past of Montenegro is enormous, inconvertible, strongest and the holiest proof that [this country] was always free, independent, and autonomous' (*Glas Crnogorca* 9/6/1873:1). '[T]his is a time to create a new epoch in the history of proud Zeta.... [T]he Montenegrin people are capable of creating a new and better future by remembering bravery of victims that were sacrificed to the altar of their freedom in five centuries of fighting with the enormous Turkish power' (*Glas Crnogorca* 10/3/1879:3).

What is distinct about these late nineteenth-century portrayals of the golden age is their top-down character. In all these cases the narratives of glorious past were created, developed, and perpetuated by state officials and cultural and political elites: the educationalists and teachers, state administrators, loyal journalists, cultural activists close to the regime, nationalist intellectuals, and representatives of the local government

(Malešević 2019; Baar 2010). This finding is partially in line with the arguments articulated by Hobsbawm. However, there is also an important difference. While Marxists such as Hobsbawm emphasise the economic aspects of this process, the focus should be on the political power and role of the state. While class dimension is important in this process, it cannot be reduced to ownership of means of production and economic power alone. Instead, the top-down nationalisation of population was a state-generated phenomenon. Furthermore, Bauman's point about the preservation of the status quo does not apply here. Instead, political, economic, and cultural elites in the Balkans were focused on enacting rather than preventing social change. The nationalist myths of the golden age were deployed not to preserve the existing order but to generate a new one.

In this context the lionisation of medieval kingdoms was not a spontaneous reflection of different social strata. Instead, this was a top-down project aimed at accomplishing two principal political goals: (1) to legitimise the very existence of the newly created states and to justify territorial expansion in the near future, and (2) to create culturally and politically homogenous populations that would be loyal to the new states.

First, the gradual independence of the Balkan states was achieved through the combination of changed geopolitical conditions and the increasingly organised resistance to imperial rule. With the organisational weakening of the Ottoman empire and the continuous pressure from the Western empires, Ottoman rulers were forced to concede independence to Greece and autonomies to Serbia, Bulgaria, Montenegro, and the two provinces that would eventually become Romania. These external geopolitical shifts fostered internal changes within local resistance movements, which became more organised and capable of challenging the local Ottoman administration. Once this process was in full motion, it accelerated until all Balkan states had become sovereign polities in the late nineteenth and early twentieth century. However, nominal independence was not the end of this process. As the borders of new polities remained contested within and outside the region, the new governments focused extensively on legitimising their claims for specific territories. This includes the legitimation of territories under their control that may have been claimed by other Balkan states or providing justification for the claims over territories that were currently controlled by other states in the region. Hence invoking the narratives of the golden age with a focus on the resurrection of the glories of medieval kingdoms was a crucial mechanism to justify territorial expansion. Referring to the 'vast' medieval kingdoms that spread throughout the Balkans in the past provided legitimacy for the envisaged enlargement of existing states. Hence many political groups in the Balkans devised elaborate programmes of state expansion that advocated unification of all members of one's ethno-nation into a single state. Starting with the Megali idea that envisioned an enlarged Greek state that would include all ethnic Greeks, other nationalist movements in the Balkans propagated the ideas of Greater Serbia, Greater Bulgaria, Greater Romania, Greater Croatia, or Greater Albania (Malešević 2019; Roudometof 2001). Golden age narratives underpinned these ideological blueprints for territorial expansion.

Second, since the majority of the population in the mid- to late nineteenth-century Balkans were still illiterate and lived in the relatively isolated countryside, their understanding of the past differed substantially from the small, yet politically much more influential, urban populace. With ever-increasing industrialisation, urbanisation, and expansion of the educational system in the major cities, urban areas had gradually become more exposed to nationalist ideas and the urban population was more nationalist than their rural counterparts. As the leaderships of the newly independent states were eager to modernise their polities, they invested primarily in the development of state structure: the administrative sector, educational institutions, military, and police. In most cases the development of the urban areas was attained at the expanse of the countryside. Although small farmers generated food and other resources for the urban population, they were regularly exploited and underpaid for their products. In addition, many governments in the late nineteenth-century Balkans were reluctant to undergo full-scale land reform, thus leaving the majority of farmers in a state of constant impoverishment (Roudometof 2001). These highly unequal structural conditions created a state of distrust between the majority rural population and the minority urban populace. This inherent distrust was countered by the governments through intensified attempts to culturally homogenise the predominantly rural population in order to increase their political loyalty to the new states. Thus, the governments of all Balkan states devoted substantial resources and energies to transform nationally ambiguous peasantry into the loyal and proud Serbs, Greeks, Montenegrins, Romanians, or Bulgarians. The key vehicles of this mass-scale nationalist transformation were the educational system, cultural institutions, mass media, and military draft. In all of these cases the myth of the golden age played an important role.

The expansion of the educational system throughout society was decisive in turning the mostly illiterate peasantry into nationally conscious Serbs, Greeks, Bulgarians, or Romanians. This was a difficult and protracted process, as all Balkan states had very low literacy rates. For example, in 1864, 95.8 per cent of population in Serbia were illiterate. In Bulgaria even in 1884 95.5 per cent of male and 98.5 per cent of female population were illiterate. Even in Greece the majority of population were illiterate: in 1840, 87.5 per cent male and 93.7 per cent female citizens (Roudometof 2001). The first primary school was opened in Montenegro only in 1834 and in Albania in 1887 (Biondich 2011; Roudometof 2001). By the beginning of the twentieth century, educational systems had developed substantially throughout the region as the states invested heavily in the establishment of new schools and other educational institutions. For example, the Bulgarian budget for education increased from 1.5 per cent in 1879 to 11.2 per cent in 1911 (Biondich 2011:54). The Serbian government also invested substantially in building schools, and the number of primary schools increased from 143 in 1843 to 441 in 1870, while the total number of pupils rose steeply from 4,400 to 23,346 (Ćunković 1971). With the expansion of education throughout the Balkans, the literacy rates also increased. In Serbia by 1903 the literacy rate was 55 per cent in the cities and 24 per cent in the countryside (Stojanović 2017:1). Hence the schools became the central medium for nationalisation of the mostly peasant children. In these schools, pupils were exposed daily to nationalist interpretations of the past, with golden age narratives featuring prominently in the curriculum. For example, history, geography, and other textbooks used in late nineteenth-century Bulgaria, Serbia, and Montenegro all devoted many lessons to their respective medieval kingdoms (Jelavich 1990). One such textbook describes Serbian emperor Dušan as a ruler who was 'wise and strong', 'loved freedom', and had 'a beautiful soul'. The textbook author insists that the emperor was 'the tallest, most handsome, and strongest man of his times' and as such he 'ennobled Serbian arms, elevated the nation's fame, and enlightened the Serbian name' (Jelavich 1990:128).

Golden age narratives also featured prominently in the new venues of 'high culture': theatres, museums, concert halls, broadcasting, literature, learned societies, and visual arts. For example, in the second half of nineteenth century, the Serbian cultural scene was inundated with theatrical plays and musical performances that glorified the medieval Serbian state and its rulers such as *Nemanja* (shown between 1892 and 1913), *The Crowning of Dušan* (1904) or *Fatherland* (1875–1912). The Serbian parliament even stipulated in 1887 that theatres increase the number of Serbian plays at the expense of foreign imports (Popović 1899:36).

Similarly, the new Bulgarian rulers invested heavily in the nationalisation of their citizens through its ever-increasing support for cultural and political programmes that glorified medieval Bulgaria. Hence theatrical plays about medieval kings including Simeon the Great, Boris I, and Ivan Assen II were staged regularly in the late nineteenth and early twentieth century. Novels and popular books about medieval rulers such as Fani Popova-Mutafova's *Ivan Assen II* or Yordan Vendikov's *Wars for the Unification of Bulgaria in the 12th Century* were supported by the ministry of education. The state-controlled mass media was also an important vehicle of nationalist images, with newspapers and periodicals regularly featuring articles exalting the virtues of medieval kingdoms in Bulgaria, Serbia, Montenegro, and other Balkan countries. For instance, the main Montenegrin information outlets in the later nineteenth century, such as *Crnogorac*, *Cetinjski vjesnik*, and *Glas Crnogorca*, would make extensive references to the ancient glories of Montenegrin, including the medieval kingdoms and rulers of Dioclea and Zeta. The period of medieval history was often characterised as being splendid and heroic: 'The Montenegrin people have a wonderful history, and its worst enemies would have to recognise that what [Montenegrins] have endured no other people would be able to endure … for the bravery and the love of their country the Montenegrin people have no equals as Montenegrin people [were able to survive] in a rugged terrain where other peoples would vanish' (*Glas Crnogorca*, 5/5/1873:3) and '[Our people] know how much precious blood has been spilled from the time Zeta fell [to the Ottomans], it was almost four hundred years, four hundred years of woes and misery, four hundred years of spilled human blood, four hundred years of glory and greatness, Montenegrin bravery is felt by … the sons of Montenegro' (*Glas Crnogorca* 10/3/1879:3).

The military draft was another important mechanism for the nationalist socialisation of the peasant population. Although in the nineteenth century conscription was mostly voluntary, with the intensification of warfare in the late nineteenth and early twentieth century more individuals were recruited. With the onslaught of the Balkan wars of 1912–1913 and World War I most Balkan states introduced compulsory military service. The military establishment played an important role in transforming young, mostly illiterate, and nationally ambiguous peasant recruits into patriotic soldiers. In this process narratives of golden age were an important didactic device used by military establishments to portray current wars as a direct continuation of medieval conflicts. Thus, the militaries were often responsible for providing mass-scale literacy courses to illiterate recruits. These courses focussed not only on enabling individuals to read but also on inculcating specific nationalist values that would turn recruits into loyal Greeks, Serbs, or Bulgarians. Military manuals and other documents that young recruits were required to read while in the military were steeped in depictions and imagery of the glorious national past (Bozeva Abazi 2007; Kaytchev 2015; Roudemetof 2001; Posen 1993).

Hence, the arguments developed by the culturalists and instrumentalists cannot adequately capture the dynamics of the golden age phenomenon. This was not an act of cultural continuity whereby all members of a nation spontaneously embraced national myths (Pantelić 2011). Neither was this an economic process driven by the self-interest of the ruling class bent on preserving the status quo. Instead, golden-ageism was a structurally driven political project focused on enacting a specific social change: in the nineteenth and early twentieth century narratives of the golden age were deployed in a top-down fashion to transform mostly nationally ambiguous peasants into a nationalist population loyal to their new states.

In this context nationalist myths of the golden age served largely as didactic stories that would help ordinary individuals navigate new nationalist realities. The key agents behind this project were the state administrators, who were focused on centralising and modernising the new polities.

Twenty-first-Century Balkans: Embedding the Golden Age Narratives

Both Bauman and Smith emphasise that the myths of the golden age serve a particular social role in the contemporary world. While for Smith they establish a sense of cultural continuity between generations and as such make nationhood meaningful, for Bauman proliferation of the imagery of the glorious past represents an attempt to make the population subservient in order to control the economic structures of society. Nevertheless, both interpretations are inadequate for explaining the changing dynamics of nationalist narratives. Although Smith develops a longue durée understanding of this process, his cultural determinism prevents him from identifying the historical and political variability of golden age narratives. In other words, for Smith (1991) nation formation is largely a one-way process – from premodern ethnies to modern nations – and in this context the myths of the golden age only facilitate this transition. For Bauman nationalism is a phenomenon of the past: a retrotopia invoked to conceal the structural irrationalities of the neoliberal present. However, neither of these two approaches is helpful for understanding how and why golden age mythologies transform across time and space and why they maintain public resonance. Rather than being stable and fixed nodal points, these nationalist narratives constantly change. To better understand the timing, intensity, and degree of their popular appeal across societies, it is necessary to focus on the long-term processes that shape the form and character of golden age narratives.

Balkan societies provide an illustrative case study for tracking these structural transformations. By comparing the late nineteenth- and early twenty-first-century Balkans one can detect how golden age narratives develop, expand, and change. This region had a very turbulent history in the twentieth century characterised by devastating wars, enormous loss of human life, and violent changes of borders. However, this period also witnessed unprecedented structural transformations, including large-scale modernisation, urbanisation, development of state infrastructure, dramatically increased literacy rates, and expansion of education systems. These structural changes played a decisive role in the form and character of nationalism in the region. Hence while in the nineteenth century the majority of the population consisted of illiterate peasantry who identified more in terms of kinship, locality, and religion than nationhood, the contemporary populations of the Balkan societies are now thoroughly nationalised and as such identify strongly with their nations. As the majority of surveys consistently show, the populations of Serbia, Bulgaria, Greece, Albania, and other Balkan societies regularly display very high levels of national pride. Recent studies indicate that between 79 and 90 per cent of respondents in Greece, Serbia, and Albania state that they feel very proud or proud to be Greeks, Serbs, Albanians, respectively (Krstić 2011; Antonsich 2009). While in nineteenth century most individuals in the region lived in remote villages and had little or no interaction with the state, today the organisational power of the state has deeply penetrated most Balkan societies.

The infrastructural capacities of all states in the region have increased substantially. For example, while in the early nineteenth century Serbia had only twenty-four civil servants (Pavlowitch 2002:35), in 2014 the Serbian state employed close to 600,000 administrators (Verheijen 2014).Whereas there were only 800 kilometres of paved roads and no railways in 1854, Serbia today possesses over 30,000 kilometres of paved roads and close to 4,000 kilometres of railways (CIA 2023). The educational system has also expanded beyond recognition: from 16 primary schools with 800 students in 1830 to 3,265 primary schools and 515,572 pupils in 2021 (www.stat.gov.rs/en-us/oblasti/obrazovanje/osnovno-obrazovanje/). While at the beginning of the nineteenth century there was only one secondary school (Belgrade Higher School, established in 1808), in Serbia today there are 517 regular secondary schools with 247,980 pupils. In addition, Serbia has twenty accredited state and private universities (www.kapk.org/en/home/?option=com_content&

task=view&id=42&Itemid=52). The situation is very similar in other Balkan societies, all of which have experienced dramatic structural transformations with an increased organisational capacity of states, development of transportation and communication networks, and huge advancements in the educational and cultural sphere (Malešević 2019:222–228). For example, literacy rates have increased from less than 5 per cent in mid- to late nineteenth-century Serbia and Bulgaria to today's almost 99 percent literacy throughout the Balkans (https://data.worldbank.org/indicator/SE.ADT.LITR.ZS).

These staggering structural changes had a profound impact on the character of nationalism in the region. While in the nineteenth and early twentieth century support for nationalist ideas was largely confined to a small sector of population –state administrators, urban middle classes, intellectuals, and businesspeople, today nationalism has become a mass-scale ideology that envelops entire societies. In this context the narratives of the golden age have proliferated and have also changed their character.

The key issue here is that in the nineteenth century, when nationalism was a preserve of the establishment, the myths of the glorious past were framed by the state employees with the aim of inculcating specific values among the nationally ambiguous populations of illiterate peasantry. In contrast, in the twenty-first century nationalism is a mass phenomenon, dispersed throughout the whole society, and as such it cannot easily be controlled by the state. As nearly all citizens are now fully nationalised, rulers do not need to engage in continuous campaigns of nationalist socialisation of adults. A completely literate population that expresses a high degree of identification with the nation creates a very different challenge for the articulation of nationalist narratives. Despite controlling much of the educational system and some mass media, ruling groups do not possess a monopoly in this domain. Instead, they must compete with a variety of other social organisations that are in a position to formulate and disseminate their own narratives of the glorious past. Hence since the narratives of the golden age do not serve the purpose they had in the nineteenth century, they have to be constantly reformulated to appeal to a wider audience. Thus, when compared with their nineteenth-century counterparts, the golden age narratives in the twenty-first-century Balkans exhibit the following two features: (1) they are developed and propagated more from within civil society groups than from the state (more from below than from above); and (2) as different social organisations have to compete for popular support, there is a tendency to articulate more radicalised versions of existing golden age mythologies.

In early twenty-first-century Serbia, Bulgaria, Greece, or Montenegro, the general population is largely well aware of the 'golden periods' in their nation's past. The public spheres of these societies are saturated with narratives and imagery that glorify their medieval kingdoms in the case of Serbia, Bulgaria, and Montenegro or the ancient and Byzantian periods in the case of Greece. School textbooks; popular culture including films, plays, and documentaries; and many other outlets constantly reproduce imagery of Simeon the Great, Tsar Dušan, King Mihailo, or Alexander the Great, respectively. Over the last 150 years the populations of Balkan countries have constantly been exposed to nationalist narratives that glorified some events and personalities from the ancient and medieval past. Even the communist era that affected all the Balkan countries except Greece was not an exception in this respect. Communist authorities also utilised some golden age narratives to increase their own legitimacy. For example, in Bulgaria, Simeon the Great's reign was celebrated with a lavish drama series indicatively named *Zlatniyat vek* (The Golden Age), which was filmed in 1984 and is still regularly shown on various Bulgarian TV channels. In addition, a brand of high-quality fruit brandy (*rakija*) bears name 'Car Simeon Veliki' (Tsar Simeon the Great), and an Antarctic peak on Livingston Island in the South Shetland Islands was named Simeon Peak on the suggestion of the Bulgarian delegation. Similarly, communist authorities in Serbia and Montenegro regularly commemorated and glorified events associated with their respective medieval kingdoms. Both Tsar Dušan and King Mihailo were incorporated into the communist narrative of resistance to foreign invasions and as such were celebrated as the predecessors of the Yugoslav project. Many theatrical performances and documentary films have been made about these medieval states, and several successful books such as the 1987 historical novel *Stefan Dušan* by Slavomir Nastasijević were published in this period.

The glorification of the ancient past has only intensified after the collapse of state socialism in the Balkans. The development of civil society together with the proliferation of new digital technologies have created a space for the expansion of golden age imagery throughout Balkan societies. What used to be a preserve of the cultural and political establishment has now become a phenomenon associated with nearly all sectors of society. By the early twenty-first century the nationalist myths of golden age have largely become a part of common knowledge in all Balkan societies. The political and cultural establishments have continued to reproduce the imagery of the glorious national past in the educational system, mass media, and public sphere. However, with the political liberalisation and democratisation of 1990s and the proliferation of new means of communication, civil society organisations have become more involved in the reinterpretation of the national past. Initially, the key members of civil society were political dissidents who challenged the communist system and who often deployed nationalist rhetoric to delegitimise communist rule. For example, a number of Serbian and Croatian intellectuals such as Dobrica Ćosić, Gojko Đogo, Franjo Tuđman, and Marko Veselica, among others, have used the golden age myths of Serbian and Croatian medieval statehood to delegitimise the Yugoslav communist project (Malešević 2006:185–202).

However, over the past three decades many political and cultural organisations have deployed nationalist narratives to enhance their own positions within society. Although references to the glorious national past are often associated with the political right or the far right (as Bauman notes with his concept of retrotopia), nationalist golden age narratives are in fact used across the political spectrum. In other words, one of the key features of twenty-first-century nationalist golden age narratives is their grounding throughout societies, across diverse social strata, and among people with very different political orientations. This expansion throughout entire societies is in part rooted in the structural changes that have taken place over the last 150 years when most institutions of nation-state habitually reproduce nation-centric understandings of everyday reality (Storm 2024; Fox & Miller-Idriss 2008; Billig 1995). Moreover, the prevalence of nationalist imagery of the golden past is also generated through the competition of organised groups within civil society that can now rely on new modes of communication to reach much wider audiences than before.

Hence in Serbia, references to Dušan's medieval state and other golden age myths are the staple of many civil society groups – from the far right to the anti-globalist left. For instance, the notion of creating 'novo Dušanovo carstvo' (new Dušan's Empire) is present among many sectors of society. Some far-right groups such as the Serbian People's Front advocate the creation of a 'new Serbian kingdom', which would cherish the values of Dušan's Empire: 'The Serbian People's Front believes that it is time for New Serbian Empire–People's State where all Serbs would live united with their faith, history and brotherhood and following their own will and not the dictates of others.' This movement is explicit in its glorification of the medieval Serbian state: 'We should unite in order to restore glory and honour of Dušan's Empire' (www.bobangajic.rs/index.php/vruce-teme-arhiva/416-novo-srpsko-carstvo-narodna-drzava). Other far right and sovereignist political organisations, such as Dveri, Oath Keepers, Leviathan, Serbian Right, Enough Is Enough, Serbian Radical Party, or Movement of Socialists, do not explicitly advocate the creation of Dušan's Empire but tend to see the medieval Serbian state as the cornerstone of the Serb national project and its values as something that should be emulated. For example, the leader of the left nationalist party Movement of Socialists, which is currently a member of the ruling coalition, advocates creation of a 'Serbian world', which would unite all Serbs into a single state (www.danas.rs/politika/vulin-srpski-svet-bi-trebalo-da-bude-jedan-politicki-prostor-jedna-drzava/).

This idea also features in the columns of influential journalists such as Miroljub Petrović, from the high-circulation tabloid *Informer*, who advocates the establishment of a new Serbian empire where playing a traditional single-stringed musical instrument (gusle) would be one of requirements for full membership. Petrović is 'certain that new Dušan's Empire is immanent' and suggests that 'there should be a shrine to gusle in the Knez Mihailova street in Belgrade where the players of gusle (guslari) would play and teach others how to play for 24 hours per day' (Informer 2017).

However, this myth is not just a part of the political programme but has also penetrated deeply into the microcosm of everyday life, including sports, entertainment, and hospitality. For example, at major sporting events such as football matches fans often shout slogans such as 'We do not want anything new but only to restore Dušan's Empire' ('Mi nećemo ništa novo samo carstvo Dušanovo'). Popular sport commentators also rely on this mythical rhetoric. For instance, reporters have described the recent failures of the Serbian basketball team, after many years of success, as an experience that resembles the history of Dušan's Empire: 'Recent fiascos and the lost chances in basketball, in this sport which is the Serbian national sport, are crossing the border between myth and reality. [Basketball fiasco] is becoming a new Dušan's Empire. If Serbian basketball continues to develop in this direction, it will become a historical story about former glories' (www.pressonline.rs/vesti/Nedeljnik/242258/bila-jednom-jedna-zemlja-kosarke.html). In 2017 the highly popular TV series *Nemanjić dynasty – Birth of a Kingdom* mythologised the main protagonists of the Serbian medieval world, including Emperor Dušan and King Stephan. Tsar Dušan is even a subject of the 'first psychobiography' where its author, psychiatrist Aleksandar Misojčić, describes the medieval ruler as being 'extremely ambitious' and having 'a strong sense of purpose and focus on the goal' (24 Sedam 2017).

This golden age myth also features in many websites created by a variety of civil society groups and ordinary citizens of Serbia where the medieval empire is often depicted as the pinnacle of Serbian history. One such video representation, 'The Serbian Empire – Czar Dušan Mighty', uses imagery from various Hollywood blockbusters to indicate the enormous size of medieval Serbian armies (Dusan Silni 2017). Other videos provide animated and documentary portrayals of the medieval Serbian state where the actions of Dušan and other medieval rulers are embellished and exaggerated. In addition, several amateur historical and archaeological groups provide extensive information on the Serbian medieval state with texts and videos that glorify this period. A typical article published on one website is entitled 'Serbian Knights Were Warriors for whom Faith, Family and Fatherland Were Sacred' (www.arheo-amateri.rs/2012/05/srpsko-carstvo/).

The prevalence of this golden age myth and its popularity are most visible in everyday activities. For example, several restaurants and coffee-shops in Serbia refer to this golden age myth in their names: 'Dušanovo carstvo 1', Dušanovo carstvo 2', 'novo Dušanovo carstvo', and 'cara Dušana' (Dušan's Empire). One can also drink a white wine named 'Tsar Dušan'. There are also a number of online games that depict the restoration of Dušan's Empire. One such game – How to Resurrect Serbian Empire – depicts battles between Serbia, Croatia, Bulgaria, and Albania (www.youtube.com/watch?v=1QrLIJY0lME). One can also buy online sweatshirts and T-shirts with the symbols of Tsar Dušan – Otačbina (fatherland) and Car Dušan Silni. There are also children's books such as *Dušan the Mighty – Childhood of the Future Czar* (Stanišić 2017). It is through these everyday outlets of micro-level realities that nationalist mythology is reproduced and reinforced. Nationalism is continuously grounded through these everyday interactions in the micro-sphere of families, kinships, and close friendships (Malešević 2019).

In all these cases and many others, the myths of the golden age are created, maintained, and continuously reproduced much more by the ordinary individuals, groups, and different sectors of civil society than by the state. This is not to say that the state is not involved in the proliferation of nationalist narratives. Instead, state authorities invest great deal of energy in channelling and contesting these alternative interpretations of golden age myths, some of which aim to radicalise the established narratives. For example, to counter the competing anti-government nationalist discourses, the Serbian government has recently invested substantially in the state-wide campaign of resurrecting the medieval heritage. Hence in 2017 it initiated building an enormous bronze monument (twenty-three meters high and weighing seventy tons) to the founder of the medieval Serbian dynasty Nemanjić, Stephan Nemanja, a king of Serbia from 1217 to 1228. The monument was completed and unveiled in January 2021. Similarly, in 2014 the government of North Macedonia financed the construction of 136 structures in Skopje in a neoclassical style, including prominent monuments to ancient and medieval rulers, such as a five-meter-high statue of Tsar Samuil and warrior statues depicting Alexander the Great (ten meters high) and Philip II of Macedon (fifteen meters high). Nevertheless, these projects have been contested not only by the anti-nationalist opposition but also by many nationalist groups within the civil society, which have challenged the official narratives of the golden age and offered a more radicalised interpretation of the medieval past (Montgomery 2018). Despite its formidable organisational capacity, the twenty-first-century state has to deal with a much more developed civil society capable of challenging and often successfully radicalising existing nationalist discourses.

Similar processes are at work in other Balkan states. In Montenegro the focus is on glories of the medieval states of Dioclea and Zeta. Just as in the Serbian case this golden age mythology features extensively in both official and popular narratives of the state's heroic past. However, since Montenegrin society is deeply divided along the ethno-political lines, this medieval heritage is interpreted differently: those who identify as Montenegrins emphasise the continuity of Montenegrin statehood and nationhood over centuries, whereas those who identify as Serbs in Montenegro perceive Dioclea and Zeta as the cradle of heroic Serbdom in Montenegro. Nevertheless, despite these mutually exclusive identifications, in both cases the medieval heritage is glorified and regularly invoked as an ethical parameter worth emulating today. Hence many political, cultural, and social movements and civil society groups make references to the golden age of Montenegrin medieval statehood. For example, the cultural association responsible for the project Montenegrina describes the legacy of the medieval state in the following terms: 'The root of the Montenegrin state and even national being can be traced back to the past that is longer than one millennium while its Christian roots are even deeper. The Dioclean archbishop is one of the oldest in Europe.' This legacy is emphasised as an ethical parameter of contemporary Montenegrin identity: 'Montenegrins have their identity, their history, millennium year old state tradition, their culture and their name. By respecting our values – historical, cultural, national that are scientifically established, we will not only help ourselves and others, but this is also our great moral responsibility' (Montenegrina 2017). Similarly, other NGOs provide detailed accounts of the Dioclean kingdom. For example, the Montenegrin movement and the Montenegrin portal offer a number of historical articles about Dioclea and Zeta (www.crnogorskipokret.org/bastina/istorija/dr-fran-milobar-zivot-dukljanske-kraljevine/). In a typical article on the Montenegrin portal provocatively entitled 'Whose Is Our Dioclea?', the author insists that 'every time when we show pride in this glorious period [of our history] there is a frustration and anger among the employees of the church whose headquarters are in Belgrade' and argues that 'Dioclea is not just a material heritage ... it is also a spiritual thread, a parameter of millennium long existence of people and the state. She is the foundation of our freedom and non-submissiveness' (https://crnogorskiportal.me/sadrzaj/1436).

Documentary and digital content produced by various civil society groups and ordinary individuals tends to celebrate the Dioclean state and its rulers such as Mihailo Vojislavljević and Constantine Bodin. There is a popular YouTube channel (Slavenska Sparta) that features many videos that glorify Dioclea and Zeta, describing them as 'the ancient homeland of Montenegrins'.

Just as in the Serbian case, golden age mythology also permeates the microcosm of friendships and family life, including sports, education, entertainment, and hospitality. One of the well-known academic associations in Montenegro is the Dioclean Academy of Sciences and Arts (Dukljanska Akademija nauka i umjetnosti), which awards an annual prize named after the ruler of Dioclea, the Saint Vladimir of Dioclea Award. There are many restaurants, clubs, and coffeehouses named after medieval states and their rulers: Dioclea, Zeta, Bodin, and knez Mihailo. There is also a popular plum brandy, Constantin Bodin. Supporters of the Montenegrin national football team called themselves Dukljani (Diocleans), and their website provides extensive information about the key battles fought by the rulers of the Dioclean kingdom (https://dukljani.me/gumno/tema/prva-crnogorska-drzava-duklja/).

Just as in Serbia and Montenegro, in other Balkan societies the legacy of medieval kingdoms permeates everyday life in variety of ways. In Bulgaria, Croatia, Bosnia and Herzegovina, Romania, North Macedonia, and Greece, many streets, squares, schools, colleges, buildings, and plazas are named after ancient and medieval rulers who symbolise the golden age period: Tsars Simeon the Great, Asparukh, and Ivan Asen II of Bulgaria; Kings Tomislav, Peter Krešimir IV, and Demetrius Zvonimir of Croatia; King Stephen Tvrtko I of Bosnia; Tsar Samuel of Macedonia; and Alexander the Great of Greece. These historical rulers are also celebrated with numerous monuments, plaques, and memorial sites. The golden age periods are also commemorated on official postage stamps, banknotes, and coins that were created by state institutions but are also used and reproduced by ordinary individuals in their everyday interactions. This imagery of the golden age also features prominently in public and private mass media. In television, radio, and social media polls medieval rulers regularly appear in the lists of greatest nationals of all time. For example, Alexander the Great usually tops the public vote on 'the greatest Greek who has ever lived', while Simeon the Great and Asparukh, the founder of the first Bulgarian empire, often top the polls in Bulgaria. The mythology of the golden age is also perpetuated in sports, entertainment, popular culture, and many everyday practices. For instance, popular baby names in many Balkan countries include Ivan and Simeon in Bulgaria, Tomislav and Krešimir in Croatia, Alexander in Greece, and Dušan and Nemanja in Serbia. The hospitality industry throughout the region is marked by frequent naming of hotels, pubs, coffeeshops, bars, and restaurants after historical figures associated with the golden age periods: Ivan Asen Restaurant, King Tomislav hotel, King Zvonimir Grill, Alexander the Great Bar, Bistro Tvrtko, and so on. Sporting events and clubs also feature names that invoke golden age mythology: Croatian football club Tomislav, sport centre Tsar Simeon the Great (ЧСУ Цар Симеон Велики)', or 'sports hall Tsar Samuel' (Спортна зала 'Цар Самоил'). There is even an astrological website that develops a horoscope for the Bulgarian nation and makes prediction about the future of Bulgaria based on its glorious past: '[Emperor] Asparuh is a living element of Bulgarian history. You do not strain your mind to remember who he is when you hear his name. In the same way, King Simeon, Khan Krum, and others. This is a living story' (http://uraniabg.com/news/interpretacia-na-mundanna-karta-Levin).

Imagery of the glorious national past now permeates everyday life in the Balkans (Montgomery 2018). The mythical medieval heritage not only is invoked in the official institutions of the state or the church, but is integral to the microcosm of family networks, kinship groups, and close friendships. The names of medieval rulers and references to the glorious past of the nation appear at baptism ceremonies, wedding and funeral ceremonies, family gatherings, barbeque feasts of friends, and even on birthday cakes. For example, one can have a wedding party at the Tsar Dušan hall at the Hilton hotel in Belgrade or can organise an annual ritual of glorification of one's family's patron saint (*slava*) that is accompanied with imagery invoking the medieval rulers of Serbia (www.ludikamen.rs/prostori/beograd/hilton-beograd).

Hence the legacy of medieval kingdoms and their rulers is still very strong in the Balkans. However, while in the nineteenth century the commemoration and celebration of this legacy was confined to a very small section of population, today the mythology of the golden age infuses many areas of everyday life and is perpetuated by millions of people throughout the region. While the state apparatus maintains an important role in the reproduction of this nation-centric imagery of the mythological past, it is the civil society groups and ordinary individuals who now have more influence in the proliferation of these myths of the golden age.

Nationalism and the Golden Age through Time and Space

Despite their pronounced differences, culturalist and instrumentalist theories of the golden age share one common feature: they both see this phenomenon as a form of nostalgic longing. For culturalists such as Smith (1997:38), the memories of the golden age entail a collective search for authenticity, a vison of 'the communal past [that] can become a fixation and evoke nostalgia for the "good old days" at a time of rapid change'. Instrumentalist perspectives such as those of Bauman see all forms of nationalist rhetoric, including golden age narratives, as practices invoked by economic and political elites to preserve the status quo. Nationalist retrotopia promises an individualised dream of return to security: 'The yearning to "return to the womb" and thereby re-enter the state of nirvana is the individualised loner's version of the nostalgia for ... Paradise' (Bauman 2017:49).

Nevertheless, to understand the sociological rationale of golden age narratives one has to move away from a literal reading of this phenomenon. These nationalist myths cannot be taken at face value but require historical contextualisation. The individuals and organisations that invoke these narratives rarely if ever show the intention of returning to medieval times. On the contrary, such narratives are mostly propagated by groups that push for a particular form of social change. Golden ageism is a political project pursued by different social organisations to enact different types of social transformation. They are not necessarily a form of reactionary politics initiated by far-right movements only. Instead, they offer an ideological matrix for a variety of groups across the political spectrum. In this sense golden age topoi sustain many different nationalist narratives. Since they operate with publicly recognisable symbols of the past, they often underpin very different political projects. In the nineteenth-century Balkans, the focus was on nation-building and golden age rhetoric was deployed to socialise the predominantly rural and nationally ambiguous population into nationalist Serbs, Bulgarians, or Greeks. Hence the institutionalisation of nationalist myths did not have a nostalgic purpose, but, on the contrary, was a mechanism aimed to intensify and speed up the modernisation process in the newly established states. Golden age rhetoric was not a return to the past but an attempt to project a long nationalist legacy in order to fully nationalise and modernise the predominantly rural and illiterate population. Similarly, the proliferation of golden age myths in the twenty-first century also has less to do with nostalgic longing and much more with competition between different social and political groups for public attention. In this context such groups deploy golden age myths precisely because they are familiar and recognisable symbols of nationhood. By using shared mythological knowledge and sometimes radicalising it in the process, such groups make themselves visible in the ideologically congested public sphere. Hence in neither of these two time periods was the golden age a form of nostalgic longing. Instead, the focus is more on the future where the link with the past provides legitimacy for a variety of prospective policies.

The nineteenth- and twenty-first century Balkan experience also indicates that the myths of the golden age are the prerogative of not only radical right-wing groups. Rather, many social and political agents relied on these nationalist idioms. In the period of early nation-building these myths were generated, disseminated, and eventually institutionalised by state authorities and political and cultural elites across the political spectrum. Glorification of medieval kingdoms in Bulgaria, Serbia, Montenegro, or Bosnia, just like veneration of ancient Greek warriors, was part of the nationalist projects across the region. As such these idioms were part and parcel of very different ideological projects. In more contemporary contexts, nationalist ideas and practices have become fully grounded through Balkan societies, and golden age narratives are now deployed by a multitude of groups and individuals, from the far right to the radical anti-globalist left and everything in between. Moreover, these symbols of nationhood are now embedded in the habits of everyday life and as such are often unconsciously reproduced in day-to-day activities – from being at home with friends drinking brandy named after a historic figure to attending football matches where fans shout chants about a former empire to eating at a restaurant named after a king. Thus, golden-ageism is not a temporary phenomenon invoked by extremists in times of deep social crises; it is a permanent feature of social and political life in the early twenty-first-century Balkans and beyond.

The gradual societal expansion and popularity of golden age narratives stems from the increased organisational and ideological powers that characterise modern social orders. In the case of south-eastern Europe one can chart profound structural transformations that have taken place over the last 200 years. These structural changes have made the proliferation of nationalist habitus possible. The development of the organisational capacities of states, private corporations, religious and cultural institutions, as well as civil society groups, has proved crucial in creating structural foundations for the expansion of golden age narratives. The growth of infrastructure, including transportation and communication networks, together with the introduction of mass education, military conscription, advanced administrative systems, mass media, and the vibrant public sphere, have all contributed to the emergence of a population imbued with nation-centric visions of the world. With dramatically increased literacy rates and later also with the development of new media technologies, the national mythologies of the golden age have become fully embedded in Balkan societies. While in the nineteenth century only a small number of literate individuals were responsive to the nationalist imagery of the past, in the twenty-first century nearly all citizens of Bulgaria, Serbia, Greece, and other countries in the region are well receptive to the narratives that portray their nations as having glorious and heroic pasts. With full literacy, mass-scale national schooling, and daily exposure to nation-centric mass media and social media, the populations of Balkan countries are now fully nationalised, and many citizens are also actively involved in the everyday reproduction of golden age narratives. None of this would be possible without the continuous expansion of organisational and ideological capacities of Balkan societies.

Finally, the deeper societal penetration of nationalist idioms and practices is also dependent on the organisational ability to imbue the informal and intimate areas of everyday life. Nationalist ideologies can mobilise mass support only when they successfully envelop the universe of micro-group solidarities. Thus, golden age narratives have more impact when they become normalised and naturalised in the ordinary habitual interactions of individuals who know each other. The case of the Balkan societies shows how the development of nationalism can dramatically change the scope of golden age mythologies. What started off in the nineteenth century as a state-sponsored project gradually developed, and by early twenty-first century transformed into a mass-scale phenomenon. Whereas the newly independent Balkan states had to invest a great deal of resources and energy to turn peasants into Bulgarians, Serbs, or Greeks, in contemporary south-eastern European societies nationalist rhetoric permeates all sectors of society. While nineteenth-century political and cultural elites lacked the organisational and ideological capacity to penetrate the micro-world of the remote countryside and had to disseminate nationalist myths through other channels, in the twenty-first century the rise of infrastructural powers and new technologies have made the nationalist envelopment of micro-group solidarities possible. In this changed social environment golden age narratives are not proscribed and disseminated from the top only but have become an object of mass production, mass dissemination, and mass reception.

6 From Civic to Ethnic Grounding of Nationhood

Introduction

One of the key topics in nationalism studies is the dichotomy between ethnic and civic nationalisms, where the former is associated with the myth of shared descent and common cultural roots and the latter is understood as a form of voluntary union defined by common citizenship and shared political rights. This conventional understanding has been criticised extensively for its very essentialist view of a phenomenon that is highly dynamic and blurry: most nationalisms contain the features of both and can be more ethnic or more civic in different historical contexts (Tamir 2019; Brubaker 2004). Critics have also pointed out that this dichotomy is often applied in a rigid, Eurocentric, or Western-centric way so that less developed parts of the world are associated with ethnic, and thus exclusive nationalisms, while 'the West' is perceived to be a beacon of liberal and inclusive forms of civil nationalism (Özkirimli 2017; Yack 2012). Some scholars have also emphasised that no nationalism can be based on universalist and inclusive principles and that civic national projects inevitably draw on shared cultural markers (Yack 2012). Furthermore, the historical record indicates that civic nationalisms can be just as exclusive, intolerant, and violent as their ethnic counterparts (Hall 2002).

These criticisms are all valid: such a sharp and mutually exclusive definition is neither analytically nor normatively sustainable. However, a distinction between the ethnic and civic forms of nationalism can still be preserved in a minimalist and sociologically flexible form. As researchers need to differentiate between nationalisms that focus exclusively on shared ethnic markers and those that invoke wider categories of membership, this typology can be still preserved in a purely descriptive sense, avoiding any normative judgements. In other words, one can recognise that ethnic and civic categories are dynamic, contingent, provisional, and not necessarily mutually exclusive. In this sense all nationalisms represent a continuum that includes both ethnic and civic dimensions. The minimalist version of this dichotomy is most applicable to multinational states, where the competing forms of state-centred and regional nationalisms tend to shape the character of social order (Basta 2021). Using the example of the Yugoslav national project one could explore how this dichotomy operates in practice. Furthermore, the application of the civic-ethnic dichotomy in its minimalist form is also highly useful in tracing the transformation of nationalist subjectivities across long periods of time. Hence, this chapter aims to explore how and why civic national projects can be overpowered by ethno-national subjectivities.

The violent implosion of Yugoslavia in the early 1990s generated a voluminous academic literature that aims to explain this phenomenon. There are many valuable studies that dissect different aspects of Yugoslavia's collapse, including the political, economic, military, geo-political, cultural, and ideological processes that contributed to the break-up of this complex polity (Baker 2015; Jović 2003). However much of this scholarship has focused on the character and viability of the state itself, while there was less focus on understanding the historical dynamics of nation formation. In other words, we now know great deal about the processes that led towards the formation and collapse of the Yugoslav state, but there is not enough knowledge about the rise and fall of the Yugoslav national project.

This chapter focuses on the development and transformation of Yugoslav nationalism with a spotlight on its two main incarnations: the Yugoslav idea as articulated in the centralised and monarchic state of Serbs, Croats, and Slovenes[1] (1918–1941), and the development of the Yugoslav project during the state socialist period (1945–1991). I will explore the social dynamics of Yugoslav nationalism as it changed its form during the twentieth century. More specifically, the chapter zooms in on the key historical processes that have shaped the organisational, ideological, and micro-interactional grounding of Yugoslav nationalism. I argue that despite the relatively strong nominal commitment towards building civic nationhood, the Yugoslav project has paradoxically provided organisational, ideological, and micro-interactional mechanisms for the relatively continuous rise of ethnic nationalisms. The failure of Yugoslav nationalism stems in part from its uneven, underdeveloped, or misdirected grounding. It is this structural unevenness that also contributed to the relatively continuous proliferation of much better-grounded ethnic nationalisms.

[1] The state was renamed Yugoslavia in October 1929 following the introduction of the dictatorship of King Alexander.

The Impossibility of Yugoslav Nationhood?

The idea of Yugoslav nationhood has been dismissed by many on a variety of grounds. Some argue that the two Yugoslav states were the artificial product of two world wars and as such a Yugoslav nation was always an impossibility. In Simpson's (2008:49) view, 'Yugoslavia was an artificial state created by the Treaty of Versailles in 1919.' For Payne (1995:171), 'Yugoslavia was essentially an artificial nation-state held together by Tito's domineering personality and the power of the League of Communists of Yugoslavia.' Similarly, Ørstrøm Møllerm (2008:321) argues that 'the artificial nation-state, Yugoslavia, created after WWI, started to fall apart in 1991'. Nevertheless, this type of essentialist reasoning is deeply flawed as it sharply differentiates between the allegedly 'natural' and 'artificial' forms of nationhood and statehood. It is a view that perpetuates the early nineteenth-century distinction between historical and ahistorical peoples, a view most clearly espoused by Hegel and Engels (Nimni 1991). Contemporary scholarship on nationalism demonstrates clearly that there are no natural nations or states. Nation-formation is a dynamic historical process. All nations are modern phenomena forged through the assimilation of local and regional cultural differences. They are products of wars, revolutions, domestic state policies, external influences, and economic, cultural, and political transformations (Gellner 1983; Breuilly 1993; Mann 1993; Malešević 2013). In this sense all nations and states are artificial projects; they are products of political engineering, historical contingencies, and geopolitical changes. So, the project of Yugoslav nationhood was historically just as viable as building the Argentinian, Israeli, or Pakistani nation.

Some scholars have identified deep economic disparities between the north and the south of Yugoslavia or the historically late timing of Yugoslav unification as being crucial for the weakness of national sentiment (Plestina 2019; Voyles-Burks 1971). However, such arguments cannot be squared easily with many cases of successful nation-building that have occurred very late and in societies with pronounced regional and economic differences. The cases of Italy, Germany, Romania, and Vietnam, among others, indicate clearly that successful unification and nation-formation is possible despite the late historical timing. Italy, Mexico, Turkey, and Hungary also show that pronounced regional differences in economic development are not unsurmountable obstacles to nation formation (Özkirimli 2017; Smith 1998).

Others have singled out 'inherent' cultural and religious divides as the key obstacles towards building a single Yugoslav nation. For example: 'Yugoslavia was something of an artificial state, composed of a number of very different nations, with different languages and different alphabets.... [I]ts peoples, Serbians, Croatians, Slovenians and so on – practice different religions' (Collado-Schwarz 2012:58). The idea that cultural and religious differences are an intractable hindrance for nation-formation goes against everything that is known in nationalism studies (Özkirimli 2017; Smith 1998). Many classical studies show convincingly that in the majority of European cases nationhood was forged through coercive and assimilationist practices. From the French Revolution onwards, state authorities devised a variety of policies that led towards standardisation of cultural practices and consequently the obliteration of the local, regional, religious, and linguistic differences (Malešević 2020; Weber 1978). In other contexts, cultural and religious differences have been tolerated and successfully integrated into the national project. Today much of the world consist of nation-states that are not ethnically or religiously homogeneous. The fact that the German population has historically been relatively equally split between Catholics and Protestants has not prevented successful nation-formation. India, Australia, Singapore, Malaysia, Brazil, and many other societies are culturally and religiously highly diverse, yet they were able to forge single nationhood. So, Yugoslavia was not an exception.

Some analysts have focused on the historical legacies and differences in political traditions that can be traced back to living under two different imperial projects – the Habsburgs and the Ottomans. However, this also is not particularly unique to the Yugoslav case. Many contemporary nation-states have emerged from populations that have been colonised by different empires and were still able to forge a single nationhood. For example, several African and Asian states (e.g., Rwanda, Burundi, Togo) are composed of territories and populations that were colonised by different European powers, and despite these different historical legacies many were able to avoid the emergence of separatist movements. Even in Europe some states were colonised by different empires and were still successful at forging a single nation. Poland was divided between Austrian, German, and Russian empires. Finland was first colonised by Sweden and then by Russia, while parts of Romania were ruled by the Habsburg empire and the rest by the Ottomans. Thus, a single Yugoslav nation was still possible under these historical conditions.

Although all these individual factors have certainly played some role in the preventing the development of a single Yugoslav nationhood, none of them can be singled out as a decisive factor in this process. While recognising the complex, historically contingent, and multi-causal nature of Yugoslav nation-formation, my approach will focus on the social dynamics of nationalist grounding. In other words, I argue that the project of forging Yugoslav nationalism was a failure because either it was not able to attain a high level of organisational, ideological, and micro-interactional grounding that is necessary for successful and historically viable nation-formation, or this grounding was misdirected and uneven. Unlike ethno-nationalist projects, Yugoslav nationalism was characterised by uneven, low-level, or misdirected grounding, which prevented society-wide development of Yugoslav nationalism. Moreover, Yugoslav nationalism often developed not in opposition to ethno-nationalisms but as an overlay on existing ethno-nationalist projects. Simply put, despite nominal commitment to civic Yugoslavism,[2] the institutions of the two Yugoslav states provided the ideological and organisational scaffolds for the rise of the Serbian, Croatian, Slovenian, and other ethno-nationalist projects. These organisational and ideological developments, together with the rise of micro-interactional grounding, have played a decisive role in the eventual dominance of ethno-national over civic ideologies of political legitimacy in the Yugoslav political space.

Grounding Nationalism before Yugoslav Statehood

To understand the historical dynamics of the Yugoslav and ethno-national projects, I will focus on the processes of nationalist grounding. As elaborated in Chapter 1, grounded nationalism stands for an array of historical processes that make nationhood an organisationally, ideologically, and micro-interactionally embedded phenomenon. Organisational grounding is premised on the idea that the proliferation of nationalist discourses and practices is dependent on the rise of coercive and organisational capacities – from the initial congregations of nationalists in the saloons, beer houses, and private clubs to the development of well-organised secret revolutionary societies and emergence of large-scale social movements, political parties, cultural associations, and paramilitary

[2] This is not to say that Yugoslavism was always articulated as a civic nationalism only. Some strands of Yugoslavism had strong ethnic elements that emphasised shared language, Slavic roots, and common cultural practices. Furthermore, the Yugoslav national project in all its incarnations was not particularly inclusive towards the non-Slavic ethnic minorities such as the Albanians, Hungarians, Germans, Italians, or Turks. State socialist Yugoslavia made substantial provisions to accommodate ethnic minorities, including recognition of their languages; establishment of primary, secondary, and in some cases tertiary education; development of cultural institutions; and a degree of political autonomy (in Kosovo and Vojvodina). This was a major improvement when compared with its monarchist counterpart. However, the Yugoslav national project always remained (South) Slavic-centred (Greble 2021; Hajdarpasic 2015). My focus here is mostly on the civic aspects of Yugoslav nationalism in relation to the ethno-nationalist projects of its six constitutive nations.

organisations. Ultimately, organisational grounding increases substantially once nationalism becomes the dominant operative ideology of the state, as modern states possess a formidable bureaucratic apparatus and a monopoly on the legitimate use of violence. Organisational grounding allows nationalism to become embedded across societies, as 'ideas can't do anything unless they are organised' (Mann 2005:346–347).

Ideological grounding is rooted in the narratives that promote the idea of nationhood as the only legitimate form of territorial political association where nation is conceptualised as the transhistorical community of fate. In ideological terms, nationalism espouses grand visions of salvation, emancipation, liberation, and an authentic life. By relaying on an increasing organisational capacity (including the educational systems, mass media, and the public sphere), these ideas are disseminated to a wider audience. Nationalist rhetoric regularly deploys the language of righteousness and invokes the moral principles of equality, justice, and solidarity (e.g., all nations should be free). In this sense ideological grounding becomes a vehicle of mass mobilisation and gradually attains the status of a hegemonic discourse of political legitimacy.

Micro-interactional grounding captures the realm beyond the large-scale structural processes that are the organisational scaffolds and ideological narratives. Nationalism becomes a potent ideological force only when it successfully permeates the microcosm of everyday life. Nationalist idioms are regularly reproduced through an array of habitual practices that constitute daily experiences of most human beings in the contemporary world – routinised forms of nation-centric communication, consumption, and interaction. More than any other ideological discourse, nationalism normalises and naturalises a particular form of group membership (nation) through personalised experiences and intimate relationships with significant others (i.e., family members, close friend, peer groups, etc.). It is no accident that nationalist rhetoric often deploys metaphors of kinship and comradeship such as 'our Ukrainian brothers and sisters', 'Mother Russia', and 'fatherland'.

The success of nationalist projects is dependent on the interaction of organisational, ideological, and micro-interactional grounding. Effective organisational grounding presupposes a high level of coercive-organisational power, while the scale of ideological grounding is determined by the ability of nationalism to permeate the social sphere. While these two large-scale processes provide structural conditions for proliferation of nationalism, their success is ultimately dependent on micro-interactional grounding – the ability of nationalist doctrines to tap into local attachments, including the emotional and moral dynamics of the everyday micro-universe (Malešević 2023, 2020, 2019).

The Kernels of Early Yugoslav Grounding

The view that the Slavic populations of Southeast Europe constitute or could become a single nation has a long history. Early concepts of South Slav unity can be traced back to the sixteenth-, seventeenth-, and early eighteenth-century writings of Juraj Križanić, Pavao Ritter Vitezović, Ivan Gundulić, and Andrija Kačić Miošić, among others. These authors often wrote about the inhabitants of this region, and in some cases of all populations from the Adriatic to the North Sea, as belonging to one group – the Slavic people (*slovinski narod*) (Fine 2006). However, the first ideologically and organisationally coherent movement that propagated the idea of South Slavs as belonging to a single collective was the Illyrian movement (1835–1863).

In terms of ideological grounding the Illyrian movement provided the framework for cultural integration. Several prominent intellectuals based in the Habsburg empire, including Ljudevit Gaj, Ivan Mažuranić, Petar Preradović, and Stanko Vraz, among others, have articulated a pan–South Slavic programme of cultural unification.[3] The Illyrian movement perceived the South Slavs as a population with a shared origin and language and as such representing a single 'Illyrian' nation. This was primarily a cultural movement influenced by the ideas of Enlightenment and Romanticism. However, some members also articulated specific political ideas, with a focus on the unification of the 'Croatian provinces' with the Habsburg empire and eventual unification of all South Slavs in a single polity that would be either a part of the empire or an independent state (Despalatović 1975). Franjo Rački and the Roman Catholic bishop Josip Juraj Strossmayer were the main proponents of the Illyrian project who perceived South Slav unification as a bulwark against ever-increasing Germanisation and Magyarisation in the Habsburg empire (Šidak 1990). Elements of ideological grounding were visible in the establishment of the first Croatian/Illyrian newspaper (*Novine hrvatsko-slavonsko-dalmatinske*, later renamed *Ilirske novine*) in 1834, which was edited by Gaj, as well as in the publication of a literary magazine (*Danica Ilirska*), novels, epic poetry, and opera. The Illyrian movement was highly successful in the cultural sphere, as it spearheaded the standardisation of the Serbo-Croat language, and it also galvanised the expansion of new literary and other artistic works in the region. The standardisation of the

[3] 'Illyrian national thought' has a longer history. It articulated the pre-national ideas about the linguistic unity of the South Slavs. This helps explain the relative success of this project among the educated elite (Stergar 2017; Blažević, 2008).

common literary language, based on the Shtokavian and Ijekavian dialects, with a unified orthography, was later codified by the Vienna literary agreement (1850). However, the ideological grounding remained confined to an exceedingly small section of the population. This was essentially an elite movement that had little resonance outside the intellectual and some middle-class groups (Wachtel & Štiks 2019). Nevertheless, its cultural project remained highly influential in the long term, as it directly impacted other pan–South Slav movements in the late nineteenth and twentieth century.

The organisational grounding of the Illyrian movement was much more modest. Although the key representatives of the movement have established various cultural and some political associations, the movement did not create secret revolutionary societies, political parties, paramilitary organisations, nor any other entities possessing visible coercive-organisational capacity.[4] Some members of the parliament (Sabor) were influenced by the Illyrian ideas and were even involved in the Zagreb 1845 street unrests, but as they did not control the state apparatus their impact was minimal.[5] They were members of the small and poorly organised associations that could not extend their ideological programme to the wider sections of society. There were some organisational seeds planted, such as count Janko Drašković's establishment of a reading room in Zagreb as a regular meeting place for the representatives of the Illyrian movement. Furthermore, in the 1860s Strossmayer met the Serbian Foreign Minister, Ilija Garašanin, where they both supported the creation of an independent state for South Slavs (Rusinow 2003). However, after the revolutions of 1848 the imperial state imposed stricter censorship regulations, which prevented further activities of the Illyrian movement.

The weakest link of the Illyrian project was its inability to penetrate the world of everyday life among the majority of population, most of whom were uneducated peasants. In the 1830s, 80 per cent of the population of what is today Croatia and Slovenia were illiterate (Kamusella 2009). Thus, micro-interactional grounding was extremely limited as it impacted a very small section of population – some cultural and political

[4] In the mid-nineteenth century Josip Jelačić raised a peasant militia to fight against the Hungarian national movement, but these peasants were neither inspired nor had any knowledge of the Illyrian cultural project (Šidak 1990; Despalatović 1975).

[5] The only relative exception here is the short period when the Illyrians took control over the Sabor, just before the revolution of 1848. During this period, they replaced Latin with the 'national language' as its official language, but this made their project even less viable as they focused on Croatia-Slavonia only while neglecting Dalmatia, the Military Border, and the so-called Slovene lands.

elites. Illyrian ideas had no resonance in the everyday interactions of people living in remote villages of Slavonia, Dalmatia, or Zagorje.

Early Forms of Ethno-Nationalist Grounding

Although the Illyrian movement was relatively successful in the cultural sphere, its political impact was much more modest. Nevertheless, its legacy was later preserved through the different articulations of the Yugoslav project, which developed in opposition to the ever-rising ethno-nationalist movements throughout south-eastern Europe. Once Serbia attained full statehood in 1878 Serbian ethno-nationalism gained momentum and was a much more influential ideology than the project of pan-Yugoslav unification. The legacy of Serbian medieval statehood together with the Serbian Orthodox religion were the cornerstones of this national programme. The aspirations towards unification were articulated in terms of the Greater Serbian project where many inhabitants of the Balkans were perceived to be Serbs. In Croatia too the Yugoslav idea was weakened by the rise of the Croatian ethno-nationalism, which centred on the idea of Croatian state rights associated with the legacy of Croatian medieval kingdoms. The ethno-nationalist movement was headed by Ante Starčević's Party of Rights, which advocated an idea of Greater Croatia that would incorporate many South Slav lands, as their residents were perceived to be Croats (Uzelac 2006).

In organisational terms, the ethno-national associations and movements had already an upper hand in unifying South Slav organisations. Despite some elite clergy being sympathetic to the Yugoslav idea, most religious institutions including the Serbian Orthodox Church, the Roman Catholic Church, and Islamic organisations fostered the rise of ethno-nationalist ideologies, as they all prioritised ethno-religious differences in their teachings, education, communication, and mass media (Jelavich 1983). Although some political parties espoused policies advocating the unification of South Slavs and in rare cases even the creation of a single Yugoslav nation, ethno-national parties had much more influence across the region, as they were able to gradually mobilise larger sectors of the population around ethno-national markers. For example, the Serbian Radical Party under Nikola Pašić was particularly effective in combining social egalitarianism with Serbian ethno-nationalism to mobilise large sectors of rural population in Serbia. Similarly, Antun and Stjepan Radić had created the Croatian Republican Peasant Party in 1904, which, after 1918 when universal male franchise was introduced, attracted large support among the rural and small-town populations in Croatia (Gross 1981:209–225). The Slovene People's Party, established in 1892, also deployed recognisable ethnic markers to mobilise mass support.[6] Many civil society groups were also successful in drawing on ethno-national imagery to influence popular opinion. For example, to counterbalance pan-Slavic civic movements such as the Sokol gymnastic societies, the Catholic Church in Croatia created alternative youth societies such as the Eagles (Orlovi) and Catholic Action (Katolička Akcija) (Nielson 2014).

In ideological terms the ethno-nationalist programmes were able to successfully draw upon the historical legacies of the medieval Serbian empire of Stefan Uroš IV Dušan (reigned 1331–1346), the Croatian medieval kingdom under Tomislav (910–925), and Slovenian claims to the principality of Carantania that emerged after King Samo's kingdom fell apart (623–658), among other historical 'predecessors'. These programmes were also able to invoke the proto-ideological heritage of Christianity, which was gradually becoming a potent cultural and nationalising marker – the Serbian Orthodox religion, Roman Catholicism, and Sunni Islam as ethno-national unifiers and potential civic dividers. Despite the similarity of South Slav languages, ethno-nationalist projects were able to successfully utilise some linguistic differences to politicise the language policies. Hence the standardisation of vernaculars together with the rise in the literacy rates contributed towards the proliferation of ethno-nationalist projects.

In micro-interactional terms, ethno-nationalists also had an advantage over civic-oriented associations. For one thing, the entrenched traditionalism, conservatism, and patriarchal environment of south-eastern Europe proved less conducive towards the Enlightenment-inspired ideas and practices associated with the development of civic nationhood. Instead, traditional extended families and groups such as *zadrugas*, village communes, and clan and tribal networks were all more in tune with the inward looking ethno-national projects, as they were strongly associated with traditional institutions such as those of religion, kinship, and patriarchal authority (Stein-Erlich 1964). Nevertheless, ethno-nationalism was still a highly underdeveloped project. These were elite-based movements that could not penetrate deeply within the countryside, as they lacked substantial organisational capacity, including transportation and communication networks and coercive bureaucratic power, and their ideological dissemination was largely limited to urban areas and a small section of the literate middle class. In contrast, the majority of the

[6] As Zajc (2008:103–114) shows, this Sloveneness was often presented as part of the larger, Croat or Yugoslav, whole, but Yugoslavianism was more an afterthought than an essential part of their self-image in everyday politics.

predominately peasant and illiterate population had little understanding of what either ethnic or civic nationhood was. They still identified much more in local, kinship, clan, and religious-based terms (Stergar & Scheer 2018; Gross 1981). All of this indicates that in the second half of the nineteenth century, a Yugoslav nation was still a viable option. Although ethno-national projects had a better starting position, they were, just as the Yugoslav project, a minority ideology in the Balkans. Both ideological projects were still largely confined to elites and the higher echelons of society, and as such either could have had become the dominant form of nationalism in the region.

The Under-Grounding of Monarchist Yugoslavism

The idea of South Slav unification was popular among some groups across the region, and many intellectuals and activists were working towards the creation of such a polity (Djokić 2007). However, the first Yugoslav state emerged because of war. The collapse of Austro-Hungary together with Serbia's military victories in World War I had generated new geopolitical realities that led towards swift and highly uneven unification. The provisional government of the hastily created and internationally unrecognised State of Slovenes, Croats, and Serbs, which emerged in the wake of Austro-Hungarian collapse, decided to join the Kingdom of Serbia and the Kingdom of Montenegro to create a new state: the Kingdom of Serbs, Croats, and Slovenes (1918). However, the results of war impacted substantially on the character of negotiations between the two sides, as the Serbian government was able to dictate the terms of the new settlement. So, the new state inherited Serbia's political system and become a highly centralised monarchy headed by the Serbian dynasty of Karađorđević. Despite being a culturally very diverse society that had no clear ethnic majority, the new state was dominated by the Serbian political establishment. This situation generated a society-wide dissatisfaction, most pronounced in Croatia where the majority of political parties advocated a federal and republican organisation of the state. Furthermore, as the north-western parts were economically and socially much more developed than the rest of the country, this become a source of constant tension, as some groups argued that they were exploited by others. Hence the new state was beset by internal political, ideological, and economic conflicts. This swift and unsymmetric unification ultimately hindered rather than fostered the formation of a single Yugoslav nation .

Neither the new state nor the civil society was particularly effective in the ideological and organisational grounding of Yugoslav nationalism.

Ideologically, the new polity articulated and promoted the idea that Yugoslavs were one nation composed of three tribes. As Djokić (2007:21) emphasises: 'That Serbs, Croats, Slovens belonged to the same ethnic group was not even questioned. They were considered 'tribes' [*plemena*] of a single 'trinominal nation' [*troimeni narod*].' When the Kingdom of Serbs, Croats and Slovenians was proclaimed on 1 December 1918, Prince Regent Aleksandar also expressed a similar view as he invoked a single nation in his speech: 'Long live the entire nation, Serb, Croat, and Slovene!' (Petranović & Zečević 1988:138). The term 'Serbo-Croato-Slovene nation' was used often by many politicians and intellectuals. The first constitution of the kingdom, narrowly approved by the Constitutional Assembly in 1921 and with the opposition boycotting the vote, also adopted the unitary concept of a trinominal nation. Even the official language of the state was declared to be Serbo-Croatian-Slovenian. While the king and the Belgrade-centred political establishment conceptualised the Yugoslav project in unitary terms, oppositional groupings offered an alternative model of Yugoslav nationhood. For example, the leaders of several Croatian, Slovenian, and Serbian parties together with some prominent intellectuals initially advocated the notion of 'national unity' or 'national oneness' (*narodno jedinstvo*) that stood for South Slav unification on politically equal terms, while also preserving cultural differences (Lampe 2000). The adoption of a new constitution that lacked legitimacy in much of the country impacted negatively on the idea of a single South Slav nation in the north-western parts of the country.

In addition to these persistent political disagreements, ideological grounding was even more underdeveloped on the structural level. The literacy rates were generally low, with only 54.8 per cent of population being able to read and write in 1918 (Roucek 1954). More importantly, there was an enormous divide between the predominantly literate north-western and large urban congregations, and the mostly illiterate rest of the country. For instance, in 1918 only 10 per cent of the Slovenian population was illiterate, while at the same time more than 80 per cent of citizens living in Bosnia and Herzegovina and Macedonia could not read and write. Furthermore, in 1920 an overwhelming majority of population (78.9 per cent) were working in agriculture, many of whom were impoverished small landowners or landless peasantry. As Gellner (1983) emphasises, the peasantry are not particularly receptive to either civic or ethnic forms of nationalism.

Despite the strong nominal commitment to the Yugoslav project, the new rulers failed to transform the educational system, another important pillar of ideological grounding. Instead of developing a robust system of primary and secondary education with a clearly articulated pan-Yugoslav curriculum, each region largely maintained the educational practices they had used before they become part of the new unified state. As Nielsen (2014:96) emphasises: 'in 1929 schools in Yugoslavia were still not using the same textbooks ... [S]tudents in former Habsburg areas often learned from textbooks that featured overtly hostile coverage of Serbia.' Jelavich's (1990) analysis of primary and secondary school textbooks used in Serbia, Croatia, and Slovenia after 1918 indicates clearly that the Yugoslav project was either a marginal or a non-existent topic in the curriculum. Instead, the focus was on the ethno-national interpretations of the 'glorious past' and in the Serbian case also the promotion of the idea that Serbs were the dominant nation in the new state. In the Slovenian part of the state, Slovene remained the language of instruction.

Similarly, the mass media remained mostly regionalised and centred on the audience from one part of the country only. Since the Slovene language is markedly different, most of the Slovenian audience was reading material, and later also listening to radio programmes, that targeted only Slovenian readers and listeners. The same applies to large minority groups such as Hungarians, Germans, Albanians, and Turks. Although Croatian and Serbian dialects are very similar, most audiences of Zagreb-based mass media were in Croatia and Bosnia and Herzegovina. While the Belgrade-based media had a wider network of readers and listeners, most of their audience was still based in Serbia and among Serbs living outside Serbia.

In addition, the Yugoslav project also faced strong competition from other ideologies, including not only the rising ethno-nationalisms, but also highly entrenched conservatism reinforced by religious discourses and practices, many of which were either hostile or indifferent to pan-Yugoslav nationalism. For example, the leaderships of both the Serbian Orthodox and the Roman Catholic Church were generally not sympathetic towards the idea of forging a Yugoslav nation, as this was perceived to be a potential vehicle for proselytising across religious lines (Calic 2019). Similarly, key representatives of Muslim, Protestant, and Jewish organisations were less interested in promoting the Yugoslav project and more centred on establishing ideological monopolies among their religious followers. The communist movement, which was very successful in the first elections and was then quickly banned in 1920, was also antagonistic towards the idea of creating a single Yugoslav nation.[7]

[7] The official position of the communist movement on the Yugoslav project has changed several times during this period. See Gužvica (2021), Calic (2019), and Banac (1984).

Even agrarian and peasant populist-oriented movements, including Pašić's People's Radical Party and Radić's Croat Republican Peasant Party, were opposed to the idea of a Yugoslav nation (Djokić 2007; Biondich 2000).

The organisational grounding of Yugoslav nationalism was just as ineffective and underdeveloped. The infrastructure of the newly unified country was devasted by World War I and the Balkan wars of 1912–1913. Although the new state invested in the development of key state apparatuses, the focus was on Belgrade and to some extent other urban centres, while the rural areas, the majority of the country, remained neglected. The new state was poorly integrated and largely continued the project of uneven modernisation that characterised Serbian state formation since mid-nineteenth century (Malešević 2019). In this system priority was given to the development of the military, police, and state bureaucracy at the expense of industrialisation, urbanisation, education, economic growth, and the creation of the welfare institutions. Consequently, by the 1930s civil service posts had doubled in size, reaching 350,000 individuals, or 'every ninth citizen'. This was an enormous tax burden on a poor state (Banac 1984:220). Following the unification, many former Habsburg civil servants and teachers were removed from their posts and replaced with less qualified individuals. For example, in 1921/22, 600 teachers were pensioned or transferred in Croatia-Slavonia alone (Banac 1984:220). The state created a relatively large military and police force but there was little attempt to reform these coercive organisations to make them genuinely pan-Yugoslav. Instead, they mostly continued in the form they attained in the Kingdom of Serbia. 'The uniforms, ranks and regulations, as were the principal military and civilian medals, the Order of White Eagle, the Order of Saint Sava, and Karadjorde's Star' were all preserved in the new Yugoslav military (Banac 1984:150). The officer corps was completely dominated by individuals from Serbia: in 1938, of the 10,000 officers of the Yugoslav army, only 1,000 were Croat. The percentage of non-Serb officers remained very small until the end of the kingdom: out of 191 staff officers in 1941, only 53 were non-Serbs (Banac 1984:152). The government was also sympathetic to paramilitary groups that espoused aggressive Yugoslavism, such as the Organisation of Yugoslav Nationalists (ORJUNA), which was engaged in violent activities against individuals considered to be Croatian ethno-nationalists, separatists, or communists. Financial policies, such as the conversion from the old Habsburg crown to the new dinar at a very disadvantageous rate, generated further dissatisfaction in the north-western regions of the country. The country did not possess a single legal code for much of its existence (Nielsen

2014:72). Hence the new state remained organisationally very weak and unintegrated. For example, the communication and transportaation networks of the kingdom were among the least developed in Europe (Calic 2019), and as Weber (1978) emphasises, railways had played a central role in making peasants into Frenchmen.

After King Alexander dissolved the parliament and established a dictatorship in 1929, the new government embarked on a more intensive campaign to forge a single Yugoslav nation. This was reflected in changing the name of the country to the Kingdom of Yugoslavia and introducing an even more centralised system of rule. Nominally, these political changes were meant to boost the organisational and ideological grounding of the Yugoslav project. Hence new laws and regulations were introduced that banned organisations promoting ethno-national causes. The new Law on the Protection of the State (1929) was explicit in stating that all associations that deployed tribal (*plemenska*) or religious (*verska*) names including the political parties, were required to disband (Nielsen 2014:173). The government also disbanded local peasant assemblies and choral societies that were popular in Croatia and banned the use of the Croatian national anthem (Nielson 2014:115). The administrative structure of the country was completely redesigned. The existing thirty-three regions (*oblasti*) were replaced with nine provinces (*banovine*) that deliberately crossed the ethno-national territories (Grgić 2018:458–470). Furthermore, all references to Serbian, Croatian, Slovenian, and other ethno-national toponyms disappeared, with the nine regions being named after the main rivers (and Littoral). The dictatorship relied more visibly on coercive power to police everyday life and to inculcate the Yugoslav project among ordinary people. For example, the new prime minister Živković centralised administrative appointments and replaced all disloyal civil servants with those espousing strong pro-Yugoslav views. The new government introduced several draconian laws that prevented most public gatherings, and severely censored mass media and cultural production. All meetings were strictly regulated, and a police agent was required to attend such meetings, which could be dispersed instantly if the agent considered them to be involved in illegal activities. The police monitored activities of many politicians, intellectuals, trade unionists, and activists. The most influential public figures and proponents of ethno-national projects were either imprisoned or under constant surveillance. The traditional ethno-national days of celebrations were now considered 'tribal holidays', which were largely replaced by highly contested all-Yugoslav state holidays such as Unification Day and the king's birthday. Local officials were responsible for enforcing the celebration of these holidays across the country, but as British diplomatic sources indicate, these actions were mostly counterproductive, as many individuals expressed disdain for new holidays (Falina 2023; Nielsen 2014:123).

The state also supported some civil society movements and paramilitary organisations that glorified the king and his version of integral Yugoslavism. For example, the Yugoslav Sokol movement, a youth physical fitness organisation with branches throughout the country, was spearheading royalist and Yugoslav unitarist ideas. The ethno-national Sokol organisations were disbanded and replaced with the Union of Sokols of the Kingdom of Yugoslavia whose leader, a Slovene, Engelbert Gangl, proclaimed that unified Sokol stands for unified Yugoslav nation: 'One people, one state, one Sokol!' (Zec 2015). The state financially supported the movement, encouraged all students to join it, and shortened the compulsory military service for members of the movement. Similarly, the government sponsored the Yugoslav Peasant Movement, led by Karla Kovačević, a former vice president of the Croatian Peasant Party. This movement promoted integral Yugoslavism while claiming to be an heir of Stjepan Radić's teachings and was involved in organising highly choreographed, large-scale peasant meetings (Troch 2012). The same applies to other pro-government organisations such as Yugoslav Action or the Union of Slovene Soldiers.

However, despite the marked intensification of coercive policies and the promotion of unitarist Yugoslav rituals, the organisational and ideological capacity of the state remained weak. As Nielsen (2014:203) shows convincingly, this was 'a weak state masquerading as a strong state'. Despite increasing its police and judiciary apparatus, the dictatorship was mostly ineffective in creating new organisational vehicles for the development and expansion of Yugoslav nationalism. The civil service was bloated, highly inefficient, and corrupt. The police and intelligence forces lacked competence and would waste time and resources on protecting the authoritarian façade rather than contributing towards the institutional transformation of the country. There was a constant shortage of resources to fund new organisational projects. The country remained underdeveloped, poorly integrated with sharply uneven modernisation, with low levels of urbanisation and industrialisation, and inadequate transport and communication networks – all of which are key pillars of organisational grounding. The same applies to ideological grounding. The state had created many new rituals and cultural practices aimed at glorifying the king and integral Yugoslavism. However, the key props of ideological grounding such as the educational system, the mass media, and the public sphere were still either underdeveloped or unintegrated across the country. On top of that, half of the population was still illiterate. Thus, both the organisational and ideological grounding of the Yugoslav national project remained feeble.

Since integral Yugoslavism was largely imposed from above, it tended to provoke political resistance that ultimately associated the Yugoslav national idea with the dictatorship. Building a unified nation through crude coercive policies and without political legitimacy was bound to backfire. Consequently, and paradoxically, the government's attempt to intensify the Yugoslav national project eventually diminished the cause of the South Slav unification while simultaneously strengthening the organisational, ideological, and most of all the micro-interactional grounding of ethno-nationalisms.

Although most ethno-national movements were excluded from state structures, they were still able to operate through alternative official institutions, informal networks, or clandestine organisations. For example, leading ethno-national political parties such as the Croatian Peasant Party, Slovene People's Party, or Independent Democratic Party were all officially disbanded and their leaders were prosecuted, but they continued their activities through clandestine channels. During this period their support had substantially increased, as evident from the election results after the end of the dictatorship (Djokić 2007). This clandestine experience was crucial in expanding the organisational capacity of these movements. So, by 1936 some of these parties were able to create their own paramilitary forces such as the Croatian Peasant Defence and the Croatian Civil Defence (both entities of the Croatian Peasant Party), which indicates that the Yugoslav state lacked the ability to establish a monopoly on the legitimate use of violence and was organisationally rather weak. The hostile policies of the central government also bolstered support for other non-state organisations such as churches, mosques, and synagogues. The Catholic Church gained substantial organisational and ideological powers: because many Croats had no access to other institutions, banned Croatian political and cultural groups encouraged their supporters to meet in churches. As Nielsen (2014:92) emphasises: 'The government's firm stance against the banned Croatian Peasant Party (Hrvatska Seljacka Stranka, HSS) and against Croat societies more generally often had the perverse effect of herding Croats into the Roman Catholic Church and towards hard-line Croat nationalists. Desperate to avoid fortifying property to the state, even secular organisations such as Napredak (Progress), a Croat cultural organisation, transferred their holdings to the Roman Catholic Church.'

Ideologically, the Yugoslav national project was also delegitimised as it was quickly perceived by many non-Serb organisations to be much more lenient towards Serbian ethno-nationalism while demonstrating hostility towards most other ethno-nationalist projects. For example, out of the nine new *banovinas*, or provincial governments, six had a Serb majority and were governed by a Serb ban; two had a Croat majority with a Croat ban; and one had a Slovene majority with a Slovenian ban. Other ethno-national collectivities had no political representation at this level (Greble 2021; Hajdarpasic 2015). Moreover, in the rhetoric of integral Yugoslavism Serbs were often perceived to be the backbone of the Yugoslav project. This was clear in many speeches of leading government officials, including the king (Calic 2019). At the same time the coercive policies of the state were not symmetrically applied to all groups. For instance, non-Serbs were more likely to be persecuted by police than Serbs: between 1929 and 1935 out of 3,356 convictions for crimes against the state, 66.4 per cent (2,229) were Catholics, 23.9 per cent were Orthodox, and 4.6 per cent (155) were Muslim (Dobrivojević 2006:148–149).[8]

Nevertheless, it is in the micro-level domain where ethno-nationalist projects have completely overpowered integral Yugoslavism. Although organisational and ideological grounding provide structural scaffolds for the development of nationalism, this doctrine cannot became a dominant ideological practice until it successfully permeates the everyday life of most people (Malešević 2020, 2019). Since the Yugoslav state was organisationally and ideologically feeble, it had no means to deeply penetrate the countryside where most of its population lived. In this context micro-interactional grounding was dependent on one's ability to permeate the daily activities of ordinary people. In the highly traditional and conservative world of the early twentieth-century Balkans, much of daily life revolved around kinship, tribe, clan, and village-based small networks of face-to-face interaction. Micro-level groups were involved in shared religious rituals and practices and their knowledge of external world was largely confined to information provided by respected local individuals such as priests, imams, teachers, or traditional village leaders. The Yugoslav state attempted to impart its ideological massages to the peasantry by policing the celebrations of the king's birthday and other Yugoslav holidays and by promoting the Yugoslav unitarist project in schools and local gatherings while simultaneously preventing ethno-national agitation. However, it could not successfully compete with well-established local practices that often contravened the official ideology. As local priests, imams, and traditional village leaders were generally

[8] The statistical offices were not allowed to collect information on ethno-national groups, so religious affiliation was the only available category used to identify differences in the population.

unsympathetic towards integral Yugoslavism, which was associated firmly with the dictatorship, they gradually expressed more dissatisfaction towards these ideas. Once state authorities started harassing such individuals and clamping down on dissent, the local population become more receptive to alternative ideological projects and most of all to ethno-nationalism. For example, the government banned 'tribal activities', including the anniversary commemorations of Stjepan Radić's death, and performances of 'tribal songs', display of 'tribal symbols', and participation in 'tribal events'. Hence villagers could only attend religious ceremonies, which ultimately become the spaces of dissent. As Nielsen (2014:145) points out, such 'demonstrations proceeded without interference as long as the participants did not speak openly against the regime, display Croatian flags, or refer to Radić [and later Macek] as vodja (leader) … In all cases, however, the police took note of the identities of those who participated in the ceremonies.' The use of coercion against individuals considered to be disloyal or hostile to the Yugoslav government generated dissatisfaction, which often led towards passive resistance and occasionally to active dissent. In one such case, when asked by the authorities to sing the Yugoslav national anthem to celebrate the tenth anniversary of king's reign, the Croatian choral group Zrinjski from Osijek claimed that they don't know the song and thus could not perform (Nielsen 2014:182).

With ever-increasing, but highly inefficient, police surveillance of everyday life, the population gradually became more receptive towards ethno-nationalist resistance against the dictatorship. As the clandestine activities of ethno-nationalist groups found refuge in religious and other non-state institutions and as these institutions expanded their organisational capacities, they were better able to ideologically permeate the micro-worlds of the peasantry but also dissatisfied groups in the cities. To use Mann's (1993) terms, while the Yugoslav state increased its despotic power its infrastructural capacity remained low. In addition, as the royal dictatorship lacked political legitimacy, its ideological influence was quite weak . In contrast the ethno-nationalist movements benefited enormously from the environment of fear and distrust – they utilised alternative organisational channels, including religious and cultural organisations as well as sporting and entertainment associations to imbue everyday life with ethno-nationalist discourses of resistance.

The Mis-Grounding of Socialist Yugoslavism

Just as in the case of its monarchist counterpart, the state socialist Yugoslavia was a product of war. In both instances military victories determined the character of state organisation. While in 1918 the Serbian military success was the backbone of the monarchist project, in 1945 it was the victory of the communist-led National Liberation Army and Partisan Detachments of Yugoslavia that shaped the structure of the new state. The political legitimacy of the new government was derived from its ability to defeat the Nazis, fascists, and their local collaborators. Yugoslav partisans were the only significant civic and pan-Yugoslav-oriented political movement that advocated equal rights of all ethno-national collectivities, while most other political and military forces represented only one ethno-national group. Moreover, as the local collaborators such as Ustashas and Chetniks were involved in the mass-scale massacres of civilians, the partisan movement attained more support once they were perceived to be the only political movement capable of preventing inter-ethnic killings (Bergholz 2016). In this post-war context the Yugoslav state project acquired a new, state-socialist form while the idea of the Yugoslav nation received a new boost. Hence in the early post-war years Yugoslav nationhood was conceptualised in terms of 'Yugoslav socialist patriotism', which recognised individualities of different nations within the new state but also emphasised the common socialist future (Wachtel & Štiks 2019:63). However, as this was a partocracy where power was highly centralised within the central committee of Communist party, there was not much actual space for the transformation of ethno-national relations. In these early years the communist leadership was committed to proletarian internationalism and perceived 'the national question' as a leftover from the capitalist world, which was bound to lose its significance once socialism became fully developed (Lampe 2000). Until 1948 Yugoslav communists largely imitated the Soviet policy of developing individual nations within the federal state that will be 'socialist in content, national in form' (Malešević 2002). After the Stalin/Tito split of 1948 and Yugoslavia's isolation from the communist bloc, the Yugoslav leadership devised a variety of new policies that, on the one hand, gradually decentralised power structures by enhancing the capacity of individual republics and, on the other, pursued a distinct socio-economic policy associated with the ideology of socialist self-management. In this context the focus was less on building a common Yugoslav nation and much more on achieving the ideological aims of workers' self-management as articulated by the chief Yugoslav communist ideologue – Edvard Kardelj. Drawing on the works of early Marx and Engels, Kardelj developed policies that prioritised workers' participation in decision-making at the local levels while envisaging that socialist self-management would contribute towards the 'withering away'[9] of the state and the long-term de-politicisation of ethno-national attachments (Jović 2003). These ideological and structural changes were fully reflected in the four Yugoslav constitutions (1946, 1953, 1964, and 1974), which all contributed to the decentralisation of political and economic power, culminating in the 1974 constitution that transformed Yugoslavia into a semi-confederate state structure.

Although the Yugoslav national project went through several very different phases of development, its organisational, ideological, and micro-interactional grounding experienced similar trends (Iveŝić 2021). In organisational terms state socialism was much more successful than its monarchist counterpart. While the kingdom of Yugoslavia had achieved very modest progress in this area, the socialist state dramatically transformed the organisational structure of Yugoslav space. For one thing, the new government invested heavily in the development of economic, educational, social welfare, transportation, and communication systems. In 1945 the country was destroyed by war, and a large number of educated people emigrated abroad. Many households lacked basic provisions such as sanitation or running water. The majority of the population consisted of impoverished peasants, many of whom still used wooden ploughs on the land. Hence the new state had to rebuild the infrastructure but also create a new civil service, new police force, new judiciary, new educational system, and so on. Consequently, new positions were filled by individuals lacking the requisite skills: in the early 1950s 'two-thirds of the leading personnel came from the working and peasant classes' and 'every second low-level civil servant and employee had little or no schooling' (Calic 2019:163; Milić et al. 1981:135).

In the early post-war years the Yugoslav government nationalised much of the economy, including industry, banking, and trade. The focus shifted towards intensive development of the entire country. In a short period of time Yugoslavia's economy experienced record levels of growth: 'Between 1953 and 1960, industrial production increased yearly by an impressive 13.83 percent, which meant Yugoslavia held the world record, ahead of even Japan' (Calic 2019:183). In two decades after the war the agricultural sector was reduced from 75 to 57 per cent while the industrial sector grew sixfold, to 21 per cent, and the service sector to 22 per cent (SGSJ 1979). The new regime was also eager to urbanise the population and to develop better infrastructure including proper transportation and communication networks. Thus twenty-five years after the war more than five million people had migrated from the countryside to the cities (Puljiz

[9] The concept of 'withering away' of the state was originally developed by Fredrich Engels in *Anti-Dühring* (1877). See Nimni (1991).

1977:119), and all capital cities of the Yugoslav republics experienced unprecedented population growth. The size of the civil service kept constantly increasing, so by 1970 there were more than half a million lower and middle ranking officials servicing the ever-expanding state structure (Milić 1981:200ff.). The coercive apparatus of the state also increased substantially over the years. At the end of war, the People's Liberation Army consisted of 800,000 soldiers, many of whom were demobilised (Malešević 2002:128). However, Yugoslavia still had one of the largest militaries in Europe, and its police force was also quite large. The Yugoslav People's Army was composed of 2,500,000 regular soldiers, 500,000 reservists, and up to 900,000 individuals who were registered with the territorial defence units (Živković 1986). The socialist state spearheaded the intensive modernisation, which contributed substantially towards better organisational grounding of Yugoslav national project. Although the state was nominally committed towards the Marxist project that advocated 'the withering away of the state', the sociological reality was very different: the organisational capacity and the power of the state over society dramatically increased. Unlike its highly inefficient monarchist counterpart, the new state socialist apparatus was able to penetrate the social order by taxing its citizens at the source, by regularly collecting information on the whereabouts of its citizenry (e.g., via official statistics, conscription data, birth certificates, passports, compulsory registration for place of residence, registration with health boards) and by policing its borders and collecting data on 'suspicious' activities. As in all modern states, socialist Yugoslavia expanded its organisational power over many areas of everyday life such as education, labour and employment, fiscal policy, health, urban surveillance, environmental planning, mass media, culture, and migration.

Yet despite this impressive organisational capacity, the new state did not facilitate an intense organisational grounding of Yugoslav nationalism. There were two main obstacles to this: (1) the inefficiency of over-bureaucratisation and (2) the decentralised character of state organisation. While in the first two decades of its rule the communist government had radically and successfully transformed the Yugoslav state and society, the rest of its rule was defined by stagnation and overproduction of inefficient bureaucracy across the economy, politics, and culture. As Calic (2019:244) emphasises, by the 1970s the state introduced no fewer than 1.5 million new regulations, while the civil service 'grew eight to eleven times the size of bureaucracies in countries of comparable size'. The implementation of the socialist self-management project generated a plethora of new and unnecessary bureaucratic bodies, which made most social organisations highly inefficient. For example, the air traffic control authority was composed of 52 different bureaucratic units, while the postal service consisted of no fewer than 291 separate organisations (Calic 2019:244; Jović 2003:209). The state was crippled by the constant proliferation of useless bureaucratic units with popularly incomprehensible names such as the Basic Organisation of Associated Labour (OOUR), the Complex Organisation of Associated Labour (SOUR), or the Basic Organisation of the League of Communists (OOSK). So, organisational grounding of nationalism can be undermined not only by the lack of organisational capacity but also by the overexpansion of ineffective bureaucracy. This was a clear case of organisational mis-grounding that undermined the development of civic nationalism.

A second and more important development was the fact that the organisational grounding was decentralised, with power constantly being devolved to the party leaderships of individual republics. In 1969 in a new statute of the ruling party, the decision was made to decentralise power by redefining branches of League of Communists of Yugoslavia (LCY) in each republic as independent organisations that would meet and create their own policies before the general federal congress of the party. Following the 1974 constitution the leaderships of the republics gained even more autonomy whereby each republic operated as a semi-independent entity with full control of the economy, political system, education, health, policing, and even some aspects of defence. Representatives of individual republics were even involved in autonomously borrowing from the international banks and redirected their trade away from the internal Yugoslav market and towards foreign markets. Hence for the much of the 1970s the exchange of goods between the Yugoslav republics 'dropped from 27.7 per cent to 21.1 per cent and four-fifths of production either remained in the place of origin or was shipped abroad' (Calic 2019:241). Ultimately, these policies strengthened ethno-nationalist organisational grounding while simultaneously weakening the Yugoslav national project. As Calic (2019:245–246) rightly points out: 'Political careers were pursued exclusively in the institutions and party organisations of each of the republics, where things were not run any more democratically than they were at the national level. Instead, the system encouraged ethnic pillarization. Except for the military, there were practically no channels for advancement in an integral Yugoslav context and no institutions with a nationwide base of legitimacy.' So, state socialist Yugoslavia generated a very high level of organisational grounding, but this was an uneven and distinctly decentralised grounding that eventually contributed not to the growth of Yugoslav nationalism but to the rise of ethno-nationalist projects.

The situation was very similar with ideological grounding. Unlike the leadership of monarchist Yugoslavia, which struggled to develop a coherent narrative to justify its very existence, the Yugoslav communists were the proponents of a clearly defined ideology – the Marxist theory of history. In this understanding class was prioritised over nation and other forms of group attachments and the state was perceived to be no more than a vehicle for abolishing capitalism and establishing socialism. In this context, building a unified Yugoslav nation was not one of the central aims of the new government. Furthermore, since communists were fierce critics of the Yugoslav unitarist project, as developed during the dictatorship of King Alexander, the new government was eager to emphasise that they aimed to protect the rights of all ethno-national groups. So, the new government recognised not only Serbs, Croats, and Slovenes but also Montenegrins, Macedonians, and eventually in 1968/1971 Bosnian Muslims as the constituent nationalities of Yugoslav federation. Nevertheless, to preserve a modicum of unity while respecting the individual differences of each, the government initially, after the war, promoted the idea of 'Yugoslav socialist patriotism'. Yet from early on it was clear that this concept did not imply forging a single nation. In the words of an influential communist politician: 'We are not talking about creating a new "Yugoslav nation" ... but ... affirming common interests on the bases of socialist relations. Such Yugoslavism [*jugoslavenstvo*] does not inhibit the free development of languages and cultures; on the contrary, it requires these' (Pleterski 1986; Šuvar 1970:10).

To navigate successfully between the Yugoslav project and 'the emancipation of nations', the government promoted the idea of 'brotherhood and unity'. This guiding principle was articulated during the war but gained full traction in the post-war period. 'Brotherhood and unity' stood for the full equality and interdependence of Yugoslav nationalities. The focus was on recognising cultural differences of all groups while striving towards a common socio-political project. This doctrine was also institutionalised through the adoption of a national quota system throughout all public institutions to secure full ethno-national representation. The key unifying symbols of this doctrine were the charismatic leadership of Tito and the collective remembrance of partisan sacrifices and victories during Worl War II (Malešević 2002).

The new state provided highly effective structural foundations for ideological grounding. Literacy rates dramatically increased in a very short period: while in 1945, 50 per cent of the population were illiterate, by 1961 illiteracy was confined to 21 per cent, and by 1981 only 9.5 per cent of population were illiterate (Milošević 2017). New systems of education were put in place, which substantially increased the number of primary and secondary schools. In 1958 compulsory eight-year primary school education was introduced, and by the mid-1970s there were close to three million pupils in primary schools. The secondary school system was also expanding quickly. So, while in 1953 only 6.6 per cent of the population had completed a secondary level education, by 1981 this number rose to 25.5 per cent (Milošević 2017). University-level education experienced the most substantial transformation: while there were only three universities and two institutions of higher learning in 1945, by late 1970s Yugoslavia had 158 such institutions. From 1945 to 1960 the country increased the number of university graduates tenfold: to half a million people (Calic 2019:207; Milić et al. 1981:269).

Mass media experienced a similar boom. Whereas in 1947 there was one radio set per seventy listeners, by 1965 it was already just seven people per radio set. By the 1970s there were nine TV stations and over 190 radio stations, while Yugoslav publishers were printing over 13,000 new book titles per year. At that time there were also around 2,000 different newspapers and magazines and 1,150 periodicals (Calic 2019:198). Such an abundance of educational opportunities, book production, and mass media has historically been an important catalyst of ideological grounding of nationalism in many European societies (Gellner 1983; Anderson 1983; Malešević 2019, 2013). However, just as with organisational grounding here too the structural transformations facilitated the rise not of the Yugoslav but of ethno-nationalist projects. For one thing, the gradual and steady devolution of power allowed for the almost complete cultural independence of each republic. The educational boards of each republic were in charge of devising the school curricula, approving and publishing their own school textbooks, and deciding on which cultural institutions would be financially supported, which monuments would be built, and which mass media would operate on its territory. Ultimately, this created a situation where citizens of each republic were completely oriented on their own ethno-national narratives, including historical, geographical, and contemporary knowledge. Students learned mostly about their own republic/nation while acquiring only basic information about the rest of the country. As Calic (2019:246) illustrates, in Macedonia's secondary schools 'pupils spent twenty-one class hours learning about Macedonian literature and only five hours about the literature of the rest of the country'. As most Yugoslav republics, apart from Bosnia and Herzegovina, had a clear majority of one ethno-national group, the curricula tended to reinforce ethno-nationalist interpretations of the past and present. Although textbooks espoused a socialist self-management doctrine, this ideology was often couched in subtle ethno-nationalist discourses. While the normative ideology was universalist and socialist, its operative discourse was largely particularistic, as it successfully combined self-management ideas with nationalism (Malešević 2002).

Even in Bosnia and Herzegovina, ethnic categorisation was integral to ideological grounding. A key feature of this were the ethnic quotas that were implemented for all significant state appointments, from membership in the central committee of the League of Communists of Yugoslavia to key posts in the economy, military, police, and judiciary. While the use of this 'national key' as it was called centred on attaining equal representation of the three main groups (Bosnian Muslims, Serbs, and Croats), this mechanism also inadvertently contributed to the reification of ethno-national categories in everyday life. Hence as Brubaker noted (2004) in other cases across Eastern Europe, here too state socialist policies facilitated the rise of nationalism. After Tito's decision to remove local communist leaders in Croatia and Serbia in the 1970s, the LCY attempted to regain a degree of political legitimacy through further decentralisation. Thus, federalisation was often used as a mechanism to diffuse political tensions and resistance. Instead of democratisation and liberalisation of the political space, the LCY leadership opted for further decentralisation, thus enhancing ethno-nationalist grounding. For example, even though Tito had purged the leaders of the Croatian Spring in 1971, he eventually agreed to change the federal constitution in 1974, which gave more power to the individual republics, thus accepting many of their demands. This change was also reflected in the ideological sphere, including the 1972 constitutional amendment that recognised 'Our Beautiful Homeland' as the official national anthem of Croatia. From this period until the end in 1991, the Yugoslav national project experienced a relatively continuous decline. As Calic (2019:218) notes perceptively, one's individual success become ever more linked to ethnicity and not to the Yugoslav idea: 'Since upward social mobility was effectively affixed to nationality, the Yugoslav system reproduced the ethnic stratification and competition that actually aspired to transcend with a supernational state of Yugoslav citizens.' With the death of Tito in 1980, Yugoslavia lost one of the most important unifying ideological symbols, and ethno-national grounding gained impetus. Hence ever-increasing ideological grounding was largely detrimental to the Yugoslav project as it enhanced the symbolic identification with ethno-nation groups, not with Yugoslavia.

Paradoxically, the weakness of the Yugoslav national idea was most pronounced on the micro-interactional level. However, in contrast to its monarchist counterpart, socialist Yugoslavia was highly capable of penetrating the realm of everyday life. Intensive urbanisation and industrialisation substantially transformed the patterns of communal living. As people moved from relatively isolated rural areas to the expanding cities, the traditional ties of village, tribe, clan, and extended kinship lost much of their significance in daily life. The *zadruga* type of communal dwellings were gradually replaced by single households populated by nuclear families where both partners had full employment. The number of children born in such families had markedly shrunk: while in 1950 the birth rate for the whole country (per 1,000) was 30.2, in 1991 it was only 13.8 (https://publikacije.stat.gov.rs/G1991/Pdf/G19912003.pdf). Thus, the weakness of micro-interactional grounding was not a product of structural underdevelopment, as was the case in monarchist Yugoslavia. Instead, the new social order had generated novel forms of micro-level attachments, which generally were not strongly linked to the ideological and organisational scaffolds of the federal state. Instead, intense modernisation largely proceeded at the level of individual republics, which ultimately facilitated not the Yugoslav but mostly the ethno-national micro-grounding. Migration waves involving permanent re-settlement from the countryside to the cities largely followed the ethno-national pattern, with the Serbs moving to Belgrade, Novi Sad, and other Serb-dominated urban areas; Croats moving to Zagreb, Spilt, and other Croatian-dominated cities; Slovens moving to Ljubljana; and so on (Jović 2003). There were also significant waves of economic migration (e.g., from Bosnia and Herzegovina to Slovenia), but these were understood to be mostly seasonal or temporary migrations. Furthermore, most Yugoslav citizens did not travel much or live outside their own republics. Close friendship networks were mostly built with people from the local community, who often happen to be from the same ethno-national background. The rare opportunity to live in another republic was almost solely associated with compulsory military service that all men had to complete for one to three years between the ages of eighteen and twenty-seven (Petrovic 2024). However, in most cases they would stay in barracks and socialise with other recruits. Although some former soldiers maintained lifelong friendships, in most instances the links fizzled out once the service was completed. Furthermore, once former recruits were integrated into the reserve forces, they continued to operate in local areas only with people from their regions. Local interactions were often shaped by a variety of ethno-national markers. For example, the fan base of the main sporting teams in football, basketball, handball, water polo, and other popular sports had a strong ethno-national base, with most Croatian youths supporting Dinamo Zagreb or Hajduk Split and most Serbian youths supporting Belgrade teams such as Red Star or Partisan (Brentin & Zec 2018). Hence the deep friendship networks formed through regular participation in sporting events tended to enhance ethno-national over Yugoslav attachments.

Similarly, key family-centred events involving rites of passage such as births, weddings, funerals, and other important events were also mostly disconnected from the Yugoslav project while simultaneously promoting some ethno-national markers. In some cases, this was linked with the religious practices that accompanied these rites of passage, which re-affirmed the ethno-national divides between Yugoslav groups. In other instances, such events offered regular micro-bonding of close friends and family members who usually were from the same ethno-national collective. This was even more pronounced in rural settings, where family life was still shaped by religious practices and ethno-national differences as most villages were mono-ethnic. This is not to say that there were no elements of Yugoslav-centred micro-grounding. In some parts of the country, such as urban areas of Bosnia and Herzegovina and Vojvodina, there was great deal of inter-ethnic mixing in the housing estates, schools, colleges, and places of employment, as well as in sports and entertainment. In these contexts, micro-level ties did cross ethno-national boundaries and multi-ethnic friendships and kinships were successfully formed. It is no coincidence that these urban areas reported the highest level of inter-ethnic marriages and the highest number of individuals who declared themselves in the national census as Yugoslav (Botev 1994). Nevertheless, as Smits (2010) and Botev (1994) show, between 1961 and 1981 only 12 per cent of all marriages were inter-ethnic, and they remained at a similar level for several decades before the collapse of the Yugoslav state. The number of people who identified only as Yugoslav increased slightly, from 1.7 per cent in 1961 to 5.4 per cent in 1980s, but this type of self-identification remained a marginal phenomenon (Dugandžija 1985).[10]

So, despite the impressive organisational capacity of the Yugoslav state and its ability to ideologically penetrate some areas of the wider society, its activities and policies did not strengthen Yugoslav nationalism. This was an acute case of nationalist mis-grounding. The socialist project unwittingly provided effective organisational, ideological, and micro-interactional channels for the proliferation of ethno-nationalist discourses and practices.

[10] R. Petrović's (1987) work indicates that in addition to this relatively low level of ethnic intermarriage outside the large urban congregations, migration patterns show a similar mono-ethnic trend. Since the 1960s one could identify an ethno-national pattern of migration whereby Bosnian Serbs were moving more to Serbia, Bosnian Croats to Croatia, Kosovar Serbs to Serbia, and so on.

Ethno-Nationalism and the Yugoslav National Project

There is no doubt that the failure of the Yugoslav national project was a product of many different factors. However, by zooming in on the key mechanisms of nationalist grounding it is possible to trace the historical dynamics of this process. This perspective allows us to track the long-term trajectories of competing nationalist discourses and practices while also recognising the contingent and ever-changing character of nationalism. This approach calls attention to the conditional, ongoing, and uncertain features of nation-formation. Nationalist grounding is an open-ended, reversible, and always incomplete process that is shaped by dynamic historical forces. Thus, the failure of Yugoslav nationalism was not predetermined, nor was the rise of ethno-nationalist projects in its place a historical inevitability. Instead, by focusing on the dynamics of grounding it is possible to see that Yugoslav nationalism failed twice for very different reasons. While the project of monarchist Yugoslavism fumbled because of its undergrounding, communist Yugoslavism faltered because of its mis-grounding.

The bureaucratic apparatus of the monarchist state never developed an adequate organisational capacity to foster the society-wide rise of Yugoslav nationalism, while its ideological grounding was mostly shallow and reduced to crude propagandistic programmes that had little appeal outside the narrow circle of monarchist supporters. The Kingdom of Serbs, Croats and Slovenes was a disorganised state characterised by profound structural differences. The economic, institutional, and literacy rate disparities between the north-west and the rest of the country contributed to the uneven and weak grounding of the Yugoslav project. Repressive policies against ideological opponents of the new state further polarised already a highly fragile polity. The abolition of democratic institutions during the king's dictatorship only amplified all the structural differences while also delegitimising Yugoslav nationalism in the process. Most of all, the Yugoslav project could not successfully penetrate the micro-universe of everyday life. Instead, the aggressive imposition of unitarist policies associated with the integral Yugoslav nationalism of King Alexander largely backfired as they opened the ideological, organisational, and even micro-interactional space for the rise and expansion of Serbian, Croatian, Slovenian, and other ethno-nationalist projects.

In direct contrast, state socialist Yugoslavia never articulated nor promoted a coherent Yugoslav nationalism. While post–World War II governments invested a great deal in the creation of robust organisational capacity that could successfully sustain the Yugoslav national project, this did not happen as the focus was on the ever-expanding decentralisation and devolving of state power to the individual republics. In this way organisational and ideological grounding proved to be highly beneficial for the emergence of ethno-nationalist projects. Initially, they were monopolised by the communist leaderships of each republic but eventually they facilitated grounding of society-wide ethno-nationalist discourses and practices. With the dramatic rise of literacy rates, the growth of ethno-centric educational systems, and the proliferation of mass media, ethno-nationalism successfully trumped a more civic, and organisationally and ideologically less focused, Yugoslav idea. Moreover, as the ideological and organisational grounding were directed towards the republics and not the federal state, they ultimately contributed to the rise of mass-level ethno-nationalist projects. This nationalist mis-grounding was particularly pronounced at the micro-interactional level: the politics of decentralisation inadvertently stimulated and strengthened the networks of kinships and close friendships that often reproduced ethno-nationalist rituals in everyday life.

These two very different historical experiences of Yugoslav nation-formation clearly indicate that the success and failure of nationalist grounding can originate in very different policies, practices, and discursive frames. There was nothing in Yugoslav nationalism that would historically predestine it for collapse. Instead, its decline and failure were shaped by historical dynamics of uneven, underdeveloped, or misdirected grounding. For much of the twentieth century, Yugoslav nationalism was rarely articulated in direct opposition to ethno-nationalist projects. Rather, it was often conceptualised as something that was lightly superimposed on existing ethno-nationalisms. Even in the period of open hostility to the 'tribal politics' during the dictatorship of King Alexander, there was no attempt to dispense with some ethno-national symbols, distinct cultural traditions, different commemorations of historical events, diverse religious affiliations associated with ethno-national attachments, or distinct language practices. Even at the hight of integral Yugoslavism the focus was not on obliterating existing cultural differences but on incorporating them into the shared Yugoslav project. In this context the main complaint of oppositional forces was not that Yugoslavism aims to annul existing ethno-national collectivities but that it incorporates too much from the Serbian ethno-nationalist traditions while marginalising other ethno-national projects. Hence monarchist Yugoslavism was delegitimised not as anti-national or a-national but as being the Great Serbian project.[11]

[11] It is highly indicative that the political enemies of monarchist Yugoslavia were regularly labelled 'antinational elements' (Nielsen 2014).

To avoid any such potential accusations, the government of socialist Yugoslavia was extremely sensitive towards ethno-national practices, ideas, and symbols. Thus, from the very beginning the new communist rulers were clear that they had no intention of downgrading the rights of ethno-national groups or creating a single Yugoslav nation. Instead, the emphasis was on producing the structural conditions for the further development of all six constitutive nations of the federal state. Even the ethnic minorities received substantial cultural and political rights, including their own academies of sciences and arts, educational systems, and national flags. In this way the Yugoslav project was envisaged not as a replacement but as an overlay on ethno-national projects. In other words, the Yugoslav national idea was lightly superimposed on ethno-national foundations. Hence the organisational, ideological, and micro-interactional development of Yugoslav project did not transpire at the expense of individual ethno-national projects. Instead, they were instituted so as to grow and expand together. To balance between this Scylla of ethno-national rights and the Charybdis of Yugoslav unity, the communist government initially promoted the idea of 'brotherhood and unity of Yugoslav peoples'. Nevertheless, for the most part this kinship metaphor failed to penetrate the micro-universe of everyday life. Later, this idea was gradually replaced by the blueprint of socialist self-management, which devolved all central instruments of power to the leaderships of individual republics and thus unwittingly strengthened ethno-nationalist grounding. So, by avoiding democratisation through decentralisation, communist leaders undermined the political legitimacy of the Yugoslav national project. Ultimately, the lack of democratisation fostered more intensive conflicts between the republics, thus further weakening Yugoslavism while strengthening ethno-national ideologies. In the end the ethno-nationalisms triumphed while shedding the Yugoslav national idea as a lizard's old skin.

7 Nationalising War Victories and War Defeats

Introduction

In *On the Genealogy of Morality* (2023 [1887]:90), Nietzsche argues that 'there is perhaps nothing more fearful and more terrible in the entire prehistory of human beings than the technique for developing his memory. We burn something in so that it remains in the memory. Only something which never ceases to cause pain remains in the memory.' Inspired indirectly by this idea, many scholars of nationalism have focused on the role military defeats have played in the development of collective memories of specific nations. From the quashed Jewish Revolt against the Romans at Masada (66–77 CE) to the defeat of the Bohemian army at the Battle of White Mountain (1620) to the massacre of the ANZAC forces on the battle of Gallipoli in World War I, large-scale tragedies have become the cornerstone of national commemorations. There is now a substantial scholarship on the role major military defeats play in the development of national rituals of collective remembrance (Smith 2003, 1999, 1981; Hastings 1997; Hutchinson 2017, 2005; Macleod 2008; Mock 2011). However, it is still not clear how military defeats impact the character of specific nationalist discourses and whether such discourses differ significantly from nationalisms shaped by war victories. Hence in this chapter I focus on the impact of war victories and war defeats on the nature of dominant nationalist narratives. I argue that winning or losing of a particular war rarely determines the character of nationalist narratives in the post-war context. Instead, nationalism is shaped much more by the role a specific war legacy can play in the post-war social and political environment. More specifically, I argue that the legacies of previous wars are moulded by the historical dynamics of coercive-organisational, ideological, and micro-interactional grounding. I illustrate this point by comparing one case of victorious nationalism (Croatia) with one case of nationalism shaped by the military loss (Ghana). Furthermore, my argument challenges dominant culturalist and state-centric interpretations. Instead of perceiving war defeats and victories as acts of heroic and traumatic martyrdom for the nation or as the caging mechanism of state prestige, I emphasise the organisational, ideological, and micro-interactional role of victories and defeats in nationalist narratives.

Nationalism and War Defeats

There is a certain paradox that underpins the study of the relationship between nationalism and war. Nationalist rhetoric and practice have traditionally been associated with an aggressive foreign policy, leading to wars and the uninhibited glorification of military victories and heroic deeds in the name of the nation. However, scholars of nationalism have focused more on the role that military defeats, rather than victories, have played in the construction of national identities. The central question here has been: 'Why do so many nations elevate symbols signifying their own defeat to the centre of their national mythology?' (Mock 2011:7). There are two main and highly compatible perspectives that have attempted to provide a systematic answer to this question: the ethno-symbolist approach and the cultural trauma perspective.

Ethno-symbolists such as Anthony D. Smith (2003, 1999, 1981), John Hutchinson (2017, 2005), and Steven Mock (2012) analyse military defeats through the prism of collective remembrance rituals. For Smith (2003), nationalism is a form of civil religion that necessitates the periodic worship of sacrificial symbols that sustain a shared normative universe and bind members of national communities together. In this context, war defeats and other large-scale tragedies are framed as acts of national sacrifice. For example, the commemorations of the 'glorious dead' establish and sustain moral parameters that invoke a sense of moral responsibility towards ancestors who made the ultimate sacrifice for future generations. In Smith's (2003:54) words: 'The cult of the glorious dead gives the most tangible expression to the idea of the nation as a sacred communion of the dead, the living and the yet unborn. But, more important, the cult of the glorious dead, and the rites and ceremonies of national commemoration that accompany it, are themselves seen and felt as sacred components of the nation intrinsic to its "sacred communion" of history and destiny.' Military defeats generate a sense of collective sacrifice that is regularly commemorated in ceremonies of national remembrance. For Smith (2009:78) such commemorations for fallen soldiers combine a private grief with collective traumas and in this way celebrate 'the survival of the nation in the face of its enemies and of repeated blood sacrifice of its youth to ensure the regeneration of the nation'.

In a similar vein, Hutchinson (2017:13) conceptualises nations as communities of sacrifice. He also argues that military defeats can play a central role in nation-formation: 'although warfare can produce an integration of state and nation, it is frequently in the defeat or the breakdown of states that a sense of national consciousness is heightened'. He argues that war defeats help crystallise and revigorate national identities: 'the recurring historical revivals were driven by the need to overcome radical uncertainty, by finding concrete models to redefine collective goals and myths of destiny by which to unify and energise populations in the task of regeneration' (Hutchinson 2017:35).

Mock (2012) extends these ethno-symbolist arguments further to show how the symbols of defeat often assume a foundational role in the mythologies of many nations. Nationalist movements often draw on religious myths of blood sacrifice to generate new moral frameworks of national belonging. For Mock (2012:8), the shared myths of defeat are a potent cohesive force: 'It is my view that the prominence of such symbols first demonstrates the efficacy of theories that place mechanisms of sacrifice at the centre of social order but also, more to the point, serves as a convenient way for nations in particular to manage the function that the sacrificial mechanism provides, essential to the cohesion of any social system or communal identity.'

The cultural trauma perspective focuses less on the role of sacrifice in the foundational myths of nationhood and more on the collective perceptions of national tragedies. This approach traces the transgenerational sense of collective traumatic events, which are deemed to be a form of cultural trauma. As Jeffrey Alexander (2013:18) explains, 'cultural trauma occurs when members of a collectivity feel they have been subjected to a horrendous event that leaves incredible marks upon their group consciousness, making their memories forever and changing their future identity in fundamental and irrevocable ways'. Nevertheless, not all traumatic episodes become codified as a collectively meaningful experience of shared pain. Instead, only some historical events acquire this status. As Alexander emphasises, cultural trauma does not automatically emerge from traumatic experiences. Rather, this is 'socially mediated attribution' that entails specific cultural framing and institutional codification. All traumatic events are socially constructed, and cultural trauma is a social process through which events attain social representation. For Alexander (2004:88), 'it is the meanings that provide the sense of shock and fear, not the events in themselves'. In this context war defeats do not automatically engender nationalist narratives of any kind. Instead, the traumatic war events must be framed and codified as such through the specific ritualistic norms and practices. The nationalist narratives can work only when 'collective actors "decide" to represent social pain as a fundamental threat to their sense of who they are, where they come from, and where they want to go' (Alexander 2004:93).

Similarly, Philip Smith (2008, 2005) and Piotr Sztompka (2000) interpret military defeats through the prism of cultural traumas. Sztompka (2000:458, 452) sees cultural trauma as 'a culturally interpreted wound to cultural tissue itself' that transpires in the aftermath of a radical social change such as 'collapse of an empire' or 'lost war'. Sztompka also emphasises the transgenerational aspect of recurring forms of organised violence: new wars tend to awaken traumatic experiences that have been 'preserved in collective memory or hibernating in collective consciousness'. Nevertheless, such events attain full traumatic expression only when they are framed and institutionalised as such. Philip Smith (2005) applies this theoretical model to the study of war discourses in several major violent conflicts, including the 1956 Suez Crisis, 1991 Gulf War, and 2003 Iraq War. These traumatic events are analysed through the prism of different cultural coding. By zooming in on the different portrayals of these conflicts in US, British, French, and Spanish media, Smith aims to show how all wars are dependent on specific and disparate cultural frames. For Smith (2005:2012), 'war is not just about culture, it is all about culture'. In this context cultural trauma depends on the application of diverse binary codes that articulate different conflicts through a variety of cultural genres – from the mundane and the tragic to the romantic and the apocalyptic.

Beyond Heroic Sacrifice and Cultural Trauma

The ethno-symbolism and the cultural trauma perspectives help us understand how war experiences and particularly major military defeats shape society-wide narratives of sacrifice and shared moral responsibility towards one's nation. There is no doubt that many nationalist narratives draw extensively on the myths of collective sacrifice to generate a degree of social cohesion. Traumatic experiences from the past certainly do require specific cultural coding and narrating so they could resonate successfully across the wider sections of the population. It is difficult to imagine nationalism without commemorations, rituals, and sacrificial symbolism. Nevertheless, there is much more to wars than cultural framing. War victories and defeats are first and foremost material events that involve a wide gamut of political, economic, ideological, and military processes. As I have argued before, neo-Durkheimian approaches such as ethno-symbolism and the cultural trauma perspective combine structural functionalism with cultural determinism and as such cannot adequately explain the complexity and historical variability of social action (Malešević 2019, 2010:68–70). These perspectives overemphasise culture at the expense of political motives, economic interests, social conflicts, geopolitical factors, and many other variables. Hence culturalist explanations cannot account for the uneven historical experiences of military defeats and victories. Why are some war defeats extensively commemorated while others are ignored or marginalised? Culturalist perspectives also cannot explain the timing, direction, and the scale of war commemorations: Why are some military defeats extensively commemorated in some years and almost completely neglected in other years? Why is the same event commemorated differently in different decades? For example, as Brubaker and Feischmidt (2002:738–739) show, Hungarian, Slovak, and Romanian commemorations of the 1848 revolutionary defeats have constantly changed – from aggressive and particularistic ethno-nationalist celebrations that glorify national liberation to more universalist-focused narratives where '1848 stands for a civic, democratic, modernizing Eastern Europe, casting off the vestiges of feudalism, autocracy, and Empire, and joining the West on a progressive developmental trajectory leading to the modern market economy and liberal democratic polity'. More recently, such commemorations have shifted towards ethno-nationalism yet again (Molnar 2023).

Second, the culturalist perspectives overemphasise the integrative quality of cultural traumas and the myths of collective sacrifice. The epistemological idealism that underpins these perspectives leaves no room for the political manipulation, social polarisation, or competing organisational logic that can shape the character of such commemorations. The framing of cultural traumas and the myths of blood sacrifice entails the presence of effective political agents and potent social organisations capable of generating and managing such public events. These activities often involve political contestation, disagreements, and rival claims among different groups. For example, the 1916 Easter Rising has traditionally been commemorated differently and separately by political adversaries in Irish society: while the government parties such as Fianna Fail and Fine Gael tended to glorify the independence of the existing Irish state and downplay the violent character of this military defeat, oppositional groups including Sinn Fein or other left-wing movements tend to emphasise the unfinished project of Irish unification (Averill 2019). Thus, there is nothing automatic and self-evident in the commemorations of military defeats.

Third, neo-Durkheimian approaches tend to exaggerate the role of sacrifice and trauma in forging a sense of shared nationhood. Anthony Smith (1998:128) emphasises that one's willingness to die for their nation is a powerful indicator of the role sacrifice plays in nationalist narratives, 'the frequent willingness on the part of the unlettered and poor to make great sacrifices and even court death to defend their countries'. However, the link between the actual sacrifice and symbolic framing of national martyrdom is rarely, if ever, direct. Instead, as Alexander rightly acknowledges, trauma, including sacrifice, can become a society-wide phenomenon only as a 'socially mediated attribution'. There have been many acts of self-sacrifice for others that have never been codified as instances of national martyrdom. On the other hand, many nationalist narratives glorify acts of self-sacrifice that have a dubious or no historical record, such as the case of Serbian prince Lazar, who in nationalist narratives dies on Kosovo Polje by opting for death and 'heavenly kingdom' over 'worldly wealth and betrayal of his nation to a foreign oppressor' (Silber & Little 1995:75). The key issue here is that the acts of self-sacrifice can become socially meaningful only when specific groups and social organisations invest time, resources, and energy to make such acts publicly visible, politically meaningful, and institutionalised by specific social organisations. Alexander recognises this relatively arbitrary character of narratives that invoke collective sacrifice and trauma, but he does not analyse the organisational logic that underpins this process. In other words, neo-Durkheimian perspectives tend to overemphasise the norm-governed behaviour and ignore the political, ideological, and economic processes that make these myths of traumatic sacrifice believable.

Finally, the hard culturalist interpretations of war defeats often conflate the macro and micro social worlds and as such cannot account for the direction of the causal links between the two. For the neo-Durkheimians, nationalism is a phenomenon that permeates entire societies as a single, uniform, and synchronised group sentiment. In this sense, for Anthony D. Smith, nations resemble religious groups – they are all sacred communions of citizens who display similar if not identical national values. However, nationalism is a complex and uneven sociological phenomenon that entails continuous and forceful organisational and ideological work. Rather than operating as a vast collective conscience, nationalist ideology is most effective when it taps into existing networks of micro-level solidarities (Malešević 2019, 2013). There is nothing natural or organic in nationalist projects; they are abstract principles that become normalised through ideological penetration and organisational embedment. Hence, there is a significant difference between the micro-universe of everyday life where individuals are emotionally and morally rooted in networks of genuine solidarity with their close family and friends and the anonymous and emotionally detached macro-organisational world of states and other organisations that aim to penetrate this micro-universe. It is highly revealing that nationalist discourses deploy metaphorical and emotional language such as trauma and sacrifice to appeal to the wider population. These terms, borrowed from medical and religious vocabulary, respectively, and originally devised for individual behaviours, are now transformed into collective nouns that address millions of people as if they are members of the same family or friendship circle. In this context the military defeat of a specific and distant social organisation (e.g., the nation-state, the armed forces, the insurgency) becomes transformed into a personalised tragedy involving one's close friends and family members.

Nationalism and War Victories

In contrast to this relative abundance of theories centred on explaining the relationship between nationalism and military defeats, there is a paucity of theoretical analyses focused on the impact war victories have on the character of nationalism.[1] In some respects, this is understandable, as the celebration of major war victories such as the Battle of Waterloo or the Battle of Stalingrad is regularly taken for granted and normalised. It is often assumed that such acts of commemoration are self-explanatory and do not require much analysis. Thus, instead of exploring the link between nationalism and war victories, the focus is much more on the role of warfare in the rise and transformation of modern states. Among the existing scholarship, two approaches have been most influential: the bellicist perspective and the state prestige approach.

The key representatives of the bellicist perspective such as Charles Tilly (1992), Michael Mann (2023, 1986), and Miguel Centeno (2002) primarily focus on the impact of warfare on state formation. For Tilly, war-making and state-making are mutually constitutive processes where war victories determine the patterns of state development. By zooming in on the European experiences from the seventeenth century onwards Tilly aims to show how protracted and destructive military campaigns forced European rulers to reorganise their states and societies. For Tilly, war played a decisive role in the birth of nation-states. As early modern warfare intensified, aristocratic rulers were forced to borrow money from town-based bankers and merchants

[1] Obviously, there is a rich empirical scholarship in history, geography, political science, and area studies that deals with some of these issues, but there are very few systematic theoretical studies that are focused exclusively on the relationship between war victories and nationalism.

to fund these expanding and ever more expensive wars. They also required more resources, better weapons, and larger numbers of soldiers. Hence to accomplish all these tasks, rulers had to centralise the governance, build a larger and more effective civil service, and develop state-wide transportation and communication networks to increase their tax intake. Eventually, the states had to extend citizenship rights to expand the much wider pool of recruits who would fight in these protracted wars. For Tilly (1992), state formation was an unintended consequence of intensified wars, and this process ultimately reduced the number of polities from around 1,000 in fourteenth-century Europe to only thirty nation-states in the early twentieth century. Tilly also emphasises that the cycles of war-making and state-formation were instrumental in the development of two forms of nationalism: the top-down model where the state authorities fostered a state-enforcing nation formation and the bottom-up model where minority elites opposed the imperial centre and propagated the establishment of independent nation-states. For Tilly, war victories shaped the character of nationalism in European modernity: the winning states created the hegemonic narratives that justified the new geopolitical order.

Mann (1986) and Centeno (2002) argue along the similar lines, but focus more on the different forms of state structure. Mann (1986:2) challenges the conventional views that see societies as unitary and relatively homogenous entities and analyses social order through the prism of 'multiple overlapping and intersecting power networks'. More specifically, he differentiates between four types of social power – political, economic, military, and ideological – and argues that all these forms of power shape the character of state structure. However, in his analyses he is particularly interested in the way states increase their administrative, coercive, and territorial capacities. In this context Mann (1986) traces what he terms the process of social caging – how states gradually impose restrictions on individual liberties and spatial mobility via different social mechanisms that generate military protection, regular access to economic resources, and a relative social well-being for their citizens. For Mann, war has been one of the most important catalysts of state formation, and the modern nation-state, in particular, emerged as a forceful 'war making machine'. It is through warfare that states increased their social powers and transformed from city-states, patrimonial kingdoms, and empires into nation-states. This enhanced military capacity of victorious states has often developed in tandem with increased ideological legitimacy (i.e., nationalism) and substantial control of economic resources. The victories in protracted inter-state wars enhanced the dominance of nationalism in modernity.

Centeno (2002:35) applies this bellicit argument to Latin America and argues that the lack of society-wide, protracted inter-state warfare resulted in a relatively weak nationhood and ineffective administrative structures. In his words: 'Latin America has experienced low levels of militarisation, the organisation and mobilisation of human and material resources for potential use in warfare. Latin Americans have frequently tried to kill one another, but they have generally not attempted to organise their societies with such a goal in mind.' For Centeno, the prevalence of local rebellions, coups, civil wars, and revolutions instead of protracted inter-state wars generated weak and incohesive polities. Furthermore, in an environment where most of the Latin American states share the same cultural foundations (i.e., shared history, the same language, Bolivar as the same national hero), a strong sense of continental identity has historically undermined the development of national identities. Thus, the lack of war victories in Latin America had a detrimental impact on the development of nationalism.

The state prestige approach was originally formulated by Max Weber (1968) and has recently been developed and applied most consistently by Randall Collins (1999, 1990). Weber was adamant that nationhood is a relational phenomenon without a fixed essence. He emphasised its contextual ambiguity and its emotional character. In his words: 'The term nation could probably only be defined as: an emotion-based community (*Gefülsmäßige Gemeinschaft*), whose adequate expression would be a common state, which therefore normally has the tendency to produce just such a state. The causal components however which lead to the emergence of this national feeling can have very different roots' (Lehne 2010:224). In this context Weber argues that nations should be conceptualised as status groups that struggle over prestige. In this understanding, prestige is associated with a collective sense of superiority: 'the prestige of power means in practice the glory of power over other communities' (Weber 1968:911). Prestige is also linked with specific cultural values (*Kulturgüter*) that are perceived to represent a particular group. Weber identifies the notion of irreplaceability as an anchoring point for national prestige. In this view nation-states are locked in the never-ending status struggle that can range from economic successes and cultural achievements to military victories. Wars in particular have proved to be a potent mechanism for the rise and fall of national prestige.

Collins (1990:154–155) develops these insights further and argues that nationalism is usually enhanced by war victories. In his view 'political success is the generator of nationalism … [I]t is a vote of confidence in the ability of one's state to defend one against outside enemies, and relatedly, in its ability to expand and conquer others'. For Collins the nations that win wars resemble the football fans of the winning team: 'the loyalty of political subjects to their state depends on its victories … [A] victorious state experiences the greatest nationalism … [while] a long string of defeats saps national loyalty.' Collins (1999:81) also links the internal political legitimacy of the nation-state to its successes in the international realm: 'the power-prestige of the state in the external arena affects the legitimacy of its rulers in the internal arena … [T]he prestige of state rulers rises with military success; even in the absence of war, the ability of a strong state to dominate other states in diplomacy reinforces the legitimacy of its rulers.' Hence for the state prestige approach, war victories tend to enhance nationalist ideologies and increase the reputation of nations that win wars.

Beyond Social Caging and State Prestige

The bellicist and state prestige approaches are very useful in pinpointing the historical impact warfare had on state and nation formation. There is no doubt that nation-states and nationalisms as they exist today have substantially been shaped by the legacies of many wars. The organisational and ideological transition from empires and patrimonial kingdoms to the now hegemonic system of nation-states owes a great deal to protracted warfare over the past three centuries. As Wimmer's empirical studies (2018, 2013) show convincingly, warfare was the central catalyst for the transformation of empires into nation-states.

Nevertheless, the bellicist and state prestige perspectives do not offer much in terms of helping us understand the relationship between nationalism and victorious wars. First, the tendency in both perspectives is to focus much more on state formation processes and less on the character of nationalism that emerges after war victories. Even when they identify differences between nationalisms, as Tilly does with the top-down versus bottom-up models, they do not single out specific mechanisms that foster differences between victorious and non-victorious nationalisms.

Second, these approaches often engage in a 'post hoc, ergo propter hoc' form of reasoning where the analysis focuses only on historically 'successful' cases. This retrospective type of argumentation is problematic as it ignores the complexity and contingency of historical transformation. As Spruyt (2017:86) points out: 'without explicit comparison between successful states and forms of organisation that did not survive, we can suggest that failures lacked the attributes of those that survived, but we do not know for sure … [I]t is equally plausible to argue that shifts in artistic mentality, belief systems or economic changes caused the emergence of the state.'

Third, these state-centric perspectives cannot explain the historical variation that characterises the link between war victories and nationalism. The key issue here is the overly structuralist explanation that leaves no room for different actions of specific agents. The decisions of specific rulers impact on the trajectory of this relationship. For example, the military successes of Prussia and Chile that later had a significant impact on the development of their respective nationalist ideologies cannot be reduced to structural forces alone, as other states were affected by similar structural changes (e.g., Peru had a very similar imperial legacy to Chile). Instead, different trajectories of Prussia and Chile are in part a consequence of successful elite bargaining, while in other similar states different agents prevented such elite agreements (e.g., in Peru large landowners were opposed to such agreement as they feared the native population) (Spruyt 2017).

Finally, state prestige and bellicist theories overemphasise the European experience while neglecting the historical examples outside Europe where wars have not played a decisive role in nation-state formation. For example, in Central and South America, the bellicist argument falters completely as countries that have experienced fewer wars such as Costa Rica and Uruguay have developed much more effective state structures than those that had a history of protracted warfare such as Guatemala, El Salvador, or Nicaragua. Holden (2017:254) sums up this difference with the European experience: 'by the 1920s Costa Rica had allowed its armed forces to shrink to the point that the national military establishment could be abolished after the 1948 civil war with scarcely a word of dissent and replaced with a national gendarmerie. Tilly's dictum would suggest "no military, so no war, and therefore no state". But this is exactly the opposite of Costa Rica's experience.'

Grounding Nationalism in the Aftermath of Wars

Existing scholarship on war victories and defeats contributes to better understanding of the impact organised violence has on nationalism and vice versa, but it does not offer adequate answers to some key questions. Not only do nationalism scholars tend to focus primarily on military defeats and only sporadically and indirectly on war victories, but, more importantly, there is not much systematic analysis of the relationship between the two in the context of nationalist ideas and practices. The following key questions remain unanswered: Is there more nationalism in the wake of military victories or defeats? What kind of nationalism emerges after victories and defeats? Why are military defeats and victories commemorated selectively? Why do public acts of war remembrance change through time?

To answer these questions adequately, it is necessary to move away from overly culturalist explanations of military defeats as well as a too materialist and state-centric understanding of war victories. To explain the changing dynamics of nationalism in the wake of victories and defeats, it is necessary to develop an integrated sociological analysis that aims to capture the variation in social experiences after major wars. In other words, it is important to articulate an alternative theoretical framework that aims to explore the impact warfare has on the character of nationalism in the context of both war victories and defeats. The key points will be illustrated with a paired analysis of two historical case studies: Ghanian nationalism with the legacies of defeat in the War of the Golden Stool (1900), and Croatian nationalism as articulated after the victory in the War of Independence (1991–1995).

One should start from the premise that both warfare and nationalism are historical phenomena shaped by the three distinct, interdependent, and open-ended processes: coercive-organisational grounding, ideological grounding, and micro-interactional grounding. I argue that these three processes impact the character of nationalism in the wake of military defeats and victories. More specifically, my key point is that the character of nationalism is less determined by whether a particular war was victorious or not but by the coercive-organisational, ideological, and micro-interactional logic of post-war societies. These three processes impact substantially on the choice of which wars will be commemorated, as well as when and how these acts of remembrance will feature in the dominant nationalist narratives.

As elaborated in Chapter 1, coercive-organisational grounding stands for an enduring and an incomplete historical process that involves the relative continuous increase in the capacity of social organisations to coerce individuals to comply with their demands and implement the tasks set by these organisations. As all complex social organisations rely on division of labour, established social hierarchies, discipline, and complex systems of control and coordination of tasks, they tend to rely on coercive powers to implement specific organisational goals. Complex social organisations such as the military, police, and judicial systems, but also veterans' organisations, trade unions, political parties, NGOs, nationalist movements, and religious organisations, can deploy coercive powers to stifle disobedience and insubordination. Although this process can be dated to pre-state formations such as chiefdoms, coercive-organisational grounding has accelerated with the rise of the state. Warfare has been one of the key catalysts of this process, as many rulers used organised violence to expand their imperial orders by acquiring new territories and populations. In this process, some states were incorporated into other, larger, polities or have simply disintegrated and vanished (Davies 2011). However, the process itself remained cumulative, as the coercive capacities of social organisations have generally continued to increase over the last 10,000–12,000 years and particularly in the last 200 years as the nation-states gradually established their territorial monopolies on the legitimate use of violence, taxation, and educational and judiciary systems (Malešević 2017; Giddens 1986; Gellner 1983). This process is neither evolutionary nor teleological, as many social organisations experience periods of rise and decline. However, its cumulative character stems from its isomorphic qualities – the tendency to replicate efficient social organisations: from novel military inventions to the latest technological breakthroughs. In the last two centuries coercive-organisational grounding is most clearly visible in the capacity of various social organisations, and states especially, to increase their social penetration within society, expand their surveillance and control, and enhance their infrastructural reach (Malešević 2017, 2010). Hence the key issue is that the historical relationship between war and nationalism has been moulded by the ever-increasing coercive-organisational capacities of states and other powerful entities. It is this bureaucratic coercive capacity that often impacts profoundly not only on the outcome of wars but just as much on the dominant nationalist interpretations of specific war experiences. The effective remembrance of past wars and their visibility in the public sphere are completely dependent on the dynamics of coercive-organisational grounding. This applies equally to victorious wars and tragic military defeats, as there could be no large-scale and regular commemorations of these wars without specific social organisations (e.g., states, social movements, political parties, NGOs) involved in coordinating such events. It is no accident that there are many more public memorials of the Holocaust and the Armenian genocide than those commemorating the genocides of Namibia's Herero/Namaqua or the Romas killed in World War II, as those arranging for the former memorials possess a formidable organisational capacity in numerous state and non-state organisations, while the latter lack such organisational structures.

While coercive-organisational grounding is central for the manifestation of nationalism in the wake of major wars and defeats, it in itself is not enough for the long-term articulation and institutionalisation of nationalism. Another important process that facilitates the direction of nationalism during and after wars is ideological grounding. This concept stands for a historical process through which large sections of population become gradually influenced by abstract principles through which different social organisations provide normative justification for their action. Although the premodern world also operated through specific normative codes including mythologies, religious belief systems, or imperial creeds, these proto-ideological doctrines usually divided rather than united the highly distinct worlds of the aristocracy and those of the peasantry (Gellner 1983). Furthermore, political legitimacy was very narrowly defined as the rulers were primarily focused on justifying their actions to their fellow aristocrats. It is only under modern social conditions that ideological grounding becomes centrifugal and, in this way, starts to successfully permeate entire social orders. Ideological grounding regularly takes place in a competitive environment where different social organisations aim to fend off their ideological rivals. In other words, modern ideologies such as liberalism, socialism, conservatism, republicanism, and, most of all, nationalism attain society-wide justification and become potent principles around which social organisations can mobilise a large section of population. Ideological power can expand only in modernity, when mass-scale educational systems generate fully literate citizenry, where mass media and publishing industries foster the emergence of politicised individuals, and where the democratisation of the public sphere creates an environment for ideological polarisation (Anderson 1983; Gellner 1983). Among the modern ideological doctrines, nationalism has proved to be the most successful in projecting utopian visions of transcending internal conflicts, political polarisation, and social discord. In addition, as nationalist ideology is rooted in the principle of popular sovereignty, it was well posed to acquire society-wide appeal. As such it has become the dominant operative ideology of modernity, which attracts equally the rulers and the ruled. Most of all, nationalism in all its forms has become the only legitimate mode of territorial rule in the contemporary world (Malešević 2013, 2006). The scale and depth of ideological grounding often determine which wars will be commemorated and which conflicts will largely remain neglected or even forgotten. Whether a particular war victory or defeat is memorialised in the public sphere has less to do with actual historical experiences and much more with ideological suitability to fit into the existing nationalist narrative.

The historical dynamics between warfare and nationalism is not only shaped by coercive-organisational and ideological grounding but also by specific micro-interactional processes. The states and many non-state organisations are by and large bureaucratic, anonymous, and abstract entities governed by the principles of efficiency and instrumental rationality. In direct contrast, human beings are emotional and meaning-oriented creatures who often achieve emotional, moral, and cognitive fulfilment through interaction with small groups of people who matter to them – family members, lovers, friends, neighbours, work colleagues, or peer groups. Hence to successfully penetrate these micro-networks of deep personalised bonds, social organisations must mimic their language, rules, rituals, and practices. Sociological research on small group dynamics has demonstrated convincingly that human behaviour is strongly influenced by an individual's sense of attachment to their micro-level groups (Collins 2022, 2004). This is even more the case in the context of organised violence: human beings are often willing to make enormous sacrifices for significant others to the point of giving their own life for their micro-groups. Front-line soldiers, revolutionaries, insurgents, terrorists, and many other individuals involved in violence are often motivated by a sense of responsibility towards their comrades, family, and friends (Della Porta 2013; Atran 2010; Sageman 2004; Lynn 1997).

Many individuals engage in organised violence and join different violent organisations as members of close-knit friendship and kinship networks. So, to motivate people to participate in wars, social organisations often emulate the emotional and moral ties of micro-level groups. In this context, many military organisations have implemented policies that recruit and train new soldiers not as individuals but as members of small groups. For example, the US Army's COHORT system and the Buddy Team Enlistment Option have been designed to recruit and train close friends and family members together (Malešević 2022:232). Atran (2010) also shows how in many cases terrorist cells are composed of people who have strong family or friendship links: 'they frequently come from the same neighbourhoods and interact during sporting activities, such as playing soccer together or becoming camping and hiking companions who learn to take care of one another under trying conditions'. Furthermore, micro-group interactions are just as important for the commemorations of past wars. The narratives of heroism and sacrifice resonate well only when they are couched in the language and practices of micro-level solidarities. It is here that nationalism and war remembrance rituals coalesce together with interpersonal ties. The nationalist discourses project made family and friendship tragedies into society-wide narratives of heroism and sacrifice. While soldiers fight and die for their comrades in arms or their family and friends at home in nationalist narratives, these acts are always framed as instances of national martyrdom. It is no accident that nationalist ideologies tend to co-opt kinship terminology, where bureaucratic and abstract units that are nation-states become 'motherlands' and 'fatherlands', while inter-personal bonds between actual friends and family members are transformed into 'national brotherhood and sisterhood' between 'the sons and daughters of our nation'. Thus, social organisations envelop the networks of micro-level solidarities to ideologically project a sense of society-wide national bonds. By relying on their coercive-organisational capacities and ideological grounding, social organisations can blend macro-organisational aims with micro-interactional and deeply personal attachments. This is how micro-interactional grounding operates. In the next section, I will apply this model to war victories and defeats to show why winning or losing is not central for the character of nationalism in the post-war contexts.

War and Nationalist Narratives in Ghana and Croatia

Obviously, an analysis of only two case studies cannot allow for statistical generalisations about war and nationalism. However, as Yin (2009:18) emphasises, a case study is a not a data collection method, but a specific research strategy aimed at in-depth analysis of particular social phenomena in their real-life contexts. The value of this research strategy is not in its ability to generate replicable findings but instead to provide tools for analytical generalisations that would help us develop and refine our explanatory models. Hence, I aim to apply my theoretical model to the paired analysis of two very different war legacies: the development of the Ghanian nationalism in the wake of defeat in the 1900 War of the Golden Stool and the rise of Croatian nationalism after victory in the War of Independence (1991–1995). This is an exploratory attempt aimed at illustrating the value of providing a sociological interpretation that integrates the study of war defeats and victories in the context of nationalism.

Much of the scholarship on these two wars overemphasises their cultural foundations (Mock 2011:134–141; Boahen 2003; Anzulovic 1999; Mestrovic 1996). In (nationalist) narratives the focus is on the myth of unwavering resistance against unjust foreign rule. In these accounts the War of the Golden Stool (1900) is depicted as a struggle over a specific cultural symbol – the royal throne. The Asante uprising is perceived to have started as an act of disobedience against the demand of British colonial administrator Frederick Hodgson that Asante rulers surrender the Golden Stool, the royal throne of the Asante kings, considered to be divine and the ultimate symbol of power among the Asante people. As this demand was rejected by the Asante, British colonial authorities attempted to crash the rebellion. Despite strong resistance by the Asante and several British military setbacks, the colonial armies eventually captured the city of Kumasi and defeated and occupied the

Asante empire, which become an integral part of the British Gold Coast. Nevertheless, the British never found the Golden Stool and experienced strong resistance led by the queen mother Yaa Asantewaa, who rejected the legitimacy of British rule and as such was exiled to the Seychelles (Mock 2012; Day 2001). These acts of defiance were later integrated into the Ghanian nationalist narrative where Yaa Asantewaa and the Asante military defeat became potent images of heroic sacrifice for the national cause. Although the conflict was initially associated only with the heritage of the Asante people, once Ghana became an independent state, this war was commemorated as a powerful symbol of Ghanian nationhood.

Similarly, the Croatian case is often interpreted through the prism of centuries-old national resistance to Serbian domination. Some strands of scholarship emphasise the cultural differences between the Croats and Serbs and the long-term attempts to assimilate Croats into Greater Serbia (Mestrovic 1996; Anzulovic 1999). Although the Croatian War of Independence (1991–1995) was a stage in the collapse of the Yugoslav communist federal state, this wider context is regularly downplayed at the expense of culture-centred views that posit the Croatian struggle for independence as a 'thousand-year-old dream' (Malešević 2002). Furthermore, nationalist accounts portray the conflict as a relentless struggle against the Serbian invaders, while the conflict itself was more complex and uneven. It initially involved war between the remnants of the Yugoslav People's Army (YPA), which controlled substantial parts of Croatia, mostly inhabited by the local Serb population, and the newly formed Croatian Army. The first year of the Croatian war was associated with large-scale destruction and the siege of several cities such as Vukovar and Dubrovnik by the YPA and Serbian paramilitaries. Both cities later became key cultural symbols of Croatian resistance. However, for the next three years there was not much fighting in Croatia as war operations moved to Bosnia and Herzegovina, where Croatian soldiers fought against Serbian and later Bosnian forces. After several years of military stalemate, during which the YPA in Croatia was transformed into the Serbian Army of Krajina (SAK), in 1995 the Croatian Army defeated SAK; recaptured its capital city, Knin; and integrated the occupied territories into the Croatian state. The Croatian military victory became the cornerstone of the Croatian nationalist narrative from 1995 until the present. The reintegration of Croatian territory is celebrated in many annual events, including the central state commemorations in the city of Knin (Žunec et al. 2013).

The cultural interpretations of these wars often take the nationalist narratives at face value. While the scholars might dissect and question the actual content of these narratives, they rarely take into account the different trajectories of nationalism in the wake of military victories and defeats. Hence, the dominant cultural interpretations cannot explain the variation of nationalist narratives and practices during and after the wars. Thus, to track down these different trajectories it is paramount to explore how nationalist projects are shaped by coercive-organisational capacities, the degree of ideological grounding, and their links with micro-level solidarities.

Coercive-Organisational Grounding

Coercive-organisational grounding is decisive in making any war narrative prevalent and viable. Without the organisational powers of states and many non-state entities, nationalist accounts would remain invisible and ineffective. The War of the Golden Stool and the Croatian War of Independence are regularly commemorated precisely because the apparatuses of the state are involved in the organisation and promotion of such commemorations. Even though the borders and the population of contemporary Ghana do not overlap substantially with the former Asante confederacy, the war's legacy has been firmly incorporated into the contemporary Ghanian national project. Although Ghana is a multiethnic society where the Akan ethnic group, which the Asante are a part of, constitute only 45 per cent of population, the heritage of the Asante empire is well institutionalised throughout the educational system, the state administration, judiciary, military, police, and many other state sectors (Fuller 2014). The War of the Golden Stool is commemorated annually, including re-enactments of the Kumasi battle, concerts, plays, museum exhibitions, and other state-sponsored events (Day 2001). Many of these commemorations are centred on glorifying the sacrifices of Yaa Asantewaa. Such commemorations may include descendants of the queen mother who would often be involved in the government-sponsored events. For example, in 2000 a Yaa Asantewaa descendent headed the centenary coordinating committee together with the government regional minister. He was cast in the role of 'chief mourner', and the event involved the funeral and reinterment of Yaa Asantewaa's remains, which were brought back for this occasion from the Seychelles (Day 2001:5–7). The Ghanian state was not the only entity using its coercive-organisational capacities to institutionalise these commemorative practices. Religious organisations, political parties, NGOs, and sports societies were just as involved in the centenary: 'Other events included an international conference, a football match, the opening of the Yaa Asntewaa museum, a mass rally of women, an interdenominational church service, a tour of craft villages in the region, a concert, a play, a beauty pageant, a gala dinner dance, and a book launch' (Mock 2012:139).

However, there is nothing automatic in memorialising this war defeat. For much of Ghanian postcolonial history, the War of the Golden Stool did not play such a prominent role in the nationalist narrative. In the early years of Nkrumah's rule the focus was more on the pan-Africanist project that combined socialist ideas with the decolonial paradigm that centred on the entire continent. In the later years of his rule Nkrumah fostered a personality cult that prioritised his own role in the independence and success of his Convention's People's Party (Fuller 2014; Day 2001). Nevertheless, Nkrumah's rule was highly instrumental in developing the administrative state apparatus, transportation and communication networks, mass media, and educational system, which would later be used effectively to institutionalise the legacy of the War of the Golden Stool. After the 1966 violent coup d'état, Pan-Africanism was replaced with a stronger version of Ghanian nationalism, but this was resisted by representatives of various ethnic groups. Asante leaders were particularly hostile to President Jerry Rawlings's attempt to incorporate the legacy of the War of the Golden Stool into the Ghanian nationalist project (Fuller 2014). Nevertheless, their objections were rejected, and any signs of organised resistance were quashed. From early 1990s authoritarianism was replaced by a more democratic model of rule, which allowed the Ghanian state to accelerate the coercive-organisational grounding that was reflected in the greater centralisation of power, the development of nation-centric policies and institutions, and the proliferation and dominance of Ghanian nationalism across society. Hence the role of coercive-organisational power was central in institutionalising and nationalising the symbols of the War of the Golden Stool. It did not really matter whether this war resulted in victory or defeat; its organisational value stemmed from its ability to operate as a unifying nodal point for the proliferation of Ghanian nationalism.

The Croatian case also shows how indispensable coercive-organisational grounding is for the development of nationalism. Although Croatian nationalism was an important source of political legitimacy for the rulers even during the state socialist period (1945–1990), it become the dominant ideological discourse through the 1991–1995 War of Independence. In the highly polarised political environment of late 1980s Yugoslavia, the winner of the first democratic elections in Croatia was the hard nationalist Croatian Democratic Community (HDZ). Once in power in 1990, the HDZ quickly embarked on the institutionalisation of ethno-nationalist policies in the state apparatus with sweeping changes in the police, judiciary, educational system, and mass media. It also created a new military force, which was soon to be involved in war with the remnants of the YPA that was by then largely controlled by Serbian nationalists who were focused on carving parts of Croatia mostly inhabited by a Serbian population. The new government was eager to remove ethnic Serbs from the state institutions and invested substantial resources to increase the size of the police and military forces. Hence by 1991 the Croatian police grew to a staggering 20,000 members, and by 1995 tiny Croatia had an enormous army with around 250,000 soldiers (CIA 2002:86; Žunec et al. 2013:33). With the end of war in 1995, ethno-nationalism did not evaporate. Instead, the war victory intensified its presence throughout Croatian society. The central role in this process can be attributed to the increased coercive-organisational capacities of the state as well as the increased influence of some non-state or para-state organisations such as veterans' groups, patriotic societies, and religious organisations (Milekić 2022). Victory in the War of Independence became the organisational cornerstone of the new nation-state. Hence in the Croatian, just as in the Ghanian, case, coercive-organisational grounding was a central organising vehicle for the institutionalisation and reproduction of nationalism throughout the society. Nevertheless, different levels of coercive-organisational grounding in Ghana and Croatia impacted differently on the direction of ideological grounding. These differences have also played an important role in the intensity of nationalism.

Ideological Grounding

These differences were shaped in part by diverse patterns of ideological grounding in the two cases. When Ghana attained full independence in 1957, most of its population consisted of illiterate peasantry whose principal source of identification was locally rather than nationally based. The key sources of group attachment were the clan, village, kinship, or tribe. Although literacy campaigns intensified after independence, even in 1970 UN estimates indicated that 70 per cent of population above the age of fifteen were illiterate (57 per cent males and 82 per cent females) (UNESCO 1980). The levels of adult literacy improved substantially in the twenty-first century: in 1990 57.9 per cent population was literate, while in 2020 the adult literacy rate attained fairly high levels with 80.4 per cent of population being literate (Knoema 2023). After independence the government had invested extensively in building educational institutions, and the number of primary and secondary level students substantially increased. However, the completion rate has remained uneven: in 2020, 71 per cent of pupils complete primary-level education, but only 47 per cent complete lower secondary and 35 per cent complete upper secondary education (MISC 2020). The post-independence state also supported many cultural projects centred on the promotion and development of national literature, theatre, art, science, and other areas that are central for the emergence of what Gellner (1983) calls 'high culture'.

However, the relative underdevelopment of the coercive-organisational capacities of the new state prevented the proliferation of these cultural products beyond major cities in Ghana. In other words, the lack of transportation and communication networks across the country proved to be a major impediment to the growth of national identification. In this context nation-centred ideological grounding was much slower and uneven, with regional and ethnic attachments often overriding a sense of shared nationhood. This is also reflected in commemorations of the War of the Golden Stool. The event was initially marginalised and to some extent monopolised by leaders of the Asante ethnic group. It was only in the last twenty years or so that this war attained greater ideological significance in the Ghanian nationalist narrative. During Rawlings' presidency Yaa Asantewaa was institutionalised as the Ghanian rather than an Asante national heroine. Despite not being Ashante himself, Rawlings was eager to place the War of the Golden Stool at the heart of national commemorations. The legacy of this war was promoted extensively in the mass media, educational system, and public sphere. For example, Yaa Asantewaa's defiant speech on the eve of the war has been reproduced in numerous media outlets, textbooks, and artistic exhibitions: 'How can a proud and brave people like the Asante sit back and look while white men took their king and chiefs and humiliate them with demand for the Golden Stool. The Golden Stool only means money to the white man.... If you, the chiefs of Asante, are going to behave like cowards and not fight, you should exchange your loincloths for my undergarments' (Boahen 2003:118). The heroism of Yaa Asantewaa was commemorated in public rituals including re-enactments of major battles with face-painted warriors, war drums, and cannon blasts (Day 2001). Popular writers, artists, and journalists were encouraged to produce works that celebrate the martyrdom of those who fought in the War of the Golden Stool. Hence in one such popular book Yaa Asantewaa and her warriors were depicted as martyrs for Ghanian independence: 'patriotic Ghanaians, Asantes in particular, exhibited a high degree of nationalism by sacrificing their lives in defence of their motherland against imperial domination. The Yaa Asantewaa war provides a typical example of such a high degree of nationalism ... [warriors] who shed their blood in defence of the nation'

(Danquah 2002: xi–xii). Thus, in the Ghanian case ideological grounding was uneven and slow. In this context the sacrificial nationalism associated with the War of the Golden Stool never attained a hegemonic position. It was gradually incorporated into the Ghanian civic nationalist narrative, but its significance and ownership remained contested by different groups within Ghana.

In direct contrast, the Croatian War of Independence attained a hegemonic role within the Croatian nationalism immediately after the war and this has continued until the present. The war victory played an important role in this process, but this in itself was not enough to achieve such a hegemonic position. One of the key factors for this dominance was the scale of ideological grounding. Croatia achieved independence in very different historical circumstances to that of Ghana. In 1991 an overwhelming majority of Croatian citizens were fully literate – 96.7 per cent – and this number has increased to 99.45 per cent by 2021 (www.macrotrends.net/countries/HRV/croatia/literacy-rate). The state-run and highly centralised education system evenly covers the entire country. Primary and secondary schools use the state-approved and standardised curricula where pupils learn from nation-centric textbooks. The number of people who have completed secondary and tertiary education has constantly been increasing: from 36.5 per cent and 9.5 per cent, respectively, in 1991 to 55.5 per cent and 24.1 per cent in 2021 (https://dzs.gov.hr/news/continuous-growth-of-the-share-of-highly-educated-population/1599).

Although Croatian institutions of 'high culture' have been developing and expanding since the early nineteenth century, the post-independence period witnessed the mass proliferation of many cultural, educational, artistic, and academic institutions that are centred on the promotion of Croatian nationhood. Croatian-centred mass media outlets have also increased substantially. While in 1991 there were only three state-wide TV channels and a handful of radio stations and newspapers, by 2016 this had increased to 31 TV channels, 158 active radio stations, and over 800 registered print publications (IREX 2016). All these institutional outlets are involved in the reproduction of nationalist narratives that glorify the Croatian War of Independence. Primary and secondary school textbooks, much of the mass media, and all state institutions continuously present a nearly uniform view of this war where the focus is on triumphalism. For example, speeches of politicians and leaders of the veterans' organisations regularly invoke a sense of military and moral superiority: 'We are celebrating the 21st anniversary of the victory over Greater Serbian pretensions. How we will celebrate is our decision and no one will be able to order us. With the leadership of Tuđman, Oluja [the military action that brought the final war victory] was the biggest jewel in the crown of the Homeland War [War of Independence]; it was a fight for modern Croatia' (https://n1info.ba/regija/a108076-govor-predstavnika-branitelja-u-kninu/). 'The Croatian defender is our hero. We defended our homeland with morality. Croatia is free, and we are the winners! We must transfer patriotism to our youth' (www.index.hr/vijesti/clanak/plenkovic-i-milanovic-na-proslavi-oluje-poslali-poruke-srbiji-necemo-to-dopustati/2385281.aspx). The war is also regularly commemorated in numerous public events where leading politicians make speeches that invoke acts of national heroism. Government officials are present at various national and local commemorations that often take place in different parts of the country. From 1995 until the present, an enormous number of new monuments were built to honour the soldiers and civilians who died in the war. In addition to the state authorities, the Catholic Church, veterans' organisations, and many patriotic associations have been involved in the process of war commemoration. Croatian veterans of the War of Independence have been at the forefront of such activities and have also been the most influential pressure group involved in public policing of the dominant war narrative. As Milekić (2022) shows, veterans' organisations have often covertly and overtly cooperated with the leading right-wing party (HDZ)[2] to contain any form of public dissent on the interpretation of the 1991–1995 war. Hence, despite nominal acceptance of pluralism in a formally democratic society, any attempts to challenge the dominant ethno-nationalist narrative of this war have been fiercely condemned. The deep ideological grounding that has permeated the educational system, mass media, state institutions, NGOs, and the public sphere has largely prevented the visibility of alternative interpretations of the war.

Micro-Interactional Grounding

Finally, the intensity and direction of nationalism are shaped by the ability of social organisations to penetrate the micro-world of everyday life. Although modern nationalist ideologies were articulated at the end of the eighteenth and beginning of the nineteenth century, it took another two centuries for these ideological discourses to fully permeate the everyday interactions of ordinary people (Weber 1978). Hence, the commemorations of war victories and defeats remain dependent on the size and commitment of their audience. There are numerous wars fought in the

[2] It is important to emphasise that HDZ has been the ruling party in Croatia for much of the post-independence period.

history of nearly any society, yet only some war victories and a very small number of war defeats are commemorated. Why have Masada, Kosovo Polje, or the Battle of White Mountain become the epicentre of national remembrance in Israeli, Serbian, and Czech nationalism, respectively, while hundreds of other war defeats are largely ignored? The same applies to war victories. Coercive-organisational and ideological grounding certainly play a central role in the selection and institutional reproduction of such war commemorations. However, these macro structural forces cannot succeed unless they envelop the micro-universe of everyday life. The triumphs and tragedies of previous wars can resonate in the public eye only when they are couched in personalised stories where ordinary people can recognise their significant others. Thus, the War of Croatian Independence and the War of the Golden Stool have attained central positions in their respective nationalist narratives when coercive-organisational and ideological powers were able to penetrate and enfold micro-level solidarities. It is no coincidence that war commemorations often focus on acts of sacrifice and heroism of ordinary individuals, who are regularly depicted as 'our brothers and sisters', 'our fellow comrades', or 'our mothers and fathers'. The speeches that accompany war remembrance ceremonies in Croatia tend to invoke this language of kinship and close friendship. In many of their speeches, Croatian government representatives rely on kinship metaphors. For instance, former president Grabar-Kitarovic often made reference to the '200,000 Croatian sons and daughters who, led by the Commander-in-Chief and the first Croatian President Dr. Franjo Tuđman, broke the backbone of the Great Serbian policy of Slobodan Milošević and his cohorts in Croatia' (https://dnevnik.hr/vijesti/hrvatska/govor-predsjednice-grabar-kitarovic-u-kninu—395526.html). Similar kinship-based language is often used by leading representatives of the Catholic Church in Croatia: 'Brothers and sisters, with that sense of faith we look at the names and lives of these brothers and sisters of ours. We owe deep and sincere gratitude to all our brothers and sisters who died as Croatian soldiers' (https://splitsko-dalmatinska-policija.gov.hr/vijesti/u-hrvacama-obiljezena-31-godisnjica-pogibije-hrvatskih-redarstvenika-i-policijskih-sluzbenika/39095). Leaders of veterans' organisations often use nearly identical reference points: 'I admit that I took up arms with my brothers to stop the Serb Chetnik hordes, I admit that now I would do it with even greater zeal' (https://n1info.ba/regija/a108076-govor-predstavnika-branitelja-u-kninu/). By invoking emotional ties to the networks of micro-group solidarity and framing them as acts of national solidarity, these representatives of powerful social organisations can successfully link inter-personal attachments with wider nationalist ideologies (see Chapter 9).

Despite the war loss, Ghanian nationalism relies on similar ideological and organisational tropes, which are framed in the discourse of kinships and deep friendships. In this context Yaa Asantewaa is regularly depicted as a mother or grandmother of all Ghanaians. Her statues throughout Ghana invoke this perception: 'The juxtaposition of both statues presents Yaa Asantewaa as the Mother of the Nation and Kwame Nkrumah as the Father of the Nation' (Fuller 2014:66). Politicians and the community leaders often refer to Yaa Asantewaa through kinship metaphors that link her motherly role with her children and grandchildren: 'Yaa Asantewaa's name brings goose pimples to some of us because we cherish the heroism of this great Queen mother. Yaa Asantewaa brought dignity to the Ghanaian and African woman.... May our children, and our children's children grow stronger each day to fight injustices, indignities, and greed' (Fuller 2014:69). Similarly, during the centenary commemorations a local Asante dignitary had 'positioned himself to declare Yaa Asantewaa his own "grandmother" and thus establish a close familial tie' (Day 2001:8).

In the Ghanian case the strong link with micro-level solidarities was also instrumental in overcoming the tension between the Asante and the Ghanian nationalisms. Since the War of the Golden Stool has historically been a source of friction between national and regional governments, a focus on interpersonal and kinship-based attachments allowed for relatively frictionless war commemorations in the last twenty years. Hence the 2000 centenary war celebrations successfully combined coercive-organisational, ideological, and micro-interactional powers to foster a stronger sense of Ghanian nationalism. 'The very public coverage of the afternoon's events, with many national and regional dignitaries, and GTV video cameras guaranteeing a national television audience, lifted the Asantes' war against British out of the realm of local legend and into the ranks of national myth' (Day 2001:10). This national stage was then used to promote the queen mother's heroism and sacrifice as national virtues to be emulated: 'to embrace the ideals of Yaa Asantewaa' for all Ghanaians and to build on the ideas that 'Asante has a history that engenders a spirit of nation building, brotherliness, sacrifice, and devotion to the common good' (Day 2001:7).

The post-Nkrumah era has been defined by a much stronger integration of the legacy of the War of the Golden Stool into the Ghanian nationalist narrative. During his presidency Rawlings showed great effort to bring Asante symbolism into the Ghanian national project. This had often been achieved by relying on the language and practices that facilitated micro-interactional grounding. Hence, despite being a member of another ethnic group (Ewe) he named one of his daughters after Yaa

Asantewaa. He also invoked the sacrifice of Yaa Asantewaa in his speeches and was critical of previous governments that were often in conflict with Asante (Mock 2012:137). Rawlings would often visit the Asante region and even attended the funeral of Yaa Asantewaa's granddaughter when she died in the early 1980s. This highly personalised symbolism that linked national project with the kinship line would resonate well in the region: 'They [the Asante] were proud to show a visitor the photo taken of young-looking Jerry Rawlings in his military uniform at the bedside of Yaa Asantewaa's granddaughter laid in state' (Day 2001:4). Thus, just as in the Croatian case, nationalism was able to grow and expand by enveloping the micro-universe of the local and personal bonds.

Hence both war victories and defeats can serve a very similar purpose for the development of nationalist narratives. To understand the trajectories of nationalist commemorations the focus should shift from examining the outcome of the particular war and towards the coercive-organisational, ideological, and micro-interactional processes through which nationalism becomes fully grounded in contemporary societies.

Conclusion

Scholars of nationalism have devoted a great deal of attention to the impact war defeats have on rituals of national remembrance. Major tragedies such as Masada, Kosovo Polje, or the Battle of White Mountain have attained an aura of national martyrdom that is periodically displayed through annual commemorations and pilgrimages to the sites where these events took place. Similarly, there are studies that explore how major war victories such as the Battle of Waterloo or the Battle of Stalingrad have become nodal points of heroic national narratives that are memorialised and celebrated. However, there is a lack of comparative analyses that attempt to integrate the study of war victories and defeats to understand their impact on nationalism. This chapter brings these two strands of scholarship together to provide a critical assessment of existing perspectives. Furthermore, I offer an alternative interpretation that shifts the attention from the outcome of a particular war towards the social processes that make specific war commemorations central pillars of nationalist narratives. Hence, the emphasis is not on whether a particular war resulted in victory or defeat but how a specific war experience becomes socially meaningful through coercive-organisational, ideological, and micro-interactional grounding. The key arguments are illustrated with a paired analysis of Croatian and Ghanian nationalisms in the context of the two very different war experiences.

8 Warriors, Civilians, and the Spirit of Nationalism

Introduction

Nationalism and warfare are often depicted as conceptual twins. The onset of contemporary wars is regularly accompanied with virulent discourses that prioritise one's own nation at the expense of others. Moreover, the war environment is highly conducive to nationalist dehumanisation of the enemy nation, which often goes hand in hand with the uncritical veneration of one's own nation. In times of war, soldiers are particularly singled out as the beacons of 'patriotic ethos', that is, as individuals who willingly and altruistically place themselves in the mortal danger to 'protect their fatherland/motherland/homeland'. In other words, more than any other group members of the armed forces are firmly associated with the spirit of nationalism. In direct contrast, the civilian population is often perceived to be ideologically much more heterogenous and less consistent in their nationalist commitments. Whereas modern soldiers are assumed to be patriotic by default, civilian nationalism is expected to oscillate – from high devotion during wartime to less dedication or relative indifference during peacetime (Collins 2022). In this chapter, I question this common-sense assumption. I argue that in war situations nationalism is substantially less present on the battlefields than in the domains of civilian life. Rather than being the prerogative of warriors, nationalism is, for the most part, an artefact generated and reproduced in the civilian sphere. As nationalist subjectivities are created in the civilian sphere and are sustained by coercive-organisational, ideological, and micro-interactional processes that are developed in that realm, civilian life remains central for the proliferation of nationalism.

The chapter is divided into three sections. First, I explore the attitudes of combatants towards nationalist ideology. Drawing on different historical and contemporary examples I aim to show that in most cases nationalist discourses play a marginal role on the battlefield. Instead, soldiers tend to be motivated more by micro-level solidarities that are often integrated into the norms of the warrior ethos. Second, I zoom in on the role nationalism plays in the civilian sphere. The focus is on the historical processes that foster the rise and reproduction of the habitual nationalist ideas and practices in state institutions, civil society, and the interpersonal domain. Here my ambition is to demonstrate that nationalism is first and foremost a phenomenon of civilian life. Finally, the last part of the chapter brings together the military and civilian world to analyse how they operate together in the aftermath of war.

Are Combatants Nationalists?

In most contemporary societies, armed forces are strongly associated with nationalism. The raison d'être of all modern military organisations is to protect the population and territory of their respective nation-states. For example, the British Army specifies this explicitly: 'protecting the nation and its dependent territories will always be our first role' (www.army.mod.uk/what-we-do/). Similarly, the key task of the Chinese People's Liberation Army (PLA) is 'to safeguard national sovereignty, unity, territorial integrity and security'. More specifically, one of the central objectives of the PLA's defence policy is 'to solve the Taiwan question and achieve complete reunification of the country', which is deemed to be 'in the fundamental interests of the Chinese nation and essential to realising national rejuvenation' (http://eng.mod.gov.cn/xb/DefensePolicy/index.html). These institutional values are also reflected in the views of the recruits, who often describe their motivations to join the military in similar terms. For instance, in a survey conducted among US soldiers in 2002, a majority identified 'to serve country' (65.8 per cent) and 'patriotism' (54.95) as important in their decision to join the army (Woodruff et al. 2006:359). Similar responses have been recorded in other surveys of US recruits (Griffith 2008; Woodruff et al. 2006; Eighmey 2006; Griffith & Perry 1993). Research on motivations to join the military in other countries indicates a remarkably similar trend. For example, Israeli secondary school students have shown a strong commitment to serve in the Israel Defense Forces in order 'to fight Israel's enemies' and 'to serve the state' (Amit et al. 2007). UK recruits who join the British Armed Forces also tend to be inspired significantly by nationalist motivations (UK Government 2022). The view that most soldiers are primarily motivated by 'patriotic values' is widespread among the general public in many societies. For example, in a recent study that surveyed both military personnel and the civilian population, it was found that 'many Americans continue to subscribe to an idealized image of service members as moved by self-sacrificing patriotism' (Krebs &

Ralston 2022:25). Similarly, in British public opinion, members of the armed forces generally are associated with strong patriotic commitments, and the public displays positive feelings that 'are inspired by respect for their bravery and sacrifice' (UK Government 2022). In many other countries, civilians perceive their own militaries as being infused with strong patriotic dedication (Mann 2023; Hall & Malešević 2013).

Nevertheless, the attitudes of ordinary soldiers are usually much more complex than this. While recruits generally invoke patriotism as an important incentive to join the armed forces, this is usually just one among several sources of motivation to join the military. Other significant incentives include the material and symbolic benefits received from military service, a sense of duty, occupational development and education, job stability, the lack of better options, experiencing a personal crisis, getting to see the world, having an adventure, and experiencing military life, among others (Woodruff 2017; Mann 2023; Kleykamp 2006; Griffith 2008). Furthermore, there are pronounced differences between different ranks within the military, with ordinary recruits being more inspired by nationalist rhetoric than higher-ranked officers: 'Rank groups differed in patriotism ... with junior-ranking sergeants and then corporals and privates scoring highest, followed by officers and senior-ranking sergeants' (Griffith 2008). On this issue the views of established soldiers differ substantially from the views of the younger recruits and civilian perceptions. For instance, a recent survey shows that whereas civilians tend 'to embrace a patriotic narrative' as a primary source of motivation to join the armed forces, military personnel 'are more likely to acknowledge that pay and benefits are a primary motivation for service' (Krebs & Ralston 2022:25). This study also points out that 'the respondents with military experience ... more frequently endorse extrinsic motivations [pay, benefits, no other options] as service members' primary reason for enlistment' and 'they less often attribute military service to either patriotism or exemplary citizenship' (Krebs & Ralston 2022).

However, joining the armed forces as a recruit is a very different experience to being a seasoned combatant. Military sociologists and psychologists have studied extensively how human beings change in times of war and particularly how the battlefield experience transforms social attitudes. Much of the existing research indicates that soldiers who had direct and extensive experience of warfare and particularly those who fought on the front lines tend either to downplay any ideological commitments or to prioritise a sense of loyalty and attachment to their micro-level groups over that of their nation-state (Malešević 2022, 2010; Collins 2022, 2008; Bourke 2000; Lynn 1997; Holmes 1986; Dollard & Horton 1943). As Graves (1980:157) emphasises, during World War

I, British soldiers expressed strong resentment towards young recruits who deployed nationalist language: 'patriotism, in the trenches, was too remote a sentiment, and at once rejected as fit for civilians, or prisoners. A new arrival who talked patriotism would soon be told to cut it out.' Frédéric Rousseau's analysis of letters, memoirs, and fictional writings of more than sixty World War I French soldiers indicates an almost identical attitude. Many of these former combatants state that 'there is no patriotism in the trenches', and Rousseau's study shows that 'the so-called consent of the soldiers was expressed within a space of extreme dependence, constant surveillance, and heightened coercion' (Mann 2023:343). Similarly, during World War II prolonged exposure to combat situations was linked with indifferent or negative attitudes towards nationalist sentiments. The first systematic surveys among World War II US soldiers fighting in European theatres of war showed that patriotism was a very a marginal factor, with only 2 per cent of US soldiers being motivated to fight for patriotic reasons (Stouffer et al. 1949). In the words of one World War II American soldier: 'there is no patriotism on the line. A boy up there 60 days in the line is in danger every minute. He ain't fighting for patriotism' (Varin 2015:43). Many combatants 'declared that such "bullshit" was what civilians spouted, ignorant of the realities of war' (Mann 2023:371). This was also recognised by commanding officers, who could not rely on nationalism to motivate their soldiers to fight. Hence Brigadier Thompson states that patriotism represents 'a very fragile foundation on which to base morale, because in the stress of battle it evaporates. Whereas, if you're fighting for yourself, your comrades, for each other, that sustains you in the moments when you think you might be losing' (Moore 2009:246).

The experiences of US soldiers during the Korean and Vietnam Wars were similar, which led leading military sociologists such as Moskos and Little to conclude that 'ideological sentiments' and 'patriotic rhetoric' were no more than 'latent beliefs' that lack clear articulation on the battlefields (Moskos 1970:147; Little 1964:204–205). The shift towards professional, contract-based soldiers has not changed the front-line combatants' attitudes towards nationalism. US and UK soldiers who fought in Iraq and Afghanistan downplayed the importance of patriotic ethos as a driving force in the combat environment. Instead, as King (2011:296) shows, they often emphasised their sense of professional obligation: they were motivated not by 'patriotism but by mission-specific forms of preparation which fuse intellectual and moral imperatives in the immediate task. A self-referential ideal of professionalism motivates the troops.'

The front-line experience of being constantly exposed to life-threatening situations impacts substantially on the collective perceptions of war and nationhood. Thus, combatants feel much more attached to their front-line comrades than to abstract and distant constructs such as the nation or the state. In nearly all modern wars, combatants emphasise a strong sense of attachment to their military unit – squad, section, patrol, platoon, company, regiment, or battalion (Mann 2023; Khaiko 2018; Keegan 1993). Shared war experience usually fosters strong social bonds in such small military units. However, direct exposure to everyday bloodshed on the battlefields forges fervent and durable attachments that are often perceived to equal or surpass close family ties. For example, in the wars of Yugoslav succession most soldiers emphasised the centrality of these micro-group bonds: 'we were like brothers', 'I was ready to die for them and they would do the same for me', and 'we shared everything, helping each other as much as we could … we were all like a family' (Malešević 2022:211).

The development of strong micro-bonds has also been recorded outside formal military organisations. Clandestine groups involved in violent conflicts, terrorist networks, insurgency units, paramilitaries, gangs, criminal syndicates, and many other entities whose members have a shared experience of violence often display very similar bonding practices and values (Malešević 2022, 2017; Shire & Hersi 2022; della Porta 2013; Atran 2011). When interviewed about their motivation to fight, former members of the IRA regularly downplay nationalism and emphasise a sense of moral responsibility and emotional attachment towards their comrades: 'you have to have a sense of your comrades and that's very, very important and the sense of comradeship that comes from actual involvement in stuff, that you then come to, there are bonds which are built from your activism … [T]he bonds that you would develop with people who you're working with on active service would, yeah it would, you would develop a relationship with them unlike any that, outside of that.… You knew that they were rock solid and that they wouldn't let you down.' 'So, we would all have known each other, we all became friends and then that sort of friendship and comradeship would have built up among, as you're going along' (Malešević & Ó Dochartaigh 2018:318–322).

Much of the existing scholarship also indicates that many combatants did not join armed organisations or participate in violent conflicts because of long-lasting animosities towards the ethno-national others. War-time surveys and interviews with soldiers who fought in World War II, the Korean War, the Vietnam War, and in Iraq and Afghanistan demonstrate that front-line soldiers often showed substantially less prejudice and even more empathy towards the enemy than the civilians did (Malešević 2010; Collins 2008; Bourke 2000:137–170; Stouffer et al.

1949:158–165; Dollard & Horton 1943). They were more immune to propagandistic and dehumanising images of the enemy. Being able to directly see and interact with their adversaries during the Vietnam War, US soldiers realised that they were not facing bloodthirsty monsters but human beings who were in the similar predicament to their own. This experience 'gave the enemy the humanity I wished to deny him', as the adversary soldiers were 'young men … just like us' (Caputo 1977:117). In some cases, soldiers developed a sense of mutual respect and even admiration of the enemy. The experience of fighting in World War I left a lasting impression on Thomas Edward Lawrance, who expressed a strong sense of empathy and even praise for his German foes: 'I grew proud of the enemy who killed my brothers. They were two thousand miles from home, without hope and without guidelines, in conditions bad enough to break the bravest nerves. Yet their sections held together … when attacked they halted, took position, fired to order. There was no haste, no crying, no hesitation. They were glorious' (Lawrence 1935:634).

The shared battlefield experience can re-humanise rather than de-humanise social relationships. In an environment where individuals are directly facing other human beings, established ideological and propagandistic tropes can evaporate. For example, the wars of Yugoslav succession were characterised by mass-scale violence, ethnic cleansing policies, and even acts of genocide. All these instances of violence were inspired by ethno-nationalist ideologies that saturated the public sphere and mass media. However, this ethno-national animosity was much less present on the battlefield, where ordinary soldiers would often interact across the front lines, trade or share music tapes and jokes, jointly smuggle prohibited goods, and even play football during a ceasefire (Malešević 2010:225). When interviewed about their attitudes towards the 'enemy nations', many combatants emphasised their lack of animosity: 'I did not know who was who [in ethno-national terms]'. A Serb soldier shared that 'I was not burdened by it … my godfather is a Muslim, my best friend was a Muslim'; or 'half of my friends were Muslims and Croats' (Malešević 2022). Very similar responses were recorded in interviews with former IRA volunteers: 'Everybody knew that we were Catholics now from West Belfast, never had any problem with all these wee Protestant guys you know. Made us very welcome.' 'I'd very, very many Protestant friends. It wasn't a sectarian thing by no means, absolutely not.' 'I would have spent time on a Protestant estate. … I'd have hung around with Protestants' (Ó Dochartaigh 2015). In all of these, and many other, cases the direct experience of combat impacted negatively on nationalist dehumanisation. As Bourke (2000:236–237) summarises this process: 'Dehumanisation worked quite well in basic training, not so well in battle. In combat situations, where human slaughter was ubiquitous, atrocities were difficult to define and were often ignored. It was impossible to maintain the fiction that the enemy was any different from oneself for very long.'

However, none of this is to say that combatants will automatically become less hostile towards their adversary. The direct experience of fighting can also generate strong negative feelings towards the enemy. For example, when losing a close comrade, a soldier or the entire unit can engage in the revenge killings. Collins (2022, 2008) has analysed many such instances where ordinary soldiers and even police officers embark on rampage violence that he calls 'forward panic'. Nevertheless, these acts of hatred and violence usually do not stem from the ideological framing associated with nationalist discourses. Instead, such acts represent what Fiske and Rai (2014) call 'virtuous violence' – violence that is morally motivated to regulate social relationships. In other words, instead of killing through the dehumanisation of the enemy, these acts of violence entail full humanisation of the adversary. This is a process aimed at rebuilding the moral order.

Arguing that ideology, and nationalism in particular, play a marginal role on the battlefield does not suggest that ideas and principles do not matter for the combatants. On the contrary, shared values are crucial for any armed organisation. However, such values either are primarily linked with an inter-personal sense of moral obligation and emotional attachment between combatants or are part of the wider warrior ethos. In most cases these two overlap as the warrior ethos is often underpinned by specific ethical principles that prioritise responsibility towards others in the military unit.

For example, the US Army defines the warrior ethos along the following lines: 'I will always place the mission first. I will never accept defeat. I will never quit. I will never leave a fallen comrade' (www.army.mil/values/warrior.html). It is clear here that in addition to specific military tasks such as accomplishing a particular military mission, or not accepting a defeat, there is also a strong commitment to comradeship – never leaving a fallen comrade. As Coker (2007:5) emphasises, 'sacrifice is the key to warrior ethos. Through it, the bond that the warrior forges with his community, his unit and country, becomes a sacred one.' Nevertheless, this link between the military unit, community, and country is a very late historical development. While the warrior ethos has existed for thousands of years, nationalism is a distinctly modern ideology (Gellner 1983; see Chapter 9). Nearly all known armed forces have adopted a version of the specific warrior ethos that governed their conduct and fostered a shared sense of belonging (Coker 2007; Keegan 1993). The warrior ethos was present in very diverse armed organisations ranging from the Greek hoplite armies, the Roman legionaries, Aztec calpulli, Japanese daimyo and samurai to the Ottoman mamluks or European mounted knights, among many others. All these military organisations nurtured a strong sense of group attachment, a commitment to military tasks, stoicism and fighting commitment on the battlefield, a sense of the warrior's honour, and loyalty to their military organisation. It is only in modernity that such values were amalgamated with nation-centric principles. In the world of nation-states, the warrior ethos, just as many other social doctrines, becomes nationalised. While in the medieval Europe the warrior ethos implied a sense of moral obligation between fellow aristocrats while excluding all other social strata, in modern warfare this moral code applies to all those who fight for their nation-state (Hall & Malešević 2013; Posen 1993). For example, in US Army manuals the warrior ethos is now strongly tied to nationalist ideals: 'Every Soldier that has entered into the Army family has been taught that the Warrior Ethos is rooted in Army values and founded on the premise that service to our nation is an honor and a responsibility that requires self-sacrifice-belonging to and giving to something larger than ourselves.... [Soldiers] will find great gratitude in serving a profession dedicated to protecting the American people and our nation's national interests' (www.army.mil/article/50082/warrior_ethos).

Nevertheless, this organisational push to tie the warrior ethos to nationalism is regularly resisted on the battlefields. The front-line experience often tends to enhance the significance of the warrior ethos, while at the same time most combatants are wary of nationalist rhetoric (Mann 2023; Malešević 2022). As Collins (2013:42) demonstrates convincingly, rather than improving military performance nationalist ideologies often undermine fighting efficacy: 'Troops motivated chiefly by nationalism and unsupported by workable techniques of combat performance tend to lose their nationalist fervour fairly soon ... and become cynical or alienated'.

The Civilian Sphere and the Spirit of Nationalism

In conventional wisdom, experienced combatants are perceived to be more patriotic and hostile towards the enemy than the civilians. However, this view is wrong on both accounts. Not only is the battlefield experience often inversely proportional to nationalist sentiments and animosity towards the adversary, but during war the civilian population is usually much more nationalist and hostile than the ordinary combatants. Many war-time surveys indicate that distance plays an important role in one's attitude towards enemy nations. The further away from the battlefield people are, the more they show loathing towards the enemy (Macmillan 2020:78–79; Bourke 2000:155–170; Stouffer et al. 1949:158–165). For example, Gallup polls taken only a few days after Hiroshima and Nagasaki were bombed show that '85 percent of Americans supported use of the atomic bomb against Japanese urban targets' (Lotchin 2015:412). In other Gallup surveys conducted in late 1944, 43 per cent of respondents supported the use of poisonous gas against Japanese cities, and when asked, 'What do you think we should do with Japan, as a country, after the war?' 13 per cent answered, 'Kill all Japanese people.' Attitudes were even more extreme towards Japanese leaders, with 88 per cent demanding retribution and many respondents advocating torture: 'we should string them up and cut little pieces of them – one peace at the time' or 'torture them to a slow and awful death' (Lotchin 2015:413). In contrast, surveys conducted with US soldiers in 1943 indicate that only 21 per cent expressed animosity towards the enemy, and this number would be probably lower if the survey was done on the front-line combatants only (Dollard & Horton 1943).

Similarly, during the 1990s Yugoslav wars of succession, surveys of university students, who had no direct experience of war, found that 15.3 per cent (in 1992) and 14.1 per cent (in 1993) agreed with one of these two statements: 'I would like someone to kill them all' or 'I would personally exterminate them all.' On top of that, 12.2 per cent (in 1992) and 7.7 (in 1993) agreed with the statement 'they should be forbidden to enter my country' (Malešević & Uzelac 1997:294–295). As indicated above, these views differ substantially from the attitudes expressed by combatants who fought in the Yugoslavs wars and who often expressed much more tolerance and even empathy towards the enemy (Malešević 2022; see Chapter 9). The direct experience of fighting usually moderates attitudes towards enemy nations. For instance, surveys with US soldiers in Vietnam conducted after their first combat show that the battlefield environment changed their views about the adversary: while only 27 per cent hated the enemy more after the battle, 38 per cent respected their adversary more or hated them less than before (Bourke 2000:157). The research done during World War II points in the same direction: while civilians were very receptive towards the propagandistic and dehumanising images of the enemy as 'unscrupulous monsters' who fight in a 'dirty or inhuman' way, only 13 per cent of US soldiers who fought in Europe shared this view (Stouffer et al. 1949:162). Even among the civilian population, attitudes differ according to the extent of their exposure to violence. For instance, during World War II, citizens of British cities that were bombed by the Luftwaffe were less supportive of reprisals than the public living in the unaffected rural areas of Britain such as Westmorland, Cumberland, and Yorkshire (Garrett 1993:95). Bourke (2000:160) summarises the results of many similar studies conducted on soldiers and civilians: 'Civilians were more prone to articulate virulent hatred toward the enemy, leading many commentators to conclude that reading or writing about killing was more likely to stimulate hateful feelings than actual participation in the slaughter.'

During wartime, not only is the civilian population more hostile towards enemy nations, but civilians also tend to identify more strongly with their own nations than the combatants. Public polls conducted during inter-state wars often indicate that the war environment regularly increases a sense of national pride and stronger feelings of attachment with one's nation. For example, in surveys conducted during World War II, an overwhelming majority of US civilians expressed a strong sense of pride in their nation (Lotchin 2015). A similar attitude was recorded for many other twentieth- and early twenty-first-century wars. During the 2003 Iraq War, 90 per cent of US citizens agreed with statements that they were either extremely proud (70 per cent) or very proud (20 per cent) to be American (Bowman et al. 2011:3). When directly asked about their patriotic feelings in 2005, 70 per cent of US citizens described themselves as either extremely patriotic (27 per cent) or very patriotic (43 per cent), and an additional 24 per cent opted for the category 'somewhat patriotic', with only 5 per cent stating that they were not especially patriotic (Bowman et al. 2011:8). The post-9/11 environment generated many overt displays of nationalism among the civilians, with the extensive deployment of the national flag and other symbols, singing of 'The Star-Spangled Banner' at many public events, and organising commemorative rituals and declarations of national solidarity (Collins 2022). 9/11 and the onset of the Afghan War generated an intense proliferation of flag-waving rituals: 'The [US] flag was raised, lowered and waved; flown from buildings, porches and balconies; pasted on to windows, walls and doors; pinned to suits, shirts and sweaters; stitched onto t-shirts and school bags; and even draped over the columns of the New York Stock Exchange' (Taylor Woods &Tsang 2014:1). In 2011 public polls recorded 61 per cent of US citizens describing themselves as extremely proud and 25 per cent as very proud to be Americans (Bowman et al. 2011:3).

Other war contexts generated a similar proliferation of nationalist exuberance. For example, in the United Kingdom, the Falkland/Malvinas war sparked an unprecedented level of public animosity against the enemy nation – Argentina. Even before the violence unfolded, 89 per cent of British respondents supported military intervention, with 70 per cent advocating sinking of Argentine ships. Once the conflict developed, hostility towards Argentinians further increased, with 'one in three people want[ing] to bomb the Argentine mainland', while one in five thought British troops should invade Argentina itself (Ipsos MORI 1982). The mass media was deeply involved in stoking this nationalist frenzy with tabloid headlines such as '"WE'LL SMASH 'EM" printed with pictures of Winston Churchill and a bulldog or "Gotcha", celebrating the sinking of the Argentinian ship General Belgrano or printing a picture of the British nuclear missile with the caption "STICK THIS UP YOUR JUNTA"' (Horrie & Chippindale 1999). The Falkland war victory had an enormous impact on the rise of British nationalism: 'In the public imagination, victory in the Falklands provided a new national myth to rank alongside Dunkirk and the Battle of Britain' (Sandbrook 2019). This was also reflected in public polls in 1982 and 1983, in which 91 and 92 per cent of population, respectively, expressed pride in being British, with 61 per cent and 60 per cent, respectively, stating that they are very proud of their Britishness (Tilley & Heath 2007:665).

More recently one could notice a similar trend in Ukraine. The Russian occupation of Crimea and parts of Donbass together with war-related activities in 2014 impacted substantially on the sense of national identification. While before the war many citizens did not have a particularly strong sense of being Ukrainian, this changed profoundly during the war. While in 2012, 51.7 per cent of Ukrainian residents identified as Ukrainian only, in 2017 this had increased to 66.2 per cent. The onset of the large-scale war with Russia in 2022 shifted this sense of national identification further, with now 82.8 per cent of population identifying solely as Ukrainian (Kulyk 2023). In addition, as Kulyk (2023:1) shows, in the war environment 'national identity not only became more salient to Ukrainians, it acquired a more radical meaning, thus imbuing the supposedly civic attachment to homeland with potentially exclusive ethnocultural content'.

In contrast, the available surveys and interviews with front-line combatants show that micro-group attachments regularly trump a sense of identification with one's nation (Mann 2023; Malešević 2022, 2017, 2010; Collins 2022, 2008). In a large-scale survey conducted in 1944 among US troops fighting in Europe, a majority of soldiers downplayed the role of ideology. Instead, the dominant responses were to get the war done (44 per cent) and to support their war comrades and family members (24 per cent), while ideological reasons including patriotism were marginal motivation (5 per cent in total) (Stouffer et al.

1949:98–100, 135–140). Similarly, King (2011) and Junger (2011) found that professionalism and micro-group attachments played a more important role for most US and UK soldiers who fought in the Afghanistan and Iraq Wars. As Junger (2011:229) summarises his findings: 'the shared commitment to safeguard one another's lives is unnegotiable and only deepens with time. The willingness to die for another person is a form of love that even religions fail to inspire, and that experience of it changes a person profoundly.'

This discrepancy in the views of the combatants and civilians is not only a product of different personal experiences of war and violence. It is also a reflection of different organisational, ideological, and micro-interactional logic that operates in civilian and military spheres. For one thing, as soldiers and other combatants live and work in social organisations that are perceived to be the backbone of the national project, they do not need to legitimise their actions by invoking strong nationalist discourses. Being a member of an organisation that is viewed as a beacon of patriotism frees the combatants from any potential external attempts to delegitimise their actions as being insufficiently patriotic. As the combatants are the only group that willingly exposes themselves to mortal danger to protect the nation, their patriotic credentials are rarely questioned. Moreover, as all combatants face and share this threat of death, invoking patriotic language in such an environment would undermine the very foundation of the military unit – the micro-group solidarity. It is no accident that members of nearly all fighting units in the world dislike individuals whose 'heroic' acts endanger their comrades. As Mann (2023:371) summarises findings of studies on front-line combatants in different conflicts: 'soldiers shared a taboo against flag-waving patriotism … they were uncomfortable with civilian notions of "heroism", knowing their own imperfect behaviour. They disliked having "heroes" as comrades, since their conspicuous bravery drew enemy fire like a magnet to the whole group.'

In contrast, the civilian sphere operates according to a very different logic. Modern inter-state warfare is defined by the large-scale public mobilisation of all citizens. Since the Napoleonic wars all members of society are expected to participate in the war effort – either as soldiers, workers, or active cheerleaders for their nation. The two world wars were the epitome of total warfare where entire societies were mobilised to fight, and the states were able to direct most of the economy, industry, technology, science, transportation, and communication for the war machine. In this context all those who were not recruited to fight on the front line could be suspected of being indifferent towards the national war aims or even siding with the enemy. Hence demonstrating one's patriotism on a daily basis often becomes a norm for civilians. The public expectation is that all citizens have to participate in nationalist rituals (e.g., displaying flags, singing the national anthem, supporting the troops), and any perceived lack of the patriotic commitment can be deemed disloyal or even treasonous.

However, this level of public commitment is only possible under modern conditions where citizens are already primed in the nation-centric understanding of their world. In premodern contexts soldiering was usually associated with relatively small sectors of society: the feudal obligation of the vassals, nobility, and knights; the armies of aristocrats where ordinary soldiers had a relatively marginal role; the mercenaries, privateers, corsairs, or marauders. In this type of social order, the majority of the population consisted of illiterate peasantry, whose primary source of identification was local, kinship-based, or religious (Anderson 1983; Gellner 1983). The peasantry did not identify with their polities. As such they could not be armed, as they might use those weapons to turn against their feudal rulers.

In direct contrast, in modernity, all citizens can be recruited to fight in times of war, or if unable to fight they are expected to work for and support the war effort. Thus, nationalism and modern warfare are deeply interlinked. The nation-state differs from its premodern counterparts such as patrimonial kingdoms, city-states, city-leagues, free towns, tribal confederacies, or empires, as its very existence is premised on the idea of popular sovereignty. While traditional social orders are rooted in deep societal hierarchies that are justified in mythological, religious, or imperial doctrines, nation-states are built on the idea that power resides in people and as such all citizens are of equal moral worth. Furthermore, whereas traditional social orders had neither political interest, organisational capacity, nor ideological know-how to mould very heterogenous populations into a culturally and politically uniform society, the nation-state is a homogenising machine (Malešević 2019, 2013; Anderson 1983; Gellner 1983). As argued in Chapter 1, nationalist grounding underpins much of social life in the contemporary world. Nationalism is not only modern; modernity itself is nationalist. Over the last 200 years or so, much of the globe has been experiencing waves of organisational, ideological, and micro-interactional grounding of nationalism. Organisational grounding entails the presence of robust coercive-organisational powers that can promote and eventually institutionalise nationalist discourses and practices. Historically, this process starts with intellectual associations and secret revolutionary societies such as Carbonari, Philiki Etaireia, or Young Poland and gradually transforms into mass-scale social movements, political parties, paramilitary groups, and/or cultural organisations. Once nationalism becomes the dominant state ideology, its coercive-organisational capacity increases substantially. As the modern states possesses legitimate monopolies on the use of violence, taxation, legislation, and education, they can rely on the military, police, and judiciary to ground nationalist principles and practices across all institutions under state control.

Ideological grounding is rooted in narratives that promote the idea of nationhood as the only legitimate form of territorial political association, where the 'nation' is conceptualised as the transhistorical community of fate. In ideological terms, nationalism espouses grand vistas of salvation, emancipation, liberation, and an authentic life. By relying on increasing organisational capacity (including of the educational systems, mass media, and public sphere), these ideas are disseminated to the wider audience. Nationalist rhetoric regularly deploys the language of righteousness and invokes moral principles of equality, justice, and solidarity (e.g., that all nations should be free). In this sense ideological grounding becomes a vehicle of mass mobilisation and gradually attains the status of the hegemonic discourse of political legitimacy (Malešević 2019:11–12).

Micro-interactional grounding captures the realm beyond large-scale structural processes that are the organisational scaffolds and ideological narratives. Nationalism becomes a potent ideological force only when it successfully permeates the microcosm of everyday life. Nationalist idioms are regularly reproduced through an array of habitual practices that constitute the daily experiences of most human beings in the contemporary world – the routinised forms of nation-centric communication, consumption, and interaction (Storm 2024; Fox 2017). More than any other ideological discourse, nationalism normalises and naturalises a particular form of group membership (nation) through personalised experiences and intimate relationships with significant others (e.g., family members, close friends, peer groups). It is no accident that nationalist rhetoric often deploys metaphors of kinship and comradeship such as 'our Italian brothers and sisters', 'Mother India', or 'Albanian fatherland'.

Hence, the modern civilian sphere is saturated with nation-centric images and practices. We are all born into the world of nation-states, are socialised to be members of specific nations, and are often involved in reproducing nationhood in our everyday lives. Not only do nationalist principles underpin the cultural, economic, and geopolitical structures of the modern world; they are just as important in social practices that shape public policy, the judiciary, mass media, policing, cultural policy, education, welfare, migration laws, border controls, or tourism. Citizens of contemporary societies are involved in continuous and often taken-for-granted practices through which nationhood is discursively constructed and reproduced in routine talking practices, through ritual enactments of nationhood, and through banal forms of nation-centric consumption (Storm 2024; Fox 2017; Billig 1995). As nationalist idioms, in many diverse forms, remain the only legitimate sources for the justification of political rule over a specific territory, they dominate the public sphere of modern societies. In this context it is very difficult, if not impossible, for civilians to escape the discourse and practices of nationalism. Nation-centric idioms are created, reproduced, and maintained in the civilian sphere, while military organisations are just a segment of this ongoing and society-wide process.

In times of war and other large-scale calamities, the everyday and banal forms of nationalism attain a more volatile shape. Habitual reminders of a nation-centric world such as weather reports, postal stamps, coins, culinary practices, or decorative flags are suddenly accompanied by loud national battle cries, displays of irredentist and expansionist national maps, singing of national anthems, and fervent waving of flags (Malešević 2013; Billig 1995). This rapid shift from cold to hot nationalism is often characterised by intense ritualism. Collins (2022) describes this phenomenon as the 'time-bubble' of nationalism. In his view a time-bubble 'is an emotional mood produced by a sudden event focusing public attention into a massive interaction ritual'. He shows how after 9/11 the US population was involved in an intense, protracted, and shared ritual of national solidarity that was characterised by strong emotional displays of nationalist exuberance. These rituals are in part triggered by external conflict, but internal social dynamics are just as important, as such 'an emotional upsurge of national identity is used to legitimate insurgent crowds and discredit regimes'. However, Collins argues that such nationalist time-bubbles cannot last for more than a few months: 'Conflict-mobilized national solidarity lives in a time-bubble of three to six months, when emotions are most extreme and the most polarizing attacks – both physical and symbolic – on opponents are made' (Collins 2022:96). Obviously, more protracted conflicts such as inter-state wars that last for years can prolong such nationalist rituals. However, the intensity of nationalist rituals is bound to experience highs and lows, as it would be difficult to maintain such highly intense nationalist rituals over several years. Thus, warring states provide an organisational and ideological scaffold for the proliferation of nationalist ideas and practices and simultaneously aim to tap into micro-interactional dynamics where emotional attachments and moral commitments are developed. While the intensity of nationalist displays may wax and wane during the war, states and civil societies police social practices to make sure that nationalist rhetoric remains dominant in the public sphere.

Both the state and civil society can deploy the nationalist card to delegitimise civilians who are deemed not to be patriotic enough. The spirit of nationalism is forged and maintained primarily in the civilian sphere.

Turning Warriors into Nationalists

If nationalism is a phenomenon born and reproduced primarily in the civilian sphere, why are many military organisations, outside the combat zone, strongly associated with the patriotic rhetoric and practice? Many veterans' organisations; private military contractors; political, cultural, and economic associations representing soldiers; and some civil society groups firmly link military service and combat experience to nationalist values. For example, the largest US veterans' organisation, the American Legion, lists 'American values and patriotism' as one of its core principles. Its constitution emphasises the centrality of the nationhood: 'For God and country we ... uphold and defend the Constitution of the United States of America ... foster and perpetuate a one hundred percent Americanism ... [and aim to] ... inculcate a sense of individual obligation to the community, state, and nation' (www.legion.org/preamble). In addition, the Legion advocates honouring 'military service by observing and participating in memorial events' and by paying 'perpetual respect for all past military sacrifices to ensure they are never forgotten by new generations'. The organisation invokes a sense of national solidarity by celebrating all who 'contribute to something larger than themselves and inspires others to serve and strengthen America' (www.legion.org/vsa). In a similar vein, the Indonesian veteran organisation LVRI defines its primary role as to 'continue to preserve the soul, spirit and values of the 1945 struggle' for the independence of Indonesia. Its mission also singles out nationalist goals: 'inheriting the soul, enthusiasm and values of the 1945 struggle, playing an active role in national development,... and consistently maintaining the honour and improving the welfare of veterans of the Republic of Indonesia' (https://veteranri.go.id/index.php/lvri/detail/4). The largest Croatian veteran organisation, HVIDRA, also identifies nationhood as one of its core values: 'the promotion of Croatian national, historical, cultural, economic and other values, and the promotion and refinement of the moral and ethical values of the Croatian people'. In addition, the organisation sees its role as preserving the nation-centric view of the 1990s war: 'promoting the truth about the Homeland War in the Republic of Croatia and abroad' (https://hvidra.hr/statut/). Similar rhetoric is also present in organisations representing former combatants who were involved in insurgencies, paramilitarist actions, and terrorism. For instance, the Irish Republican

Prisoners Welfare Association, which represents former IRA combatants and prisoners, regularly invokes nationalist principles in its public campaigns. One of its central aims is 'highlighting POW issues and campaigns [as the] Republican Prisoners are amongst those that suffer the most in the struggle for Irish freedom' (https://irpwa.irish/about-us).

Even private military contractors invoke patriotic language to justify their activities. For instance, in a recent survey of US-based private military and security contractor personnel, 96 per cent see their job as 'a calling where I can serve my country', and 83 per cent agree with the view that 'citizens should show strong allegiance to their country and be willing to fight for their country' (Franke & von Boemcken 2011:734). The largest private military contractors such as Constellis/Academii, G4S, DynCorp, or the Wagner group all frame their activities in terms of defending and promoting the national interests of their respective nation-states. For example, the website of Constellis features a large US flag, while Eric Prince (2011), a former owner of Academi (Blackwater), described his life mission as 'to serve God, serve my family and to serve the United States with honor and integrity'. Key representatives of the Wagner group have always emphasised strongly that they fight for Russian national interests and have regularly displayed Russian nationalist symbols. In many of his speeches, the former leader of Wagner, Yevgeny Prigozhin, emphasised that this private military organisation was fighting for the Russian nation and aims: 'fighting traitors and mobilizing our society' (Jochecova 2023:1).

The key issue here is that the war veterans' organisations and other associations that represent former combatants do not operate on the battlefields but are pursuing specific political or social goals in the civilian public sphere. In other words, such organisations are part and parcel of the civilian world, and they deploy the language and practices that dominate the civilian life – nationalism. Political elites and state representatives can also use the experiences of former combatants for their own political purposes. For example, the Chinese government regularly frames actions of former soldiers through nationalist lenses in order to boost its own political legitimacy: 'Chinese authorities on Monday released a list of people who were awarded the "Most Beautiful Veterans" title, highlighting the exemplary deeds of retired military personnel who have selflessly dedicated themselves to the Communist Party of China, the nation and the people' (http://eng.chinamil.com.cn/CHINA_209163/TopStories_209189/16269428.html).

In some respects such organisations exploit the symbolic military capital of the former combatants to position themselves better in the civilian sphere. In this process, veterans' organisations or state authorities reframe the personal and collective experiences of ex-soldiers through well-elaborated ideological narratives. Hence, the original focus on micro-level solidarities becomes reformulated through dominant nationalist discourses as 'a sacrifice for our country'. The organisational and ideological grounding of nationalism provides the structural scaffold for this transformation, while the micro-interactional grounding 'translates' the small group bonds into potent and society-wide directed nationalist narratives (Malešević 2019; see Chapter 9).

Since nationalism is a structural force that operates through potent social organisations, it is often able to draw former combatants into its nation-centric vortex. The motivations of combatants to fight on the battlefields were primarily centred on a sense of moral obligation and emotional attachment to their micro-level groups –platoon comrades, close family members, and friends. Yet in the aftermath of wars and other violent conflicts, former warriors often embrace ideological language and practices to reframe their own battlefield experiences in nation-centric terms. Although some former combatants firmly reject this nationalisation of their war experiences, many eventually assent to or even enthusiastically promote this ideological reframing of their military past (Milekić 2022). This process is often a reflection of civilian social and political contexts. As veterans' organisations pursue specific political, economic, or ideological goals, they extensively rely on socially recognised cultural capital that their members have generated in the war. In the civilian sphere, where nationalism is the dominant operative ideology and the principal source of political legitimacy, one's war experience becomes a powerful bargaining chip in everyday political struggles. The same logic operates for the state authorities, who often excessively praise the contributions of former combatants to legitimise their own policies. In this context state representatives and veterans' organisations, among many other groups, invoke a sense of moral responsibility that society has towards those who 'willingly sacrificed themselves for the nation'. For instance, in a recent speech commemorating seventy years since the Korean War, US president Joe Biden framed the battlefield experiences of US and South Korean soldiers in distinctly nation-centric terms: 'This year marks the 70th anniversary of the alliance between our two nations. It's an unbreakable bond, forged in bravery and the sacrifice of our people, sanctified by the blood of American and Korean troops who fought and defended liberty. And I'm proud we are joined today by veterans of the Korean War. Those veterans are the reason we can stand here today.... We stand as strong, proud, and free because of them' (Biden 2023).

This nationalist framing and uniformisation of the very diverse personal war experiences of combatants fosters a mutually reinforcing two-fold moral obligation. On the one hand, the civilian population is obliged to respect the martyrdom of soldiers whose sacrifice for 'us' is 'sanctified by blood'. Hence, any civilian who might question these war sacrifices is bound to be seen as ungrateful, selfish, traitorous, and immoral. On the other hand, former combatants are also obliged to frame their own personal war experiences as a willing sacrifice for the nation. Something that is 'sanctified by blood' cannot be devalued as a diverse and historically contingent personal experience. Any attempt to present their wars past in non-national, a-national, or micro-group bonds would equally be perceived as self-interested, dishonourable, and thus immoral. This endless moral loop does not have much to do with the rhetoric of specific politicians, generals, administrators, or the leaders of veterans' organisations. Instead, such moral loops are a structural product of nationalist grounding. In a nation-centric world many war experiences become nationalised. Ongoing organisational, ideological, and micro-interactional grounding provides the institutional channels for the transformation of personally heterogeneous experiences into a homogeneous nationalist narrative.

In addition to being chained to this moral loop of nationalism, former combatants are also motivated to reinterpret their past by various incentives. Once their war experience is codified as heroic, it is likely to generate substantial status privileges and political, ideological, and even economic benefits for many former combatants. Obviously, these incentives operate only if former soldiers go along with this ideological transformation of their war experiences. Once this symbolic military capital is established, ex-combatants can also use it to delegitimise government policies, to demand better material or symbolic conditions for war veterans, or to pursue specific ideological projects. For example, dissatisfied veterans from World War I were the key political group undermining legitimacy of the post-war governments in many European countries: 'army veterans were the core of all fascist movements, which also had large paramilitaries' (Mann 2023:219; Mann 2005). More recently in Croatia and Zimbabwe, war veterans were involved in large-scale public events where they were able to directly influence government policies on many issues. The Zimbabwean war veterans' organisation (ZNLWVA), with the close links to the ruling ZANU-PF, was involved in the illegal occupation of farms and has often attacked and killed white farmers and opposition politicians. Their political activities were regularly framed in nationalist rhetoric that invokes their war sacrifices (Kriger 1993). Croatian war veterans' organisations have also relied on their symbolic military capital to shape many government polices or to force resignation of specific ministers. From 2014 to 2016 war veterans have organised a 555-day-long protest in front of the Croatian Ministry of Defence where they set up tents, demanded a change of government, and were involved in violence against police. Their rhetoric too was couched in the language of nationalism and war sacrifices (Milekić 2022).

Thus, the dominance of nationalist discourses that is present in military organisations, veterans' associations, governmental institutions, civil society groups, and even private security companies has very little to do with actual war experiences. Instead, all these organisations operate in the civilian public sphere and their actions are shaped by the nation-centric ideas and practices that dominate this world. In this context, the tangible battlefield motivations of former combatants often undergo radical transformation. Organisational, ideological, and micro-interactional grounding changes the genuine sense of micro-level solidarity into a nationalist project. The civilian-isation of combatants goes hand in hand with the nationalisation of the warrior ethos.

Conclusion

Since Horace's famous dictum that it is sweet and fitting to die for one's homeland ('Dulce et decorum est pro patria mori'), the common perception has been that most soldiers fight for patriotic reasons. In this chapter I have tried to show that such views are wrong for two main reasons: (1) while armed forces are regularly imbued with strong nationalist discourses, this is not the case with ordinary combatants, who are often more motivated by their sense of moral obligation and emotional attachment to their micro-groups; and (2) nationalist ideologies are much more prevalent in the civilian than in the military sphere. In the contemporary world, where the nation-state is the only legitimate form of territorial organisation of political sovereignty, nationalism is generated and constantly reproduced in state institutions, civil society, and the ordinary habits of everyday life. Hence, it is the civilians rather than soldiers who are the backbone of nationalist subjectivities. The warrior ethos that regularly directs the conduct of ordinary combatants existed long before the emergence of nationalism. Although modern states and military organisations have invested extensively in making this warrior ethos as nationalist as possible, the direct experience of the battlefield often generates situations where the two become decoupled. It is only in the aftermath of war and the reintegration of the civilian and military sphere that nationalism regains its primacy yet again.

9 From Deep Comradeship to Nationalist Subjectivities

Introduction

In his magnum opus, Ben Anderson (1983:7) emphasises the fraternal aspect of nationhood. A nation 'is imagined as a community, because, regardless of the actual inequality and exploitation that may prevail in each, the nation is always conceived as a deep, horizontal comradeship. Ultimately it is this fraternity that makes it possible, over the past two centuries, for so many millions of people, not so much to kill, as willingly to die for such limited imaginings.' Although Anderson is adamant that all groups 'larger than primordial villages of face-to-face contact' are imagined communities, he sees nationhood as being distinctively tied to the idea of 'deep horizontal comradeship'. Hence in his view nationalism is much closer to 'kinship' or 'religion' than other secular ideological projects (Anderson 1983:5–6). Anderson is right that fraternal imagery underpins all forms of nationalism. Nationhood is unimaginable without references to group solidarity. Nevertheless, it is not completely clear how group solidarity develops, operates, expands, contracts, or is maintained at the level of large-scale entities such as nation-states. Is it possible to generate and sustain deep social bonds between millions of people, most of whom, as Anderson emphasised, will never meet each other?

In this chapter I focus on the relationship between micro-level bonds and nationalism. I argue that deep-level solidarity is always limited by the size of the groups involved. As such, nationalism cannot arise from acts of spontaneous collective solidarity but only as a product of coercive-organisational, ideological, and micro-interactional work. In other words, as the emotional and cognitive capacities of human beings are built for life in very small groups, any attempt to project these bonds onto large-scale abstract entities such as a nation requires the presence of potent organisational and ideological capacities that can penetrate and operate within this micro-world. Nationhood can periodically be perceived as a form of fraternal tie, but this is a highly contextual experience shaped by the historical interplay between the coercive-organisational capacity, ideological penetration, and ongoing interactional dynamics. To fully understand how nationalism operates, it is crucial to explore how micro-level group bonds, including close kinships and friendship networks, are transformed into believable macro-level narratives of national solidarity. In this chapter, I analyse the experiences of soldiers who fought in the 1990s wars in Croatia and Bosnia and Herzegovina to identify how, when, and under which conditions deep comradeships can gradually be transformed into nation-centric attachments.

Origins and Scope of Group Solidarity

In Anderson's famous phrase a nation is conceived as a form of 'deep horizontal comradeship'. However, can micro-level deep bonds ever be vertical, or are all forms of comradeship inevitably horizontal? One could pinpoint some historical instances where people have developed strong bonds across the established social hierarchies (e.g., European feudal masters and their serfs or the children of American slave owners and their enslaved black nannies), but such ties cannot involve deep comradeship. As Hegel argued potently in the *Phenomenology of Spirit* (2018 [1807]), master and slave are engaged in an asymmetrical recognition where neither is free: the master possesses authority without responsibility, while the slave has responsibility without authority. Such a non-reciprocal and non-commensurate relationship can in some instances evolve to the point of a shared social tie, but it can never acquire the form of horizontal relationship that deep comradeships imply. Deep comradeship is a reciprocal and equal relationship, and as such all deep comradeships are horizontal, or they are not comradeships. It is true that one can imagine a particular relationship with their superior as a form of friendship, but this is a very different phenomenon than the actual deep bonds generated through mutual reciprocity and relative parity within the relationship. Deep comradeship can be defined as an intense and lasting social bond between small groups of people that involves a shared sense of social reciprocity, mutual moral obligations to the point of willing self-sacrifice, deep-rooted solidarity, and a strong emotional attachment. This point is central to understand the historical dynamics of micro-level bonding and its organisational and ideological impact in the development of nationalism.

One of the crucial issues for understanding the dynamics of micro-level solidarity is the size of the group. Archaeological, anthropological, and psychological research indicates clearly that the natural habitat of human beings are small groups. British psychologist Robin Dunbar

(2021, 1993, 1992) has pioneered research on the size and dynamics of group ties, and one of his better-known findings is that humans tend to have a fairly small and stable number of close friends.[1] The Dunbar number stands for the limits to the quantity of individuals with whom one can maintain long-standing social relationships. This finding was initially generated through the study of primates and was then repeated on numerous occasions with human subjects. In his early studies, Dunbar (1993, 1992) identified a strong positive correlation between the brain size of primates and the size of groups populated by these primates. The research on humans generated similar results, indicating that an average human being can maintain around 150 stable relationships. Several scholars from other disciplines have found a similar number being associated with the typical hunter-gathering and early horticultural societies (Casari & Tagliapietra 2018; Hill & Hurtado 2017; Hamilton et al. 2007). For example, a census commissioned in 1086 by William the Conqueror that was published in the Domesday Book shows that most villages in England at that time were around 150 people (Dunbar 2021:31). The sociological research also indicates that human beings cannot maintain too many strong ties with other humans, as this involves a great deal of interactional labour (Collins 2022, 2008; Goffman 1967). New technologies have allowed much more daily interaction between individuals who do not know each other. However, even on social media it is difficult to maintain regular, deep, and meaningful interactions with more than 150 individuals. Recent studies tracking social behaviour on Twitter, Facebook, and regular email communication indicate that despite the wider range of interaction, most individuals settle on maintaining regular contact with between 150 and 250 individuals (Haerter et al 2012; Goncalves et al. 2011).

Although some other species display a high level of social behaviour, primates are distinct in the intensity of their bonded relationships. As Dunbar (2021:54) points out: 'The overarching principle that bound anthropoid primate social groups with monogamous pair-bonds of the carnivore, ungulate, bat and bird families was that all these groups depend on personalised relationships in which individuals are committed to each other by a form of trust, reciprocity and obligation.' However,

[1] Dunbar's studies on group size have initiated vibrant research across many academic disciplines. These studies generally confirm that there are cognitive and emotional limits to the scale and intensity of human interactions (Collins 2022, 2008; Casari & Tagliapietra 2018; Hill & Hurtado 2017). However, Dunbar's analysis is also prone to biological determinism, as it does not allow much room for social, cultural, and historical variability in group ties (Malešević 2022:36–43).

primates differ substantially from others as 'all primates have bonded social relationships, whereas only a few ungulates and carnivores have these kinds of relationships' (54). Human beings also develop highly sophisticated and layered networks of friendships. Most people usually have a circle of friends, who range from close comrades to companions to associates and acquaintances. The scope and hierarchy of friendship is dynamic and changeable, as during our lifetimes we acquire new friends and lose some old ones.

This psychological research together with many anthropological and archaeological studies has demonstrated convincingly that social solidarity develops in relatively small groups. Human beings are biologically predisposed to operate in small-scale, face to face, social environments. Our cognitive and emotional capacities have developed through everyday interactions with such small groups. Many studies have shown that close-range interaction between small groups of friends, such as shared laughter, dancing, or singing, often generates the release of endorphins in our bodies, hormones that can help improve a body's well-being, relieve pain, and reduce stress (Malešević 2022:16–44). As Turner and Maryanski (1993) indicate, the evolution of *Homo sapiens* was shaped by the small size of groups our predecessors populated. As the birthplace of the modern human, the African savannah, was an open plain where it was difficult to hide and was also inhabited by many predatory species, early humans could not survive in large groups. Hence movement in small packs was the best survival strategy. These small groupings were also crucial in fostering emotionally attuned individuals who have also gradually developed significant cognitive capacities. Archaeologists have made clear that for 99 per cent of human existence on this planet, humans have lived in small and highly malleable groups that rarely included more than 150 people (Fry 2007). Thus, for much of prehistory group solidarity was forged, shaped, and reinforced on the level of micro-groups – close kinship and friendship networks. As small-scale hunting and gathering communities were the dominant form of social life for nearly 1.8 million years, all forms of group solidarity were inevitably micro-level solidarities.[2] Thus, the starting point of group solidarity are micro-units such as highly mobile, non-hierarchical, fluid, kinship-based, and nomadic bands.

This all changes with the emergence of chiefdoms, the first city-states, and empires. In the wake of the Neolithic revolution, human beings start

[2] It is important to emphasise that hunting and gathering were practiced by many early forms of hominids and as such they are much older than modern *Homo sapiens*, who originated ca. 160,000 years ago.

inhabiting a very different world. Once the agricultural production and sedentary lifestyle gradually replaces hunting and gathering and nomadic subsistence, the patterns of group solidarity also experience a significant transformation.[3] The rise of the populous cities, political and religious hierarchies, writing, technology, and the complex division of labour have all had dramatic impact on the dynamics of social bonds. Once the first, pristine forms of statehood emerged, rulers had to devise and implement new normative codes to generate social cohesion across a much larger social order[4] (Mann 1986). Hence the new state apparatuses had to develop novel organisational and proto-ideological tools to make the populations under their rule compliant and obedient to the state authorities. Typical proto-ideological doctrines involved mythologies, religions, spiritual doctrines, and imperial creeds, all of which were designed to justify existing social norms. Initially, the rulers were depicted as gods or god-like creatures such as in ancient Egypt, Assyria, or Babylon. Eventually, religious doctrines positioned deities outside of everyday life and focused on reinforcing the status quo.

The imperial model of rule was the dominant form of territorial and political organisation of the world for more than 5,000 years (Kumar 2021, 2017). Imperial power was successfully enforced through advanced organisational capacities as well as through the ability of imperial orders to represent themselves as being ideologically superior to their potential competitors. Capstone empires such as the ancient Chinese under the Hun dynasty (206 BCE–220 CE) or the Roman empire under Emperor Trajan (98–117) were depicted by their rulers as the epicentre of the world. Hence, instead of recognising other states as legitimate political entities, they ruled on the assumption that they constitute the entire world. As Munkler's (2007:5) emphasises: 'empires have no neighbours which they recognise as equals'. Consequently, their

[3] The anarchist tradition within anthropology has recently challenged the view that hunting and gathering was the dominant form of social life for much of prehistory (Graeber & Wengrow 2021). In *The Dawn of Everything* Graebner and Wengrow argue that traditional approaches espouse a linear view of historical change, while the pre-historical reality was characterised by the existence of large and complex, yet decentralised polities, for thousands of years. However, many scholars have criticised this assessment for lack of evidence, cherry-picking historical examples, and exaggerated interpretation of available data (Bell 2021; Handler 2022). Nevertheless, even if these anarchist accounts have credence, they largely ignore much of prehistory and focus mostly on the last 10,000–12,000 years of human existence. As such they seem unlikely to disprove the existing consensus on early foraging communities.

[4] This is not to deny the important role micro-level solidarities have played in the formation of pristine states. The solidarity of warriors was central in establishing military and political monopolies, which fostered the development of social hierarchies within the state structure (Malešević 2010:242–260; Mann 1986).

ideological doctrines often espoused the idea of the civilising mission as a universalist political programme centred on transforming the barbarian lands to civilised ones under imperial rule. In ancient China these ideas were initially articulated around the notion of emperor as the 'son of heaven', and later Confucian teachings were institutionalised as the official doctrine that glorified the status quo. In the Roman case the doctrine of humanitas was used to 'civilise' barbarian tribes who were conquered by the empire (Kumar 2021).

The rise of nationalism from the late eighteenth century onwards dramatically undermined the legitimacy of the imperial world. Although several European empires had managed to hold off domestic political pressure from many groups by imperialising abroad and gradually nationalising at home, once nationalism become the dominant ideology of modernity, imperial orders started to collapse throughout the world. The French and American Revolutions together with the Latin American wars of independence galvanised the large-scale structural transformations that eventually resulted in the nation-state model being established as the only legitimate form of territorial rule (Wimmer 2013; Malešević 2013). Although nationalism was a highly influential ideological discourse and practice for much of the nineteenth century, its dominance was established in the wake of the two world wars. After World War II imperial projects were completely delegitimised, and nation-states took their place. Instead of imperial creeds and civilising missions, nationalism become the dominant operative ideology of the post–World War II world.

Social Mechanisms of Nationalism

Perhaps more than any other doctrine, nationalism has gradually managed to develop into an all-encompassing ideological discourse and practice that now permeates everyday life. As emphasised in the Introduction, nationalism is a protean force that simultaneously operates as a political ideology, habitual form of everyday practice, and mode of modern subjectivity. Nationalism is premised on the idea that the nation is the principal unit of human solidarity and the only justifiable form of political legitimacy. This ideological discourse underpins the post–World War II geopolitical order as it legitimises the very existence of nation-states. As much scholarship on everyday nationalism indicates clearly, nationhood has become a fully normalised and naturalised practice in the contemporary world (Storm 2024; Kaplan 2018; Fox 2017; Skey 2011). Although nationalism is a modern project that is barely a few centuries old, once it had become the principal mode of governance, it managed to ideologically penetrate state institutions, civil society, and non-governmental agencies, as well as the interactional context of everyday life.

This pervasiveness of nationalism in the contemporary world is so powerful that many individuals assume that a nation is a normal, natural, and everlasting form of collective identification. Most social science surveys indicate that nationhood is perceived to be one of the key pillars of group identity, and large majorities of the population throughout the world express a strong sense of national attachment and high level of pride in their nation-states (Gallup 2021; Duina 2018; Medrano 2009). For example, in a study using the 2010–2014 World Values Survey, more than 80 per cent of respondents expressed that they are very proud or quite proud of their country (Beauchamp 2014). Similarly, a Eurobarometer survey shows that an overwhelming majority of European populations identify strongly with their nation-states: 'The most important identities of EU citizens are their family (81%) and national identity (73%)' (Eurobarometer 2021:1). In some cases, the sense of national identification is extremely high – ranging from 93 per cent in Portugal, 87 per cent in Hungary, 85 per cent in Slovakia, and 84 per cent in Spain, while in most other EU countries the level of attachment to their nation remains high, with the partial exception of Luxemburg (47 per cent) and Belgium (52 per cent) (Eurobarometer 2021:71). A 2021 Gallup survey of the US population indicates that almost two thirds of US adults are either extremely or very proud to be Americans: 43 per cent of the sample said that they are 'extremely proud' to be Americans (Gallup 2021). Other surveys record a similar pattern of strong national attachment across the world (Duina 2018). Hence, the key question is: How have the micro-level solidarities that shaped much of human pre-history suddenly been transformed into these macro-level nationalist identifications? If human beings are evolutionarily wired to live in small, face-to-face groups, how do they develop and sustain a sense of attachment with millions of people they will never meet?

The leading theories of nationalism successfully explain different aspects of this question. They emphasise the changing historical and structural context through which ordinary individuals become gradually socialised into the nation-centric world. Some scholars see the rise of nationalism through the prism of changing socio-economic conditions, uneven development, and the tensions between the industrialising centre and the underdeveloped periphery (Hechter 1977; Nairn 1998). In addition to these economic factors, classic studies by those such as Gellner and Anderson have also identified cultural and social transformations as contributing to the expansion of nationalism: while Gellner (1983) puts the spotlight on the standardisation of vernaculars, increasing literacy rates, and the introduction of compulsory education, Anderson (1983) links the rise of print capitalism with the proliferation of affordable books, newspapers, and a monoglot reading public. Other scholars emphasise political transformations and the role the modern bureaucratic state and warfare have played in the spread of nationalism as a form of modern politics (Breuilly 1993; Mann 1993; Giddens 1986). Some theorists such as Kedourie, Smith, and Hutchinson identify similarities between religious beliefs and nationalism. For Kedourie (1960), nationalism is a form of secular millenarianism that has successfully become a new form of salvation. Smith (2003) also sees nationalism as a 'form of political religion' and nations as 'sacred communions of citizens' that, just like traditional religions, offer 'a measure of personal immortality'. In Hutchinson's (2017) view, this link with religion is most pronounced in the context of warfare, as early modern European wars of religion have been central for the politization of ethno-national categories.

Although most of these explanations help us understand how nationalism has replaced other historical competitors as the dominant operative ideology of modern era, it is also necessary to study the specific processes that allowed for the transformation of micro-level attachments to the macro-level plane of nationhood and nation-states. More specifically, it is necessary to explore the social dynamics of solidarity: how small-group, face-to-face bonds become transformed into something perceived to be national solidarity.

I argue that this transformation is dependent on the presence of three interconnected and long-term historical processes: coercive-organisational grounding, ideological grounding, and micro-interactional grounding. Coercive-organisational grounding refers to an ongoing and open-ended historical process that involves the relatively continuous rise of coercive-organisational capacities and the ability of social organisations to internally pacify social order under their control. Historically, this process predates the emergence of pristine states and involves a variety of non-state organisations. However, once states acquire a monopolistic position, they become the primary purveyors of coercive-organisational power. This power has largely been cumulative and historically has been linked with the expansion of warfare and other forms of organised violence (e.g., slavery, serfdom, corvee labour). Although some states and other social organisations have experienced decline, destruction, or oblivion, coercive organisational power has for the most part continued to proliferate throughout the globe (Malešević 2017, 2010). This is an isomorphic process that involves continuous attempts to emulate and replicate successful coercive organisations.

This process dramatically intensified in the last three centuries. Tilly (1992) and Mann (1993) have documented well how the intensification of warfare in early modern Europe contributed substantially towards the development of historically unprecedented coercive-organisational powers of states. The increased frequency of European inter-state wars fostered the reform of the civil service and the development of science and technology, which in turn spurred investment in new weapons and building better transportation and communication networks. Moreover, the expansion of warfare forces rulers to centralise state power and increase their infrastructural reach, organisational dominance, and capacity to monopolise the use of coercive power over their territories. Once nation-states replaced empires, patrimonial kingdoms, and city-states as the only legitimate form of territorial power, their coercive-organisational capacities have only continued to increase. This organisational grounding is a precondition for the spread and embedment of nationalism throughout the social order (Malešević 2019, 2017).

Since nation-states are the 'bordered power containers' (Giddens 1986), they also provide the key institutional channels for the proliferation of nationalist discourses and practices. Hence, they foster ideological grounding, which is often framed through narratives that depict nations as the only legitimate model of territorial political association. Ideological grounding relies on organisational grounding, as the states use mass media, educational systems, military, police, judiciary, and the public sphere to promote nation-centric visions of social reality. Nationalist discourses and practices are often couched in the language of righteousness, invoking the promise of emancipation, liberation, authenticity, or salvation. Although ideological grounding is not limited to the states but includes civil society groups and many non-state organisations, the nation-state is the dominant organisational vehicle for mass mobilisation of nationalism.

Coercive-organisational and ideological grounding mostly operate as large-scale structural processes. They provide the organisational and ideological scaffolds around which nationalist discourses and practices operate. However, to successfully penetrate the micro-universe of everyday life it is necessary to rely on the process of micro-interactional grounding. As scholars of everyday nationalism have demonstrated convincingly, nationalism gains its potency from habitual reproduction in everyday practices (Storm 2024; Fox 2017; Skey 2011). Nationalist ideology not only permeates the sphere of public institutions and civil society groups, but also taps into the most intimate interpersonal relationships: close friendships, kinship and family networks, deep comradeships, and peer groups. Nationalism is reproduced daily through nation-centric interactions, consumption, and communication. It is this micro-level realm that is crucial for the naturalisation and normalisation of nationalism.

Bonding without Nationhood: Micro-Level Solidarities of Soldiers

As discussed in the Chapter 8, there is a paradox that underpins the relationship of soldiers towards nationalism. Usually, modern military organisations espouse a strong nationalist rhetoric, legitimise their existence through nation-centric idioms (e.g., defending the fatherland), and are often perceived to be the beacon of 'patriotic duty'. For example, the US Navy's website emphasises that their main purpose is to 'protect the American homeland' (US Navy 2023), while the Croatian Army defines its role as 'protecting the sovereignty and independence of the Republic of Croatia and defending its territorial integrity' (Croatian Army 2023). Similarly, the Israel Defense Forces specify that 'the soldiers of the IDF are obliged to fight and devote every effort, even at the risk of their own lives, to protect the State of Israel, its citizens and residents … while respecting the values of Israel as a Jewish and democratic state' (Israel Defense Forces 2023). However, years of extensive scholarship on the behaviour of soldiers on the battlefield indicate that they are usually averse to nationalist rhetoric (Malešević 2022, 2010; Collins 2022, 2008; Bourke 2000; Holmes 1986). While such patriotic discourse often appeals to civilians and young recruits and might be extensively deployed by veterans' organisations, most individuals participating in combat tend to be ill-disposed towards patriotic language on the front line (Mann 2023; Malešević 2022, 2010; Collins 2022, 2008; Bourke 2000; Holmes 1986; Dollard 1977). As Dollard's (1977) research on US soldiers shows, nationalism and other ideological doctrines had a minimal impact as fighting motivators; instead, 'ideology functions before battle, to get man in; and after battle by blocking thoughts of escape'. Other studies have also indicated that in many wars, soldiers tend to show less animosity towards the enemy they fight than do the civilians who have no military experience. For example, in a survey conducted in 1943/44 on a sample of 5,000 US soldiers who fought in Europe, only 13 per cent agreed with the dominant propagandistic line, widely accepted by the US public, that the enemy soldiers use 'dirty or inhuman' tactics (Stouffer et al. 1949:162).

This paradoxical situation whereby military organisations are highly nationalist while ordinary combatants generally dislike nationalist rhetoric requires more sociological analysis. Hence to explore the social mechanisms through which non-nationalist micro-level solidarities are transformed into macro-level nationalist narratives and practices, I will to analyse the data I collected during my 2011–2017 fieldwork in Croatia and Bosnia and Herzegovina. More specifically, I will analyse interviews I conducted with former soldiers who fought in the 1990s wars of Yugoslav succession. I interviewed many former combatants, but the focus here will be on thirty-five interviews with soldiers who had direct experience of combat violence: seventeen members of the Croatian Army (CA) and eighteen members of the Bosnian Serb Army (BSA).[5] I will also analyse mass media reports focused on their motivations to fight.

The wars in Croatia and Bosnia and Herzegovina were characterised by high levels of inter-ethnic violence, including the mass-scale ethnic cleansing of civilians and even genocidal killings in Srebrenica. There is an abundance of research on the role paramilitary organisations and police forces have played in these acts of violence (Nielsen 2022; Vukušić 2022; Karčić 2022). Many of those responsible for war crimes were in large part motivated by personal and ethno-national animosities towards the Other (Karčić 2022; Vukušić 2022). The main military organisations involved in these violent conflicts were also driven by intense nationalist aspirations (Malešević 2022; Žanić 2007; Bougarel 2006). However, there is a paucity of scholarship on the behaviour of ordinary soldiers in these wars, an overwhelming majority of whom were conscripts not involved in war crimes. Since this was the largest group of people involved in direct fighting and was also the largest population among the casualties of war, it is crucial to explore patterns of group solidarity and nationalism among these ordinary soldiers.

Despite the radical nationalist rhetoric and practice present during the wars of Yugoslav succession, ordinary soldiers generally tended to downplay the significance of these ideas on the battlefield. For example, when asked directly about their views of the Croats and Bosniaks/Bosnian Muslims during the war, most former Bosnian Serb soldiers were clear that there was no ethnic animosity towards their enemies: 'my best friend was a Muslim … you could not choose who will be your mother and father … before the war, even in 1991 and 1992 I did not know who was who [a Serb, a Croat or a Muslim] (Jovo, BSA). 'Half of my friends were Muslims and Croats … even today when they come from Sweden or

[5] For more information about the methodology and data collection for this project, see Malešević (2022:330–331). Some of the qualitative data used here draw on Malešević (2022). Since my focus is on combat soldiers only, I do not explore the experiences of military personnel who were employed in non-fighting roles. Hence there is a certain selection bias here, but this is done deliberately to track the links between direct war experience and a sense of group solidarity.

Denmark, we are together … so nobody thought about nationality' (Saša, BSA). 'I wasn't burdened by it … my godfather is a Muslim … when all those Muslims come from Sweden, they contact me … we hang together' (Dragan, BSA). Nevertheless, some soldiers emphasized the differences between urban and rural recruits: 'Those from the city didn't look so much at that nationalism, religion … those from the countryside … were into that Serbianness, they were more attached to it' (Saša, BSA).

The former soldiers of the Croatian Army gave a similar response: 'This war wasn't my fault, and it wasn't the fault of many of us who shared similar views as [ordinary Croats and Serbs], we would have found another way and there would have been no casualties or destruction' (Dražen, CA). 'My family came to Croatia from Bosnia, and I have family there … my wife's sister's husband is a Serb, he was on one side, and I was on the other … so we would talk to each other on the phone [during the war], how are you? What's happening with you? There is no hostility there … and now we regularly see each other' (Vjeko, CA).

The soldiers also provided many anecdotes that clearly illustrate how everyday interactions across the front lines were not shaped by hatred and animosity of the enemy. They would often communicate, trade, play football, and even joke across the battlefield. For example, in one such situation they compared their salaries: 'it was through the radio station … we entered their frequency … we were arguing about our salaries, how much they earned … although we all served regular military service, but we had a field salary of HRK 50 per day, and they had a carton of Marlboro and 10 German marks' (Zoran, CA). In another situation they shared laughter across the front line: 'Once my friend Dragan imitated Tito [a former Yugoslav president] … when it was quiet … and he talked like Tito … he talked for an hour, we were rolling with laughter … and we can hear the Muslims [across the front line] laughing too' (Dejan, BSA).

This lack of ethno-national hostility among the combatants who had a direct experience of battlefields is in line with findings from many other wars. While the states and military organisations that wage wars regularly deploy intense nationalist rhetoric for legitimisation of their actions and for the mobilisation of wider society, the combatants usually avoid such patriotic displays on the front line (Mann 2023; Collins 2022, 2008; Bourke 2000). This is not to say that most soldiers are a-national or anti-nationalist. Instead, their motivations are more complex, dynamic, and shaped by the ongoing organisational, ideological, and micro-interactional grounding. In this context nationalism is rarely if ever a primary motivator for fighting. Rather, I argue, nationalist ideas and practices tend to gradually envelop the non-nationalist motivations of combatants.

The ordinary soldiers who fought in the wars of Yugoslav succession rarely identify nationalist doctrine as an important reason for joining the military organisation and for their decisions to stay on the battlefield despite a very real possibility of losing their lives (Malešević 2022:189–222). Instead, most combatants emphasise that their motivation to fight was influenced by a sense of moral and emotional responsibility and feelings of solidarity towards their micro-groups. In most cases the primary motivation to accept the draft notice or to volunteer for military duty was linked to one's sense of solidarity with family members and close friends. For example, several Croatian and Bosnian Serb soldiers emphasised that their decision was influenced almost solely by feelings of responsibility to and fraternity with their family: 'My brother left for Canada … I thought … the parents, they sent one son, what will happen to them, and they stay here at the mercy of others … who will call them names, you took your sons away … I, due to a sense of responsibility towards my parents, stayed' (Dejan BSA). '[It was] my responsibility towards my father and mother' (Dragan, BSA). 'I felt I had to defend my family' (Mile, BSA). 'I felt fear when the military barracks in Osijek were captured [by the enemy] … I felt fear for my family much more than for myself' (Dražen, CA).

Other combatants identified a sense of loyalty to their close friends as playing a central role in their decision-making: 'All my close friends went, only one friend was not in the war' (Vjeko, CA). 'All my friends joined, my relatives, uncles' (Nenad, BSA). 'I was born in Banja Luka … and all my friends from the housing estate, and from the school joined [BSA] so did I too (Dragan, BSA). 'We all joined together … we were the same generation, kids of the same age in the same shit' (Goran, CA).

Nevertheless, the strong ties of the micro-group could also work in a different direction, as some individuals decided not to fight for the same micro-fraternal reasons – their family and friends had different views on the war. This was also linked to class differences: 'The better off people sent their children abroad … but these who stayed … it was as it was … when you fraternise with people … it would be shameful to say I am leaving [abroad]' (Zoran, CA). In some cases, the combatants were clear that their attitude towards fighting would be altered if their micro-group dynamics were different: 'when you see people dying … I've changed … the man changes and starts thinking … if I had children I probably would not fight anymore' (Vjeko, CA). In other cases, when a relative or a friend would join the enemy side the friendships were usually broken, and family loyalties ruined. However, even in these extreme situations, the micro-group fraternities could survive: 'my cousin was fighting on the Serbian side. It's not a problem because it wasn't the same battlefield …

and it's not a problem because I didn't see that cousin ten years before the war … and his own brother was with me in the same unit' (Zoran, CA).

Participation in war is regularly shaped by one's sense of moral obligation and emotional attachment to the micro-groups that were formed long ago and outside the theatres of war – one's family members and close friends. In most cases this strong sense of micro-solidarity remained as a powerful motivational driver on the battlefield. As one combatant emphasises, this motivation can overpower the fear that a majority of soldiers experience: 'you are full of fear and would run away from everything … but [you think of] your parents … you are there … your parents and everything' (Saša, BSA).

However, life shared in the extreme conditions of the front line tends to generate new forms of micro-group solidarity – the deep comradeship of combatants. This phenomenon of 'brothers in arms' with soldiers developing tight bonds of belonging and solidarity to the extent that they are willing to sacrifice their lives for their comrades has been identified across many different wars (Mann 2023; Malešević 2022; Whitehouse et al. 2014). A similar phenomenon has been detected among revolutionary cells, terrorist networks, and insurgent units (Shire & Hersi 2022; della Porta 2013; Whitehouse et al. 2014). The shared experience of everyday hardship with the constant exposure to death and suffering tends to generate deep bonds of comradeship that often resemble or even go beyond those of close family attachment. The war experience fosters unprecedented forms of micro-group attachments. The wars of Yugoslav succession have also fostered development of such tight forms of comradeship. In the words of Bosnian Serb soldiers: 'Unfortunately, tragedy brings people together. You bond with each other, you help each other. It has an impact, a lot to bring people together' (Saša BSA). 'I was ready to die for them and they would do the same for me … I would not be able to sleep otherwise' (Zoran, BSA). The same feelings were voiced by the Croatian soldiers: 'I was carrying a wounded comrade … they were shelling at us … your life was in peril, but you keep carrying him, if it hits you, it hits you' (Zdravko, CA). 'At the beginning, I was with my friends, and then they died. In 1993, I had a few more of them left, and then we split up in different units because friends die trying to rescue each other, and then more are killed because of that … one time a friend died, and we went to pull him out and two more died and two were wounded' (Vjeko, CA).

The combatants emphasise that such bonds were built very quickly and that in many cases they did not know their comrades before the war. For example, 'I was only eighteen years old and had some friends from childhood and such, but in the first ten days, maybe even less, five to six days, I formed such strong ties with people that was unbelievable … that you can be linked so much with the people that you know for only five days … later this seemed normal to me … we were dependent on each other' (Ivan, CA). 'I was thinking instantly why the fuck I need this, only yesterday I was in Sibinje, my village, drinking beer with my friends, we had a great time … I want to live a minute or two … but when he died, it would be dishonourable to leave him or any other wounded person on the battlefield … it was a code of honour' (Boris, CA). The battlefield bonds were often forged through the shared experience of fighting where solidarity was built through emotional and moral interdependence. As one Bosnian Serb soldier describes it, the continuous exposure to life and death situations was a key catalyst of deep bonds of micro-group solidarity: 'we were fighting for six hours in that hell … you don't know any more who is who … they thought they lost us all … and in these situations you get to know people … it was a simple reaction … a man reacts the way he thinks he should react … so you don't leave a man who is in danger so to save your own arse' (Dejan, BSA). Both the Croatian and the Bosnian Serb soldiers indicated that the strong sense of micro-group solidarity resembling family-like ties was a product of shared exposure to danger: 'we shared everything, helped each other as much as we could … we were all like a family' (Vjeko, CA). Although such deep bonds were often built in a very short period of time, they often last for years: 'our friendships are still strong … when I meet my friend [from war] Dragan, who has four children today, who is now serious and grey I kiss him like a brother' (Dejan, BSA).

The battlefield experiences of ordinary soldiers who fought in the wars of Yugoslav succession indicate clearly that their primary source of group solidarity were their micro-groups. They joined the military organisations, fought on the front lines, and decided to remain in war despite the fact that they could get killed at any moment. The soldiers did so because they felt a strong sense of moral obligation and emotional attachment to their micro-groups. Despite the prevalence of nationalist rhetoric, which emphasised the preservation of the nation as the central nodal point of war, most soldiers fought and died for much smaller groups – their family, friends, and their 'brothers in arms'.

Nationalist Grounding of Micro-Solidarity

The historical record indicates that the phenomenon of 'brothers in arms' is not new. In different times and places combatants have regularly developed a deep sense of micro-group comradeship (Mann 2023;

Malešević 2022, 2010; Collins 2022, 2008; Bourke 2000; Holmes 1986). However, in the premodern world war was predominantly a prerogative of aristocratic classes and such experiences of battlefield micro-solidarity were less discernible. With the advent of compulsory conscription and mass armies in the early nineteenth century, this phenomenon became more prevalent and better documented. However, once the nation-state became the dominant form of territorial organisation, such experiences of micro-group solidarity were regularly framed in nation-centric terms (Malešević 2019; Hutchinson 2017). Hence soldiers' willingness to make sacrifices for their actual mothers and fathers has regularly been reframed as an act of martyrdom for their motherlands and fatherlands. While soldiers fought for their actual brothers, sisters, and friends, ideological narratives were depicting this as a national sacrifice for their Serbian, Norwegian, or Pakistani brothers and sisters. Whereas soldiers were dying for their close comrades from their squads, sections, and platoons, in official discourses of state and military organisations they were making the ultimate sacrifice for their nation.

The wars of Yugoslav succession follow this pattern: although ordinary soldiers downplay the importance of 'patriotic calls' and emphasise their micro-group solidarities, the Croatian and Bosnian Serb military and state organisations define the hardship of their battlefield experience in distinctly nationalist terms. Nevertheless, this is not a simple case of manipulation undertaken by sinister political and military elites or an act of giant social engineering as implied by Bauman (2017) or Hobsbawm (2021). Instead, this is largely a structural and social phenomenon present in nearly all modern social orders – the organisational, ideological, and micro-interactional grounding of nationalism across society (Malešević 2020, 2019). Since the nation-state model of polity organisation has become hegemonic and the only legitimate form of territorial rule, its internal dynamic almost inevitably perpetuates nation-centric interpretations of social reality. In this context wars between nation-states are understood to be a struggle for the preservation of the nation where all individual sacrifices for significant micro-level others are predominantly understood as acts of national martyrdom. In the discourse of nationalism, actual mothers instantly become motherlands.

Nevertheless, the organisational 'translation' of micro-group solidarities into nationalist narratives is not a simple and straightforward act. Rather, this is a complex historical process that entails ongoing coercive-organisational, ideological, and micro-interactional mobilisation across societies. As many historical examples show, this process can also generate strong resistance and, in some cases, can be temporarily halted or reversed. For example, when in 1915 Bulgarian king Ferdinand decided to enter World War I on Germany's side, this provoked the large-scale riots and draft resistance. The Bulgarian population was exhausted from the 1912–1913 Balkan wars, was not yet fully nationalised, and was unwilling to participate in another war. This popular sentiment was reflected in the actions of the leading party at the time, the Bulgarian Agrarian Union under Aleksandur Stamboliyski, which strongly opposed participation in the war. The calls for 'patriotic duty' largely fell on deaf ears, and ultimately Bulgaria found itself on the losing side in the war (Malešević 2019:160–187).

However, in most other cases, including the 1990s Yugoslav wars of succession, the nationalist grounding had proved much more effective. The micro-level bonds forged in war theatres were successfully 'translated' into nationalist ideas and practices. This process of 'translation' is realised through the organisational, ideological, and micro-interactional grounding of nationalism (Malešević 2020, 2019). Organisational and ideological grounding operates through a variety of state institutions, including the military, police, courts, welfare, health, educational systems, and mass media, as well as the public sphere. Civil society including veterans' organisations, right-wing associations, and religious institutions have all contributed to the organisational and ideological grounding of nationalism in the war experiences of soldiers (Karčić 2022; Vukušić 2022). The post-war environment has been shaped by nation-centric discourses and practices that have infused nearly all state institutions and most non-state organisations. In Croatia, the War of Independence (or Homeland War, Domovinski rat) has become sacrosanct, and its key features have been codified in the Declaration on the Homeland War, adopted by the Croatian parliament in 2000. The declaration frames this conflict in uniform and nation-centric terms without making any space for non-national motivations. It interprets war through the prism of 'the long-standing aspirations of the Croatian people' for 'their own state' and states that 'the fundamental values of the Homeland War are unambiguously accepted by the entire Croatian people and all Croatian citizens' (Narodne Novine 2000:1). Similarly, the parliament of the Bosnian entity Republika Srpska has adopted several legal acts that glorify 'the War for Defence of the Fatherland'. These documents institutionalise a nation-centric interpretation of this conflict and state that war was caused by 'the discrimination of the Serbian people in Bosnia and Herzegovina' and that the parliament has an obligation 'to preserve the memory of the victims of the Serbian people' (Narodna skupština 2013, 2020). These wars are memorialised in numerous public rituals and commemorative practices where individual acts of sacrifice for one's micro-group are uniformly framed as instances of national heroism. In Croatia two key memorial days, Remembrance Day in Vukovar and the Day of Victory and Homeland Thanksgiving in Knin, are exclusively centred on the commemoration of the nation. In a similar vein, the Bosnian Serb Day of the Republic focuses entirely on the glorification of Serb nationhood. Nation-centric organisational and ideological grounding is even more pronounced in the educational systems, mass media, and public sphere, all of which are saturated with nation-centric interpretations of the 1990s wars (Uzelac 2006: Bougarel 2006).

The extent of this organisational and ideological grounding of nationalism is particularly visible in the statements from leading politicians and representatives of veterans' organisations after the war. Thus, Croatian presidents and prime ministers often refer to the brave soldiers who created an independent Croatia. For example, at an event where he presented war veterans with decorations and medals, President Zoran Milanović stated that 'the defenders' were responsible for the realisation of 'a historical project, a historical mission that generations of our people have thought about, hoped for, and dreamed about' (an independent Croatia) and that 'you participated in this with your heart' (*Večernji List*, 19/4/23). The 1990s war had become 'the cornerstone of Croatian cultural victim trauma' (Koska & Matan 2017:130) where the former soldiers of the Croatian Army were perceived to be heroic victims who made the ultimate sacrifice to establish a free Croatian homeland. Veterans' organizations also deployed similar rhetoric that portrays the 1990s war as a struggle for the nation. Combatants are glorified as the defenders of fatherland who endured hardship to liberate Croatia from Greater Serbian aggression (Boduszyński & Pavlaković 2019:803). Veterans' organisations deploy this rhetoric to constantly make further demands for the special position of 'the defenders' in the Croatian society. In this view, soldiers had earned this unique status through 'the holy sacrifice' they 'placed at the altar of the homeland' (Hranjski 1992:10). Anybody who opposes such interpretations of war and soldiers' alleged nationalist motivations is regularly silenced as 'the remnant of the Yugo-communist system' who disrespects 'the dignity of a Croatian defender' (Suša 2014). Even the images of disabled former soldiers are deployed to reinforce the nationalist narrative of war: they 'gave parts of their bodies' in 'building their homeland' (Rajković 1996:10).

Similar rhetoric dominates in institutions under Bosnian Serb control (Republika Srpska). BSA soldiers are depicted as the defenders of their homeland. The 1990s war is officially named the 'War for Defense of the Fatherland' (Odbrambeno-otadžbinski rat). Leading politicians and representatives of veterans' organisations regularly frame this conflict as a personal sacrifice for the nation. This conflict is often symbolically linked to previous Serbian wars and uprisings in order to project a historical continuity that is central for all nationalist narratives. Hence in a speech commemorating the 219th anniversary of the First Serbian Uprising against the Ottoman empire together with the official day of the 'War for Defence of the Fatherland', the prime minister of Republika Srpska, Radovan Višković, emphasized that 'the BSA fighters protected the Serbian people in times of war and defended Serbian lands'. He stated that 'we celebrate this date and dedicate it to our brave ancestors, as well as to the heroes who gave their lives in the War of Defense for the Republic of Srpska' (*Nezavisne Novine*, 18/4/23) Similarly, representatives of veterans' organizations regularly invoke the idea that BSA soldiers gave their lives and their bodies 'for creation and defense of the Fatherland' (*Blic*, 20/1/23) and as such they 'should have a position that will be commensurate with their merit and the sacrifice they made in the War for Defense of the Fatherland' (*Glas Srpske*, 14/2/23). In this view 'the Republika Srpska is an immense value that must be protected as it is soaked in the blood of those who defended the freedom of the Serbian people' (*Glas Srpske*, 14/2/23).

In addition to this ongoing organizational and ideological grounding, the battlefield experiences of soldiers have also been 'translated' in the micro-interactional domain. Thus, nationalist idioms and practices permeate everyday life, and the historical realities of front-line combat are continuously framed through the prism of key national nodal points: although most soldiers fought primarily for their close friends, family members, and battlefield comrades, their sacrifice is now reinterpreted in the strictly nation-centric terms. This is the process of micro-interactional grounding. In this sense all forms of micro-group solidarity become reformulated as acts of national solidarity. For example, in a speech commemorating fallen BSA soldiers, the mayor of Banja Luka, Draško Stanivuković, automatically reframes the deep bonds of micro-solidarity as martyrdom for the Serbian nation. The pain experienced by the families for the losses of their sons and siblings is articulated through the prism of national pride: 'apart from the sadness and pain felt by the families of the fallen fighters, they also feel pride, defiance and dignity for their members who wove their lives into the foundations of the Republika Srpska' (*Nezavisne Novine*, 18/4/23). The mayor reframes the interpersonal motivations of soldiers into an ideological nationalist narrative that invokes the Serbian myth of King Lazar's dilemma on the Kosovo field in 1389. Just as Prince Lazar allegedly chose the 'heavenly kingdom' over the 'earthly kingdom' and died in the battle with the Ottomans, so, according to the mayor, have the ordinary soldiers of BSA: 'Today we raise the Monument to 108 fallen fighters, who wove their lives into the foundations of the Republika Srpska and put the heavenly kingdom before earthly urges and fought for lasting and unquestionable values, which are certainly freedom, fatherland, patriotism and our Republika Srpska and on that we are grateful to them' (*Nezavisne Novine*, 18/4/23).

In a similar way, the inter-personal sacrifices of Croatian soldiers have been reframed as a struggle for the nation. For example, in an interview with the widely read Croatian newspaper, *Slobodna Dalmacija*, the state minister for veterans, Tomo Medved, had no doubts that all Croatian soldiers who had fought, were injured, and died on the battlefields had done this solely for their nation: 'We must never allow those who created the Croatian state, who gave the last breath of their life for it, who were wounded and became disabled, and their families who went through all the anxieties and sufferings with them, to be seen as a burden' (*Slobodna Dalmacija*, 29/7/23). The link is also made directly to the families of the former combatants by emphasizing the moral obligation to care for them: 'All of us, the entire Croatian state and every political option must be aware that without Croatian veterans there would be no independent Croatian state. This must be our guiding thought in respecting the rights of veterans and caring for their families.' Micro-interactional grounding is most effective when it can successfully tap into existing networks of micro-solidarity. Periodic commemorations of fallen soldiers provide an opportunity for representatives of the state, military, and veterans' organisations to organisationally and ideologically envelop the micro-universe of everyday life. In this way they can penetrate interpersonal relationships and re-frame the emotional bonds and moral responsibilities between close friends, family members, and war comrades as shared struggles for the nation. For example, a Croatian public representative directly invokes the language of kinship and family intimacy to frame the deaths of soldiers as an act of national martyrdom: 'Unfortunately, many of our brothers gave their lives and weaved them into the foundations of this country, and their parents are still suffering today, so we must always remember them' (Radio Slatina 2022). In a similar vein, a Bosnian Serb politician uses kinship metaphors to link the deaths of soldiers with the national project of state formation: 'today we all prayed for the souls of our fallen soldiers who built their lives into the foundations of the Republika Srpska … It is our obligation to remember their sacrifice, to remember and to pass on history to future generations who will continue to respect our work and protect the first Serbian state on this side of the Drina. The creation of a holy land for which our brothers gave their lives and blood' (Načelnik 2022).

When successful, the nationalist project naturalizes and normalizes all micro-level social relations as national acts: although soldiers primarily fought for their families, friends, and 'brothers in arms', their sacrifices are now 'translated' into actions of national martyrdom. Similarly, the deaths and injuries of these soldiers, which personally and intimately affect their families, friends, and comrades, are now removed from the private sphere and brought into the public arena and are completely infused with nationalist narratives.

The success of this 'translation' is best gauged in situations where former combatants deploy nation-centric narratives that are perpetuated by state officials and representatives of the veteran associations to pursue their own political or socio-economic aims. For example, during the veterans' political protest in 2015 in Zagreb, some former Croatian combatants reinterpreted their own war experiences using the nation-centric discourse for specific political ends. In their public speeches the original motivations centred on micro-solidarity were now transformed into nationalist rhetoric: 'The Homeland War is the foundation of modern Croatia for all the people, and especially for us, the veterans. Free, modern Croatia, where we can all now pray freely, was created during the Homeland War, on the backs, eyes, legs, and hands of every veteran. But that's why we don't need monuments to be built for us or that people bow down to us, we just need that everyone loves and builds on what we fought for and what we liberated' (Šimunić & Gusić 2015). Similarly, in their struggle for better pensions, Bosnian Serb war veterans tend to depict their war experiences through the prism of sacrifice for the Serbian nation. Hence, one former BSA combatant now proclaims, 'Everything is transient, only Republika Srpska and its people are eternal.... [W]e have already given too many lives, body parts, blood and sweat [for Republika Srpska] and there are more and more indictments for former members of the BSA, more and more lawlessness and debt slavery, and fewer and fewer Serbs in these areas and fewer and fewer in Republika Srpska' (BN 2023). In these situations, one can see how former combatants can naturalise the dominant nationalist interpretations of their own war experiences. The effectiveness of ideological, coercive-, and micro-interactional grounding is clearly visible in these acts of soldiers' own reinterpretations of the war. The organisational, ideological, and micro-interactional grounding of nationalism makes this 'translation' possible. Once soldiers leave the battlefields and re-enter the civilian world of political struggles, socio-economic competition, and status rivalry, they often rely on their symbolic war capital to enhance their own position in post-war society. In other words, the original motivations for fighting that are framed in the language and practices of deep comradeship in the civilian sphere become transformed into nationalism.

Conclusion

Perhaps more than any other classical scholar of nationalism, Anderson has focused on the fraternal character of nationalist ideology. Nationalism can have popular resonance only when it is couched in the language and practices of group solidarity. While many scholars have emphasised identity as the central feature of this ideology, it is actually the discourse of solidarity that makes nationalism alluring (Kaplan 2018). However, there is still a paucity of sociological research on the social mechanism that makes group solidarity workable and durable. Moreover, it is not clear how the ties of fraternity operate at the level of entities that consist of millions or even billions of people, such as India and China. In this chapter, I have explored how micro-group solidarities can gradually be transformed into viable and believable nation-centric narratives of fraternity. I argue that nationalism is not a form of deep horizontal comradeship, but a phenomenon engendered by historical and ongoing processes of coercive-organisational, ideological, and micro-interactional grounding. Much of the existing scholarship across many disciplines indicates clearly that human beings are wired to live in relatively small groups, and as such the networks of deep-level comradeship are limited by the size of the groups we populate. Hence one's ties with large-scale groups such as the nation entail protracted and ongoing coercive-organisational, ideological, and micro-interactional work. Drawing on ethnographic and documentary data together with interviews with ex-combatants from the 1990s wars of Yugoslav succession and mass media analysis, I have explored how group solidarity operates. In particular, I have analysed how deep inter-personal bonds of solidarity that were generated on the battlefields or through the years of shared life at home have gradually been transformed into potent narratives of national solidarity. Randall Collins (1992:25) noted that the discourse of solidarity is a powerful device of social control: 'an individual can dominate other people mainly by taking advantage of their feelings of solidarity … whoever knows how to arouse these feelings in others has a crucial weapon, to use for good or evil'. Collins is right that the rhetoric of solidarity is very strong in the mobilisation of social action. However, as I have tried to show in this chapter, rather than being solely a tool of elite manipulation, this is mostly a structural phenomenon that affects all contemporary societies. Nationalist grounding is a historical force tied to the hegemonic character of territorial and political order in the post–World War II globe. As long as the nation-state is the dominant model of polity organisation in the world, nationalism will remain the principal operative ideology capable of transforming micro-level solidarities into the acts of national martyrdom.

10 Imagined Communities and Imaginary Plots

Introduction

'Imagined communities' is one of the most quoted, yet most frequently misinterpreted concepts in nationalism studies. Many scholars who deploy Ben Anderson's (1983) famous phrase often misunderstand its meaning or ignore its wider sociological underpinnings. First, this term is regularly misconstrued to imply that nationhood is simply a form of false consciousness, something invented or completely fabricated. However, as Jenkins (2008:80) rightly emphasises, 'imagined' should not be misread as 'imaginary'. The fact that all forms of identification are social constructions, and as such are imagined, does not mean that they are not 'real' in their consequences. On the contrary, imaginations have a powerful material resonance. As W. I. Thomas and Dorothy Swain Thomas (1928:572) made it clear almost a century ago, if people 'define situations as real, they are real in their consequences'. For Anderson (1983:6), imagining was not a deed of misrepresentation and invention, but primarily an act of historical creation and collective visualisation.

Second, although Anderson devotes much of his attention to nationalism, he is clear that the concept of an 'imagined community' is not exclusively reserved for nations, a categorical distinction misunderstood by many readers. Instead, Anderson (1983:6) emphasises that 'all communities larger than primordial villages of face-to-face contact ... are imagined'. The focus here is not on the uniqueness or genuineness of the community, but on the style of imagination – while small face-to-face groups are imagined in a particularist way 'as indefinitely stretchable nets of kinship and clientship', large-scale groups such as nations, classes, or religious denominations are envisaged as abstract entities. Nations differ from other large-scale abstract communities in the way they are imagined – as political communities that are 'inherently limited and sovereign' (Anderson 1983:7). However, nationhood, religion, and class are all 'imagined communities', and his point is to explore how each of these communities is imagined.

Finally, the phrase 'imagined community' has often been misused to sharply differentiate nations and nationalism from premodern doctrines and forms of collective attachment such as kinship, mythology, or religion. In this understanding, nationalism is completely detached from traditional social organisations and their normative codes. But Anderson (1983) is unambiguous in his view that nationalism has more in common with kinship and religion than with modern political ideologies. He conceptualises nationalism as a phenomenon that appears in a variety of guises: nationalisms with a small n, not an ideology with capital N. In his view, nationalism is to be treated 'as if it belonged with "kinship" and "religion" rather than "liberalism" or "fascism"' (Anderson 1983:5). Hence despite offering a distinctly modernist theory of nationalism, Anderson differs from fellow modernists in emphasising the developmental character of organisational and ideological change. In other words, unlike classical scholars such as Gellner (1996) and Hobsbawm (1990) or contemporary modernists such as Breuilly (2016), Wimmer (2018, 2013) or Laitin (2007), who all embrace a rather narrow 'revolutionary model' of modernisation, Anderson offers a more nuanced reading of historical change. Instead of sharply differentiating between past and present, this approach emphasises that nationalism is built gradually on the ideological and organisational foundations of previous epochs (Malešević 2019:43).[1]

Taking these three points into account, one can work with the concept of 'imagined communities' in much wider and sociologically more fruitful ways. In this chapter, I explore how the discourses and practices of imagined communities change through time. More specifically, I analyse the role conspiratorial thinking has played in the development and proliferation of different understandings of one's own community and that of the external and threatening Other. By zooming in on episodes of major pandemics in world history, I aim to examine how different ideological and organisational processes have shaped popular understandings of conspiracies during times of pandemic outbreaks. The chapter compares and contrasts three broadly defined historical periods (premodern, modern, and contemporary) and argues that once nationalism becomes the dominant form of collective subjectivity, most conspiracy theories about pandemics inevitably embrace nation-centric understandings of social reality. The first section of the chapter explores

[1] However, this emphasis on gradual change does not make this perspective any less modernist or closer to ethno-symbolism, perennialism, or other anti-modernist approaches in the study of nationalism. On the contrary, as I have argued elsewhere, modernism is fully compatible with a longue durée analysis (Malešević 2019:40–69).

the relationship between pandemics and conspiracies before the age of the nation-state, while the second analyses how conspiracy theories transform in modernity and how nationalism shapes conspiratorial vistas. The final section zeroes in on recent developments and investigates how globalisation and new modes of communication have impacted the proliferation of nationalist conspiracy theories in the wake of the Covid-19 outbreak.

Pandemics and Conspiracies before Nation-States

Sudden outbreaks of deadly diseases have historically been linked with the proliferation of conspiratorial beliefs. Epidemics in particular have often been perceived as punishment from gods or evil spirits. In some cases, the resulting deaths and devastation were interpreted as signs of one's own sinful behaviour or as an indicator of insufficient commitment to one's religious or mythical beliefs and practices. When Cortez invaded the Aztec empire, the smallpox that accompanied his men completely decimated the Aztec population. This was seen by both sides as a sign of divine intervention: for the Aztecs this was divine wrath for their alleged transgressions, and for Cortez's soldiers this was a sign of divine reward for their commitment to Christianity (McNeill 1976:181–184) .

However, in most instances the blame for a pandemic was firmly associated with specific groups. These scapegoats were regularly depicted as powerful agents who were involved in a secret and sinister plot to harm or destroy one's society. Hence in the premodern context, the prime targets of blame were religious and cultural Others. In premodern Europe, outbreaks of plague, cholera, typhoid fever, salmonella, and other pandemic diseases were often linked to the conspiratorial activities of Jews, Muslims, heretics, pagans, and schismatics. For example, during the deadly pandemic of smallpox or viral haemorrhagic fever that spread through the Roman empire between 249 and 262, Jews and pagans were often blamed for this pestilence and the Christian clergy were adamant that only those who converted could potentially be saved in the afterlife. The bishop of Carthage, Cyprian, was unambiguous in his distinction between Christians and others: 'This mortality is a bane to the Jews and pagans and enemies of Christ; to the servants of God, it is a salutary departure' (McNeill 1976:108–109). Similarly, during the Crusades Muslims and Byzantines (after the eleventh century seen as schismatics) were often wrongly accused of conspiring against the Crusaders, and in some cases the spread of plagues was attributed to their joint plots (Neocleous 2010; Rosen 2007). For example, several medieval authors allege that the Byzantine emperor Isaac colluded with

Saladin to undermine the armies of the Third Crusade: Isaac 'entered into a conspiracy with Saladin, the seducer and destroyer of the holy name', whereby Saladin provided 'many presents very pleasing to mortals, in order to make a compact and agreement' (Munro 1896:20–21). The claim is also made in this story that Saladin and Isaac intended to poison the Crusaders (Neocleous 2010:270).

During the outbreak of the bubonic plague in Europe (1347–1351), Christian religious cults such as the Flagellants, Lollards, Beghards, and Cellites accused Jews and those they deemed to be heretics of spreading the plague. Jews were often denounced for deliberate poisoning of wells where Christians lived. One of the early forms of conspiracy theory that gained ground in the Iberian Peninsula was built around a claim that 'Jews were working under the orders of a conspiratorial network with its headquarters in Toledo; that the poison, in powered form, was imported in bulk from the Orient, and that the same organisation also occupied itself in forging currencies and murdering Christian children' (Ziegler 1969:100). The Jewish population was also held responsible for a variety of imaginary acts, including smearing walls and windows with a balm made from the buboes of plague victims or using the clothes of dead people. Show trials were organised to prove the existence of Jewish plots to poison wells with the plague (Ziegler 1969:102). Top clergy often initiated such trials, arguing that 'Jews deserved to be swallowed up in the flames' (Cohn 2007: 16–17). The Flagellant movement was at the forefront of these accusations and was involved in the persecution and mass killings of Jewish populations throughout Europe. In addition to Jews, Muslims and lepers were also held responsible for spreading pandemics and deliberately poisoning Christians. As Debra Higgs Strickland (2003:233) shows, sometimes three groups were blamed for plotting these acts together: 'Jews, Muslims and lepers working in tandem' and 'attempting to destroy Christendom through large-scale poisoning plots'.

Muslims and Mongols were also deemed to have brought the Black Death to Europe. In some accounts this was depicted as a sinister military plot of Saracens and Tatars. For example, in the fourteenth-century chronicle of the siege of Caffa (Crimea), Genoese Gabriele de' Mussi identifies Tatars (the name used for Mongol and Turkic populations) as the principal conspirators: 'The dying Tartars, stunned and stupefied by the immensity of the disaster brought about by the disease, and realizing that they had no hope of escape, lost interest in the siege. But they ordered [diseased] corpses to be placed in catapults and lobbed into the city in the hope that the intolerable stench would kill everyone inside.... Moreover, one infected man could carry the poison to others, and infect people and places with the disease by look alone. No one knew, or could discover, a means of defence' (Wheelis 2002:973).

Nevertheless, despite the popularity of such beliefs, these early forms of conspiracy theory were largely undeveloped. Periodic outbursts of hate against Jews, Muslims, pagans, schismatics, and heretics were rarely, if ever, articulated as intelligible narratives aimed at providing convincing and durable interpretations of pandemics. The Other was deemed to be evil and scheming on the simple account that they were not a member of one's religious community – Jews, Muslims, and heretics were held responsible for the plague because they were considered to be demons, devils, and representatives of the anti-Christ. The outbreaks of pandemics generated dread and fear, which often quickly translated into scapegoating practices.

Premodern social orders lacked robust coercive-organisational capacities and social mechanisms for the ideological penetration of entire societies. This was a deeply stratified world where the aristocracy and the top clergy completely dominated the social order and where group attachments were shaped by inherited status categories. In this social environment, group solidarity was determined by one's birth – while the nobility practiced transnational endogamy and used distinct cultural markers to differentiate themselves from the commoners, the ordinary peasant population was geographically and socially largely immobile and as such developed only a local sense of identification. This was also a world of rampant illiteracy, poor transport and communication networks, undifferentiated borders, and overlapping boundaries of political and religious authority (Breuilly 2016; Malešević 2017, 2006; Mann 1986; Gellner 1983).

Medieval and premodern Europe lacked strong organisational capacities and complex vertical ideological networks that could foster society-wide narratives of belonging. In this organisationally and ideologically inchoate setting, there was no space for the development of coherent and homogenous society-wide conspiracy theories. The spread of pandemics would usually be followed by waves of blame against the religious Other, but the nature of these accusations tended to be shaped by local superstitions and communal concerns. Each village, town, or county had its own mini-conspiracy, which would ordinarily focus on local concerns – a particular village well was poisoned, a specific Jewish family was blamed – and the sense of fear was confined to one's locality. For example, in some villages in Spain, Muslims (Moors) were held responsible for the spread of the Black Death, while in other parts of Europe lepers were the principal culprit in conspiracies on the passing of the disease. In some regions of France, traveling non-locals were blamed: 'in June 1348, a party of Portuguese pilgrims were said to be poisoning wells in Aragon … in Narbonne it was the English who were at one time accused', while in the City of London lepers were banned from entering, and in Languedoc, France, 'all lepers were burnt on suspicion of poisoning wells' (Ziegler 1969:97).

Furthermore, since religious denomination was the central dividing line of collective subjectivities during this period, local concerns were often mapped onto wider theological narratives, and imaginary conspiracists were depicted in biblical topoi, as sinners, devils, Satan, the anti-Christ, and so on. Hence during pandemics these faith-based discourses painted conspiracies as the attacks on Christianity. In this sense, outbreaks of disease temporarily generated imagined communities of Christians who framed the pandemics as conspiracies of the infidels. Nevertheless, such religiously articulated discourses would rarely attain a society-wide appeal. They were not and could not be national in content. Instead, they were primarily local and transnational. While local conspiracies targeted non-Christian members of the immediate community, transnational narratives centred on the eschatological imagery deduced from biblical narratives. Thus, in premodern Europe conspiracies helped forge imagined communities of co-religionists. However, the deeply stratified character of these social orders, combined with the underdeveloped organisational capacities and low levels of ideological penetration of society, meant that these religiously based imagined communities were temporary phenomena. Once the plague subsided and the conspiracies wore off, social status trumped religion and the world of lords and the world of serfs resumed their parallel and separate existence. In other words, the conspiracies that emerged in the wake of major pandemics could not patch the deep social and ideological divides that characterised premodern subjectivities. Most conspiratorial discourses emerged and spread locally and remained detached from the state and church structure. In many instances, political and religious authorities had to intervene to stop the massacres that followed the anti-Semitic, anti-Muslim, and anti-leper conspiracies. For example, Pope Clement VI issued two Bulls in 1348 condemning massacres and threatening excommunication for those who participated in violence against non-Christians, describing them as 'seduced by that liar, the Devil' (Skolnik & Berenbaum 2007:733). Premodern societies lacked the organisational and ideological mechanisms for the dissemination of coherent and homogenous conspiratorial narratives that would appeal to all social strata. The micro-group solidarities remained horizontal and detached from each other, with members of each social stratum living in their own moral universe. The strength of status and class divide was clearly visible in situations where the pandemic affected one social group more than others, as was the case with the sweating sickness (sudor anglicus) that disproportionally decimated the aristocracy in fifteenth- and early sixteenth-century Europe. Although this pandemic generated several conspiracy theories, such theories had little or no resonance among the ordinary people who had not been affected by this disease (Del Wollert 2017).

These sharp and entrenched social divides prevented the development of cross-class solidarity and cultural homogeneity among the populations of premodern Europe. Even though they largely shared a common religious worldview, the deeply stratified social order generated hierarchical cultural forms with the 'high', mostly Latin-based, culture of nobility and top clergy and the 'low' vernacular-based and localised oral cultures that lacked linguistic standardisation (Gellner 1983). The periodic outbreaks of pandemics and other major calamities, bolstered by fear and conspiratorial narratives, forged temporary imagined communities built around shared religion. However, these short-term shared experiences were not enough to transform premodern moments of solidarity into society-wide nationalist subjectivities. The lack of organisational capacities and the low levels of ideological penetration of society meant that the localised and status-based group solidarities never materialised into shared cross-societal imagined communities that would resemble nationhood (Malešević 2019, 2013). The classical and contemporary modernist accounts of Gellner (1983), Hobsbawm (1990), Breuilly (2016), and Wimmer (2018, 2013) are right in their assessment that there were no structural preconditions for the emergence and development of nationalism in premodern Europe. However, their excessive modernism leaves no analytical space for the transformation of religious into national imagined communities. In contrast, Anderson's (1998, 1983) restrained modernism points in the right direction: nationalism does not transpire ex nihilo but grows gradually from the structural transformations that take place in the premodern and early modern periods. In this context it is paramount to explore the role pandemic conspiracies have played in the rise and expansion of nationalism in Europe.

Pandemics, Nationalist Conspiracies, and Modern Subjectivities

Scholars of conspiracy theories trace their mass appearance to the late eighteenth century (Billig 1978; Roberts 1974). The shock that the French revolution created among aristocratic circles throughout Europe gave birth to the idea that revolution was an act of conspiracy.

Two highly influential books published in 1797, *Memoirs Illustrating the History of Jacobinism* by Augustin Barruel and *Proofs of a Conspiracy: Against All the Religions and Governments of Europe, Carried on in the Secret Meetings of Freemasons, Illuminati, and Reading Societies* by John Robinson, inaugurated a new genre of literature on modern political conspiracy theory (Byford 2011:40). The revolution was depicted as a planned and sinister undertaking of clandestine societies, including the French Philosophes, the Freemasons, the Bavarian Illuminati, and the Jacobins, allegedly all working together to establish world domination. The proliferation of secret societies[2] in the eighteenth and nineteenth centuries contributed to the expanding paranoia among aristocrats and members of government throughout Europe that powerful clandestine forces were hatching plots to take over the world. The chief protagonists in most of these early conspiracy theories were the Illuminati, a small Enlightenment-inspired organisation established in Bavaria in 1776, and the Freemasons, a fraternal organisation centred on the improvement of moral character of their members. Even though the Illuminati were dissolved in 1786, they continued to be linked to a variety of revolutionary and other political plots. The Freemasons have also been the object of numerous conspiracy theories over the past two centuries and have been blamed for the control of various governments (Roberts 1974).

The late eighteenth and early nineteenth century was also characterised by several intensive pandemic episodes in Europe and America, including 1778 dengue fever outbreak in Spain, the 1793 Philadelphia yellow fever epidemic, the 1793-1794 US influenza and typhus epidemics, the 1800–1803 Saint-Domingue yellow fever epidemic (which also spread to Spain), the 1812 typhus epidemic in Russia, the 1813 plague in Caragea, the 1817–1819 typhus epidemic in the British Isles, and two large-scale waves of cholera (1817–1824) and (1826–1837), among others (Snowden 2019). These sudden outbreaks of disease coupled with newly acquired political freedoms and the general democratisation of the public sphere contributed to the emergence of various conspiracies.

The French and American Revolutions fostered the proliferation of conspiratorial discourses on both sides: revolutionaries and counter-revolutionaries, including the representatives of the ancien régime. Many revolutionaries became obsessed with alleged plots to destroy the revolutionary legacy and to re-establish the monarchy. As Zwierlein & de Graaf (2013:20) show, many Jacobine conspiracy

[2] It is important to emphasise that most of these societies were not secret at all. Instead, the term 'secret society' was used to describe voluntary associations of people with similar interests that were not connected or funded by the state or the church (Byford 2011:41).

theories embraced the Manichean view of the world where revolutionary civil society was pitched against reactionary despotism and traditionalism. The counter-revolutionaries were seen to be the 'enemies of the liberty' and 'conspirators' ('une faction d'ennemis de la liberté', 'une secte de conspirateurs'), led by 'an Austrian Committee'. Similarly, their aristocratic and clerical enemies nurtured conspiracy theories that depicted the revolutionaries as external imposters financed and supported by foreign powers.

Many of these early conspiracies also reproduced the premodern obsession with the religious Other as the main culprit of the alleged political plots, with Jewish conspirators featuring prominently in many of the eighteenth- and nineteenth-century conspiracy theories. One of the most influential and lasting conspiracies was articulated in a mass-distributed book, *The Protocols of the Elders of Zion* (1903). This fabricated anti-Semitic document was first published in Russia and contained the alleged plan of Jewish elders to establish world domination through control of the mass media and global economy. The book plagiarised and misconstrued texts from various older sources and was already discredited by the 1920s. However, once the pamphlet was translated into numerous languages, it quickly become the cornerstone of many anti-Semitic conspiracies throughout the twentieth century.[3] This conspiracy theory replicates some of the standard religiously inspired tropes that were common in premodern conspiracies. However, the *Protocols* also articulate a new understanding of anti-Semitism, where the focus shifts from religion to nation. While the premodern anti-Jewish conspiracies combined religious eschatology with localised and parochial concerns, modern anti-Semitism was built around the idea of popular sovereignty, state borders, and national belonging. Hence unlike the traditional conspiratorial views of local Jews as infidels and the poisoners of wells, modern conspiracies envisage Jewishness as a threat to one's national project. The popularity of the *Protocols* stemmed in part from the framing of this conspiracy as a plot to abolish nation-states and create a world-state governed by Jews. This is clear from the statements that are imputed to the imaginary 'Jewish Elders': 'we shall be able, straightway, to absorb all powers of governing throughout the whole world, and to form the universal Supergovernment. In the place of existing governments, we will place a monster, which will be called Administration of the Supergovernment. Its hands will be overstretched like far reaching

[3] Many influential and wealthy anti-Semitic individuals contributed to popularisation of this pamphlet, including Henry Ford, who financed publishing of more than half a million copies of the *Protocols* in the United States in 1920s (Byford 2011:54).

pinchers, and it will have such an organisation at its disposal, that it will not possibly be able to fail in subduing all countries' (Nilus 2009:22). In this articulation, Jewishness is transformed from the religious Other into the national Other.

Many conspiracy theories formulated and disseminated in the nineteenth and twentieth centuries focus on alleged plots that strongly feature nationalist themes. For example, highly influential nineteenth-century anti-Jesuit conspiracies were centred on the question of Jesuits' loyalty to their respective nation-states. Jesuits were depicted as the remnants of the ancien régime but also as spies with transnational allegiances who corrupt the youth and who were bent on creating 'a state within a state' (Zwierlein & de Graaf 2013:23). In the mid- to late nineteenth century in France and Germany, Jesuits were often demonised as representatives of a sinister secret organisation that defied the sovereignty of nation-states and was committed to using all methods to establish a world empire ruled by the Papacy. In conspiratorial discourses, Jesuits were depicted as 'both subhuman and superhuman. Jesuits were allegedly so extreme in their submission to their order that they became like machines and, in their determination to achieve their goals, drew on powers unavailable to other men, through witchcraft. The peculiar location of the Jesuit, at the boundaries of humanity, unsettled the producers and consumers of anti-Jesuit discourse. In this sense, the Jesuit spectre haunted imperial Germany' (Healy 2003:1). Jesuits were also blamed for various calamities, from the pandemics of cholera to the sinking of the *Titanic*.

The second cholera pandemic that engulfed Europe in the 1830s gave birth to a plethora of conspiracy theories that identified Jesuits, Jews, Freemasons, and also neighbouring nations as the plotters behind the spread of this deadly disease. The pandemic originated in Asia and then quickly spread from Russia to the rest of Europe, causing hundreds of thousands of deaths (Henze 2010). As the disease proliferated throughout the continent, it generated a variety of conspiracy theories, many of which fuelled riots across Europe. Some of these conspiracies emphasised the class character of the pandemics, with the narratives of ruling classes 'masterminding a cull of the poor to lessen population pressures, with doctors, pharmacists, nurses, and government officials as the agents of this planned class mass murder' (Cohn 2017:163). For example, there were seventy-two cholera riots in the British Isles alone (Cohn 2017:164).

Nevertheless, most conspiratorial discourses targeted specific ethnic groups and nation-states as being involved in plots to deliberately spread the cholera. As the pandemic swiftly moved throughout the continent, some countries were instantly accused of plotting to infect the populations of neighbouring countries – various groups in Prussia and Austria blaming Russia, French political organisations pinpointing the states of the German confederation, representatives of the Italian civil society accusing France, various groups in Britain blaming the continental states, and so on. In addition, ethnic and religious communities were targeted. Hence in Spain the principal target of cholera conspiracies and subsequent riots were the Jesuits, while in some large Russian and Prussian cities the focus was on Jews. In France the conspiratorial narratives centred on King Louis Philippe's moderate government, with accusations that the rulers had poisoned the water. The government was attacked from both the republican left, who saw the pandemic as a weapon of class politics, and the conservative right, who blamed the reformist king and his allegedly ungodly and treasonous behaviour as a cause of the pandemic. In particular, the king was chastised for not occupying Belgium after its declaration of independence from Dutch rule. To counter these accusations and conspiracies, the self-styled 'King of the French' and 'citizen-king' relied extensively on nationalist discourse and nationalist policies to delegitimise the conspiratorial discourses. He presented himself as a man of the people who dressed modestly, was plain-spoken, and could be easily approached by any French citizen: 'Contemporary accounts famously describe how the king took walks in the park, umbrella in hand, stopping to have a chat with people of lower social rank' (Mehrkens 2019:209).

Italy also experienced cholera-related riots and conspiracies. With Sicily as the epicentre of pandemic activity in 1836–1837, conspirators deployed nationalist narratives to delegitimise the French Bourbon ruler. The Bourbons were accused of deliberately spreading the disease. One of the leading resistance leaders and an active member of the nationalist Young Italy, Mario Adorno, was adamant that the cholera epidemics were 'a devilish plot bent on poisoning the people' (Cohn 2017:163). Similarly, in the central Asian regions occupied by the Russian empire, cholera conspiracies centred on the responsibility of the Russian state. In Tashkent, Uzbekistan, conspiracy theorists organised riots on the belief that 'the cholera was the work of Russian doctors' who were bent to poison the local population (Cohn 2017:171).

Other pandemics in the late nineteenth and early twentieth century also fostered the development of nationalist conspiracy theories. Even the names of the two largest and deadliest epidemics of this period indicate how nationalist discourses have framed the diseases: the Russian flu of 1889–1890 and the Spanish flu of 1918–1920. The former, H2N2 influenza, spread quickly from Central Asia over Russia through Europe and hence to North America, resulting in over a million casualties. The rise of new transportation and communication systems contributed to the instant spread of the pandemic, with only five weeks between the first reported case and peak mortality (Ziegler 2011). This unprecedented speed of expansion generated a number of conspiracy theories. Some of the conspiratorial narratives centred on new technology, identifying electricity in telegraph wires, which were often close to train tracks, as the main transmitters of the pandemic. However, more influential conspiracy theories tended to focus on specific nations as the culprits in the creation and dissemination of the disease. Most Europeans and Americans blamed Russia for the pandemic, and some interpreted the disease as a form of biological warfare (Kolata 2011). The Spanish flu, H1N1 influenza, was the largest pandemic of twentieth century; it caused over fifty million deaths worldwide and generated an abundance of nationalist conspiracy theories. The pandemic did not originate in Spain, but as the Spanish media were the first to report the disease, while most other governments suppressed this information, the pandemic became the 'Spanish flu'. Although the nation-centric designation became universal, the name of the flu was different from country to country. Hence in Russia the mass media referred to the disease as the 'Chinese sickness'; in Germany the pandemic was known as the 'Russian plague'; in Spain many referred to the 'Naples soldier' (i.e., Italian) disease; while in Japan the public referred to the epidemics as the 'American disease' (Kolata 2011). From its detection until the end of the crisis, the pandemic was couched in the language of nationalist conspiracies.

For example, in the United States the conspiratorial narratives propagated the idea that German U-boats were responsible for the spread of the disease. The *Philadelphia Inquirer* reported the widely believed conspiracy theory of German soldiers docking in Boston and flooding the city with tainted vials, releasing the influenza virus in crowded places, including the cinemas (Kolata 2011:3–4). The people were also reluctant to take medicine, as some conspiracy theories blamed the German pharmaceutical company Bayer for poisoning their aspirin with the virus. The Spanish media also identified U-boats and Germans as plotting to disseminate 'strange bacilli, which infect people with the disease' (Aderet 2020:1).

The common pattern in most of these conspiracy theories is the focus on the nation as the object and subject of the pandemics: the disease is conceptualised as being generated by one nation to attack or destroy another nation. In some instances, minority groups, such as Jews, Jesuits, or Freemasons, are identified as the perpetrators of conspiracies, but even in these cases the emphasis is on their threat to the unity, stability, and future of a specific nation. In this sense, conspiracy theories reflect the changing dominant forms of collective subjectivity over time: while in the premodern context religion and locality were the principal source of collective attachments, in modernity nationhood becomes the central focus of collective belonging. Hence the shift from religiously to nationally based imaginary plots reveals the changed structural contexts: instead of the religious imagined communities that populated premodern world, one now encounters imagined communities built around the ideas and practices of nationhood.

This transformation was gradual and shaped by many historical factors and only fully crystallised in the twentieth century. The key structural processes that made this change possible include the cumulative increase in the organisational capacities of states and many non-state entities, the greater ideological penetration into societies, and the ability of social organisations to envelop micro-level networks of group solidarity (Malešević 2019, 2013). The establishment of a state's monopoly on the legitimate use of force, taxation, and legislation together with the centralisation of authority and increased growth of transportation and communication networks have allowed states to better control their populations. Furthermore, creation of state-wide educational systems with standardised vernaculars and dramatically increased literacy rates played a central role in fostering greater cultural homogenisation of the population. These structural processes also facilitated a greater ideological breach into the micro-world, as an abstract entity such as the nation gradually became naturalised and normalised in everyday life. The outbreaks of pandemics contributed substantially to the transformation of the religious into the national imagined communities. The change was both spearheaded and reflected in the conspiracy theories that regularly accompanied major pandemics. The proliferation of nationalist conspiracies was shaped by changing historical contexts. Political and industrial revolutions of the late eighteenth and nineteenth century opened the space for the democratisation of the public sphere, which gave birth to modern nationalist subjectivities that were also reflected in the rise of mass-scale nationalist conspiracies (Byford 2011:38–46).

Nationalist conspiracies were not the only conspiracies that emerged and proliferated in modernity. Conspiratorial discourses permeated many spheres of social life, including politics, the economy, culture, science, sports, and health. However, as nationalism become better grounded in the organisational and ideological structures and everyday lives of ordinary individuals, it generated more legitimacy and greater appeal to the conspiracies centred on nationhood (Posocco & Watson 2024; Malešević 2019). In some instances, nationalist conspiracies were state-sponsored projects, while in other cases they were initiated and disseminated by civil society groups, which offered only a more radicalised version of already existing nationalist mythologies about the sinister plots of other nations and the eternal heroism and victimhood of one's nation. The onset of deadly pandemics fostered much better reception and popularity of nationalist conspiracies. In times of unprecedented crisis, fear, and uncertainty, nationalist conspiracies offered simple cognitive maps of changing reality and identified scapegoats responsible for all calamities that beset one's nation. Knowing that there is a specific culprit and concrete political goal behind the deadly disease allowed many people to regain a sense of control over unpredictable and contingent events. Furthermore, the proliferation of nationalist conspiracies also helped reinforce the boundaries between groups; the expansion of nationally framed imaginary plots helped maintain and strengthen nationally embedded imagined communities.

Pandemics, Nationalist Subjectivities, and Global Conspiracy Theories

The twenty-first century has often been described as an era of globalisation. The rise of new technologies, improved and affordable transportation and communication networks, and the global expansion of the neoliberal economy created a novel social environment where movements and exchanges of capital, goods, services, and people have intensified and have brought different parts of the world closer together. Both critics and supporters of this process argue that globalisation has undermined the power of nation-states and the influence of nationalism. Hence Giddens (2007), Bauman (2006), and Beck (2009), among many others, insist that globalisation erodes national attachments as rampant consumerism fosters individualist and cosmopolitan identifications. In Beck's (2000:85) words, 'the cosmopolitan project contradicts and replaces the nation-state project'.

In this new context, conspiracy theories seem to have also become fully globalised. A number of highly influential conspiratorial narratives have spread throughout the world and have gained popularity among populations on different continents. For example, the chemtrails conspiracy theory, which alleges that secret government agencies are involved in water condensation experiments that use aircraft to spray toxic materials into the air has attracted substantial global support, with up to 20 per cent of individuals worldwide believing this to be true or partially true (Tingley & Wagner 2017; Cairns 2016). Other highly popular conspiracies with global resonance include a variety of topics, such as scepticism about global warming, 9/11, New World Order designs, water fluoridation, the Bilderberg Group's secret plans, the cultural Marxism conspiracy, secret plans of pharmaceutical companies (Big Pharma), and alleged international plots about vaccination and human microchipping (Butter & Knight 2020).

The sudden global outbreak of Covid-19 in early 2020 instantly generated a plethora of new conspiracy theories that have interpreted this pandemic as a secret plot by various governments, private corporations, or influential individuals to infect and then control the world's populations (Malešević et al. 2024). Thus, in many conspiratorial narratives, the coronavirus was deliberately bio-engineered in a lab and developed as a biological weapon. In some conspiracy theories the main culprit is the Chinese government,[4] while in others the focus is on the US, Russian, or Israeli governments. Other conspiracies focus on the role of private corporations – Microsoft, Amazon, or Soros Fund Management, among many others. One of the early Covid-19 conspiracies, viewed by millions through a video on YouTube, made a claim that the virus was created by the Pirbright Institute in the United Kingdom and was financed by Bill Gates. Another influential conspiracy theory popularised on Facebook and Twitter alleged that George Soros was responsible for the spread of the virus as he 'owns the WuXi PHARMA LAB located in Wuhan, China where COVID-19 was developed and conveniently Broke Out' (Funke 2020). However, the most popular recent conspiracy propagated on social media is the one identifying 5G mobile networks as playing a central role in the transmission of the disease. This conspiracy, viewed and shared by hundreds of millions of social media users, alleged that the virus was caused by electromagnetic fields and 5G wireless technologies.

Many of the conspiracy theories that spread in the wake of the coronavirus pandemic had a global character. Once a particular conspiracy develops, it can be quickly transmitted through social media all over the world, often attracting millions of individuals who believe the narrative and share it with other potential believers. Since the pandemic itself is a global phenomenon, affecting the entire world, it is no surprise that conspiracy theories centred on Covid-19 attracted a global audience. At first glance, these developments would suggest that the globalisation of conspiracy theories is yet another reliable indicator that we live in a fully globalised world. The rapid dissemination of conspiratorial

[4] According to Pew Research Center surveys, 29 per cent of the US population believe in this conspiracy theory, while 25 per cent believe that 'the coronavirus outbreak was intentionally planned by powerful people' (Pew Research Center 2020).

narratives across the world would seem to confirm the views of Giddens, Bauman, Beck, and others that globalisation has dented the power of nation-states and that nationalism has been replaced by new global ideological discourses and practices including individualism, cosmopolitanism, and consumerism. In Andersonian terms, this historical shift would signpost a transition from national imagined communities to global imagined communities. If nationalist conspiracy theories have given way to global conspiratorial narratives, that would imply that globalism has trumped nationalism as the dominant popular ideological discourse.

Nevertheless, there is no evidence that such a profound shift has taken place. Even though some conspiracy theories have a global audience, that in itself is not proof that nationalism has weakened in any meaningful sense. On the contrary the outbreak of the deadly virus has in fact reinforced the nation-centric perceptions of the world and enhanced nationalist subjectivities. The first reaction to the pandemic was the centralisation of decision-making at the national level, with the governments of individual nation-states introducing various measures to protect the citizens of their own nation-states. Despite the global character of the disease, most governments closed their borders and stopped all travel to their countries. Even though the pandemic does not differentiate between holders of different passports, both the governments and the citizens of individual nation-states clearly demonstrated that they privilege their co-nationals in terms of unhampered travel, medical protection, or economic support (Malešević et al. 2024). A good example of this behaviour is the world-wide scramble for medical ventilators that ensued in the wake of the sudden increase in the number of Covid-19 patients in intensive care units. Even highly cooperative and well-established transnational entities such as the European Union initially proved unable to provide medical aid to the most affected member states in the early days of the crisis, such as Italy or Spain. Instead, the governments of individual nation-states prioritised their own populations (Dettmer 2020).

However, the strength of nationalism was even more visible in the sphere of civil society. All over the world, citizens of individual nation-states took part in formal and informal mass-scale rituals of national solidarity (Fox 2025; Goode et al. 2020). For example, in several European countries, the public was involved in country-wide actions expressing their gratitude to the medical professionals involved in caring for Covid-19 patients. Many of these campaigns were framed through nation-centric discourses such as the weekly 'Clap for Our Carers' in the United Kingdom and Ireland or singing popular national songs from balconies in Italy and Spain. As Antonsich (2020:1) shows, in Italy, popular radio stations transmitted 'the stories of ordinary and famous Italians who directed their courage and inventiveness towards helping the nation fight the virus, emphasising that "the others cannot understand all this because … they are not Italians"'. Many civil society groups linked the coronavirus epidemic to previous examples of tragedies and tribulations facing their respective nations throughout history, and in this way framed the medical emergency as a nationalist cause. For example, in Serbia, influential public intellectuals and even some medical professionals linked the pandemic to the 1999 NATO bombing, while in Croatia and Bosnia and Herzegovina many individuals and organisations approached the coronavirus crisis through the prism of their own experience of the 1990s wars for independence (David et al. 2024; Fonet 2020; Kurspahić 2020).

The centrality of nationhood in public discourse was most clearly visible in the popularity of nationalist conspiracy theories. With the outbreak of the pandemic in the United States, existing nation-centric conspiratorial narratives have gained momentum – the idea of the Deep State and QAnon conspiracy, the white genocide, the Plan de Aztlan, and the North American Union project among many others. All these conspiracies identify a secret global elite that allegedly plots to undermine the national sovereignty of the US government and devise plans to remove Donald Trump from power. The QAnon conspiracy depicts a 'worldwide cabal of Satan-worshiping paedophiles who rule the world' and control US politicians, media, Hollywood, and many other sectors of society (Rosza 2019). The white genocide conspiracy theory, the Plan de Aztlan, and the North American Union conspiracies all focus on imaginary plots to change ethnic composition of the United States. While the white genocide idea targets large-scale non-white immigration, racial integration, and the policies of miscegenation, seeing them as the steps towards the obliteration of white majority in the United States, the North American Union and the Plan de Aztlan focus on alleged plots to cede US sovereignty to foreign powers. The Plan de Aztlan centres on a plot where Mexico would reclaim seven southwestern US states, while the North American Union plot is about merging the US, Mexico, and Canada into a continental association that would be ruled by a transnational elite. In Russia and China, the Covid-19 outbreak has often been interpreted through the 'Anglo-Saxon Revenge' conspiracy theory, which claims that although the virus originated in China it was manufactured and spread by the US government as a part of its secret bioweapon programme (Turp-Balazs 2020).

In many other countries the Deep State conspiracy theory has attracted much support. This narrative identifies nonelected conspirators who wield power behind the scenes and who, in collusion with foreign actors, undermine the national interest of their respective states. In the case of the United Kingdom, the Deep State conspiracy has been linked with the opponents of Brexit, who allegedly work in secret with the leaders of the EU to undermine the British attempt to regain full national sovereignty and independence. The 5G network conspiracy that links the spread of the pandemic with the mobile phone signals that allegedly transmit the virus has also gained a great deal of popularity in many countries all over the world – from Pakistan and Serbia to Bolivia (Goodman & Carmichael 2020). Similarly, conspiracies that invoke microchipping through vaccination have attained enormous popularity throughout the globe. This conspiracy is built around the claim that the Microsoft corporation is involved in a plot to 'inoculate' much of the world population with trackable microchips. The Deep State, 5G network, and microchipping conspiracies are all usually linked with specific individuals held responsible for the pandemics, such as Bill Gates or George Soros. However, despite their global appeal, these conspiracy theories have often been formulated in distinctly nationalist terms as a direct threat to the sovereign powers of individual nation-states. For example, in Iran, Ayatollah Ali Khamenei stated that the virus was deliberately manufactured to genetically target Iranians. In Russia, the leader of the Communist party claimed that 'globalists' were involved in 'a covert mass chip implantation, which they may in time resort to, under the pretext of a mandatory vaccination against coronavirus' (Goodman & Carmichael 2020). In Serbia many tabloid newspapers have linked the coronavirus with a plot to weaken Serbian resolve in their struggle to regain control over Kosovo. In the United States, Trump and his administration regularly referred to Covid-19 as the 'China virus' or the 'Chinese virus' and portray it as a sinister action on the part of the Chinese government against the United States.

All these examples illustrate that nationalism remains a highly potent source of ideological legitimacy in the contemporary world. Globalisation has generated new technologies and modes of communication, thus allowing the creation of a global public sphere, but it has not significantly undermined well-established nationalist subjectivities. While many individuals and groups are now able to disseminate their messages to world-wide audiences, the focus of many of these messages is, for the most part, framed by nation-centric concerns.

Although conspiracy theories are global phenomena, their articulations and their popular resonance are often rooted in their nation-centric appeals. Conspiracy theories reveal the strength of nationalist ideologies throughout the world. Not all conspiracies are centred on plots against one's nation, but even those conspiracies that nominally target science, technology, economy, or health seem to frame their message in nation-centric terms. Global conspiracies, such as those linking 5G networks to Covid-19, are spread rapidly throughout the world, but they are articulated and received differently in different societies. In some cases, these alleged plots are interpreted as a part of already existing political animosities involving threatening neighbouring states or world powers. In other cases, the focus is on preserving national freedoms against evil foreign corporations. In some contexts, conspiratorial discourses target ethnic and religious minorities by linking them to hostile foreign influence (Malešević et al. 2024; Carol et al. 2024).

There are two main reasons why nationalism often underpins many conspiracy theories. First, conspiratorial discourses often feed off the existing mainstream nation-centric narratives. All nationalist ideologies perpetuate the idea that one's own nation is unique and, in some ways, superior to other nations. Nationalist mythologies that are reproduced in educational systems, mass media, and the public sphere tend to portray one's nation through the prism of historical victimhood, sacrifice, and moral superiority. Conspiracy theories just tap into the already existing myths of exceptionalism and radicalise these narratives by identifying specific culprits of evil who are (yet again) plotting to destroy one's nation. The established nationalist mythologies depict their respective nations as irreplaceable and immemorial communities of destiny that have experienced immense suffering throughout history and have always survived. Conspiracy theories build on these recognisable and popular tropes and reshape and radicalise existing nation-centric myths. The conspiratorial narratives attain popularity precisely because they evoke cognitions and emotions that are already there. Despite being presented as a challenge to the 'normal' perceptions of reality, conspiracy theories reinforce embedded nationalist idioms and practices. Conspiratorial discourses work through the already established nationalist subjectivities. They draw upon existing nation-centric imagery and push nationalist messages to their logical conclusions. In this sense, nationalist conspiracies are not the 'weapons of the weak' (Scott 1985) who resist or subvert the dominant perceptions. Instead, they only radicalise the well-entrenched nationalist narratives and, in this way, reproduce the imagined communities of nationhood.

Second, global conspiracy theories cannot generate sustainable global imagined communities for the simple reason that they lack organisational capacities, ideological legitimacy, and the micro-interactional grounding that only nation-states possess in the contemporary world.

The strength of nationalism in modernity is rooted in the hegemony of the nation-state model of social organisation. Globalisation has not removed nation-states from their organisational pedestal and ideological dominance. There is no global organisational equivalent of the nation-state model. Although human beings are now capable of communicating and traveling huge distances and consuming a variety of services from all over the world at a much faster rate than ever before in history, this change has not undermined the potency of nation-states. On the contrary, the continuous growth of new technologies, science, and industry has reinforced the organisational capacities of nation-states and fostered greater ideological penetration of nationalist discourses and practices in everyday life (Malešević 2019:5–16). Since the end of World War II, the nation-state model of territorial and political organisation has become hegemonic and almost uncontested. It is also regarded as the only legitimate mode of territorial rule in the contemporary world. Moreover, the principal underlying ideology of nation-states, nationalism, has also established itself as the most influential doctrine of political legitimacy. Hence, we live in the world where nation-states shape social reality both internally (within their own societies) and externally (in international relations). Consequently, the citizens of such polities are constantly exposed to nation-centric interpretations of reality. Nationalist ideas and practices underpin our educational systems, our mass media, our public sphere, and all other institutions. Furthermore, nation-centric idioms are also generated and reproduced in the civil society and intimacies of micro-world – friendships, kinships, and comradeships (Malešević 2013:13–16). There are no global subjectivities that could equal the strength of nationalist subjectivities.

Conspiracy theories utilise these existing organisational capacities, means of ideological legitimacy, and micro-interactional grounding to disseminate images of clandestine plots and everlasting dangers. Such narratives emerge in the context of crises and times of uncertainty and fear. Drawing on the existing nationalist tropes, they offer certainty, control and security, which are couched in simple explanations and the crude politics of scapegoating and blame. The sudden outbreak of pandemics has historically proved to be an ideal environment for the proliferation of conspiracies. Conspiratorial narratives have played a central role in forging imagined communities. With the formation and development of nation-states, nationalism regularly shaped the content of most influential conspiracy theories. The organisational, ideological, and micro-interactional omnipotence of nationhood in modernity has contributed to the nation-centric imaginary plots that work to sustain national imagined communities.

Conclusion

Anderson (1983:6) emphasises that one of the defining features of all imagined communities is their abstract character. These imaginings project communities that are outside one's direct experience and beyond face-to-face interaction. Hence class, religion, and nation are all forms of imagined communities. However, not all imagined communities exist in the same way. In this chapter, I analysed the differences between these collective imaginings in the premodern, modern, and contemporary world through the prism of conspiracy theories. The chapter traced the long-term transformation of conspiratorial discourses in times of major pandemics and their impact on the formation of different types of imagined communities. I showed that the premodern conspiracies centre on the theological and eschatological themes and depict the imaginary plots and plotters in religious terms. The focus on the religious Other (infidels, heretics, and pagans) and the onset of epidemics is regularly associated with the attacks on one's faith. In contrast, the modern period is characterised by the dominance of the nation-centric discourses and practices, where conspiracy theories often reinforce and radicalise the existing nationalist narratives. In modernity, sudden outbreaks of pandemics regularly foster the proliferation of nationalist conspiracies. In these conspiratorial narratives the Other is usually portrayed as a threat to one's national sovereignty, cultural homogeneity, and territorial integrity. Globalisation has added another layer of complexity to the collective imaginings, but it has not undermined the power of nation-states nor the potency of nationalist subjectivities in the contemporary world. New technologies and new modes of communication have given rise to global conspiracy theories and global conspiracy communities, but these global conspiratorial narratives have a distinctly national resonance. Hence rather than creating global imagined communities, many of these conspiracy theories only reinforce nationalist subjectivities. The response to the Covid-19 pandemic illustrated quite well how central nation-states are to framing, understanding, and managing pandemics in the contemporary world. Despite the global reach and world-wide ramifications of the pandemic, its spread has been marked by very different national responses. Moreover, despite the prevalence of some common global conspiratorial narratives about the origins and responsibility for the pandemic, the principal culprits are usually framed as recognisable national enemies. Although the imaginary plots and imaginary plotters may be global, the imagined communities they face remain conspicuously national.

11 Beyond Nation-Centric Realities

Introduction

Over the last seventy years, the nation-state has become a hegemonic form of territorial and political organisation. Unlike ever before, the entire globe is now carved into independent nation-states that claim sovereignty over, and can coercively control, their territories. The nation-states also possess legitimate monopolies on violence, taxation, judiciary, and education. These powers are justified through references to popular sovereignty, protection of national identities, and the privileging of members of one's own nation over others. Hence, all nation-states legitimise their existence through nationalist principles. In this sense nationalism is not a political aberration associated with the far-right or far-left movements; it is the dominant form of collective subjectivity in the contemporary world.

Nevertheless, this nation-centric view of the world represents an obstacle for addressing the most pressing human problems, including environmental degradation, overuse of non-renewable energy resources, wars, global inequalities, and pandemics. There are no adequate nation-centric solutions for these global problems. In this chapter I explore briefly how future human societies could exist without nation-states and their foundational ideology – nationalism. I envisage several possible scenarios and identify the most realistic trajectories. The first section of the chapter briefly positions nation-states in the history of this planet. The second section engages with some recent sociological and historical accounts of the post-national futures, while in the final section I explore several scenarios for a world without nation-states.

Nationalism without Nation-States?

Fredric Jameson and Slavoj Žižek are both credited with the statement: 'It's easier to imagine an end to the world than an end to capitalism.'

In some respects this is true: the collapse of state socialism in the 1990s generated an unprecedented crisis of alternative economic systems, which was also reflected in a lack of imagination about non-capitalist futures. Hence, there is an abundance of post-apocalyptic scenarios, while visions of a world without capitalism are scarce. In other respects, this statement is limited as it describes a temporary phenomenon – the current crisis of the political left. The next big economic recession, depression, or crash of the stock markets might turn this tide and reinvigorate non-capitalist imaginations.

Nevertheless, this is not the case with nationalism. This ideological doctrine, and social practice, is experiencing continuous expansion and proliferation regardless of the changing socio-economic or geopolitical conditions. The number of new nation-states is constantly increasing, while the organisational and ideological powers of existing nation-states are incessantly growing. World-wide public polls also indicate that a sense of attachment and pride in one's own nation has continuously been on the rise (Duina 2018; Gallup 2021). This unremitting global upsurge of nationalism has not been negatively affected by economic downturns, wars, revolutions, pandemics, natural disasters, waves of migration, or even intensified socio-economic growth. Moreover, the nation-centric view of the world has become fully institutionalised, naturalised, and normalised, so that most of the world's population perceives nation-states as the only legitimate form of territorial rule and nationhood as the most significant form of collective identity. The world of nation-states is now hegemonic and generally envisaged as the only viable form of international order. Even in popular perceptions there is no viable alternative to nationhood as the dominant form of modern subjectivity. Hence, Jameson's and Žižek's formulation applies more accurately to nationalism than to capitalism: it is easier to imagine an end to the world than an end to nationalism.

Nevertheless, this current dominance of nation-states and nationalisms conceals an important historical fact: for 99.99 per cent of their existence on this planet human beings have not lived in nation-states, nor have they identified in national terms. Rather than being a natural, standard, or optimal form of social organisation, the nation-state is a historically highly atypical and peculiar form of social order, while nationalism is an unusual and distinctly modern ideological discourse. Despite the dominant popular primordialist views of nationhood as a timeless phenomenon, the overwhelming majority of our ancestors have lived in a non-national world. Since the emergence of *Homo sapiens* at least 200,000 years ago, there have been a minimum of 8,000 generations[1] of human beings. Out of these 8,000 generations a mere six have known the ideology of nationalism in its rudimentary form, and only four generations have lived under the hegemony of a nation-state. In other words, 7,994 human generations had no experience of nationhood in any form. Differently put, for more than 98 per cent of time our predecessors lived as nomadic hunter gatherers, and once social life had become predominately sedentary, around 12,000 years ago, they lived in a variety of state formations that have no resemblance to the nation-state: chiefdoms, city-states, tribal confederacies, patrimonial kingdoms, and, most of all, empires. It has been only in the last two centuries or so that nation-states have gradually started replacing imperial orders[2] as the principal from of territorial organisation. Only after the end of World War II has nationhood become the hegemonic and only legitimate form of political sovereignty on this planet.

These swift and very recent historical transformations indicate that nation-states and nationalism are not inevitable nor permanent historical fixtures. The world beyond nation-states is not only possible, but is very likely. If the confluence of historical forces that gave birth to nationalism and nation-states disappears or these forces experience a radical change, one can expect the emergence of a very different, and non-national, world. The key issue here is the time frame. Although the current strength of the nation-state system impedes dramatic and sudden transformations of global order, long-term trajectories can be very different, probably resulting in the gradual demise of nation-states and nationalisms.

However, before exploring these processes it is important to differentiate between these two phenomena: nation-states and nationalisms. Although they are interdependent and regularly prop each other up, it is possible to foresee the decline or disappearance of one and the continuous presence of the other phenomenon. As they have developed and spread throughout the world separately, they can also experience different pathways in the future. As an intellectual movement, nationalism precedes the emergence of nation-states. Its ideological and organisational development starts with small local initiatives – from congregations

[1] Some archaeologists argue that *Homo sapiens* has been around for 300,000 years. If a generation is assumed to be twenty-five years long, that would mean around 12,000 generations of humans, which would make nationhood even more historically insignificant.

[2] It is important to emphasise that nation-states did not simply replace empires in some teleological way. Instead, the relationship between empires and nation-states is complex and contradictory, with many powerful nation-states retaining some important imperial features (see Hall 2024; Kumar 2021).

of cultural and political elites in coffeehouses and pubs to secret revolutionary societies to well-organised social movements and political parties (see Chapter 1). Nationalist discourses and practices were well developed before the emergence of nation-states, as they were regularly deployed to challenge the existing imperial, feudal, or monarchic social orders. While initially nationalism was an oppositional project, with the rise of nation-states it became a principal mode of state legitimacy.

Once the nation-state model had become hegemonic in the global order, nationalism came to be its principal ideological glue. In this context it is difficult to envisage the downfall of nationalism without the demise of nation-states. Since nation-states cannot legitimise their existence outside of nationalist principles, the disappearance of nationalism would nearly automatically unravel the nation-state order. So, despite the enormous coercive capacities of nation-states, it is ideological power that is more likely to last longer. In other words, it is easier to envisage the end of nation-states than the end of nationalisms. This difference is rooted in the historical reality in which nationalism has become a distinct way of life. Although nation-states provide coercive-organisational shells that foster and preserve nationalist views of reality, their collapse would not inevitably abolish a particular way of life.

Distinct ideological practices and beliefs can exist even when their key social organisations are destroyed. For example, many contemporary nation-states such as Canada, Brazil, or Australia have made numerous attempts over the last two centuries to assimilate and integrate the indigenous populations. Native populations were subjected to various coercive policies since Portuguese and British colonisation, and in this process have been decimated. However, these coercive and other less coercive practices deployed by the successive Canadian, Brazilian, and Australian governments have largely proved unsuccessful at assimilating their native populations. The indigenous cultures have continued to exist, often in direct opposition to the policies of their respective nation-states.

Similarly, the collapse of imperial orders including the Habsburg and the Ottoman state structures did not automatically remove a sense of attachment that some groups had towards these empires. Ottoman and Habsburg nostalgia continued for decades, and many groups expressed deep dissatisfaction with the new nation-states that emerged in the imperial ruins. Moreover, many individuals preserved the cultural practices that existed in the imperial world (Schlipphacke 2014; Yavuz 2020). Similar attitudes have persisted in the wake of the collapse of federal, multi-national, states such as the Soviet Union, Czechoslovakia, and Yugoslavia. In each of these cases a large segment of population remained attached to political entities that no longer exist. This phenomenon has often been described as 'Yugonostalgia', 'Soviet nostalgia', or 'Czechoslovak nostalgia' (Boele et al. 2019; Velikonja 2013).

Religious belief systems have also proved resilient after the collapse of the main social organisations that promoted such beliefs. For example, despite near-cataclysmic events that followed the destruction of Jerusalem and the Second Temple in 70 CE as well as the destructive Jewish–Roman wars, Judaism continued to exist and even prosper for the next 2,000 years. Similarly, Hinduism, Jainism, Sikhism, and other beliefs have successfully survived protracted occupations by Mughal and British rule from the eleventh until the twentieth century.

In this sense nationalism as a way of life is likely to outlive the collapse of the nation-state model of polity organisation. Individuals who have been socialised in nation-centric environments will not so easily dispense with their sense of attachment to their respective nationhood. It is very likely that these nationalist visions of the world will remain for several generations. As research on 'the nations without states', including the Kurdish, Catalan, Scottish, Flemish, and other populations, indicates, nationalist subjectivities remain resilient and durable even when they lack an independent sovereign polity (Basta 2021; Keating 2001). Obviously, the strength of these independence movements is directly linked with the dominance of the specific political order that privileges the nation-state as the only legitimate from of territorial authority. Once this order ceases to exist, such movements are likely to lose their raison d'être. Nevertheless, the nation-centric sense of attachment and corresponding practices are likely to persist much longer than these political movements. None of this is to say that nationalism will not eventually fade away. It is just that this process is likely to take much longer than the demise of nation-states.

Visons of Post-National Futures

Conventional futuristic accounts often over-emphasise sudden change and radical discontinuity with the present. Much of the mainstream science fiction literature and popular apocalyptic narratives perpetuated in video games, films, social media, and popular culture tend to depict the future as a social tabula rasa. In these visions the past and the present are completely obliterated, and new forms of social life start from scratch. However, the historical record shows that in most cases social change is a protracted, gradual, uneven, and long-term process, not a rapid and abrupt event. Scholarship on the downfall of civilizations indicates that an organisational collapse is regularly a long-drawn-out process that can take centuries and can also be characterised by the periods of temporary rise and gradual decline (Diamond 2005). In some instances, the deterioration can be halted, and the organisational collapse can be reversed. So, the decline of nation-states and nationalism is bound to be a slow, prolonged, and lopsided process.

Some sociological and historical accounts that look at possible futures recognise that this is likely to be gradual and asymmetrical development. For example, classics of nationalism studies such as Gellner and Hobsbawm argued that nation-states and nationalism would progressively become less significant. Hobsbawm (1990:183) used Hegel's formulation to predict the decline of nationalism once it reaches its peak – 'the owl of Minerva which brings wisdom, said Hegel, flies out at dusk. It is a good sign that it is now circling round nations and nationalism.' He believed that nation-states would eventually be replaced by larger polities and that nationalism would then wither away: 'I think it [nationalism] has no real future. Of course, there are many nationalist movements. Nationalist ideas are not dead, far from it. It would be silly to say so. I am afraid they can still cause a lot of trouble. But I do not think nationalism is a viable option in the sense that I do not believe the new, smaller nations the nationalists want to create, can have much of an independent future. The future belongs to bigger entities' (Hobsbawm 1992:39).

Gellner (1983:121–122) was more measured in his assessment, believing that nationalism would become gentler but is likely to persevere long into the future: 'The sharpness of nationalist conflict may be expected to diminish … [T]he late industrial society … can be expected to be one in which nationalism persists, but in a muted, less virulent form.' In this understanding, continuous economic growth together with technological innovations is likely to generate more social mobility and eventually greater social equality, which would stifle the use of cultural differences in politics. While offering more subtlety and recognising the longevity of nationalism, these classical accounts did not provide any specific information on how a post-national world might look.

More comprehensive accounts such as those by Halperin (2017), Burbank and Cooper (2023, 2010), and Wimmer (2021) draw on historical experience to envisage alternatives to the nation-state in the future. Hence, Halperin (2017:107) argues that 'the nation-state became the special face of capital accumulation only after the Second World War and in only those few countries were Fordist/Keynesian and social democratic policies were adopted'. In her view, for much of history it was the imperial city-state that was the dominant political and economic form of social order. Imperial city states have driven the expansion of capitalism throughout the world. For Halperin (2017:97), the wide-spread references to the 'decline of nation-state' and 'post-national spatialities' miss the historical centrality of city-states to the global economy. Thus, with the collapse of Keynesian policies she envisages the future as 'the resurgence of a durable and historically dominant form of state: the imperial city-state form'. In her view this tendency is already present throughout the globe, with city-states such as Singapore, Hong Kong, the United Arab Emirates, Bahrain, Qatar, Kuwait, and Macau but also independent financial centres such as 'The City' of London, Mexico City, Abuja, Washington, DC, Delhi, and Buenos Aires dominating the economic life of their regions. In this understanding the decline of nation-states and nationalisms is likely to bring a future where imperial city-states and neoliberal capitalism completely dominate.

Burbank and Cooper (2023, 2010) offer a different interpretation of the post-national future. Although they also draw on historical legacies to envisage long-term social change, their focus is less on the city-states and more on empires and transcontinental unions. For Burbank and Cooper (2010:2–3), imperial orders have dominated much of sedentary life and the nation-state is no more than a very short episode in human political development: 'The Ottoman empire endured six hundred years; for over two thousand years a succession of Chinese dynasties claimed the mantel of imperial predecessors, the Roman empire exercised power for six hundred years in the western Mediterranean area and its eastern offshoot, the Byzantine empire, lasted another millennium.... By comparison, the nation-state appears a blip on the historical horizon, a state form that emerged recently from under imperial skies and whose hold on the world's political imagination may well prove partial or transitory.'

They contest the conventional historiographic accounts that see nation-states and nationalisms as reaching their pinnacle in nineteenth-century Europe and argue that imperial orders remained the dominant form of political power well into the 1950s. Moreover, they insist that imperial organisational and ideological structures were not simply replaced by those of nation-states; instead, the legacy of empire lingers on: 'Empire has not given way to a stable, functioning world of nation-states. Many recent bloody and destabilizing conflicts – in Rwanda, Iraq, Israel/Palestine, Afghanistan, ex-Yugoslavia, Sri Lanka, the Congo, the Caucasus and elsewhere – emerged from failures to find viable alternative to imperial regimes' (Burbank & Cooper 2010:443).

As they see nation-states to be highly dysfunctional and temporary entities, they focus on past and future alternatives to this form of polity. In this context they explore 'post-imperial possibilities' that could have materialised in the twentieth century, including transcontinental federations or confederacies such as Euroasia, Euroafrica, and Afroasia (Burbank & Cooper 2023). The Euroasian project developed after the collapse of imperial Russia in 1917 and was revived again in the 1990s with the disintegration of the Soviet Union. Euroafrica emerged in 1940s and 1950s as a relatively viable set of proposals to replace the asymmetrical relationship between France and its former African colonies. The 1950s and 1960s Afroasian project was perhaps the least coherent in its attempt to transcend the dominance of colonial powers through the development of horizontal solidarity among former colonised populations. Although these three post-imperial alternatives all ultimately failed, they demonstrate that the nation-state is neither predestined nor a permanent form of polity: 'to describe the pathway from empire to nation-state as linear and inevitable is to ignore the complexity of how empires came apart and the multiple possibilities for post-imperial transformations' (Burbank & Cooper 2023:263). Drawing on this historical legacy, Burbank and Cooper envisage alternatives to nation-states in the future – continental federations such as the ever-evolving European Union and the variety of transcontinental confederate models that dispense with hierarchy and discrimination and allow for more horizontal structures of power.

Drawing on sociological theories of functional integration and differentiation, Wimmer (2021) articulates the most comprehensive vision of post-national futures. Unlike Halperin and Burbank and Cooper, who provide a very general accounts, Wimmer offers specific and detailed depictions of a world without nation-states. He envisages five scenarios for the world in the 2320s. In this perspective, the collapse of nation-states and nationalisms occurs at the same time that new social organisations take over the responsibilities previously associated with nation-states, such as the provision of public goods, defence, and the mechanisms of political decision-making. In Wimmer's view the possible post-national futures would range from a stateless and anarchic social order to the existence of thousands of statelets rooted in shared cultural identities to an imperial order composed of several civilizations to a universe of culturally diverse continental states and to the globe consisting of a single, world state.

The stateless social order would be a highly individualised and unequal system of free associations. It would operate in 'a nonterritorialized, networked way' where citizenship would not be inherited 'but chosen depending on what kind of membership fees one can afford – further depoliticizing national identities by dissolving the idea of nations as groups of intergenerational continuity and mandatory solidarity' (Wimmer 2021:316). The second scenario resembles in part Halperin's idea of independent city-states. However, unlike Halperin, who emphasises the centrality of capitalism, Wimmer believes that such mini-states would develop different economic and political systems where legitimacy would be centred on ethnic, racial, or gender essentialisms. The next futuristic model invokes the re-emergence of empires. In this arrangement the neo-imperial world would replace the nation-states with a handful of mega-empires waging incessant wars of conquest. Such entities would legitimise their existence in terms of civilisational superiority. The fourth scenario shares some echoes of Burbank and Cooper's vision of a future dominated by large continental state structures. For Wimmer such mega-entities could develop out of regional trade networks such as the EU but also the North American Free Trade Association (NAFTA) in North America, the Southern Common Market (MERCOSUR) in Latin America, or the Association of Southeast Asian Nations (ASEAN) in Asia. Such large continental systems would operate as federal unions run by technocratic elites who would be recruited meritocratically from across their respective societies. The final scenario invokes the project of the world state, an entity that would integrate all existing nation-states into a federal association with a single structure of governance. Such a global state could grow out of the existing institutions such as the UN or through the hegemonic domination of some existing state. This social order would dispense with nationalism and would legitimise its existence through cultural pluralism. The government structures would represent all world regions.

Wimmer (2021:321) finds all five scenarios equally plausible but also leaves room for mixed options such as 'a world state with some mini states in the peripheries, let us say Appalachia or the mountainous Cantons of Switzerland, whose populations threaten collective suicide when asked to submit to a global Leviathan. A combination of Continental states and mini-states or areas of anarchy could also be sustainable, though it is unlikely that large areas populated by mini-states could survive the competitive (and perhaps coercive) pressure. For that reason, a scenario of equally sized Continental states and empires is more likely.' These five scenarios are all developed on the assumption that the key foundations of modern social order such as capitalism, continuous reliance on technology, universalist ethics, moral equality, and the human (rather than machine) control of society will persist.

Unlike the classics of nationalism studies such as Hobsbawm and Gellner, which do not offer much elaboration on post-national futures, Wimmer, Burbank and Cooper, and Halperin provide more comprehensive visions of the world without nation-states and nationalisms. These contemporary accounts are well informed by the existing historical and sociological scholarship on past forms of social organisation and can foresee better which social orders are more likely to be viable in the future. Nevertheless, these visions of post-national futures also exhibit some analytical weaknesses.

First, they do not differentiate between nation-states and nationalisms and simply assume that the demise of one will inevitably lead to disappearance of the other. However, considering that the majority of the world's population identify strongly in national terms, have been socialised in nationalist environments, and see the world through nation-centric categories, the collapse of nation-state system will not automatically obliterate nationalism. It is very likely that nationalist ideas and practices will continue for several generations after the end of nation-states.

Second, these accounts offer too symmetric a view of the future. Both Halperin and Burbank and Cooper envisage a dominance of a singular from of social order – either the imperial city-state or continental/transcontinental unions. Wimmer is more flexible here, as he recognises the possibility of several models coexisting together. Nevertheless, even he believes that the continental and imperial state structures have more chance of survival than the rest. These accounts lack visions that allow for the parallel existence of diverse forms of sociopolitical organisation. More importantly, they leave no room for continuous social change – the models of social organisation are likely to experience ups and downs, slow or radical changes, growth, and decline, improved and deteriorated lifestyles, and so on. Just as our present is not unform but everchanging and vibrant, it is very likely that our future will be dynamic and diverse too.

Third, these three visions of post-national futures seem to be deeply inspired by the past. Halperin and Burbank and Cooper are explicit in this as they invoke the imperial city-state and empires or transcontinental models of social order as the most probable patterns for the future. Wimmer offers more variability and political imagination, but he too mostly falls back on the models of polity that have existed before: empires, small states, or pre-state societies. Even when novel social orders are imagined, they are rooted in the contemporary world – continental states resemble the EU, while the UN is the seed of the world state. Although drawing on historical experience is valid and, in some respects, plausible, the future cannot be reduced to the available realities from the past. Instead, it is necessary to go beyond what has happened before and conceptualise very different possibilities.

Finally, these accounts offer too functionalist an understanding of the future. Wimmer (2021:313) is unambiguous about this: 'functionalism is largely ineffective at explaining why political systems develop in this direction and not another', but when thinking about future possibilities 'it forces us to think in terms of alternatives ... [T]hinking of functional needs also helps to further reduce the range of imaginable futures as we do not have to consider political systems that do not fulfil these three functional tasks.' For Halperin, the imperial city-state is the most likely future model as its existence is the most functional for the spread of capitalism. Burbank and Cooper see large-scale political entities such as transcontinental unions and empires as the most effective and thus more likely to endure in the future. However, functionalism is equally problematic as an explanatory paradigm and as a tool to predict the future. In the same way as the needs are not causes, fulfilling specific functional tasks cannot help us explain the nearly unlimited future possibilities. Functionalism is too reductionist to allow for the unintended consequences of human action that can generate very diverse forms of social life.

The World beyond Nation-States and Nationalisms: Four Scenarios

Wimmer (2021:309) is absolutely right that there is 'theoretically infinite space of long-term futures'. As the interminable number of factors can influence the direction of social change, it is extremely difficult to make any predictions about the future. Long-term social dynamics often operate similarly to the butterfly effect as developed in chaos theory. Using the example of a butterfly flapping its wings, which generates small perturbations that ultimately can cause a tornado, Lorenz (1972) demonstrated how a small change in a deterministic nonlinear system can bring about a radical transformation in the long term. Since there are so many variables involved, post-national futures are just as unpredictable. Hence any such predications are inevitably provisional and speculative. Thus, in this context it makes more sense to identify some possible long-term trends rather than to provide very detailed visions of the future social order.

Such projections of future trends must go beyond the limits of conventional approaches, including their overemphasis on structure, technology, and organisational uniformity, as well as their under-emphasis of environmental destruction.

Many futuristic accounts tend to overstate the structural transformations at the expense of changed human subjectivities. It is often assumed that changing the character of the political and economic organisation will simply and automatically lead to radical alterations in how one understands the world. This relates to individual subjectivities, different belief systems, or moral codes but also to the wider social cleavages that shape every social order, including status hierarchies, class relations, educational differences, power positions, gender relations, or cultural divisions. Any scenarios of post-national futures must take human subjectivities and social divisions into account.

Contemporary visions of the future social order also regularly exaggerate the role of ever-advancing technology while downplaying or ignoring organisational, ideological, and micro-interactional dynamics. Of course, technological and structural changes are important, but they are only possible through the development of social organisations, ideological legitimacy, and via their embedment into the networks of micro-solidarities. Science and technology mostly operate as a means and a by-product of these processes.

Another important dimension that is central for envisaging the future is environmental degradation. As Conversi (2020:51) rightly points out: 'the Anthropocene spells the actually possible death of nations, in all their human, cultural and historical components'. One cannot build future post-national scenarios without considering the continuous destruction of the biosphere, global warming, loss of biodiversity, and population growth, among other factors.

To make future scenarios as realistic as possible, it is necessary to recognise that large-scale social changes are likely to remain uneven, asymmetrical, and dynamic, as they are today. The collapse of nation-states is likely to be a slow and lopsided process that will affect some parts of the world sooner and more intensely than others. One could envisage a long period of time when nation-states still dominate in some regions while having been dissolved in other regions.

Hence by focusing on the three key social processes used in this book, coercive-organisational, ideological, and micro-interactional grounding, one can envisage several scenarios for the world beyond nation-states and nationalisms.

Although we live in a world that is completely dominated by nation-states, such entities exhibit different levels of nationalist grounding. In some societies such as Japan nationalist grounding is very deep: there is high level of organisational, ideological, and micro-interactional grounding and all three processes are deeply interconnected and embedded across the social order. In contrast, in other societies such the Democratic Republic of the Congo or Somalia micro-interactional grounding is much more developed than organisational or ideological grounding, and the links between these three remain weak. Such unevenness is even more likely to be present in post-national futures.

By focusing on these three processes, it is possible to envisage several long-term scenarios for the world without nation-states: (1) the coercive world of the post-Anthropocene, (2) the world of private corporations, (3) the quasi-imperial world, and (4) the world of digital micro-communities.

The Coercive World of the Post-Anthropocene

This future scenario would transpire in a context where no long-term solution for environmental destruction has been found. In this world, temperatures would increase substantially, and weather patterns would become extreme and unpredictable. Some parts of the world, including many large port cities, would be submerged under rising oceans. Substantial parts of the globe would experience continuous drought or floods and would eventually become uninhabitable. The extreme weather conditions would generate chronic shortages of food, arable land, and water. The lack of key resources would foster political and economic instability with increased warfare, revolutions, uprisings, and coups. The world would also experience an unprecedented level of social inequality. Most social orders would be characterised by sharp social and political polarisation, and the divide between the more prosperous, environmentally less affected areas and the rest of the globe would be deeply transformed by global warming. The continuous environmental destruction would also foster an unparalleled scale of global migrations.

These radically changed environmental conditions would have a profound impact on state organisation. In an exceptionally unstable world characterised by huge structural costs for everyday survival, small states would be unable to protect their citizens, generate sufficient resources, regularly provide public goods, protect their borders, maintain law and order, keep stable governance structures, or defend their territories from hostile neighbours. Hence, the nation-state model would gradually be replaced with large-scale political entities emerging in the areas less affected by environmental degradation. So, the existing borders of nation-states would give way to new, environment-centred, political boundaries.

These new political entities would prioritise the development of their coercive-organisational capacities at the expense of democratic decision-making. The continuous demand for resources, including food, water, and safe accommodation, together with external pressure from millions of migrants hoping to settle in these more secure areas, would foster intense coercive-organisational grounding. At the same time ideological grounding would be weaker. Being composed of a very diverse, and large, population that until recently was part of different nation-states, these novel political entities would struggle to maintain ideological unity and coherence across their polities. These new political entities would not be able to rely on nationalism as the principal source of political legitimacy and would have to create a new ideological discourse to justify their existence as well as the rulers' right to consistently deploy coercive power. Such ideological grounding is likely to emphasise the bare survival of its citizens/subjects, the promise of continuous security and safety, anti-immigrant rhetoric, and the promise of continuous technological advancements that would eventually solve the environmental degradation. The permanent mobilisation of its citizens that invokes constant threats and fear would allow for the establishment and maintenance of authoritarian or semi-authoritarian models of rule.

These new polities would not be particularly effective in penetrating the universe of micro-level solidarities. Although the governments would deploy different ideological tools to mimic the language, emotions, and moralities of kinships and friendships, they would largely be ineffective in attaining durable political legitimacy through the envelopment of micro-solidarities. Instead, most of the population would find the strongest sense of attachment in their micro-groups while obeying the coercive demands of their repressive governments. So, this would be a world typified by a very high level of coercive-organisational grounding, a low level of ideological grounding, and a low level of micro-interactional grounding.

The World of Private Corporations

The inability of nation-states to deal with environmental destruction could result in their collapse. This organisational incapacity could generate a chronic lack of political legitimacy among their populations, thus also delegitimising the nationalist projects. In this environment of general insecurity and uncertainty, private corporations can step in and offer an alternative solution: the full membership in their corporate organisations. In this way large-scale private corporations would gradually and unevenly replace nation-states. They would offer key provisions associated with state governance: the regular supply of all resources required for everyday subsistence, the deployment of public goods, policing and legal services, and the defence of the company's assets, including the lands under their ownership. Individual memberships in the corporations would be based on signing legally binding contracts that would stipulate their duties and rights. The contract would also entail complete loyalty to these organisations, including commitment to the company ethos. The company would provide regular payment to their employees from which they would be required to pay for all the services and resources received from the corporation. Alternatively, the company would offer all such services on condition of signing a contract that would require individuals to work for the rest of their lives for their chosen corporation. The corporations would provide housing in huge megalopolises under their ownership. Accommodation and other provisions would be strictly based on one's position within the corporation's hierarchy. Hence, the CEOs, COOs, and members of the governing boards would live in the most prestigious and luxurious housing based in the secluded, secure, and environmentally protected areas of the cities or suburbs, while ordinary employees would live in the poorer and more polluted estates of huge mega-cities.

The new world would consist of numerous private corporations that would compete against each other for new markets and larger shares of profit. The CEOs of the largest corporations would meet annually to agree and sign various international trading treaties that would be compulsory for all corporations. The policing of such treaties, including possible court cases, would be in the hands of a special agency that would be staffed and funded by these leading corporations.

The largest corporations would possess enormous wealth, would have their own currency (or bitcoin equivalent), their own legal system, administration, and moderate but well-equipped and trained professional military and police force. In some important ways they would be the modern equivalent of seventeenth- , eighteenth-, and early nineteenth-century joint-stock trading companies such as the East India Company, Dutch United East India Company, or Hudson Bay Company. Using up-to-date advanced technology, such corporations would substantially increase their coercive-organisational capacities, including extensive surveillance techniques, border control, dispersion of protests, and systems of labour camps for disobedient employees. The corporations would also ban trade unions and political dissent. Some corporations would be run in a more democratic or oligarchical model, while others would operate an authoritarian system of organisation. However, even when more democratically run, this would not translate into mass participation in decision-making at the level of all employees. The large-scale corporations would regularly engage in hostile takeovers of smaller companies.

The corporations would also invest in building their own ideological doctrines that would justify their existence and domination. All employees would be required to attend company ethos training courses that would be examined by senior staff and with exam results serving as the key requirement for promotion. Children of company employees would attend the corporation-owned schools and universities where they would be constantly exposed to the key ideological principles of the corporation. The companies would also publish their own mass and social media that would be distributed daily to all company members and their offspring. Although initially nationalist attachments would still trump company-based ideologies, over several generations nationalism would be eventually replaced by corporate ideologies. Hence, in addition to the strong coercive-organisational grounding, this post-national future would also be characterised by strong ideological grounding.

However, micro-interactional grounding would be less developed and patchier. As the corporations would encourage individualist capitalism, consumerism, and self-fulfilment, the micro-social ties of kinships and deep friendships would fragment and weaken. With the development of new technologies, individuals would fulfil their emotional needs for social interaction with robotic, synthetic, and virtual alternatives. The development of AI, digital technologies, and automation would serve to replace human-based interactions. Nevertheless, these technological (and possibly pharmaceutical) substitutes would not in the long term facilitate the development of micro-interactional grounding. Thus, the world of private corporations would be dominated by strong coercive-organisational and ideological grounding but quite weak envelopment of micro-solidarity.

The Quasi-Imperial World

Empires have dominated this planet for more than 5,000 years and it is not unreasonable to envisage their return in some form after the collapse of the nation-state system. However, as imperial social orders have been thoroughly delegitimised in the last eighty years or so, they are unlikely to return in their traditional from. Conventional empires were profoundly hierarchical polities where the moral order was rooted in descent-based status inequalities. In such a world, only the members of the aristocracy were treated as fully-fledged human beings, while the commoners were perceived as inferior in every respect. The heritage of Enlightenment together with the political and industrial revolutions of the eighteenth and nineteenth centuries radically transformed these perceptions. With the rise of nationalisms and nation-states all citizens were deemed to be of equal moral worth. This moral quality is unlikely to automatically disappear with the collapse of nation-states. Modern subjectivities, rooted in a sense of individual self-worth, bodily autonomy, and political equality, are likely to prove stubborn even when nation-states disintegrate and are replaced by other forms of polity.

The same principle applies to another major feature of the conventional imperial orders – cultural heterogeneity. While traditional empires had neither organisational means nor interest to mould diversity into homogeneity, their post-national equivalents would have to deal with already highly homogenised populations. In a world where aristocratic lineage and religion were the main sources of political legitimacy, there was no reason to homogenise culturally diverse subjects of empire. In contrast, in the post-national world status lineage is delegitimised, while populations are highly nationalised. So, the new quasi-imperial entities would have to accommodate a modern sense of citizenship including institutionalised and embedded cultural values and practices. In this context nationalism would not go away easily or quickly. It is only when the new ideological projects become entrenched throughout the society and over several generations that nationalism would be replaced by alternative ideologies. Hence, any attempt to simply recreate the world of yesteryear empires is unlikely to succeed.

This is not to say that establishing some forms of quasi-imperial structures would be impossible. On the contrary, many structural and geopolitical aspects of the imperial order could be put in place in a relatively short period of time. With the collapse of nation-states, the mutual recognition of political borders would also evaporate. This would create a new geopolitical environment where territorial conquest could yet again become a legitimate political option. Environmental destruction and the chronic lack of resources would foster wars of territorial conquest as the new post-national polities would aim to acquire liveable habitats, arable land, and clean water and air, among other necessities. These incessant wars of conquest are likely to generate chronic instability, with many quasi-imperial polities fighting for control of different territories, resources, and populations. The result of such protracted wars would be a world dominated by several very large quasi-imperial entities with complex and multi-layered territorial structures. There would also be other, smaller territorial entities negotiating their way between the large quasi-imperial orders. Such entities could include relatively autonomous cities centred on the financial sector, with wealthy bankers and brokers; mid-sized polities, in vassal or client status in the quasi-empire, whose existence is built around extraction of specific resources; small polities controlled by different religious orders; or territorialised academic hubs centred on scientific innovation that provide services for the quasi-imperial states.

In such an unstable environment, the states would prioritise the development of military, police, and the production of weaponry. Hence, the coercive-organisational grounding of large quasi-empires would expand substantially, with the smaller polities remaining dependent on the military protection and even policing of their respective quasi-empires. All such large political entities would introduce compulsory military draft, would maintain high taxation to pay for wars, and would establish a large network of prisons and labour camps for POWs and domestic dissidents. So, the quasi-empires would have very high coercive-organisational capacities, while other polities would have mostly weak organisational grounding.

The new polities would also develop different ideological doctrines to justify their existence and dominance. Hence, instead of nationalism one could envisage rhetoric that glorifies the civilizational superiority of a particular quasi-empire and its citizens or ideological discourses that laud their technological and military prowess. The smaller polities would invoke alternative ideological projects such as the religious purity of their societies (for religious orders), the economic ascendency of their citizens (for the financial centres), or the scientific superiority of their population (for the academic hubs). All such polities would establish educational institutions, mass/social media, and the public sphere that would continuously disseminate ideas and foster specific social practices centred on worship of one's state. Thus, in most cases ideological grounding would be highly developed.

In such a world, micro-interactional grounding would be very uneven. While some smaller polities such as those based on religious orders and some mid-sized states might maintain strong networks of micro-solidarity, others, more centred on individual achievements such as the financial or academic centres, would be characterised by weak micro-interactional grounding. The quasi-empires too would struggle to integrate the networks of micro-level solidarities within their highly developed coercive-organisational and ideological capacities.

The World of Digital Micro-Communities

The final scenario is premised on the idea that the environmental catastrophe has been averted and a viable, long-term solution to nearly all ecological problems has been found. In this new world, nation-states and nationalism would gradually evaporate, but this would not be a violent process. Instead, well-informed, politically active, and educated citizens would initiate development of small-scale communities that would actively practice deliberative democracy and would shun the highly ineffective and corrupted structures of the nation-state. Such small communities would be mostly self-sufficient but not autarchic. They would produce their own resources required for everyday life, including food, water, electricity, heating, and so on. They would also provide all necessary public goods including transportation, communications, education, communal policing, and legal services. By relying on advanced technologies and hyperconnectivity, such communities would not be isolated but would interact, trade, communicate, and engage in cultural and social activities with other such communities all over the world.

The development of digital and other technologies would change the character of labour relations and global economy, with the focus shifting towards collective self-actualisation over consumerism, the amassing of material possessions, and the maximisation of profit. Such communities would foster a progressive taxation system aiming to reduce inequalities and provide for high-quality public services. Large-scale, costly public projects including major roads, the health system, and welfare provisions would be coordinated with neighbouring communities with the aim of making these systems more effective and affordable for all. The communities would be run democratically, with all major decisions being made through extensive public (including online) deliberation and electronic voting from home. The system of governance would involve all adult citizens, with coordinators for different political and social roles being elected every two years. With the development of new technologies, such communities would also rely on robotic workers that would undertake all physically demanding jobs. These communities would also foster the development of arts, science, and education in general.

The shift from the nation-state model towards such small digital communities would be protracted and uneven as some rulers of nation-states would attempt to eradicate these post-national communities. However, once such communities become highly popular, they would gradually expand throughout the world. Once such communities prove viable, more effective, and more pleasant for everyday life, their existence would gradually undermine the political legitimacy of nation-states. With ever-decreasing participation in the political, economic, and cultural institutions of nation-states, including abysmal election turnouts, disengagement from national institutions, and withdrawal from the excessively bureaucratic and extremely expensive educational system at all levels, the nation-states would eventually lose much of their organisational capacity and ideological justification.

Digital micro-communities would possess low levels of coercive-organisational power. They would not have a standing military force and would preserve order through a communal policing system. In the case of external threat or attack, such police force would be expanded through voluntary recruitment to defend the territory of the community. If the external threat is more serious, neighbouring micro-communities would develop a unified strategy of collective defence. The system of governance would shun permanent hierarchies, and all adult citizens would be involved in different aspects of political, economic, and social decision-making.

The new social order would foster proliferation of different beliefs and practices, thus preventing the emergence of hegemonic ideological discourses. Digital micro-communities would develop diverse ideational mechanisms for the justification of their specific social orders. There would be no uniform education system, but a plurality of educational practices would be recognised and practiced throughout each community. Mass and social media would have the freedom to disseminate diverse points of view. Micro-digital communities would develop their own mini-public spheres, which would also be a part of the wider, global, and digital public sphere. Thus, there would be a low level of ideological grounding.

Digital micro-communities would differ profoundly from other future scenarios in their strength of micro-interactional grounding. Such communities would encourage the development of micro-group solidarities. Since most members of community would know other individuals from their micro-community, they would be in a position to develop a strong sense of micro-group attachments. Regular face-to-face interactions together with routine digital communications would strengthen the sense of micro-communal identity and solidarity. Such communities would be composed of networks characterised by deep friendships and close kinships. The patterns of everyday life would also stimulate the advent of generational cohorts who would go together through all the key rites of passage and would develop strong inter-personal bonds. However, individuals would also interact regularly with people from other digital communities, and many would live, work, socialise, and have romantic partners in other communities.

Obviously, these four scenarios represent only a small segment of what the post-national futures might look like. It is also conceivable that some combination of these four models and many others transpires in the future with some syncretic features from different scenarios. The future offers enormous possibilities, but the key issue is that nation-states and nationalisms can and will eventually give way to alternative models of social order.

Conclusion

In a world where nation-states have become hegemonic and the only legitimate form of territorial political organisation, it might seem that no viable alternatives are possible. However, any longue durée look at human beings indicates that such a social and political order represents no more than a tiny blip in the historical experience of human subjectivities. Both nation-states and nationalisms have developed very late in history, and in many important respects they represent a highly unusual way of organising social order. There is nothing that has predetermined the formation of nationalist subjectivities. The world of nation-states is just one of many possible options that history could have generated. Human beings were initially hard-wired to live in very small, face-to-face communities, and they now inhabit political entities consisting of millions and in some cases billions of people. This historical outcome is a product of highly contingent coercive-organisational, ideological, and micro-interactional forces. It seems plausible to expect that once these forces change, one can expect emergence of very different, post-national futures. Nevertheless, it remains to be seen whether the world without nation-states and nationalisms will be better, safer, and more prosperous than the one we inhabit now.

Conclusion

Modern Subjectivities as Nationalist Subjectivities

One of the key questions that created a rift in classical scholarship on nationhood was: How old are nations and nationalisms? The pinnacle of this analytical dispute was the famous 1995 Warwick debate between Ernest Gellner and Anthony D. Smith. As the key representative of ethno-symbolism, Smith rejected the idea that nationhood is exclusively a modern phenomenon. In his understanding, the potency of nationalism in the contemporary world stems from its deep cultural roots: 'because so many nations are historically embedded in pre-modern ethnic ties, memories and heritages, we are unlikely to witness in our lifetime the transcendence of the nation and the supersession of nationalism' (Smith 1996:363). The leading modernist, Gellner (1996:366), responded bluntly that the 'world was created round about the end of the eighteenth century, and nothing before that makes the slightest difference to the issues we face'. Gellner recognised that in some instances of nation-formation cultural heritage might matter, but that in most cases a fictitious past would be just as adequate: 'the cultural continuity is contingent, inessential'.

In this book I have tried to show that neither of these two assessments is valid. While I share Gellner's view that cultural continuity is not necessary for the rise and popularity of nationalism, I disagree with his dismissal of the past. Nationalism does not emerge suddenly and out of nowhere but grows gradually from the structural transformations that take place in the premodern and early modern periods. Similarly, I believe that Smith is right that the transcendence of nationalism is unlikely to happen any time soon. However, this has very little or nothing to do with the 'premodern ethnic ties' or shared 'heritage'. Instead, as argued throughout this book, the strength and persistence of nationalism stems from coercive-organisational, ideological, and micro-interactional grounding – the processes that long predate, but also significantly intensify with, modernity.

In other words, the proliferation and dominance of nationalism in the contemporary world is not a consequence of shared memories, myths, or the cultural heritage of premodern ethnies, as nationhood can exist without such cultural resources from the past. Rather, what really matters is the coercive-organisational capacity: nation-states do not emerge ex nihilo; instead, they develop on the coercive and organisational apparatuses of their predecessors – the patrimonial kingdoms, city-states, city-leagues, chiefdoms, tribal confederacies, and empires. It is the existing political and military structure of previous polities that has proved indispensable for the development of modern nation-states. Nation-states are not built from scratch. Instead, they re-deploy, re-organise, and radically transform the existing coercive-organisational spine – the governance structures, administrative apparatuses, transportation and communication networks, judicial systems, military forces, revenue collection agencies, and many other social organisations.

In addition, to make the processes of coercive-organisational grounding smoother and less resistant, all polities rely on the ideologisation of their social orders. The process of ideological grounding confers political legitimacy and can foster mobilisation of public support. In this context coercive-organisational and ideological grounding often overlap – nation-states create, finance, and maintain the educational systems, mass media, welfare agencies, public sphere, and many other outlets that foster ideological grounding. In addition, non-state entities such as private corporations, religious institutions, civil society networks, and others also prop up the nation-centric projects – from consumerism and nationalised faiths to nation-centric sports, tourism, or cuisine. What is central here is not the specific content of ideological messages or the 'shared cultural heritage' but the process of ideologisation itself. Ideological grounding is an ongoing, dynamic, contingent, and relational historical process that helps transform individuals into proud members of their respective nations.

Finally, nationalism became the dominant way of life only when it was able to successfully penetrate the micro-universe of everyday interactions. The process of micro-interactional grounding relies on the emotional and moral ties generated in face-to-face interactions of people who care about each other, including the networks of close kinships, friendships, and deep comradeships. Since the enduring bonds of solidarity usually develop in micro-interactional contexts, large-scale social organisations such as nation-states focus on penetrating and utilising these micro-level ties. They often mimic the micro-interactional world by depicting the abstract entities that are nation-states as our 'motherlands' and 'fatherlands', while the millions of people who will never meet each other become our 'brothers' , 'sisters', and 'brethren'. In this way, coercive-organisational, ideological, and micro-interactional grounding create conditions under which modern human subjectivities become nationalist subjectivities.

However, this is far from being a teleological or predetermined phenomenon. The concept of grounding stands for the process-oriented and highly contingent character of nationalism. This is a historically dynamic, unpredictable, but also ongoing and enduring phenomenon. There is nothing inevitable in how nationalism operates. This is a phenomenon that has had no impact for much of human history and has only become a significant social force in the last three centuries. Thus, if social conditions change dramatically, nationalism can also go away in the same way it came to dominate our social and political landscape.

While the Gellner–Smith debate remains relevant today, most contemporary historical sociologists see nationhood and nationalisms as distinctly modern phenomena. What I have tried to do in this book is to shift this debate in a different direction. The classical theorists of nationalism have focused predominantly on the question of origins while paying much less attention to how nationalism preserves its centrality in the contemporary world. In other worlds, instead of asking why nationalism is modern, one should ask why modernity is so nationalist. Using the tools of an inductive middle-range perspective and moving beyond structure-versus-agency explanations, I have tried to answer this question by exploring a variety of historical and contemporary contexts to show how and why nationalism has become the dominant way of life.

In this context the book zoomed in on the multifaceted relationships between imperial and national subjectivities, explored the role religion and secularism play in the development of nationalist projects, and analysed how the administrative structures of imperial states foster the rise of nationalist movements. I also examined the use of golden age nationalist narratives and the impact of warfare and conspiracy theories on nation-formation. The book also looked at the social processes that foster the transformation of deep micro-comradeships into nationalist subjectivities and instigate different social experiences of combat soldiers and civilians in relation to nationalism. What all these very different forms of social and historical experiences have in common is that they show how modern human subjectivities have, for the most part, become nationalist subjectivities. It seems rather odd that despite enormous individual, social, political, economic, and cultural differences in the world, most people display a solid degree of similarity in their positive attitudes towards nationhood. For an overwhelming majority of individuals on this planet, their nationhood is the central category of political and cultural attachment. This is not just a matter of self-identification, categorisation of others, a sense of solidarity, or personal perceptions.

Nationhood is even more a form of lived experience and collective subjectivity that is generated, sustained, and re-constructed through the coercive-organisational, ideological, and micro-interactional processes. In this book I have tried to show why and how billions of people now see the world primarily through the prism of nationhood and also reproduce nation-centric ideas and practices in their daily lives. This hegemony of nationhood is so baffling precisely because it is historically highly atypical and rather unnatural for our species, which was built to live in much smaller groups. Yet despite these unusual features, in the early twenty-first century, nationalism has acquired such dominance in social life that no other ideological project can match. Nationalism is indeed the dominant way of life.

References

24 Sedam 2017. https://24sedam.rs/drustvo/vesti/83674/sta-se-vrtelo-u-glavi-dusana-silnog-prvi-psihobiograf-najveceg-srpskog-vladara-ogolio-carevu-licnost-video/vest.

Aderet, O. 2020. 'A Terrible New Weapon of War': The Spanish Flu Had Its Own Share of Conspiracy Theories. www.haaretz.com/israel-news/.premium-the-spanish-flu-had-its-own-share-of-conspiracy-theories-1.8713448.

Agoston, G. 2005. *Guns for the Sultan: Military Power and the Weapons Industry in the Ottoman Empire*. Cambridge University Press.

Akçam, T. 2007. *A Shameful Act*. Macmillan.

Akgül, A. 2019. *The Case of Atatürk Reforms in Early Turkish Republic Between 1923–1946: From an Educational Perspective*. Harvard Extension School.

Akmese, H. N. 2005. *Birth of Modern Turkey: The Ottoman Military and the March to WWI*. Bloomsbury Academic.

Aksakal, M. 2016. The Ottoman Proclamation of Jihad. In E. J. Zürcher (ed.), *Jihad and Islam in World War I*. Leiden University Press, 54–69.

Alexander, J. 2004. Toward a Theory of Cultural Trauma. In J. Alexander et al. (eds.), *Cultural Trauma and Collective Identity*. University of California Press.

2013. *Trauma: A Social Theory*. Polity.

Althusser, L. 1994 [1970]. Ideological State Apparatuses. In G. Elliot (ed.), *Althusser: A Critical Reader*. Blackwell.

Amit, K., A. Lisak, M. Popper, & R. Gal. 2007. Motivation to Lead: Research on the Motives for Undertaking Leadership Roles in the Israel Defense Forces (IDF). *Military Psychology* 19(3): 137–160.

Anderson, B. 1983. *Imagined Communities: Reflections on the Origin and Spread of Nationalism*. London: Verso.

1998. *The Spectre of Comparisons: Nationalism, Southeast Asia, and the World*. London: Verso.

Andras, E. 2014. Vigorous Flagging in the Heart of Europe: The Hungarian Homeland under the Right-Wing Regime. www.e-flux.com/journal/57/60438/vigorous-flagging-in-the-heart-of-europe-the-hungarian-homeland-under-the-right-wing-regime/.

Anscombe, F. 2014. *State, Faith, and Nation in Ottoman and Post-Ottoman Lands*. Cambridge University Press.

Antonsich, M. 2009. National Identities in the Age of Globalisation: The Case of Western Europe. *National Identities* 11(3): 281–299.

2016. The ‘Everyday’ of Banal Nationalism: Ordinary People’s Views on Italy and Italian. *Political Geography.* 54: 32–42.

2020. Did the COVID-19 Pandemic Revive Nationalism? Open Democracy. www.opendemocracy.net/en/pandemic-border/did-covid-19-pandemic-revive-nationalism/

Anzulovic, B. 1999. *Heavenly Serbia.* NYU Press.

Aral, B. 2004. The Idea of Human Rights as Perceived in the Ottoman Empire. *Human Rights Quarterly* 26(2): 454–482.

Archer, M. 2008. *Realist Social Theory: The Morphogenetic Approach.* Cambridge University Press.

Armstrong, J. A. 1982. *Nations before Nationalism.* University of North Carolina Press.

Asad, Talal. 2003. *Formations of the Secular: Christianity, Islam, Modernity.* Stanford University Press.

Atran, S. 2010. *Talking to the Enemy: Violent Extremism, Sacred Values, and What It Means to be Human.* Penguin.

2011. *Talking to the Enemy.* Penguin.

Austrian Census. 1910. https://austriagenweb.jimdoweb.com/info/general-information/census-data/ and https://www.statistik.at/en.

Averill, A. 2019. Rising: Reverence, Relevance, Revelry – Commemorations of the 1916 Rising in Dublin, Easter 2016. *Studies in Ethnicity and Nationalism* 19(2): 207–226.

Aydingün, A., & I. Aydingün. 2004. The Role of Language in the Formation of Turkish National Identity and Turkishness. *Nationalism & Ethnic Politics* 10(3): 415–432.

Baar, M. 2010. *Historians and Nationalism: East-Central Europe in the Nineteenth Century.* Oxford University Press.

Baker, C. 2015. *The Yugoslav Wars of the 1990s.* Palgrave Macmillan.

Balta, E., & I. N. Grigoriadis. 2024 The Evolution of Public Opinion in Greece and Turkey (2021–2023): Dynamics and Shifts in Comparative Perspective. ΕΛΙΑΜΕΠ (eliamep.gr).

Banac, I. 1984. *The National Question in Yugoslavia.* Cornell University Press.

Banton, M. 1983. *Racial and Ethnic Competition.* Cambridge University Press.

Barker, A. 1998. Austria: Nationality and the Borders of Identity. In M. Anderson & E. Bort (eds.), *The Frontiers of Europe.* Pinter.

Basta, K. 2021. *The Symbolic State.* Mcgill-Queen’s University Press.

Bauman, Z. 2002. *Society under Siege.* Polity.

2006. *Liquid Times: Living in an Age of Uncertainty.* Polity.

2017. *Retrotopia.* Polity.

BBC. 2023. Turkey Media Guide. www.bbc.com/news/world-europe-17992011

BBG Gallup. 2014. Contemporary Media Use in Turkey. www.usagm.gov/wp-content/media/2014/07/Turkey-research-brief.pdf.

Bean, R. 1973. War and the Birth of the Nation State. *Journal of Economic History* 33(1): 203–221.

Beauchamp, Z. 2014. World Values Survey at WOX. WVS Database (worldvaluessurvey.org).

Beck, U. 2000. The Cosmopolitan Perspective: Sociology of the Second Age of Modernity. *British Journal of Sociology* 51(1): 79–105.

2009. *World at Risk*. Polity Press.

Befu, H. 2001. *Hegemony of Homogeneity: An Anthropological Analysis of Nihonjinron*. Transpacific Press.

Bell, D. 2021. A Flawed History of Humanity. *Persuasion*, 20 November.

Benesch, O. 2014. *Inventing the Way of the Samurai*. Oxford University Press.

Benner, E. 2006. Japanese National Doctrines in International Perspective. In N. Shimazu (ed.), *Nationalism in Japan*. Routledge.

Bergholz, M. 2016. *Violence as a Generative Force: Identity, Nationalism, and Memory in a Balkan Community*. Cornell University Press.

Bianet. 2023. Turkey Ranks Third in Police Force Ratio in Europe. Sessiz Kalma. www.sessizkalma.org/en/news/turkey-ranks-third-police-force-ratio-europe.

Biden, J. 2023. Remarks by President Biden and President Yoon Suk Yeol of the Republic of Korea at Arrival Ceremony. www.whitehouse.gov/briefing-room/speeches-remarks/2023/04/26/remarks-by-president-biden-and-president-yoon-suk-yeol-of-the-republic-of-korea-at-arrival-ceremony/.

Billig, M. 1978. *Fascists: A Social Psychology of the National Front*. Academic Press.

1995. *Banal Nationalism*. Sage.

Biondich, M. 2000. *Stjepan Radić, the Croat Peasant Party, and the Politics of Mass Mobilization, 1904–1928*. University of Toronto Press.

2011. *The Balkans*. Oxford University Press.

Birmingham, D. 2003. *A Concise History of Portugal*. Cambridge University Press.

Blažević, Z. 2008. *Ilirizam prije ilirizma*. Narodne novine.

BN. 2023. Ratni veterani poručili Dodiku: Neka te brane tvoji tajkuni i kriminalci, mi nećemo! www.rtvbn.com/4049662/ratni-veterani-porucili-dodiku-neka-te-brane-tvoji-tajkuni-i-kriminalci-mi-necemo.

Boahen, A. A. 2003. *Yaa Asantewaa and the Asante-British War of 1900–1*. James Currey.

Boduszyński, M. P., & V. Pavlaković. 2019. Cultures of Victory and the Political Consequences of Foundational Legitimacy in Croatia and Kosovo. *Journal of Contemporary History* 54(4): 799–824.

Boele, O., B. Noordenbos, & K. Robbe. 2019. *Post-Soviet Nostalgia: Confronting the Empire's Legacies*. Routledge.

Botev, N. 1994. Where East Meets West: Ethnic Intermarriage in the Former Yugoslavia, 1962 to 1989. *American Sociological Review* 59(3): 461–480.

Bougarel, X. 2006. The Shadow of Heroes: Former Combatants in Post-War Bosnia and Herzegovina. *International Social Science Journal* 58(189): 479–490.

Bourdieu, P. 1990. *The Logic of Practice*. Stanford University Press.

Bourke, J. 2000. *An Intimate History of Killing*. Granta.

Bowman, K., E. Rugg, & J. Simmonds. 2011. *Polls on Patriotism and Military Service*. American Enterprise Institute for Public Policy Research.

Bozeva Abazi, K. 2007. *The Shaping of Bulgarian and Serbian National Identities 1800–1900*. Institute for National History.

Brass, P. 1991. *Ethnicity and Nationalism*. Sage.
Brentin, D., & D. Zec. 2018. *Sport in Socialist Yugoslavia*. Routledge.
Breuilly, J. 1993. *Nationalism and the State*. Manchester University Press.
2016. Nationalism and National Unification in 19th Century Europe. In J. Breuilly (ed.), *The Oxford Handbook of the History of Nationalism*. Oxford University Press.
Broadbridge, A. 2008. *Kingship and Ideology in the Islamic and Mongol Worlds*. Cambridge University Press.
Brockett, G. D. 2011. *How Happy to Call Oneself a Turk*. University of Texas Press.
Brooke, S. 2022. Constructing National Identity: Japanese Narratives and Triadic Discourses. *Electronic Journal of Contemporary Japanese Studies* 22(3): 1–11.
Brown, D. M. 1993. *The Cambridge History of Japan*. Cambridge University Press.
Brubaker, R. 1996. *Nationalism Reframed: Nationhood and the National Question in the New Europe*. Cambridge University Press.
2004. *Ethnicity without Groups*. Harvard University Press.
2015. *Grounds for Difference*. Harvard University Press.
Brubaker, R., & M. Feischmidt. 2002. 1848 in 1998: The Politics of Commemoration in Hungary, Romania, and Slovakia. *Comparative Studies in Society and History* 44(4): 700–744.
Brubaker, R., J. Fox, L. Grancea, & M. Feischmidt. 2006. *Nationalist Politics and Everyday Ethnicity in a Transylvanian Town*. Princeton University Press.
Bukh, A. 2007. Japan's History Textbooks Debate: National Identity in Narratives of Victimhood and Victimization. *Asian Survey* 47(5): 683–704.
Burbank, J., & F. Cooper 2010. *Empires in World History*. Princeton University Press.
2023. *Post-Imperial Possibilities: Eurasia, Eurafrica, Afroasia*. Princeton University Press.
Butcher, T. 2014. *The Trigger: Hunting the Assassin Who Brought the World to War*. Vintage.
Butler, M., & P. Knight (eds.) 2020. *Routledge Handbook of Conspiracy Theories*. Routledge.
Byford, J. 2011. *Conspiracy Theories: A Critical Introduction*. Palgrave.
Cagaptay, S. 2006. *Islam, Secularism and Nationalism in Modern Turkey: Who Is a Turk?* Routledge.
Cairns, R. 2016. Climates of Suspicion: 'Chemtrail' Conspiracy Narratives and the International Politics of Geoengineering. *Geographical Journal*. 182(1): 70–84.
Calhoun, C. 1997. *Nationalism*. Open University Press.
2007. *Nations Matter*. Routledge.
Capezza, D. 2009. Turkey's Military Is a Catalyst for Reform. *Middle East Quarterly* 16(3): 5–10.
Carol, S., L. David, S. Malešević, & G. Uzelac. 2024. Pro-social Attitudes towards Ethno-religious Out-groups during the COVID-19 Pandemic: A Survey Experiment in Five Countries. *International Sociology* 39(1): 113–137.

Calic, M.-J. 2019. *A History of Yugoslavia*. Purdue University Press.
Caputo, P. 1977. *A Rumour of War*. Ballantine.
Casari, M., & C. Tagliapietra. 2018. Group Size in Social-ecological Systems. *Proc Natl Acad Sci.* 115(11): 2728–2733.
Cederman, L. E. 1997. *Emergent Actors in World Politics: How States and Nations Develop and Dissolve*. Princeton University Press.
2024. Nationalism and the Transformation of the Sstate. *Nations and Nationalism* 30(3): 380–396.
Celik, M. 2020. Reforming Criminal Justice in the Ottoman Empire: Police, Courts and Prisons in Rusçuk, 1839–1864. *American Journal of Legal History* 60(2): 109–136.
Centeno, M. 2002. *War and Debt*. Pennsylvania State University Press.
CIA. 2002. *Balkan Battlegrounds: A Military History of the Yugoslav Conflict, 1990–1995*. Central Intelligence Agency.
2023. Serbia. www.cia.gov/the-world-factbook/about/archives/2023/countries/serbia/.
Clark, C. 2012. *The Sleepwakers: How Europe Went to War in 1914*. Penguin.
Cohn, S., Jr. 2007. The Black Death and the Burning of Jews. *Past & Present* 196: 3–36.
Cohn, S. K. 2017. Cholera Revolts: A Class Struggle We May Not Like. *Social History* 42(2): 162–180.
Coker, C. 2007. *The Warrior Ethos: Military Culture and the War on Terror*. Routledge.
Cole, L., & P. Unowsky (eds.) 2009. *The Limits of Loyalty: Imperial Symbolism, Popular Allegiances, and State Patriotism in the Late Habsburg Monarchy*. Berghahn Books.
Collado-Schwarz, A. 2012. *Decolonising Models for the America's Last Colony*. Syracuse University Press.
Collins, R. 1986. *Weberian Sociological Theory*. Cambridge University Press.
1992. *The Sociological Insight*. Oxford University Press.
1999. *Macro-History*. Standford University Press.
2004. *Interaction Ritual Chains*. Princeton University Press.
2008. *Violence: A Micro-Sociological Theory*. Princeton University Press.
2013. Does Nationalist Sentiment Increase Fighting Efficancy? A Skeptical View from the Sociology of Violence. In J. A. Hall & S. Malešević (eds.), *Nationalism and War*. Cambridge University Press.
2014. Time-Bubbles of Nationalism: Dynamics of Solidarity Ritual in Lived Time. In R. Tsang & E. T. Woods (eds.), *The Cultural Politics of Nationalism and Nation-Building*. Routledge.
2022. *Explosive Conflict: Time-Dynamics of Violence*. Routledge.
Connelly, J. 2020. *From Peoples to Nations*. Princeton University Press.
Conversi, D. 1997. *The Basques, the Catalans and Spain: Alternative Routes to Nationalist Mobilisation*. University of Nevada Press.
2020. The Future of Nationalism in a Transnational World. In J. Stone et al. (eds.), *The Wiley Blackwell Companion to Race, Ethnicity, and Nationalism*. Wiley.
Cooper, F. 2005. *Colonialism in Question: Theory, Knowledge History*. University of California Press.

Coulmas, F. 2007. *Population Decline and Ageing in Japan: The Social Consequences*. Routledge.

Craib, I. 1992. *Anthony Giddens*. Routledge.

Croatian Army. 2023. OSRH – Glavna. www.osrh.hr.

Crone, P. 1989. *Pre-industrial Societies: New Perspectives on the Past*. Oxford University Press.

2003. *Pre-Industrial Societies: Anatomy of the Pre-Modern World*. Oneworld.

Cronin, M.., W. Murphy, & P. Rouse (eds.) 2009. *The Gaelic Athletic Association, 1884–2009*. Irish Academic Press.

Crvcek, T. 2020. *Schooling under Control: The Origins of Public Education in Imperial Austria 1769–1869*. Mohr Siebeck.

Ćunković, S. 1971. *Školstvo i prosveta u Srbiji u XIX veku*. Pedagoški muzej.

Dale, P. N. 1988. *The Myth of Japanese Uniqueness*. Routledge.

Danquah, A. 2002. *Yaa Asantewaa: An African Queen Who Led an Army to Fight the British*. Asirifi-Danquah Books.

David, L., S. Carol, S. Malešević, & G. Uzelac. 2024. Heroes, Villains and Naked Nations: Micro-Solidarity and Grounded Nationalism in Times of Crisis. Ethnic and Racial Studies, 1–22. https://doi.org/10.1080/01419870.2024.2380928.

Davies, N. 2011. *Vanished Kingdoms: The History of Half-Forgotten Europe*. Allen Lane.

Day, L. 2001. Long Live the Queen! The Yaa Asantewaa Centenary and the Politics of History. *JENDA* 1(2): 1–12.

Deak, J., & J. Gumz. 2017. How to Break a State: The Habsburg Monarchy's Internal War, 1914–1918. *American Historical Review* 122(4): 1105–1136.

de Condorcet, N. 1988. *Sketch for a Historical Picture of the Progress of the Human Mind*. Greenwood.

De Donno, F., & N. Srivastava. 2006. Colonial and Postcolonial Italy. *Interventions: International Journal of Postcolonial Studies* 8(3): 371–379.

della Porta, D. 2013. *Clandestine Political Violence*. Cambridge University Press.

Del Wollert, E. 2017. An Assessment of the 'Sweating Sickness' Affecting England During the Tudor Dynasty. PhD thesis, Oregon State University.

Despalatovic, E. 1975. *Ljudevit Gaj and the Illyrian Movement*. East European Quarterly.

Dettmer, J. 2020. European Governments Scramble for Ventilators, Urge Shoppers to Stop Panic Buying. www.voanews.com/science-health/coronavirus-outbreak/european-governments-scramble-ventilators-urge-shoppers-stop.

Diamond, J. 2005. *Collapse: How Societies Choose to Fail or Succeed*. Viking Press.

Djokic, D. (ed.) 2003. *Yugoslavism: Histories of a Failed Idea, 1918–1992*. Hurst.

Djokić, D. 2007. *Elusive Compromise: A History of Interwar Yugoslavia*. Hurst.

Djurić, M. 2013. Istorija medija novinske fotografije u Crnoj Gori od 1840-1940. *Medijski Dijalozi* 16(6): 729–741.

Dobrivojević, I. 2006. *Državna represija u doba diktature kralja Aleksandra 1929–1935*. IZSI.

Doherty, B. 2007. *Radicals for Capitalism: A Freewheeling History of the Modern American Libertarian Movement*. Public Affairs.

Dollard, J., & D. Horton. 1977 [1943]. *Fear in Battle*. Institute of Human Relations, Yale University.

Dugandžija, N. 1985. *Jugoslavenstvo*. Mladost.

Duina, F. 2018. *Broke and Patriotic: Why Poor Americans Love Their Country*. Stanford University Press.

Dunbar, R. 1992. Neocortex Size as a Constraint on Group Size in Primates. *Journal of Human Evolution* 22(6): 469–493.

1993. Coevolution of Neocortical Size, Group Size and Language in Humans. *Behavioral and Brain Sciences* 16(4): 681–694.

2021. *Friends*. Little, Brown.

Dusan Silni. 2017. www.youtube.com/watch?v=-yorGk2nZbk&t=334s.

Dvorakova, D. 2002. Knight Culture in the Life of the Hungarian Nobility at the Turn of the 14th and 15th Centuries. *Historický časopis* 50(4): 569–586.

Dwyer, J. C. 1998. *Church History: Twenty Centuries of Catholic Christianity*. Paulist Press.

Edensor, T. 2002. *National Identity, Popular Culture and Everyday Life*. Berg.

Eighmey, J. 2006. Why do Youth Enlist? Identification of Underlying Themes. *Armed Forces & Society* 32(2): 307–328.

Ekinci, E. B. 2015. Literacy in Ottoman Society Was Higher than Believed. Daily Sabah. www.dailysabah.com/feature/2015/09/11/literacy-in-ottoman-society-was-higher-than-believed.

Elias, N. 2000. *The Civilising Process: Sociogenetic and Psychogenetic Investigations*. Oxford: Blackwell.

Engel, P. 2001. *The Realm of St Stephen: A History of Medieval Hungary, 895–1526*. I. B. Tauris.

Esen, B. 2024. Impact of Türkiye's demographic transformation on family structures. Opinion. Dailysabah.com.

Eurobarometer. 2021. Values and identities of EU citizens. November. Eurobarometer survey (europa.eu).

FAI (Football Association of Ireland). 2024. Ireland Women's Team Triumph in 2024 Homeless World Cup. www.fai.ie/latest/ireland-womens-team-triumph-2024-homeless-world-cup/#:~:text=The%20Ireland%20Women's%20Team%20will,goals%20across%2010%20games%20overall.

Falina, M. 2023. *Religion and Politics in Interwar Yugoslavia: Serbian Nationalism and East Orthodox Christianity*. Bloomsbury Academic.

Feinstein, Y. 2024. The Tempest Within: The Origins and Outcomes of Intense National Emotions in Times of National Division. *Theory & Society* 53(1): 729–763.

Ferejohn, J. A., & F. M. Rosenblut. 2010. *War and State Building in Medieval Japan*. Stanford University Press.

Findley, C. V. 1980. *Bureaucratic Reform in the Ottoman Empire: The Sublime Porte, 1789–1922*. Princeton University Press.

1989. *Ottoman Civil Officialdom: A Social History*. Princeton University Press.

Fine, J. V. 2006. *When Ethnicity Did Not Matter in the Balkans*. University of Michigan Press.

Fiske, A., & T. S. Rai. 2014. *Virtuous Violence: Hurting and Killing to Create, Sustain, End, and Honor Social Relationships*. Cambridge University Press.

Fodor, P., & A. Pok. 2020. The Hungarians in Europe: A Thousand Years on the Frontier. *Hungarian Historical Review* 9(1): 113–139.

Fonet. 2020. Danica Grujičić: Kao društvo nemamo imunitet na kovid 19. Danas. www.danas.rs/drustvo/danica-grujicic-kao-drustvo-nemamo-imunitet-na-kovid-19/.

Foster, B. A. 2016. *The Age of Agade: Inventing Empire in Ancient Mesopotamia*. Routledge.

Fox, J. 2017. The Edges of the Nation: A Research Agenda for Uncovering the Taken-for-Granted Foundations of Everyday Nationhood. *Nations and Nationalism* 23(1): 26–47.

2018. Banal Nationalism in Everyday Life. *Nations and Nationalism* 24(4): 862–866.

2025. Clapping the Nation, or, From a Global Pandemic to National Imaginaries via Local Solidarities. *Nations and Nationalism* 31(1): 96–112.

Fox, J., & C. Miller-Idriss. 2008. Everyday Nationhood. *Ethnicities* 8(4): 536–563.

Fox, J., & P. Vermeersch. 2010. Backdoor Nationalism. *European Journal of Sociology* 51(2): 325–357.

Franke, V., & M. von Boemcken. 2011. Guns for Hire: Motivations and Attitudes of Private Security Contractors. *Armed Forces & Society* 37(4): 725–742.

Fry, D. 2007. *Beyond War*. Oxford University Press.

Fukuoka, K. 2017. Between Banality and Effervescence? A Study of Japanese Youth Nationalism. *Nations and Nationalism* 23(2): 346–366.

Fuller, H. 2014. *Building the Ghanaian Nation-State: Kwame Nkrumah's Symbolic Nationalism*. Springer.

Funke, D. 2020. Conspiracy Theory Falsely Connects George Soros to COVID-19. www.politifact.com/factchecks/2020/mar/19/facebook-posts/conspiracy-theory-falsely-connects-george-soros-co/.

Gailey, C. 2016. Locating Primitive Communism in Capitalist Social Formations. *Dialectical Anthropology* 40: 259–266.

Gallup. 2014. Contemporary Media Use in Turkey. www.usagm.gov/wp-content/media/2014/07/Turkey-research-brief.pdf.

2021. https://news.gallup.com/poll/351791/american-pride-ticks-last-year-record-low.aspx.

Ganchev, D. 1888. *Uchebnik po Balgarskata Istoria za Dolnite Klasove na Gimnaziite i za Triklasnite Obshtinski Uchilishta*. Hristo G. Danov.

Garrett, S. A. 1993. *Ethics and Airpower in World War Two: The British Bombing of German Cities*. Macmillan.

Gary, R. 2009. Land Reform and the Hungarian Peasantry, 1700–1848. PhD thesis, University College, London.

Gat, A. 2013. *Nations: The Long History and Deep Roots of Political Ethnicity and Nationalism*. Cambridge University Press.

Gazete tiraj rakamları. 2016. gazeteciler.com.

Geertz, C. 1973. *The Interpretation of Cultures*. Basic Books.

Gellner, E. 1983. *Nations and Nationalism*. Blackwell.

1988. *Plough, Sword, and Book: The Structure of Human History*. University of Chicago Press.

1996. 'Do Nations Have Navels?' *Nations and Nationalism* 2(3): 366–370.

Gerolymatos, A. 2002. *The Balkan Wars*. Spellmount.

Giddens, A. 1984. *The Constitution of Society: Outline of the Theory of Structuration*. Polity.

1986. *Nation-State and Violence*. Polity.

2007. *Europe in the Global Age*. Polity Press.

Gilmore, H. 2019. 'In the Open Country': Nature and the Environment during the 'Monster' Meeting Campaign of 1843. In M. Kelly (ed.), *Nature and the Environment in Nineteenth Century Ireland*. Liverpool University Press.

Glosserman, B., & S. Snyder 2008. Confidence and Confusion: National Identity and Security Alliances in Northeast Asia. *Issues and Insights* 8(16): 1–42.

Go, J. 2011. *Patterns of Empire*. Cambridge University Press.

Goffman, E. 1967. *Interaction Ritual: Essays in Face-to-Face Behavior*. Routledge.

Goncalves, B, et al. 2011. Modeling Users' Activity on Twitter Networks: Validation of Dunbar's Number. *PLoS ONE* 6(8): e22656.

Goode, P., D. R. Stroup, & E. Gaufman. 2020. Everyday Nationalism in Unsettled Times: In Search of Normality during Pandemic. Nationalities Papers, 1–25. doi:10.1017/nps.2020.40.

Goodman, J., & F. Carmichael. 2020. Coronavirus: 5G and Microchip Conspiracies around the World. BBC News. www.bbc.com/news/53191523.

Graeber, D., & D. Wengrow. 2021. *The Dawn of Everything: A New History of Humanity*. Farrar, Straus and Giroux.

Graves, R. 1980 [1957]. *Goodbye to All That*. Doubleday.

Greble, E. 2021. *Muslims and the Making of Modern Europe*. Oxford University Press.

Grehan, J. 2014. *Twilight of the Saints: Everyday Religion in Ottoman Syria and Palestine*. Oxford University Press.

Grgić, S. 2018. Pantheon on a Tablecloth: Yugoslav Dictatorship and the Confrontation of National Symbols in Croatia (1929–1935). *Nationalities Papers* 46(3): 458–470.

Griffith, J. 2008. Institutional Motives for Serving in the U.S. Army National Guard: Implications for Recruitment, Retention, and Readiness. *Armed Forces & Society* 34(2): 230–258.

Griffith, J., & Perry, S. 1993. Wanting to Soldier: Enlistment Motivations of Army Reserve Recruits before and after Operation Desert Storm. *Military Psychology* 5(2): 127–139.

Grosby, S. 2005. *Nationalism: A Very Short Introduction*. Oxford University Press.

Gross, M. 1981. On the Integration of the Croatian Nation: A Case Study in Nation Building. *East European Quarterly* 15(2): 209–225.

Grunert, H. 2020. The Inner Enemy in Wartime: The Habsburg State and the Serb Citizens of Bosnia-Herzegovina, 1913–18. In M. Cornwall (ed.), *Sarajevo 1914: Sparking the First World War*. Bloomsbury Academic.

Gutierrez, J. A. 2021. The Counter-insurgent Paradox: How the FARC-EP Successfully Subverted Counter-insurgent Institutions in Colombia. *Small Wars and Insurgencies* 32(1): 103–126.

Gužvica, S. 2021. Jugoslavija ili Balkanska federacija? Dileme jugoslovenskih komunista u doba Oktobarske revolucije. *Tragovi* 4(1): 102–133.

Hadžijahić, M. 1950. Emigracije muslimana Bosne i Hercegovine u Tursku u doba austro-ugarske vladavine 1878.–1918. God. *Historijski zbornik* 3: 175–188.

Haerter, J. O., et al. 2012. Communication Dynamics in Finite Capacity Social Networks. *Physical Review Letters* (109): 168701.

Hajdarpašić, E. 2015. *Whose Bosnia? National Movements, Imperial Reforms, and the Political Re-ordering of the Late Ottoman Balkans, 1840–1875.* Cornell University Press.

Halden, P. 2020. *Family Power: Kinship, War, and Political Orders in Eurasia, 500–2018.* Cambridge University Press.

Hall, J., & S. Malešević. 2013. Introduction: Wars and Nationalisms. In J. Hall & S. Malešević (eds.), *Nationalism and War*. Cambridge University Press.

Hall, J. A. 1986. *Powers and Liberties: The Causes and Consequences of the Rise of the West.* Blackwell.

1993. Nationalisms: Classified and Explained. *Daedalus* 122: 1–28.

2002. A Disagreement about Difference. In S. Malešević & M. Haugaard (eds.), *Making Sense of Collectivity*. Pluto Press.

2013. *The Importance of Being Civil.* Princeton University Press.

2017. Taking Megalomanias Seriously: A Rough Note. *Thesis Eleven* 139: 30–45.

2024. *Nations, States and Empires.* Polity.

Halperin, S. 2017. The Imperial City-State and the National State Form: Reflections on the History of the Contemporary Order. *Thesis Eleven* 139(1): 97–112.

Halpin, J., et al. 2018. Is Turkey Experiencing a New Nationalism? www.americanprogress.org/article/turkey-experiencing-new-nationalism/

Hamilton, M. J., et al. 2007. The Complex Structure of Hunter–Gatherer Social Networks. *Proceedings of the Royal Society, London* 274B: 2195–2202.

Handler, R. 2022. Prehistory without Hierarchy. Times Literary Supplement. www.the-tls.com/history/the-dawn-of-everything-david-graeber-david-wengrow-book-review-richard-handler.

Hastings. A. 1997. *The Construction of Nationhood.* Cambridge University Press.

Healy, R. 2003. *The Jesuit Spectre in Imperial Germany.* Brill Academic.

Hearn, J. 2006. *Rethinking Nationalism: A Critical Introduction.* Palgrave.

Hechter, M. 1977. *Internal Colonialism.* University of California Press.

2000. *Containing Nationalism.* Oxford University Press.

Hedström, P., & L. Udehn. 2009. Analytical Sociology and Theories of the Middle Range. In P. Hedström & P. Bearman (eds.), *The Oxford Handbook of Analytical Sociology.* Oxford University Press.

Hegel, G. W. F. 2018 [1807]. *The Phenomenology of Spirit.* Cambridge University Press.

Henze, C. 2010. *Disease, Health Care and Government in Late Imperial Russia: Life and Death on the Volga, 1823–1914.* Routledge.

Hill, K., & A. M. Hurtado. 2017. *Ache Life History: The Ecology and Demography of a Foraging People*. Routledge.

Hitchins, K. 2014. *A Concise History of Romania*. Cambridge University Press.

Hobsbawm, E. 1990. *Nations and Nationalism since 1780*. Cambridge University Press.

1992. The Future Belongs to Bigger Entities. https://peervries.com/resources/Eric-Hobsbawm.pdf.

2021. *On Nationalism*. Little, Brown.

Hobson, J. M. 2004. *The Eastern Origins of Western Civilisation*. Cambridge University Press.

Hofer, T., & E. Fell 2008. *Proper Peasants: Social Relations in a Hungarian Village*. Routledge.

Holden, R. 2017. Beyond Mere War: Authority and Legitimacy in the Formation of the Latin American States. In L.Kaspersen & J. Strandbjerg (eds.), *Does War Make States?* Cambridge University Press.

Holmes, R. 1986. *Acts of War: The Behaviour of Men in Battle*. Free Press.

Horrie, P., & C. Chippindale 1999. *Stick It Up Your Punter! The Uncut Story of The Sun Newspaper*. Pocket Books.

Horváth, A., Z. Vidra, & J. Fox. 2012. Hungary. CIDOB. www.cidob.org/en/articulos/monografias/discursos_sobre_tolerancia/hungary.

Howard, D. A. 2017. *A History of the Ottoman Empire*. Cambridge University Press.

Hranjski, H. 1992. Vaša je žrtva sveta. *Slobodna Dalmacija*, 26 April, p. 10.

Hroch, M. 2015. *European Nations: Explaining Their Formation*. Verso.

Hungarian Constitution 2011. www.constituteproject.org/constitution/Hungary_2011.

Hutchinson, J. 2005. *Nations as Zones of Conflict*. Sage.

2009. Warfare and the Sacralisation of Nations: The Meanings, Rituals and Politics of National Remembrance. *Millennium*. 38(2): 401–417.

2017. *Nationalism and War*. Oxford University Press.

Ichijo, A., & R. Ranta 2016. *Food, National Identity and Nationalism: From Everyday to Global Politics*. Springer.

IISS. 2023. The Military Balance. www.iiss.org/publications/the-military-balance/the-military-balance-2023.

Imber, C. 2002. *The Ottoman Empire, 1300–1650: The Structure of Power*. Palgrave.

Informer 2017. https://informer.rs/vesti/kolumne/338255/bam-bam-bam-nova-video-kolumna-miroljuba-petrovica-stranci-koji-zele-novo-Du%C5%A1anovo-carstvo-morace-otvore-poglavlje-nauce-sviraju-gusle.

International Trade Administration. 2024. Turkey Country Commercial Guide. www.trade.gov/country-commercial-guides/turkey-information-and-communication-technology.

Ipsos MORI. 1982. The Falklands War: Panel Survey. Ipsos MORI. www.ipsosmori.com/researchpublications/researcharchive/poll.aspx?oItemId=49.

IREX. 2016. Croatia. Media Sustainability Index. www.irex.org/sites/default/files/pdf/media-sustainability-index-europe-eurasia-2016-croatia.pdf.pdf.

Israel Defense Forces. 2023. Israel Defense Forces | IDF. uwww.idf.il.

Ivešić, T. 2021. The Yugoslav National Idea under Socialism: What Happens When a Soft Nation-Building Project Is Abandoned? *Nationalities Papers* 49(1): 142–61.

Iwasaki, I. 2008. Development of Mass Media in Japan & Its Background. Japan Spotlight. January/February, 5–7.

Japanese Constitution. 2024. https://japan.kantei.go.jp/constitution_and_government_of_japan/constitution_e.html.

Jelavich, B. 1983. *History of the Balkans*. Cambridge University Press.

Jelavich, C. 1990. *South Slav Nationalisms: Textbooks and Yugoslav Union before 1914*. Ohio State University Press.

Jenkins, R. 2008. *Rethinking Ethnicity*. Sage.

Jochecova, K. 2023. Wagner Boss Yevgeny Prigozhin Resurfaces with New Message. Politico. www.politico.eu/article/wagner-boss-prigozhin-message-russia-war-reappear-belarus/.

Jones, E. 1987. *The European Miracle: Environments, Economies and Geopolitics in the History of Europe and Asia*. Cambridge University Press.

Jović, D. 2003. *Jugoslavija – država koja je odumrla: Uspon, kriza i pad Kardeljeve Jugoslavije (1974.–1990.)*. Prometej.

Judson, P. 2006. *Guardians of the Nation: Activists on the Language Frontiers of Imperial Austria*. Harvard University Press.

2016. *Habsburg Empire: A New History*. Harvard University Press.

Junger, S. 2011. *War*. Twelve.

Juzbašić, D. 2002. *Politika i privreda u Bosni i Hercegovini pod Austrougarskom upravom*. ANU BiH.

Kaihko, I. 2018. Broadening the Perspective on Military Cohesion. *Armed Forces & Society* 44(4): 571–586.

Kamusella, T. 2009. *The Politics of Language and Nationalism in Modern Central Europe*. Palgrave.

2016. Upper Silesia in Modern Central Europe: On the Significance of the Non-National/a-National in the Age of Nations. In J. Bjork et al. (eds.), *Creating Nationality in Central Europe, 1880–1950: Modernity, Violence and Belonging in Upper Silesia*. Routledge.

Kaplan, D. 2018. *The Nation and the Promise of Friendship: Building Solidarity through Sociability*. Plagrave.

Karčić, H. 2022. *Torture, Humiliate, Kill: Inside the Bosnian Serb Camp System*. University of Michigan Press.

Karsh, E., & I. Karsh. 1999. *Empires of the Sand: The Struggle for Mastery in the Middle East, 1789–1923*. Harvard University Press.

Kaytchev, N. 2015. Children into Adults, Peasants into Patriots: The Army and Nation-Building in Serbia and Bulgaria (1878–1912). In B. Fortna (ed.), *Childhood in the Late Ottoman Empire and After*. Brill, 115–140.

Keating, M. 2001. *Plurinational Democracy: Stateless Nations in a Post-Sovereignty Era*. Oxford University Press.

Kedourie, E. 1960. *Nationalism*. Hutchinson.

Keegan, J. 1993. *A History of Warfare*. Alfred Knopf.

Kia, M. 2011. *Daily Life in the Ottoman Empire*. Greenwood.

King, A. 2011. *The Combat Soldier: Infantry Tactics and Cohesion in the Twentieth and Twenty-first Centuries*. Oxford University Press.

King, B. 2019. *The Life of Mazzini*. Good Press.

King, J. 2002. *Budweisers into Czechs and Germans: A Local History of Bohemian Politics, 1848–1948*. Princeton University Press.

Kirby, F. 2000 [1960]. *The Village Institute Movement of Turkey*. Columbia University Report.

Kitromilides, P. 2010. The Orthodox Church in Modern State Formation in South-East Europe. In W. van Meurs & A. Mungiu-Pippidi (eds.), *Ottomans into Europeans*. Hurst.

Kleykamp, M. A. 2006. College, Jobs, or the Military? Enlistment during a Time of War. *Social Science Quarterly* 87(2): 272–290.

Knoema. 2023. Literacy. https://knoema.com/atlas/Ghana/topics/Education/Literacy/Adult-literacy-rate.

Knott, E. 2015. Everyday Nationalism: A Review of the Literature. *Studies in National Movements* 3: 1–16.

2023. Sociological and Grounded, but Everyday? *Nationalities Papers* 51(1): 229–232.

Koen-Sarano, M. 2015. *Folktales of Joha, Jewish Trickster*. Jewish Publication Society.

Kohn, H. 1958. *The Idea of Nationalism*. Macmillan.

Kolata, G. 2011. *Flu: The Story of the Great Influenza Pandemic of 1918 and the Search for the Virus That Caused It*. Touchstone.

Kopp, M. 2021. Hungarians Are Proud of Being Hungarian. www.koppmariaintezet.hu/docs/press-en/2021/20210825_Hungarians_are_proud_of_being_Hungarian.pdf.

Koska, V., & A. Matan. 2017. Croatian Citizenship Regime and Traumatised Categories of Croatian Citizens: Serb Minority and Croatian Defenders of the Homeland War. *Croatian Political Science Review* 54(1–2): 119–149.

Kotsonis, Y. 2025. *The Greek Revolution and the Violent Birth of Nationalism*. Princeton University Press.

Krebs, R. R., & R. Ralston. 2022. Patriotism or Paychecks: Who Believes What about Why Soldiers Serve. *Armed Forces & Society* 48(1): 25–48.

Kriger, N. 1993. *Guerrilla Veterans in Post-war Zimbabwe: Symbolic and Violent Politics, 1980–1987*. Cambridge University Press.

Krstić, Z. 2011. Odnos nacionalnog i evropskog identiteta Srba. *Bezbednost Zapadnog Balkana* 6(20): 31–51.

Kulyk, V. 2023. National Identity in Time of War: Ukraine after the Russian Aggressions of 2014 and 2022. *Problems of Post-Communism* 71(4): 296–308.

Kumar, K. 2017. *Visions of Empire: How Five Imperial Regimes Shaped the World*. Princeton University Press.

2021. *Empires: A Historical and Political Sociology*. Polity.

Kurspahić, K. 2020. Korona virus i duhovi devedesetih. www.slobodnaevropa.org/a/kurspahic-korona-virus-i-duhovi-devedesetih/30512627.html.

Laitin, D. 2007. *Nations, States, and Violence*. Oxford University Press.

Lalkov, M. 1997. Tsar Simeon the Great (893–927). In *Rulers of Bulgaria*. Kibea.

Lampe, J. 2000. *Yugoslavia as History*. Cambridge University Press.

Lane, E. 1973. *An Account of the Manners and Customs of the Modern Egyptians.* Dover Publications.

Laver, M. S. 2011. *The Sakoku Edicts and the Politics of Tokugawa Hegemony.* Cambria Press.

Lawrence, T. E. 1935. *Seven Pillars of Wisdom.* Cape.

Leerssen, J. 2006. *National Thought in Europe.* Amsterdam University Press.

Lehne, J. 2010. Max Weber and Nationalism: Chaos or Consistency? *Max Weber Studies* 10(2): 209–234.

Lewis, R. 1971. *Everyday Life in Ottoman Turkey.* B. T. Batsford.

Little, R. 1964. Buddy Relations and Combat Performance. In M. Janowitz (ed.), *The New Military.* Norton.

Lorenz, E. N. 1972. *Predictability: Does the Flap of a Butterfly's Wings in Brazil Set off a Tornado in Texas?* American Association for the Advancement of Science.

Lotchin, R.W. 2015. A Research Report: The 1940s Gallup Polls, Imperial Japanese, Japanese Americans, and the Reach of American Racism. *Southern California Quarterly* 97(4): 399–417.

Loyal, S., & S. Malešević. 2020. *Contemporary Sociological Theory.* Sage.

Lu, D. J. 1997. *Japan: A Documentary History.* M. E. Sharpe.

Lugones, M. 2003. *Pilgrimages/Peregrinajes.* Rowman & Littlefield.

Lynn, J. A. 1997. *The Bayonets of the Republic: Motivation and Tactics in the Army of Revolutionary France.* Routledge.

Lyon, J. 2014. Habsburg Sarajevo 1914: A Social Picture. *Contributions/Prilozi Instituta za istoriju Sarajevo* 43: 23–40.

Macleod, J. 2008. *Defeat and Memory.* Palgrave.

Macmillan, M. 2020. *War: How Conflict Shaped Us.* Random House.

Macrotrends. 2025. Turkey Literacy Rate. www.macrotrends.net/global-metrics/countries/tur/turkey/literacy-rate.

Malešević, S. 2002. *Ideology, Legitimacy, and the New State.* Routledge.

2004. *The Sociology of Ethnicity.* Sage.

2006. *Identity as Ideology: Understanding Ethnicity and Nationalism.* Palgrave.

2010. *The Sociology of War and Violence.* Cambridge University Press.

2012. Did Wars Make Nation-States in the Balkans? Nationalisms, Wars and States in the 19th and Early 20th Century Southeast Europe. *Journal of Historical Sociology* 25(3): 299–330.

2013. *Nation-States and Nationalisms: Organisation, Ideology and Solidarity.* Polity Press.

2017. *The Rise of Organised Brutality: A Historical Sociology of Violence.* Cambridge University Press.

2019. *Grounded Nationalisms: A Sociological Analysis.* Cambridge University Press.

2020a. Grounded Nationalism and Cultural Diversity. In F. Höhne & T. Meireis (eds.), *Neo-Nationalism and Religion.* Nomos.

2020b. Nationalist Conspiracies. Yugosplaining the World Project. https://thedisorderofthings.com/2020/07/05/nationalist-conspiracies/.

2022. *Why Humans Fight: The Social Dynamics of Close-Range Violence.* Cambridge University Press.

2023. Grounded Nationalisms in Time and Space. *Nationalities Papers* 51(1): 237–241.

2024. The Many Faces of Nationalism. *Nationalities Papers* 52(3): 487–496.

Malešević, S., & N. O'Dochartaigh. 2018. Why Combatants Fight: The Irish Republican Army and the Bosnian Serb Army Compared. *Theory and Society* 47(3): 293–326.

Malešević, S., & G. Uzelac. 1997. Ethnic Distance, Power, and War: The Case of Croatian Students. *Nations and Nationalism* 3(2): 291–298.

Malešević, S., G. Uzelac, S. Carol, & L. David. 2024. Plotting against Our Nation: COVID-19, Nationalisms, and Conspiracy Theories in Five European Countries. *National Identities* 26(2): 141–171.

Mango, A. 1999. Atatürk and the Kurds. *Middle Eastern Studies* 35(4).

Mann, M. 1986. *The Sources of Social Power, vol. I: A History of Power from the Beginning to A.D. 1760*. Cambridge University Press.

1993. *The Sources of Social Power, vol. II: The Rise of Classes and Nation-States, 1760–1914*. Cambridge University Press.

2005. *Fascists*. Cambridge University Press

2012. *The Sources of Social Power, vol. III: Global Empires and Revolution, 1890–1945*, Cambridge University Press.

2023. *On Wars*. Yale University Press.

Marcassa, S., J. Pouyet, & T. Trégouët. 2020. Marriage Strategy among the European Nobility. *Explorations in Economic History* 75.

Masashi, T. 2000. Maturing of a Literate Society: Literacy and Education in Edo Period. Journal of Japanese Trade and Industry, March–April: 44–48.

Mass, J. P. 1999. *Yoritomo and the Founding of the First Bakufu: The Origins of Dual Government in Japan*. Stanford University Press.

Masters, B. 2001. *Christians and Jews in the Ottoman Arab World: The Roots of Sectarianism*. Cambridge University Press.

Maxwell, A. 2019. *Everyday Nationalism in Hungary: 1789–1867*. De Gruyter Oldenbourg.

McLeod, H. 2015. Christianity and Nationalism in Nineteenth-Century Europe. *International Journal for the Study of the Christian Church* 15(1): 7–22.

McNeill, W. H. 1976. *Plagues and Peoples*. W. W. Norton.

Medrano, J. D. 2009. The Public Sphere and the European Union's Political Identity. In J. T. Checkel & P. Katzenstein (eds.), *The Public Sphere and the European Union's Political Identity*. Cambridge University Press.

Mehrkens, H 2019. Teacher, Father, King: Royal Representations of Louis-Philippe I. *Francia. Forschungen zur westeuropäischen Geschichte* 46(1): 207–230.

Merton, R. 1968. *Social Theory and Social Structure*. Simon & Schuster.

Mestrovic, S. 1996. *Genocide after Emotion*. Routledge.

Mevius, M. 2005. *Agents of Moscow: The Hungarian Communist Party and the Origins of Socialist Patriotism 1941–1953*. Clarendon Press.

Meyer, J., et al. 1997. World Society and the Nation-State. *American Journal of Sociology* 103(1): 144–181.

Michaels, A. 2004. *Hinduism: Past and Present*. Princeton University Press.

Mijatović, Č. 1880. *Despot Djuradj Brankovic, gospodar Srbima, Podunavlju i Zetskom Primorju*. Državna štamparija.

Milekić, S. 2022. A Protest, Coup d'État, or Internal Party Power Struggle: What Motivated Croatian War Veterans to Hit the Streets? *Croatian Political Science Review* 59(4): 215–250.

Milić, A., et al. 1981. *Domaćinstvo, porodica i brak u Jugoslaviji*. IZSI.

Milios, J. 2023. *Nationalism as a Claim to a State: The Greek Revolution of 1821 and the Formation of Modern Greece*. Brill.

Mills, C. W. 1959. *The Sociological Imagination*. Oxford University Press.

Milošević, S. 2017. Od stagnacije do revolucije: Društvo Jugoslavije 1918–1991. In L. Perović et al. (eds.), *Jugoslavija u istorijskoj perspektivi*. Helsinki Federation for Human Rights Serbia, 327–367.

MISC. 2020. Country Data: Literacy Rate. www.country-data.com/cgi-bin/query/r-5253.html#:~:text=The%201970%20figure%20was%20a,literacy%20rate%20of%2025%20percent.

Mock, S. 2011. *Symbols of Defeat in the Construction of National Identity*. Cambridge University Press.

Molnár, G. 2023. Nationalism and Sport Intersection in Hungary. *National Identities* 25(4): 305–322.

Molnar, M. 2001. *A Concise History of Hungary*. Cambridge University Press.

Montenegrina. 2017. www.montenegrina.net/pages/pages1/istorija/duklja/dukljanska_drzava_crnogorski_iskon_i_korijeni_b_sekularac.htm.

Montgomery, D. 2018. *Everyday Life in the Balkans*. Indiana University Press.

Mooney, K. 1991 Military Intervention, Kemalism, and Politics in Turkey. https://apps.dtic.mil/sti/tr/pdf/ADA236024.pdf.

Mooney, T. K. 1984. Military Intervention, Kemalism, and Politics in Turkey. Thesis, State University of New York at Binghamton.

Moore, D. 2009. *The Soldier: A History of Courage, Sacrifice and Brotherhood*. Icon Books.

Morley, J. W (ed.) 1999. *Driven by Growth: Political Change in the Asia-Pacific Region*. Routledge.

Moskos, C. 1970. *The American Enlisted Man: The Rank and File in Today's Military*. Russell Sage Foundation.

Mosse, G. 1991. *The Nationalization of the Masses: Political Symbolism and Mass Movements in Germany from the Napoleonic Wars through the Third Reich*. University of Wisconsin Press.

Moutsoglou, V. 2020. *The Greek Revolution of 1821: The Transition from Slavery to Freedom*. Independent Publishers.

Munkler, H. 2007. *Empire*. Polity.

Munro, D. C. 1896. Letters of the Crusaders. In *Translations and Reprints from the Original Sources of European History*, vol. 1:4. University of Pennsylvania Press.

Murata, H. 2014. How the Japanese Are Emotionally Attached to Their Country. www.nhk.or.jp/bunken/english/reports/summary/201405/02.html.

Mylonas, H., & M. Tudor. 2023. *Varieties of Nationalism*. Cambridge University Press.

Nacelnik. 2022. Boračka rganizaciji opštine Sokolac obilježila krsnu slavu – Mitrovdan. https://nacelnik.net/boracka-organizacija-opstine-sokolac-obiljezila-krsnu-slavu-mitrovdan/.

Nairn, T. 1981. *The Break-Up of Britain*. Verso.
1998. *Faces of Nationalism: The Modern Janus*. Verso.
2011. *The Enchanted Glass: Britain and Its Monarchy*. Verso.
Narodna skupstina RS. 2013. www.narodnaskupstinars.net/?q=la/akti/ostali-akti/deklaracija-o-uzrocima-karakteru-i-posljedicama-tragi%C4%8Dnog-oru%C5%BEanog-sukoba-u-bosni-i-hercegovini-od-1992-do-1995-godine.
www.narodnaskupstinars.net/?q=la/vijesti/narodna-skup%C5%A1tina-usvojila-20-zaklju%C4%8Daka-odba%C4%8Dena-rezolucija-parlamentarne-skup%C5%A1tine-bih-zbog-prekrajanja-istorijskih-%C4%8Dinjenica.
Narodne Novine. 2000. Deklaracija o Domovinskom ratu. https://narodne-novine.nn.hr/clanci/sluzbeni/2000_10_102_1987.html.
Neocleous, S. 2010. Byzantine-Muslim Conspiracies against the Crusades: History and Myth. *Journal of Medieval History* 36(3): 253–274.
Nielsen, C. A. 2014. *Making Yugoslavs: Identity in King Aleksandar's Yugoslavia*. University of Toronto Press.
2022. *Mass Atrocities and the Police: A New History of Ethnic Cleansing in Bosnia and Herzegovina*. Bloomsbury.
Nietzsche, F. 2023 [1887]. *On the Genealogy of Morality*. Broadview Press.
Nilus, S. 2009. *The Jewish Peril: Protocols of the Learned Elders of Zion*. Martino.
Nimni, E. 1991. *Marxism and Nationalism*. Pluto.
Nolte, C. E. 2002. *The Sokol in the Czech Lands to 1914: Training for the Nation*. Palgrave Macmillan.
Novaković, S. 1870. *Zakonik Stefana Dušana Cara Srpskog. 1349 i 1354*. Državna štamparija.
Ó Dochartaigh, N. 2015. Interviews with Former IRA Combatants (unpublished).
O'Donnell, D. 2024. Irish Women's Team Return Victorious from Homeless World Cup. www.rte.ie/news/ireland/2024/0930/1472816-homeless-football/.
Okey, R. 2007. *Taming Balkan Nationalism: The Habsburg 'Civilising Mission' in Bosnia, 1878–1914*. Oxford University Press.
Ooms, H. 2009. *Imperial Politics and Symbolics in Ancient Japan: The Tenmu Dynasty, 650–800*. University of Hawai'i Press.
O'Rourke, E. 2024. Bambie Thug Says 'No One Screams Louder than the Irish'. www.rte.ie/entertainment/2024/0512/1448675-eurovision-was-bambie-thugs-night-in-irish-eyes/.
Ørstrøm Møllerm, J. 2008. *European Integration*. ISAS.
Özgen, K. 2008. The Ottomans History. www.theottomans.org/english/family/index.asp.
Özkirimli, U. 2017. *Theories of Nationalism: A Critical Introduction*. Palgrave.
Palairet, M. 1993. *The Habsburg Industrial Achievement in Bosnia-Hercegovina, 1878–1914: An Economic Spurt That Succeeded?* Austrian History Yearbook, XXIV: 133–152.
Pamuk, S. 2023. The State and Industrialization in Turkey since the Nineteenth Century. www.hoover.org/sites/default/files/2023-10/LRP%20WP%202312.pdf.
Pantelić, B. 2011. Memories of a Time Forgotten: The Myth of the Perennial Nation. *Nations and Nationalism* 17(2): 443–464.

Pap, M. 2023. 'The True Love of the People and the Motherland': The Concept of Socialist Patriotism, Socialist Nation and Anti-nationalism in Hungary in the 1960s and 1970s. *Nations and Nationalism* 29(3): 992–1006.

Pavlowitch, S. 2002. *Serbia: The History behind the Name*. Hurst.

Payne, R. 1995. *The Clash with Distant Cultures*. State University of New York Press.

Pejić, O. 2018. The Treatment of History in Austrian-Hungarian State Primary School Textbooks for Bosnia and Herzegovina. *Sprawy Narodowościowe. Seria nowa* 50: 1–11.

Perez, L. G. 2009. *The History of Japan*. Greenwood Press.

Peter, L. 1992. The Aristocracy, the Gentry and Their Parliamentary Tradition in Nineteenth-Century Hungary. *Slavonic and East European Review* 70(1): 77–110.

Petranović, B., & M. Zečević. 1988. *Jugoslavija: 1918–1988: Tematska zbirka dokumenata*. Rad.

Petrović, R. 1987. *Migracije u Jugoslaviji i etnički aspekt*. IIC CCO Srbije.

Petrović, T. 2024. *Utopia of the Uniform: Affective Afterlives of the Yugoslav People's Army*. Duke University Press.

Pew Research Center. 2020. Coronavirus Disease (Covid 19). www.pewresearch .org/topics/coronavirus-disease-2019-covid-19/.

Plestina, D. 2019. *Regional Development in Communist Yugoslavia*. Routledge.

Pleterski, J. 1986. *Narodi, Jugoslavija, revolucija*. Državna založba Slovenije.

Pohl, W. 1998. Conceptions of Ethnicity in Early Medieval Studies. In Lester K. Little & Barbara Rosenwein (eds.), *Debating the Middle Ages: Issues and Readings*. Blackwell.

Popov, C. 2004. *Evropa i srpska revolucija: 1804–1815*. Platoneum.

Popović, P. 1899. *Nacionalni Repertoar K.S. Narodnog pozorista u Beogradu*. Narodno Pozoriste.

Posen, B. R. 1993. Nationalism, the Mass Army, and Military Power. *International Security* 18(2): 80–124.

Posocco, L. 2022. *Museums and Nationalism in Croatia, Hungary, and Turkey*. Routledge.

Posocco, L., & I. Watson. 2024. Conspiracy Theories and Nationalism: Exploring the Intersections and Implications. *Politica & Società* 1(1): 89–122.

Prince, E. 2011. *Civilian Warriors: The Inside Story of Blackwater and the Unsung Heroes of the War on Terror*. Random House.

Pryke, S. 1998. The Popularity of Nationalism in the Early British Boy Scout Movement. *Social History* 23(3): 309–324.

Puljiz, V. 1977. *Eksodus poljoprivrednika*. IDIS.

Radio Slatina. 2022. Udruga HVIDR-a Slatina svečano obilježila 30. Obljetnicu osnutka. www.radioslatina.hr/fotogalerija-udruga-hvidr-a-slatina-svecano-obiljezila-30-obljetnicu-osnutka/.

Rajković, Z. 1996. Savez HVIDR-a. *HVIDRA: Glasilo Saveza HVIDR-a*, June.

Rath, R. 1964. The Carbonari: Their Origins, Itition Rites, and Aims. *American Historical Review* 69(2): 253–273.

Rébay, M., & T. Kozma. 2015. Hungary. In W. Hörner, H. Döbert, L. Reuter, & B. von Kopp (eds.), *The Education Systems of Europe*. Springer.

Reis, J. 2005. Economic Growth, Human Capital Formation and Consumption in Western Europe before 1800. In R. C. Allen, T. Bengtsson, & M. Dribe (eds.), *Living Standards in the Past: New Perspectives on Well-Being in Asia and Europe*. Oxford University Press, 195–225.

Reuters. 2023. Turkey to Allocate 150% More to Defence Budget in 2024. www.reuters.com/world/middle-east/turkey-allocate-150-more-defense-budget-2024-minister-2023-10-17/.

Révész, L. 2014. *The Era of the Hungarian Conquest*. Hungarian National Museum.

Rex, J. 1980. The Theory of Race Relations: A Weberian Approach. In *Sociological Theories*. UNESCO.

Rietbergen, P. 2018. Not of This World…? Religious Power and Imperial Rule in Eurasia, ca. Thirteenth – ca. Eighteenth Century. In M. van Berkel & J. Duindam (eds.), *Prince, Pen, and Sword: Eurasian Perspectives*. Brill.

Ritzer, G. 1993. *McDonaldisation of Society*. Sage.

Roberts, J. M. 1974. *The Mythology of the Secret Societies*. Paladin.

Rose, C. 2006. The Battle for Hearts and Minds: Patriotic Education in Japan in the 1990s and Beyond. In N. Shimazu (ed.), *Nationalisms in Japan*. Routledge.

Rosen, W. 2007. *Justinian's Flea: Plague, Empire and the Birth of Europe*. Jonathan Cape.

Rozsa, M. 2019. QAnon Is the Conspiracy Theory That Won't Die. Salon. www.salon.com/2019/08/18/qanon-is-the-conspiracy-theory-that-wont-die-heres-what-they-believe-and-why-theyre-wrong/.

Roucek, J. 1954. Yugoslavia's Higher Institutions of Learning. *Journal of Higher Education* 25(9): 478–503.

Roudometof, V. 2001. *Nationalism, Globalization and Orthodoxy*. Greenwood Press.

RTÜK. 2024. www.rtuk.org.tr/sayfalar/English.aspx.

Rusinow, D. 1977. *Yugoslav Experiment 1948–1974*. Hurst.

2003. The Yugoslav Idea before Yugoslavia. In D. Djokic (ed.), *Yugoslavism: Histories of a Failed Idea 1918–1992*. Hurst.

Rustow, A., & R. Ward. 2015. *Political Modernization in Japan and Turkey*. Princeton University Press.

Ruthner, C. 2018. Habsburg's Only Colony? Bosnia-Herzegovina and Austriahungary, 1878–1918. *SEEU Review* 13(1): 2–14.

Sageman, M. 2004. *Understanding Terror Networks*. University of Pennsylvania Press.

Sandbrook, D. 2019. Falklands Feelgood Factor. www.pressreader.com/uk/bbc-history-magazine/20191003/281556587550625?srsltid=AfmBOoqAI7pj5gORDf4um1pfrwPAO9ln21lv1eGtvjpjbfgSAHT7Pjod.

Schindler, J. R. 2004. Defeating Balkan Insurgency: The Austro-Hungarian Army in Bosnia-Hercegovina, 1878–82. *Journal of Strategic Studies* 27(3): 528–552.

Schlipphacke, H. 2014. The Temporalities of Habsburg Nostalgia. *Journal of Austrian Studies*. 47(2): 1–16.

Scott, J. C. 1985. *Weapons of the Weak: Everyday Forms of Peasant Resistance*. Yale University Press.

2017. *Against the Grain: A Deep History of the Earliest States*. Yale University Press.
Sezer, O. 2022. *Forming the Modern Turkish Village: Nation Building and Modernization in Rural Turkey during the Early Republic*. Transcript Publishing.
SGSJ. 1979. Statisticki godisnjak. Jugoslavija Savezni Zavod za Statistiku.
Shimazu, N. 2006. Reading the diaries of Japanese conscripts: Forging national consciousness during the Russo-Japanese war. In N. Shimazu (ed.), *Nationalism in Japan*. Routledge.
Shire, M. I., & A. Hersi. 2022. Brothers in Arms: The Phenomenon of Complex Suicide Attacks. *Terrorism and Political Violence* 34(2): 263–284.
Shutler, A. 2023. Why It's Never Been a Better Time to Be a UK Metalhead. www.nme.com/features/music-features/uk-metal-scene-new-bands-pupil-slicer-heriot-interview-radar-3459515#.
Šidak, J. 1990. *Hrvatski narodni preporod- Ilirski pokret*. Skolska knjiga.
Silber, L., & A. Little. 1995. *The Death of Yugoslavia*. Penguin Books.
Simmonds, P. L. 1841. Statistics of Newspapers in Various Countries. *Journal of the Statistical Society of London* 4(2): 111–136.
Simpson, A. 2008. Nations and States. In T. C. Salmon & M. F. Iber (eds.), *Issues in international Relations*. Routledge.
Šimunić, M., & V. Gusić. 2015. Branite, gradite, volite! www.pastoralmladih.hr/Fokus/Razgovori/Branite%2C-gradite%2C-volite%21.aspx.
Skey, M. 2011. *National Belonging and Everyday Life*. Palgrave.
Skolnik, F., & M. Berenbaum. 2007. *Encyclopaedia Judaica*. Macmillan & Keter Publishing.
Smith, A. D. 1981. War and Ethnicity: The Role of Warfare in the Formation, Self-Images, and Cohesion of Ethnic Communities. *Ethnic and Racial Studies* 4(4): 375–397.
1986. *The Ethnic Origins of Nations*. Blackwell.
1991. *National Identity*. Penguin.
1996. Nations and Their Pasts. *Nations and Nationalism* 2(3): 358–365.
1997. The 'Golden Age' and National Renewal. In Geoffrey Hosking & George Schopflin (eds.), *Myths and Nationhood*. Routledge.
1998. *Nationalism and Modernism*. Routledge.
1999. *Myths and Memories of the Nation*. Oxford University Press.
2003. *Chosen Peoples*. Oxford University Press.
2009. *Ethno-Symbolism and Nationalism: A Cultural Approach*. Routledge.
2013. *The Nation Made Real*. Oxford University Press.
Smith, P. 2005. *Why War?* Chicago University Press.
2008. *Punishment and Culture*. University of Chicago Press.
Smits, J. 2010. Ethnic Intermarriage and Social Cohesion. What Can We Learn from Yugoslavia? *Social Indicators Research* 96(3): 417–432.
Snowden, M. 2019. *Epidemics and Society: From Black Death to the Present*. Yale University Press.
Snyder, L. 1968. *The New Nationalism*. Cornell University Press.
2000. *From Voting to Violence: Democratization and Nationalist Conflict*. Norton.

Spohn, W. 2003. Multiple Modernity, Nationalism and Religion: A Global Perspective. *Current Sociology* 51(1): 265–87.

Spruyt, H. 2017. War and State Formation: Amending the Bellicit Theory of State Making. In L.Kaspersen & J. Strandbjerg (eds.), *Does War Make States?* Cambridge University Press.

Stanišić, S. 2017. *Dušan Silni: Detinjstvo budućeg cara*. Pčelica.

Statista. 2021. Hungary. www.statista.com/topics/2459/hungary/.

2022. Turkey. www.statista.com/study/48360/turkey/.

2024. Turkey. www.statista.com/markets/422/topic/525/turkey/.

Stein-Erlich, V. 1964. *Obitelj u transformaciji: Studija u tri stotine jugoslavenskih sela*. Naprijed.

Steinmetz, G. 2023. *The Colonial Origins of Modern Social Thought: French Sociology and the Overseas Empire*. Princeton University Press.

Stephanov, D. 2018. *Ruler Visibility and Popular Belonging in the Ottoman Empire, 1808–1908*. Edinburgh University Press.

Stergar, R. 2012. National Indifference in the Heyday of Nationalist Mobilization? Ljubljana Military Veterans and the Language of Command. *Austrian History Yearbook* 43: 45–58.

2017. Illyrian Autochthonism and the Beginnings of South Slav Nationalisms in the West Balkans. In A. De Francesco (ed.), *In Search of Pre-Classical Antiquity: Rediscovering Ancient Peoples in Mediterranean Europe (19th and 20th C.)*. Brill.

Stergar, R., & T. Scheer. 2018. Ethnic Boxes: The Unintended Consequences of Habsburg Bureaucratic Classification. *Nationalities Papers* 46(4): 575–591.

Stojanović, D. 2017. *Kaldrma i asphalt*. Čigoja.

Stojanovic, Lj. 2004. *The First Serbian Uprising and the Restoration of the Serbian State*. Istorijski muzej Srbije.

Storm, E. 2024. *Nationalism: A World History*. Princeton University Press.

Stouffer, S. A., E. A. Suchman, L. C. Devinney, S.A. Star, & R. M. Williams, Jr. 1949. *The American Soldier: Adjustment during Army Life*. Princeton University Press.

Strayer, J. R. 1970. *On the Medieval Origins of the Modern State*. Princeton University Press.

Strickland, D. H. 2003. *Saracens, Demons, & Jews: Making Monsters in Medieval Art*. Princeton University Press.

Sugar, P. 1963. *Industrialization of Bosnia-Hercegovina, 1878–1918*. University of Washington Press.

Sugimoto, Y. 2010. *An Introduction to Japanese Society*. Cambridge University Press.

Sunar, M. M. 2009. 'When Grocers, Porters and Other Riff-raff Become Soldiers': Janissary Artisans and Laborers in the Nineteenth-Century Istanbul and Edirne. *Kocaeli Üniversitesi Sosyal Bilimler Enstitüsü Dergisi* 17(1): 175– 194.

Surak, K. 2012. *Making Tea, Making Japan: Cultural Nationalism in Practice*. Stanford University Press.

Suša, L. 2014. Branitelji su blokirali Savsku ulicu, traže ostavku ministra. 24sata.hr, 20 October.

Šuvar, S. 1970. *Nacije i međunacionalni odnosi u socijalističkoj Jugoslaviji*. Nase teme.
Sztompka, P. 2000. Cultural Trauma: The Other Face of Social Change. *European Journal of Social Theory* 3(4): 449–466.
Taeuber, I. B. 1958. Population and Modernization in Turkey. *Population Index* 24(2): 101–122.
Tamir, Y. 2019. *Why Nationalism*. Princeton University Press.
Tanabe, S. 2021. Sociological Studies on Nationalism in Japan. *International Sociology* 36(2): 171–182.
Tang, W., & B. Barr. 2012. Chinese Nationalism and Its Political and Social Origins. *Journal of Contemporary China* 21: 77.
Taylor Woods, E.., & R. Tsang. 2014. Ritual and Performance in the Study of Nations and Nationalism. In E. Taylor Woods & R. Tsang (eds.), *The Cultural Politics of Nationalism and Nation-Building*. Routledge.
Teschke, B. 2017. After the Tilly Thesis: Social Conflict, Differential State-Formation and Geopolitics in the Construction of the European Systems of States. In L. B. Kaspersen & J. Strandsbjerg (eds.), *Does War Make States? Investigations of Charles Tilly's Historical Sociology*. Cambridge University Press.
Tesser, L. M. 2024. *Rethinking the End of Empire: Nationalism, State Formation, and Great Power Politics*. Stanford University Press.
Thomas, D. S., & W. I. Thomas. 1928. *The Child in America: Behavior Problems and Programs*. Knopf.
Tilley, J., & A. Heath. 2007. The Decline of British National Pride. *British Journal of Sociology* 58: 661–678.
Tilly, C. 1992. *Coercion, Capital and European States, AD 990–1990*. Blackwell.
Tin-Bor Hui, V. 2005. *War and State Formation in Ancient China and Early Modern Europe*. Cambridge University Press.
Tingley, D., & G. Wagner. 2017. Solar Geoengineering and the Chemtrails Conspiracy on Social Media. *Palgrave Communications* 3(1): 12.
Tocco, M. C. 2003. Norms and Texts for Women's Education in Tokugawa Japan. In D. Ko, J. K. Haboush, & J. R. Piggott (eds.), *Women and Confucian Cultures in Premodern China, Korea, and Japan*. University of California Press.
Tomasevich, J. 1955. *Peasants, Politics, and Economic Change in Yugoslavia*. Stanford University Press.
Toshio, K. 1996. Buddhism and Society in the Medieval Estate System. *Japanese Journal of Religious Studies* 23(3–4): 287–319.
Totman, C. 2014. *Japan: An Environmental History*. I. B. Taurus.
Troch, P. 2012. Education and Yugoslav Nationhood in Interwar Yugoslavia. PhD thesis, Ghent University.
Trode, R. 2022. The Sarajevo Tobacco Factory Strike of 1906: Empire and the Nature of Late Habsburg Rule in Bosnia and Herzegovina. *Central European History* 55(4): 493–509.
Turkish Minute. 2021. Turkey Sees Record Rise in Number of Civil Servants under AKP Rule. www.turkishminute.com/2021/02/11/turkey-saw-record-rise-in-number-of-civil-servants-under-akp-rule/.

Turner, J., & A. Marynski. 1993. *The Social Cage: Human Nature and the Evolution of Society*. Stanford University Press.

Turner, J. H. 2007. *Human Emotions: A Sociological Theory*. Routledge.

Turner, J. H., & J. Stets. 2005. *The Sociology of Emotions*. Cambridge University Press.

Turp-Balazs, C. 2020. The Conspiracy Theories Made in Russia Spreading Faster than Covid-19. Emerging Europe. https://emerging-europe.com/news/the-conspiracy-theories-made-in-russia-spreading-faster-than-covid-19/.

UK Government. 2022. The Perceptions of UK Armed Forces Ex Service Personnel. www.gov.uk/government/publications/perceptions-of-uk-armed-forces-ex-service-personnel/ova-public-perceptions-report-241122-html.

UNESCO. 1980. *Literacy, 1972–1976: Progress Achieved in Literacy throughout the World*. UNESCO.

US Navy. 2023. United States Navy > About > Our Core Values. www.secnav.navy.mil/ethics/pages/corevaluescharter.aspx#.

Uzelac, G. 2006. *The Development of the Croatian Nation: An Historical and Sociological Analysis*. Edwin Mellen.

Van den Berghe, P. 2001. Sociobiological Theory of Nationalism. In A. Leoussi (ed.), *Encyclopaedia of Nationalism*. Transaction.

Van Ginderachter, M., & J. Fox. 2019. Introduction: National Indifference and the History of Nationalism in Modern Europe. In M. Van Ginderrachter & J. Fox (eds.), *National Indifference and the History of Nationalism in Modern Europe*. Routledge.

Varin, C. 2015. *Mercenaries, Hybrid Armies and National Security*. Routledge.

Velikonja, M. 2013. The Past with a Future: The Emancipatory Potential of Yugonostalgia. In S. Pavlović & M. Živković (eds.), *Transcending Fratricide*. Nomos Verlagsgesellschaft mbH, 109–128.

Verheijen, T. 2014. *Serbia: State Employees Galore, but Where Is the Private Sector?* World Bank.

Vojinović. 2018. Political Ideas of Young Bosnia: Between Anarchism, Socialism, and Nationalism. In W. Höpken & W. van Meurs (eds.), *The First World War and the Balkans: Historic Event, Experience, Memory*. Peter Lang.

Voyles-Burkes, R. 1971. *The National Problem and the Future of Yugoslavia*. Rand Corporation.

Vukušić, I. 2022. *Serbian Paramilitaries and the Breakup of Yugoslavia State Connections and Patterns of Violence*. Routledge.

Wachtel, A., & I. Štiks. 2019. Squaring the South Slavic Circle: Ethnicity, Nationhood and Citizenship. In J. Trautsch (ed.), *Civic Nationalism in Global Perspective*. Routledge.

Ward, J. 2002. *Women in Medieval Europe: 1200–1500*. Routledge.

Warren, J. N. 2024. In the Shadows of the Commonwealth: Catholicism, Religious Tolerance, and Nineteenth-Century Polish Independence. *East European Politics and Societies* 38(2): 553–575.

Web Japan. 2024. Mass Media: Pillars of the 'Information-Oriented Society'. https://web-japan.org/factsheet/en/pdf/e41_mass.pdf.

Weber, E. 1976. *Peasants into Frenchmen: The Modernization of Rural France, 1870–1914*. Stanford University Press.

1978. *Peasants into Frenchmen: The Modernisation of Rural France, 1870–1914*. Stanford University Press.

Weber, M. 1968. *Economy and Society*. Bedminster Press.

1992. *Protestant Ethics and the Spirit of Capitalism*. Routledge.

Weiker, W. F. 1992. *Ottomans, Turks and the Jewish Policy: A History of the Jews of Turkey*. University Press of America.

Wert, M. 2014. 'The Military Mirror of Kai': Swordsmanship and a Medieval Text in Early Modern Japan. *Das Mittelalter* 19(2): 407–419.

Wheelis, M. 2002. Biological Warfare at the 1346 Siege of Caffa. *Historical Review* 8(9): 971–975.

White, J. 2009. *Muslim Nationalism and the New Turks*. Princeton University Press.

Whitehouse, H., et al. 2014. Brothers in Arms: Libyan Revolutionaries Bond like Family. *PNAS* 111(50): 17783–17785.

Williams, L. 2024. Ireland's Non-binary Eurovision Act Bambie Thug Sparks Fury with 'Sick and Satanic' Routine. www.gbnews.com/celebrity/eurovision-ireland-bambie-thug-witch-satanic-ritual.

Wimmer, A. 2013. *Waves of War: Nationalism, State Formation, and Ethnic Exclusion in the Modern World*. Cambridge University Press.

2018. *Nation-Building: Why Some Countries Come Together while Others Fall Apart*. Princeton University Press.

2021. World without Nation-States: Five Scenarios for the Very Long Term. *Nations and Nationalism* 27(1): 309–324.

Wittek, P. 2013. *The Rise of the Ottoman Empire: Studies in the History of Turkey, Thirteenth–Fifteenth Centuries*. Routledge.

Woodhead, C. 1982. From Scribe to Litterateur: The Career of a Sixteenth-Century Ottoman Katib. *British Society for Middle Eastern Studies Bulletin* 9(1): 55–74.

Wooding, L. 2015. *Henry VIII*. Routledge Historical Biographies. Routledge.

Woodruff, T., R. Kelty, & D. R. Segal. 2006. Propensity to Serve and Motivation to Enlist among American Combat Soldiers. *Armed Forces & Society* 32(3): 353–366.

Woodruff, T. D. 2017. Who Should the Military Recruit? The Effects of Institutional, Occupational, and Self-Enhancement Enlistment Motives on Soldier Identification and Behavior. *Armed Forces & Society* 43(4): 579–607.

Woolf, G. 1998. *Becoming Roman: The Origins of Provincial Civilization in Gaul*. Cambridge University Press.

Yack, B. 2012. *Nationalism and the Moral Psychology of Community*. University of Chicago Press.

Yavuz, H. 2020. *Nostalgia for the Empire: The Politics of Neo-Ottomanism*. Oxford University Press.

Yildirmaz, S. 2017. *Politics and the Peasantry in Post-War Turkey: Social History, Culture and Modernization*. I. B. Tauris.

Yılmaz, G. 2011. The Economic and Social Roles of Janissaries in a Seventeenth Century Ottoman City: The Case of Istanbul. PhD thesis, McGill University.

Yin, R. 2009. *Case Study Research*. Sage.

Yoshino, K. 1992. *Cultural Nationalism in Contemporary Japan*. Routledge.

Zahra, T. 2008. *Kidnapped Souls: National Indifference and the Battle for Children in the Bohemian Lands, 1900–1948*. Cornell University Press.

2010. Imagined Noncommunities: National Indifference as a Category of Analysis. *Slavic Review* 69(1): 93–119.

Zajc, M. 2008. Jugoslovanstvo pri Slovencih v 19. stoletju v kontekstu sosednjih 'združevalnih' nacionalnih ideologij. *Evropski vplivi na slovensko družbo, Zbirka Zgodovinskega časopisa* 35: 103–114.

Žanić, I. 2007. *Flag on the Mountain: A Political Anthropology of War in Croatia and Bosnia*. Saqi.

Zec, D. 2015. The Sokol Movement from Yugoslav Origins to King Aleksandar's 1930 All-Sokol Rally in Belgrade. *East Central Europe* 42(1): 48–69.

Zhao, D. 2015. *The Confucian-Legalist State: A New Theory of Chinese History*. Oxford University Press.

Ziegler, M. 2011. Epidemiology of the Russian Flu, 1889–1890. Contagions: Thoughts on Historic Infectious Disease. https://contagions.wordpress.com/2011/01/03/epidemiology-of-the-russian-flu-1889-1890/.

Ziegler, P. 1969. *The Black Death*. Harper & Row.

Zielenziger, M. 2006. *Shutting Out Sun: How Japan Created Its Own Lost Generation*. Vintage Books.

Živković, M. 1986. Razvoj oružanih snaga SFRJ 1945–1985. Teritorijalna odbrana. Vojnoizdavački i novinski centar.

Žunec, O., et al. 2013. *Oficir i casnik*. HSN.

Zupka, D. 2016. *Ritual and Symbolic Communication in Medieval Hungary under the Árpád Dynasty (1000–1301)*. Brill.

Zwierlein, C., & B. de Graaf. 2013. Security and Conspiracy in Modern History. *Historical Social Research* 38(1): 7–45.

Internet Sources

www.statista.com/statistics/1250277/hungary-poll-on-identifying-as-european-or-hungarian/

www.koppmariaintezet.hu/en/allarticles/530-hungarians-are-proud-of-being-hungarian

web.archive.org/web/20080111092617/http://www.theottomans.org/english/family/index.asp

www.iiss.org/publications/the-military-balance/the-military-balance-2023

https://web.archive.org/web/20151219145010/http://www.gazeteciler.com/gazete-tirajlari.html

www.bobangajic.rs/index.php/vruce-teme-arhiva/416-novo-srpsko-carstvo-narodna-drzava

www.danas.rs/politika/vulin-srpski-svet-bi-trebalo-da-bude-jedan-politicki-prostor-jedna-drzava/.

https://informer.rs/vesti/kolumne/338255/bam-bam-bam-nova-video-kolumna-miroljuba-petrovica-stranci-koji-zele-novo-Dušanovo-carstvo-morace-otvore-poglavlje-nauce-sviraju-gusle.

www.pressonline.rs/vesti/Nedeljnik/242258/bila-jednom-jedna-zemlja-kosarke.html.
https://24sedam.rs/drustvo/vesti/83674/sta-se-vrtelo-u-glavi-dusana-silnog-prvi-psihobiograf-najveceg-srpskog-vladara-ogolio-carevu-licnost-video/vest
www.youtube.com/watch?v=-yorGk2nZbk&t=334s.
www.arheo-amateri.rs/2012/05/srpsko-carstvo/
www.youtube.com/watch?v=1QrLIJY0lME.
www.montenegrina.net/pages/pages1/istorija/duklja/dukljanska_drzava_crno gorski_iskon_i_korijeni_b_sekularac.htm.
www.crnogorskipokret.org/bastina/istorija/dr-fran-milobar-zivot-dukljanske-kralje vine/.
https://crnogorskiportal.me/sadrzaj/1436.
www.youtube.com/watch?v=zJ0zxbXSHRg.
https://dukljani.me/gumno/tema/prva-crnogorska-drzava-duklja/.
http://uraniabg.com/news/interpretacia-na-mundanna-karta-Levin.

Index

Printed by Integrated Books International,
United States of America